En

MW00531975

6.00

EHJ

EMPIRES OF MUD

ANTONIO GIUSTOZZI

Empires of Mud

War and Warlords in Afghanistan

Columbia University Press
New York

Columbia University Press
Publishers Since 1893
New York   Chichester, West Sussex
Copyright © 2009 C. Hurst & Co (Publishers) Ltd
All rights reserved

Library of Congress Cataloging-in-Publication Data

Giustozzi, Antonio.
Empires of mud : war and warlords of Afghanistan / Antonio Giustozzi.
   p. cm.
   Includes bibliographical references and index.
   ISBN 978-0-231-70080-1 (alk. paper)
   1. Warlordism—Afghanistan—History. 2. Warlordism and international
relations—Afghanistan. 3. Civil-military relation—Afghanistan. 4. Military
government—Afghanistan. 5. Jihad—Afghanistan. 6. Qa'immaqami, 'Abbas.
7. Masud, Ahmadshoh, 1953-2001. 8. Afghanistan—Politics and government—
1989–2001. 9. Afghanistan—Politics and government—2001– I. Title.

JQ1763.5.C58G58 2009
958.104—dc22

2009024414

♾

Columbia University Press books are printed on permanent and durable
acid-free paper. This book is printed on paper with recycled content.
Printed in India

c 10 9 8 7 6 5 4 3 2 1

References to Internet Web sites (URLs) were accurate at the time of writing.
Neither the author nor Columbia University Press is responsible for URLs
that may have expired or changed since the manuscript was prepared.

CONTENTS

v

CONTENTS

LIST OF MAPS, GRAPHS, TABLES AND PICTURES

MAPS

PREFACE AND ACKNOWLEDGEMENTS

Empires of Mud is the result of a four year effort that started in 2003 with a month-long research visit, the modest aim of which was to produce a paper on Afghanistan's non-state actors. I then served for a year in UNAMA, to return to academic research at the end of 2004. Since then I have regularly travelled to Afghanistan three times a year to complete what had in the meanwhile become a book project. Much has changed during these four years in Afghanistan. At the same time, my views have evolved as I immersed myself deeper and deeper into the subject, although there is still a degree of continuity with my earlier writings on the topic (2003). Part of the material used derives from a previous study, which I carried out in the 1990s as part of my doctoral research. At the core of this project is the conviction that for analytical purposes it is important to distinguish between warlords and other 'non-state actors'; but is part also of a wider effort to contribute to the understanding of contemporary Afghan politics. Like anything contemporary, Afghan warlordism is a moving target, but it has been around long enough to merit this study. Non-state actors, moreover, are becoming frequent objects of scholarly analysis and I feel that it is about time to start 'zooming in' with specific, in-depth, analyses of particular periods and individuals.

In writing this book I have tried to skirt around morally charged statements, which would have been quite easy, given the topic. This is in part due to selfish reasons (I wish to return to Afghanistan), but also to a more general 'Weberian' conviction that the scholar has to try to assume an unbiased position. I do not see who would stand to gain from another easy libel against the 'warlords'; it is about time to undertake serious analysis and reflection on these many years of war.

The methodology of this book is mostly based on semi-structured interviewing carried out between 2003–2007 with hundreds of individuals unsually linked in one way or another, directly or indirectly, with the 'warlords'. I usually avoided interviewing the warlords themselves, in the belief that apart from being unlikely to produce much useful information such a move would have drawn unwarranted attention to my research. The information gathered was used to determine not just events, but also the extent of the influence of different players. I also used those written sources I could find, mostly memoirs by participants in the civil wars and works by fellow scholars, among which Gilles Dorronsoro's book and articles were the most useful. Inevitably, researching such a topic was problematic to some extent, not least because many of the people mentioned in the book were still around. In this regard serving in UNAMA for a year was very helpful, as it gave a near 'immunity' at a crucial time. Operating under UNAMA's banner also facilitated the gathering of information, although at that time I did not have a book project in mind yet. While in UNAMA I also had access to classified information which I did not directly use, but proved very useful in directing future information gathering. Even then, there were major constraints in this research effort. Although Afghans are usually quite open, and information circulates widely, checking the veracity of facts was always difficult. This is why I have tried whenever possible to cross-reference information in order to verify it and to identify more trustworthy sources. In part I have circumvented the problem by focusing on aspects of Afghan political life that are least controversial, such as territorial control.

Compared to my other recent book, *Koran, Kalashnikov and Laptop*, the present volume presents greater challenges to the reader. Although I tried to make it more readable, the subject is very complex. Trying to unravel the dynamics of Afghan warlordism prompted me to rewrite the book twice; I hope that the results will be judged worthwhile.

As always in these cases, it is difficult to be fair to all those who have helped me in bringing this book to life. I will do my best in the hope that those who have been overlooked will forgive me. The present version incorporates suggestions and advice from Jonathan Goodhand, Chris Cramer, Andreas Lövold and William Maley, all of whom I thank for making the effort to read an earlier version of the manuscript. As in the case of my previous book on the Neo-Taliban, special thanks go to Mina Moshkiri and her colleagues at LSE's cartography department, who once again patiently redrew my maps in higher resolution. Special thanks must also go to the director of the Crisis States Research Centre, James Putzel, who funded my research before and after my stay in UNAMA. A number of Afghans accompanied me in my research trips and I thank them all, beginning with Niamatullah Ibrahimi of the CSRC. Wendy Foulds, the administrator of the CSRC, efficiently managed the logistical and administrative side of my research. Special thanks should also go to Noor Ullah, with whom I co-authored some works on southern Afghanistan, in part included in some chapters of this book, to David Azadifar and Vikram Parekh for their hospitality and help in Kunduz and Kabul, Talatbek Masadykov for hosting me in Kabul and Guy Griffin in Mazar. Particularly invaluable in the early days of my research was the help given by Eckart Schiewek and Ghulam Sakhi. I also wish to thank the following for their help and advice (in alphabetical order): Mohammad Ayoub, Yakub Ayubi, Martine van Bijlert, Sergey Illarionov, Abas Kargar, Dr Latif, Sarah Lister, Mervyn Patterson, Mohammad Purdel, Thomas Ruttig, Michael Semple, Barbara Stapleton, Oliver Vick, Asadullah Walwalji and of course Michael Dwyer and his team at Hurst.

INTRODUCTION

WARLORDS AND STATES

Of all provinces of Afghanistan, probably none deserved to be called the 'warlord hotbed' more than Faryab, in the north-west. Its extreme levels of violence during the 1980s and 1990s, the deadly competition among military leaders and its role as a 'border province' between areas under the influence of Abdul Rashid Dostum and Ismail Khan all highlighted its particular importance. Indeed, it is in Faryab in the summer of 2004 that I first conceived this book, although the project underwent major changes over the four years of its evolution. On one occasion I visited a police station in a district north of the provincial capital, Maimana. The outpost was a small and decrepit building atop a hill, where were based twenty or thirty policemen, but I could not help but noting how it was overlooked by a similar building on a neighbouring, higher hill. The latter was occupied by a group of men who were not displaying weapons but observing us intently. While above the police station fluttered the Afghan national flag, the other building was topped by the black, red and green flag of Junbesh-i Milli-ye Islami, the party of Gen. Dostum, Afghanistan's most famous 'warlord'. Although I was advised against talking to the men in the other building, it was immediately apparent that there was a highly symbolic meaning in the positioning of the two buildings. Indeed, had I spoken to them I would have learnt that, to the extent that there was security in Faryab, it was more likely to be maintained by Dostum's men than by the ragtag hilltop police. Soon afterwards I took part in a meeting in the provincial capital of Maimana, together with some colleagues from UNAMA and Afghan civilian and military authorities. I was at that time just beginning to become acquainted with the recent history of Faryab, but many of the names that were mentioned to me already sounded familiar. None of the major protagonists of the 1980s and 1990s was present, as all were either dead or in exile, but those who were there had already accumulated quite a pedigree. The leading figure among them, Fataullah, had once given his allegiance to men like Rasul Pahlawan, his brothers and then their nemesis, Hashim Habibi. He was now running the game in alliance with Abdul Rashid Dostum. I observed silently as Fataullah, now commander of a division, led

1

the former gunmen's effort to present a reasonable face and contribute to the orderly running of Faryab province. In a sense, they were seemingly engaged in state-building. Ever since the question in my mind (and no doubt in the mind of many others) has been how genuine or sustainable was this effort; was is it is possible to entrust state-building to warlords?

From the vantage point of four years of research and writing on the subject, I now view my initial thoughts on the subject as being quite simplistic. Having seen the goings-on in other parts of Afghanistan, and in Kabul too, and having been exposed to the views and contributions of colleagues in academia and in the policy world, the problem of state-building in the context of 'very late development' has assumed in my mind an altogether different magnitude. In the case of Afghanistan, moreover, the problem is still state-formation more than state-building. Gradually I came to think that the formation of a 'modern' and 'diplomatically recognisable' state in the context of Afghanistan has little chances of succeeding unless it relies on the establishment of an international protectorate, with all the difficulties that come with that. For example, has the 'international community' the stamina to commit itself to such kind of enterprises for a long period of time and with ultimately uncertain results? And even if it had, does it really know how to do it? What kind of reaction will a prolonged effort of this kind elicit among sections of the Afghan population?[1]

I believe that the chances of success of the international community's attempt to re-establish the Afghan state are diminished by its inability to understand and analyse Afghan politics. Many among the well-meaning agents of the 'international community' seem to think that it might be possible to grow a state exclusively on a diet of Locke and Kant, particularly among those from a legal background. My purpose with this book is to inject a fair dose of Hobbes, Machiavelli and Ibn Khaldun in the mix, as well as contemporary authors, and at the same time to bring into the debate a specific understanding of Afghanistan's recent history. We should clearly distinguish between the ideology of state-building as we experienced it in Europe, which at its most attractive incarnation took a liberal-idealistic shape, and the historical reality.

The title of this book, *Empires of Mud*, sums up in a way the impact of warlords on state formation in the absence of interaction with other social forces. I borrowed the title from a Nine Inch Nails song covered by Johnny Cash[2] in order to convey the sense of polities which leave nothing behind in their wake, as well as to pay homage to Afghanistan's omnipresent mud. The first core argument of the book is indeed that as long as warlords stick to their military origins and build nothing durable (including metaphorically) on their mudbrick forts, they cannot contribute much to state formation and state-building. At the same time, there is evidence both in Afghanistan and in other places before it that in some instances warlords participated in processes of cross-fertilisation conductive to state formation, whether by cooptation, conquest, coercion or cooperation, openly or surreptitiously. This is the second main point of the book.

INTRODUCTION

The convention which abhors 'warlords', but accepts their like once they adopt a façade of respectability, might well be a diplomatic necessity, but it is the task of scholars to throw light into the most remote recesses and help understand how these 'façade' states work. I will deal in the conclusion with the policy implications, but I can already point out that the tendency to rely on international recognition as the primary criterion for the definition of a state does not exempt us from trying to discern how such a state is going to sustain itself politically, militarily and economically. My thought back in 2004 that one day such knowledge might be useful has been vindicated sooner than I had expected. The state-making patterns which I shall identify in this book will mostly horrify the right-minded, but this is the material of which not only almost all the states that have ever existed were once made, but also of which many states are still made today, possibly beneath a superficial façade. This book thus concerns itself with the 'dirt' of state-making, the dark side of an often idealised process.

The book follows the paths of Afghanistan's main warlords from the outset of their careers to 2008, when the manuscript was completed. Two of them, Abdul Rashid Dostum and Ismail Khan, feature here most prominently, but along with them many other characters. The purpose is to show how Afghan warlordism came into being, giving a fair weight to both the character of individual actors and structural causes, and how it evolved and impacted on the process of state (re-)formation in Afghanistan. This is an utterly complex task, since this is an almost virgin ground. In the rest of this introduction, I sum up the theoretical debate about warlordism and draw some preliminary conclusions from it, as well as illustrate some analytical categories of my own on which I will draw throughout the text. Part I then provides a discussion of Afghan society and history from the perspective of explaining the rise of warlordism. Inevitably the focus will be on recent history, with the period starting in 1980 being followed in quite a great detail. The structure of chapters 2–5 is loosely chronological, not least in the attempt to help the reader find his way through the thickets of Afghan history and politics. Part II, by contrast, is a detailed analysis of the two leading Afghan warlords and the polities which they created: Abdul Rashid Dostum (chs 6–13) and Ismail Khan (chs 14–21). Because they embody two different 'models' of warlords, they are suitable for a comparative study. The analysis therefore follows a roughly consistent pattern, trying to isolate specific aspects of these polities in line with the analysis produced in the introduction. A single chapter (22) is dedicated to Ahmad Shah Massud and his polity, Shura-i Nezar. Some readers might be surprised to see such a limited treatment of one of Afghaistan's most popular figures, but as I explain in the text I do not consider Massud a warlord. There were, however, some aspects of Massud's *Shura-i Nezar* that resembled warlordism and I decided to include a short study for comparative purposes. The conclusion follows.

Both the media and a majority of scholars have been using the term 'warlord' in a pejorative sense.[3] This is not too surprising given that when it first

3

gained currency in China in the 1910s it was already used in the political debate as a term of abuse.[4] As a result, the use of the term 'warlord' with reference to a particular period of Chinese history, has not been without controversy.[5] While scholars of contemporary conflicts too have often fallen prey to the hegemony of the mass media and used the term in vague, ill-defined and morally charged ways, historians have been more restrained. For example, the term has been used by historians of medieval Europe to indicate a blurred category of local rulers who entertained an ambiguous relationship with the central government towards the end of the Roman Empire and emerged as fully independent rulers after its collapse. The most advanced theorisation of late Roman warlordism comes from Dick Whittaker,[6] who describes a process in which officers on active service were becoming increasingly powerful locally, through their acquisition of land ownership in regions where they were serving, while state control over the exercise of private patronage weakened. At the same time landlords were turning to militarism, and with the increasing concentration of property ownership came the control of large numbers of dependants, who could be mustered for military action. Whittaker sees in this process something very similar to what happened in China in 1911–1939, which in his interpretation was the product of two separate forces, the raising of local militias by the gentry (still remaining loyal to the Beijing government), and the breakdown of the Chinese army into the personal armies of various generals. Not only did the two start to merge, but the gentry and their networks, including local bureaucrats, turned out to be necessary instruments for the warlords to extract surpluses and secure control of the land, and with it the supply of soldiers. This would also explain why Chinese warlords had no radical political goals. In the case of the Roman Empire, the merging took place between the militarised rural gentry and the Germanic war-leaders (*Kriegsherren*) and their invading tribal armies. Other historians have identified warlords as a category of pre-feudal or post-feudal rulers in parts of Europe.[7]

While the controversies and the tendency to use the term disparagingly suggest that abandoning it altogether might not be unwise,[8] such an approach would leave intact the problem of naming and defining a category of military-political actors and processes, characterised by peculiar characteristics and dynamics. For example, it can be argued that militarism and militarisation, which are terms sometimes used to indicate warlordism, would more appropriately be confined in their use to processes leading to the expansion of military structures and capabilities and to their rise in importance vis-à-vis political power, albeit still within a state framework. There is instead a need specifically to study the role of military leaders in state-making or state decentralisation/disintegration. In the case of the latter, military leaders replace political and/or bureaucratic legitimacy with its military corollary by effectively taking over political power in parts of the old state. In processes of state-making, military leaders can often play a key role, particularly in the early stages. I have therefore decided to stick to terms such as 'warlord' and 'warlordism' for the purposes of this book.

My main interest in *Empires of Mud* is indeed to explore the relationship between warlordism and state building/state crisis. Although state-making as described in the historical literature cannot be repeated in contemporary times due to the modified environment, it is still worth bearing in mind what the process of formation of early states looked like. Within the context of the debate on the origins of the early state, it has been argued that early political leadership is connected with personal qualities and not with the development of economic differences.[9] There is little question that among the factors triggering the development of the early state was war or the threat of war,[10] alongside others such as population pressure, conquest, incentives provided by ideology and legitimisation, progress in the production of surplus and the influence of existing states. Power, which is one of the key components of government, is achieved through a mix of persuasion, threats, physical force and indirect control.[11] Even more than that, early states achieved their legitimisation both through ideology and 'repeated actions of military nature', which served to show that protection by the state was indispensable.[12] There has been, therefore, an important role to play for military leaders in statemaking from its very early origins. Moreover, as I shall show, warlords too do not necessarily reject forms of partial institutionalisation and bureaucratisation and can in certain circumstances turn into political leaders, not least because 'extra-economic coercion' tends to be not very productive and results in modest surpluses.[13] In a sense, the historical origins of the state (and hence of politics) might often be found in the survival instinct of large military organisations and their leaders. One would certainly agree with Jackson (2003) that 'the study of government could be enhanced by the study of warlords'.

A necessary question must be what is left of the historical role of warlords in state-making in contemporary times, where the latter is constrained by international rules and by the ability of great powers to interfere in every corner of the globe. As this volume will illustrate, warlords can still turn into key stakeholders of state rebuilding, deeply affecting them in the process.

Warlord: a definition

Drawing from the historical and political science literature and keeping in mind my own aim to situate warlordism in the context of state-building and state crisis, I shall use the following ideal type of warlord in this volume:

- a legitimate,[14] charismatic[15] and patrimonial military leader with autonomous control over a military force capable of achieving/maintaining a monopoly of large scale violence over a sizeable territory.
This definition has two major implications:
- the warlord has little or no political legitimacy, but nonetheless…
- …he exercises patrimonial political power over such territory, where central authority has either collapsed or has weakened or was never there in the first place.

I exclude from the definition of warlord a number of contentious issues. The most widely disputed point is whether warlords are predominantly motivated by economic aims and financial greed. The idea was first launched by Keen[16] and found support mainly among scholars studying African conflicts, especially those with a background as economists.[17] However, it has been pointed out by others, such as Berdal, that the interest of warlords in economic profit might also be related to their need to maintain armies and reward their followers, and therefore cannot be necessarily ascribed to pure 'greed'.[18] Related to this issue is whether warlords have necessarily to be predatory. This point is made by many scholars[19] and it goes hand in hand with the assertion that warlords have no interest in providing services and public goods.[20] While it would be possible to build an ideal type of the predatory warlord, in practice few military-political actors have ever been merely predatory. Studies of some so-called Chinese warlords showed how the provision of welfare or even upholding 'progressive' ideas was not incompatible with warlordism.[21] More importantly, the stress on their predatory character misses the main point about warlords and what differentiates them from 'bandits', that is the fact that armed force and military leadership can themselves be public goods, for example when related to the provision of security, and obey different logics. In this regard as some authors have been using the term warlord as a sub-type or synonym of military/conflict/violence entrepreneur, or even as part of a wider continuum ranging from insurgents to bandits and warlords, it is best to clarify why I wish to set warlords apart even if there can be points of contact. With regard to ideological insurgents, the answer is easier: their primary concern is political, not military; their constituency is not a professional military class in search of a role and a status; the recourse to violence is not an end in itself, but a means to achieve an aim (usually power). Hence, to limit ourselves to a few Afghan examples, the Taliban or Hizb-i Islami were never warlords in any meaningful sense and their modus operandi differed radically. The entrepreneur of violence is the protagonist of political economy analyses and has been defined as:

'an individual who takes the necessary and deliberate steps to ignite a violent conflict by utilising a specific situation or in order to gain something through the exploitation of new power relationships.'[22]

The entrepreneurs are not traditional tribal or clan leaders, but

'ambitious modern politicians, former army officers, civil servants, members of parliament, merchants or university professors'[23]

and owe their position not to any military role that they might have played, or to the traditional influence exercised by their family, but to their political skills in emerging as representatives of the local population from among a larger number of elders and notables. As for bandits, Olson's discussion of their 'roving' or 'stationary' role has been very influential in recent times and is useful to my argument too in several regards, but it does not help in that it schematically lumps together actors who might well have very different ori-

gins and aims.[24] While there is some overlapping with my definition of warlord, the key difference is that entrepreneurs and to a lesser extent Olson's
bandits are assumed to be calculating figures bent on making specific gains,
seen by most authors as having to be financial in nature. The greed/grievance
dichotomy, for example, would appear to portray the behaviour of the con-
flict/violence entrepreneurs more than of the warlords or politico-military
entrepreneurs. 'My' warlord, by contrast, is prisoner of his military ethos and
cannot always afford to be calculating *homo oeconomicus*. He resembles early
political leaders in his reliance on personal loyalty and reciprocity.[25] Most if
not all of what he extracts has to be redistributed to ensure loyalty and to pay
for his armed force. Because of the specific requirements of war-making that
characterise warlords, their lives are subjected to high risks. The risk of getting
killed or captured, or of losing all that they have gained, is indeed too high
for personal enrichment to be a driving factor and the main aim of their
activities.

For similar reasons I reject a view shared by many authors, that warlords do
not aim to conquer the state, but rather to perpetuate the state of war and
state crisis.[26] This is clearly not always true, as characters like Charles Taylor
and Jonas Savimbi, classified as warlords by most writers, tried to seek legitimisation through presidential elections. Whatever Savimbi's predatory attitudes might have been,[27] his determination to conquer Luanda should not be
doubted, even if he failed to achieve his aim. The argument bears nonetheless
some relevance if we use a definition of the state largely focused on international recognition. Indeed, if warlords often fail to commit themselves to the
struggle for central state power, it may well also be because they judge their
chances of receiving international recognition too low. This would be mis-
leading. However important international recognition might be, it is just one
ingredient of state-building and focusing on it risks obscuring key internal
dynamics of state-building. As it will be discussed in Part II, often warlords
get involved in forms of state-building within their own areas of control.

Military leadership is a rare quality, and in a context of violent competition
among rival groups the skills of a military leader can be a decisive factor.
There is much debate in the military studies literature with regard to what
military leadership exactly is. The US Army defines military leadership as 'the
art of direct and indirect influence and the skill of creating the conditions for
organizational success to accomplish missions effectively.'[28] Qualities that are
often mentioned as contributing to military leadership include integrity,
courage, loyalty, selflessness, self-discipline, dedication, knowledge, intellect,
perseverance, decisiveness and ability to discipline subordinates. These qualities together are unlikely to be found in many humans, let alone warlords, but
the more a military commander manages to approach such an ideal type the
more he would have an edge over rivals who fall shorter. In practice, especially in a non-bureaucratic (Weberian) environment, the skills of a military
leader are judged on the basis of his ability to win battles. This is not merely
measured on the basis of battlefield skills, but on the ability to manage rela-

tively large military organisations, their logistics and supply. It takes many years in a regular army to mould a general and possibly even longer for a guerrilla leader to develop such skills in the field. Things get even more complicated when military organisations are in fact loose coalitions of local strongmen, former army officers, and local military leaders of various sorts. In this case the warlord might well look more like a service provider for the military class, which could be defined in Gallant's terms as 'a category of men who take up arms and who wield violence or the threat of violence as their stock in trade'.[29] I shall add to this definition that they must have acquired self-awareness of their specific role in society. Among them, a particularly important role belongs to those who are able to maintain a following of armed men. The military class as such includes both salaried armed force officers and specialists and local military leaders who have an autonomous power base. It is of course the latter who represent the natural constituency of the warlord, who could well have started his career as a *primus inter pares* among them. In the context of non-bureaucratic polities, the control exercised by the military class over armed men and territory (military patrimonialism) may be irreplaceable at least in the short and medium term and is an asset that is prized even by ideological enemies. This fact might explain why Chinese warlords were incorporated into the political factions, including the KMT and Communist parties. The warlord rises above the mass of military leaders to provide services such as coordination, planning, management, logistics, foreign relations as well as skilled military leadership (of a more strategic type). By providing them to otherwise autonomous members of the military class, the warlord improves the chances of survival and success of each of them. Moreover, to the professional of violence winning battles means more opportunity for looting, for example, or for the expansion of territorial control and hence a greater tax base.[30]

This point about military leadership brings us back to the importance of legitimacy for warlords. Political legitimacy defines the warlord by its absence. The warlord may develop it, but if a warlord succeeded in legitimising his political power, he would no longer be considered a warlord, but a king, a president, or at least a political leader. In order to understand the dynamics which lead to the emergence of warlordism and drive its development it is equally important to stress that a warlord enjoys a different type of legitimacy, namely 'military legitimacy'.[31] This could be defined as having demonstrated military leadership and enjoying support among the military class.

Military leadership and charisma are two key qualities of a warlord, which polarise the support of the military class around him. As a result of this support, the warlord becomes a key actor in the process of establishing a monopoly over large scale violence (see below). Several authors implicitly recognise this when identifying the warlords' ability to provide security to at least part of the population in a context of ongoing warfare.[32] It is an essential ingredient of state-making. In a Hobbesian environment, individuals and communities might well prize the protection afforded by the monopolist of large scale violence against external threats, particularly if it is perceived that such threats also affect civilians. Thus military leadership might be recognised by the wider population too as a useful quality and earn the warlord wider support, although not full political legitimacy.

In Afghanistan throughout the 1980s and 1990s and even after 2001, military leaders of all sorts have been popularly referred to as 'commanders' (kumandanha). In this book, in order to avoid confusion among different roles, the term 'commander' will be used only to refer to 'officers' or military leaders hierarchically incorporated in organisations and therefore devoid of effective autonomy in decision-making. Only a tightly organised insurgent organisation has commanders to lead its men in the field, as in the case for a regular army. Otherwise, terms like 'military leader' and 'warlord' will be used.

Warlordism as a process: techniques and skills

For the purpose of situating warlordism within processes of state-making, defining it is not sufficient. Warlordism has to be seen as a dynamic process, susceptible to develop into a more sophisticated type of polity as well as to culminate in outright collapse. In order to understand the origins and evolution of warlordism in Afghanistan, we need to look at both the social and political processes underpinning it and at the techniques and skills that subjectively warlords have to use in order to emerge and consolidate their power. To this end I will employ several concepts that are set out in the following pages.

In order to explain how a warlord emerges in a very competitive environment and to identify the techniques and skills required, I draw my inspiration from the analysis of Niccoló Machiavelli's *Il Principe*.[33] In his classic work, looking at the challenges facing the statesmen of Renaissance Italy, an environment only relatively friendlier than Afghanistan in the 1980s and 1990s, Machiavelli identified several characteristics as defining the chances of success for an aspiring 'Prince'. I have agglomerated these characteristics or 'virtues' in four groups and discuss them separately below: ruthlessness and deceit, diplomacy, institutionalisation and legitimisation.

Ruthlessness and deceit

As shown by a discussion of the disintegrative tendencies of warlord polities (see following paragraph), command and control is inevitably one of the key problems faced by warlords. How to implement and strengthen command and control? The feudal model is interesting in this regard, given its recognised military origins and its later consolidation into a system endowed with a specific mode of production and source of legitimisation.[34] The Carolingians controlled the fragmentation of their polity, using monetary payment for services, which had the effect of curtailing the decentralised tendencies implicit in feudalism. Local military leaders were forced to rotate residencies every few years. The king would travel throughout his territory to exercise on site control; sometimes he would use paid administrators to do the same.[35] An alternative mode of polity consolidation is the centralisation of patronage, where the ruler tries to establish exclusive control over as many sources of wealth as possible, which can be redistributed to create political support.[36] Brinkmanship is another tactic that political leaders often use to force partners and adversaries to concede as much as possible. Following Machiavelli's argument, the warlord has at his disposal a number of tools, each with different implications in terms of the characteristics that his polity will be taking. Machiavelli's main argument was that in order to secure political survival (seen as a supreme goal) the Prince should not shy away from ruthlessness and deceit. Apart from his celebrated approval of divide and rule tactics ('endeavour with every art to divide the forces of the enemy'), Machiavelli's main argument was that the Prince should inspire fear, but not hatred, and that cruelty might be necessary to prevent worse disorders from arising. Not only might the Prince have to dispose of unsavoury characters, but also 'without cruelty he would never hold his army united or disposed to its duties'. The impact of cruelty has to be minimised ('injuries ought to be done all at one time, so that, being tasted less, they offend less') but cannot be avoided.

The scope for ruthlessness and deceit were for Machiavelli to be limited as much as possible to the stage of what I refer to as primitive accumulation of power.[37] This in part at least corresponds to what Weber identified as the establishment of the monopoly of violence. With regard to this key aspect of state-making, it is important to distinguish between two aspects. What matters in terms of 'primitive accumulation of power' is the monopoly of large scale violence. Establishing control over small scale violence is by contrast the concern of the mature state, which offers policing services to its population among other reasons in order to achieve long-term legitimisation. A particular form of accumulation of power that historically played an important role in state formation is the replacement of kinship with clientage as the base of political organisation. In particular, the recruitment of uprooted social elements ('broken men') or migrant minority groups as soldiers or militiamen appears historically to have been a frequent occurrence. The result would have been to insulate the ruler from society and allow him a greater degree of arbitrary power.[38]

Institutionalisation (de-patrimonialisation)

Machiavelli was also aware of the importance of institutionalisation (meant here as de-patrimonialisation) and highlighted the need to strengthen the principality 'with good laws' and 'abstain from the property of his citizens and subjects and from their women'. He knew enough to resist patronage politics:

excessive 'liberality' should be avoided, as it 'rewards few', 'offends many' and it might not be sustainable.[39] Of course, Machiavelli has been superseded by an army of authors in terms of detailed analysis on institutionalisation or, in Weber's terms, bureaucratisation and rationalisation. For the purposes of my analysis I identify different types of processes related to institutionalisation, bureaucratisation and rationalisation. The most obvious type is institution-building: patrimonial power is stabilised through the 'formation of impersonal, relatively permanent political institutions'.[40] In its most elementary form, this means that certain tasks pertaining to the ruler, mostly related to security and the protection of the interests of some of his subjects, are devolved to purposely created agencies, such a judiciary, a police force, etc. It may also take the shape of the creation of a political organisation to take over at least some of the functions of the ruler. These processes of institution-building may also allow a shift in loyalty from local communities or local rulers to a more centralised polity, a typical process of state-building.[41] A related type of institutionalisation consists in the seizure and re-orientation of existing and possibly partially decayed state institutions by non-state agents. We could define this type as institutional seizure and it can represent either a short cut to institution-building (using existing structures) or a form of sabotage of effective institutionalisation (perverting the nature and the aims of institutions).

A quite different type is instead institutional self-cooptation. In this case a warlord or other non-state agent lobbies for his own cooptation into pre-existing state structures with a high profile job, such as governor, military officer or chief of police. The main purpose of self-cooptation is to formalise a role for non-state agents; in a sense this is akin to a form of legitimisation. Similar in its purpose is international recognition. Of course, full international recognition is unlikely to happen until a warlord has seized the national capital and convinced his international interlocutors that he is there to stay. Yet to the extent that a warlord can establish international relations with several states, he can temporarily and/or partially institutionalise and legitimise his role within the international system, with obvious advantages for himself and his polity. It this regard it is worth keeping in mind that the interaction of states and 'warlords' or other non-state actors has a long history. Indeed in the early stages they were

'deeply insinuated in the processes of state formation and state consolidation of power. […] Inlaw or outlaw, border guard or bandit, privateer or pirate were labels applied by the state, and depending on the designation chosen the activitiesof those groups were deemed either legal or illegal. If the former was chosen, these men were patriots and defenders of the state; if the latter, then they became the scourge of the nation...'[42]

A key aspect of the institutionalisation of political leadership is the establishment of mechanisms to regulate succession. A firmly established and institutionalised system of succession offers guarantees of continuity to the supporters of a ruler, as well as preventing competition among potential successors from destructively competing against each other. This can be achieved in a number of ways, of which hereditariness represents the most patrimonial option and elections the least patrimonial. The creation of a political organisation may also play a role in regulating succession.

Institutionalisation, bureaucratisation and rationalisation imply both advantages and costs to power-holders. The transfer of power to agencies and institutions, as well as any move towards the establishment of the rule of law, all represent a constraint to the arbitrariness of the ruler. If the non-state agent becomes only an intermediate member of the institution (as it can be in the case of self-cooptation), the costs are even more obvious, since he too will be asked to comply with rules and regulations that will constrain the arbitrary use of power. In the longer term, there might even be a serious danger of institutionalisation getting out of control and disempowering the ruler. Such costs and dangers explain the reluctance of many warlords to engage in institutionalisation, particularly when the costs of not engaging are seen as modest.

Legitimisation

In the early stages of the creation of a polity, that is during the primitive accumulation of power, military legitimacy plays a paramount role, as pointed out earlier. Machiavelli saw the need to guarantee the effectiveness of the army as linked to the fact that only victories and successes can be trusted to bring legitimacy, and legitimacy after the initial consolidation of power was to be the main concern of the Prince. His understanding of the intricacies of legitimisation was subtle enough for him to advise the Prince to eschew the use of allied troops, because they are controlled by leaders who may turn against their employers. Moreover, any glory they could earn would not be attributed to the Prince. Machiavelli also famously advised against the reliance on mercenary troops. I include the manipulation of warfare for political ends (to create a measure of identification with the ruler among the subjects) in what I called military legitimisation. This manipulation can take many forms, such as the production of myths of valour, and is not just limited to the troops, although the latter are the primary target.

However, the monopoly of violence alone is normally not sufficient to achieve the critical mass required by the formation of a state. The next layer of the process is political legitimisation, described by Gellner as a process meant to attract loyalty and therefore stabilise a polity.[43] Over time, this might lead to a process of 'courtisation of warriors', as spelt out by Norbert Elias, which he describes as one of the most decisive transitions in the civilising process.[44] The necessary sophistication might well elude some warlords, but there are some among them who try to legitimise their rule in various ways. Machiavelli recommended relying on popular support rather than on that of the 'nobles', because the latter 'would consider themselves equals to the prince, and because of this he can neither rule nor manage them to his liking'. Raising a degree of popular support can be achieved by appropriating an issue that has a genuine constituency among the population; in this way the warlord can turn into the representative of certain interests or agendas. I will call this legitimisation by representation. I would distinguish this type of legitimisation from another one, with which it is often confused: indoctrination. Contrary to representation, indoctrination does not pick on existing grievances or demands, but is much more manipulative and creates them ex-novo. Its impact on an adult public can be more counter-productive than anything else and it has therefore often specifically targeted the youth. As a result it requires some time to have a serious impact as well as a comparatively high degree of organisation and skilled cadres. Another variation on this theme is legitimisation by participation, which is achieved through grassroots involvement. Such involvement mostly takes place through the creation of a political organisation, but it inevitably implies to some degree shared aims between the ruler and the subjects.

Probably the strongest form of legitimisation is ideological, in which I include some forms of religious legitimisation (others might fit better in customary legitimisation, see below). In Ibn-Khaldun's words 'when people [who have a religious colouring] come to have the (right) insight into their affairs, nothing can withstand them, because their outlook is one and their object one of common accord. They are willing to die for (their objectives)'.[45] Various authors have pointed out the role of ideology in fields such as legitimisation, the development of loyalty and cohesion among 'the agents of coercion'[46] and more generally for management of collective action. In Geertz's words, ideologies are 'matrices for the creation of collective conscience'.[47] Ideology provides 'the motivation to seek [...] technical skill and knowledge, the emotional resilience to support the necessary patience and resolution, and the moral strength to self-sacrifice and incorruptibility'...[48] It is possible to carry out a mobilisation, exercise hegemony and obtain legitimisation with a relatively weak organisational/bureaucratic presence (for example, through the clergy and local notables). But as a tool of legitimisation and of sophisticated long-term management of collective action, ideology needs a specialised carrier, a mass political party/organisation.[49] As pointed out in the original definition of warlord, this is not an ideological actor, although he might allow a certain role to ideology as a legitimisation/survival strategy in specific contexts. Bear in mind too that ideology represents a constraint to the arbitrary action of the leader and as such it will always be seen with suspicion by the patrimonial ruler (see ideologisation, below).

Winning elections is another way of becoming legitimised (electoral legitimisation) that is also compatible with other types of legitimisation. Its main shortcoming is that winning elections is not easy, especially in a genuinely competitive environment. If the elections are too obviously rigged, little legitimacy will derive from them. If they are not, there will always be a chance that the elections might be lost, with disastrous effects at least on the legitimacy of the leadership. Moreover, once the principle of elections has been established, it is difficult to roll it back without great political damage.

Hence, they have to be repeated over time, so that the promise of certain victory in a given election is offset by the risk of a defeat later. Possibly the way to achieve legitimisation most discussed in the literature is the delivery of services to the population (delivery-based legitimisation). It is not very controversial politically and guarantees good results, but it is very expensive and therefore not always the first choice of rulers. The delivery of services requires a sophisticated bureaucracy in order to ensure the functionality of the syst—some services can however be delivered more easily even in the absence of bureaucratic supervision (gas, electricity).

The financial and political costs of certain types of legitimisation explain why relatively ineffective, short-term, ways to achieve some political legitimisation are relatively common: because they are cheaper. This is the case of image-driven legitimisation. Essentially a matter of public relations, it consists in projecting the image of an organisation or individual bent on doing the best for the people. It requires at least some expenditure on eye-catching public works and monuments, or social events, and its effects are unlikely to be very deep or long lasting. Machiavelli also understood the importance of public relations in legitimisation and advised the Prince to 'appear merciful, faithful, humane, religious, upright', although he then proceeded to caution him to be ready to 'do evil' if needed. It might be useful to distinguish customary legitimisation as a separate type. It consists in developing an image of respect for the traditions of the population (including religion) and appearing to be addressing the day-to-day problems faced by it. The ruler can himself pretend to have turned into a traditional notable, or he can try to woo the support of opinion-making sections of the population, such as the clergy, the notables, etc.

Diplomacy

Machiavelli was acutely conscious of the importance of diplomatic skills in state-making, recommending the selection of wise advisors and advising that deceit is acceptable when the alternative is to be disadvantaged. The point about deceit is important because it raises the issue of different forms of alliance making and coalition-building. In its most basic form, coalition-building includes the formation of temporary alliances with political organisations, local communities, leaders of armed groups, etc., in order to achieve common aims or to engage in joint activities.[50] Such temporary and loose alliances, where no coercion is involved, are not conducive to political stability and to the formation of a solid polity. Hence we have to identify more complex and solid types of coalition-building. In subaltern coalition-building the implicit threat of violence by the ruler gives a strong incentive to groups and individuals to ally with him in a subordinate position, although not without some rights and entitlements. In coercive coalition-building the ruler actually forces groups to establish relations with him, so that their bargaining position is weaker even if the ruler avoids establishing a true personal dictatorship (in which case it would be inappropriate to speak of a coalition).

While the three previous types of coalition-building (loose, subaltern and coercive) were defined on the basis of the degree of coercion involved, it is possible to form a relatively resilient coalition even in the absence of sufficient coercive powers. What I define as manipulative coalition-building incorporates a strong dose of ruthlessness and deceit, such as:

- the elimination (physical or otherwise) of reluctant allies;
- divide and rule tactics to split communities and groups and bring one of the rivals into the coalition, or to create divisions within the coalition itself in order to avoid challenges to the ruler;
- the artificial creation of links of dependency between members of the coalition and the leader (for example through patronage);
- inter-marriage among the families of members of the coalition;
- the granting of privileges to communities and groups, for example over the use of land, water rights, access to resources, access to specific professions, etc.

If successfully managed, manipulative coalition-building may lead to the formation of power blocs,[51] which can be very resilient. This explains why nepotism has often been used as a strategy to build or consolidate polities. Coalition-building can take many shapes, across international borders and across opposed factions. Reno repeatedly stressed the point in his writing that in West Africa warlords (and military-political entrepreneurs) are often former members or collaborators of the old state elite who are trying to maintain or increase their influence through 'non-conventional' means, once the old system becomes increasingly inefficient in building at least a degree of consensus; they often maintain links to the state apparatus or to the rival coalition even when they are formally opposed to it.[52] In these cases we might speak of informal coalitions. In Hendryk Spruyt's account of the rise of the state, social alliances play a key role. In his interpretation, weak kings ally with early capitalists in trading property rights for financial support in building a centralised state.[53] The formation of social groups, however, is the result of a relatively advanced stage of state formation.

Warlordism as a process: social and political dynamics

The emergence of a warlord is not just a matter of his skills and of the techniques he uses. A favourable environment must exist to allow his emergence. Then, the interplay of his actions with social and political dynamics will determine whether he will successfully consolidate his polity and develop it or not. What follows is an outline of social, economic and political processes affecting the development of warlordism, introducing concepts that will be used in the two main parts of the book.

The origins of warlordism

The most common source of warlordism is the weakening or disintegration of the security and political institutions of a state, especially if such a state is weakly integrated, either because of its large size, difficult geography, or complex ethnic/religious make-up. Within this process of weakening of the state, the most typical instance in which warlordism arises is when political power collapses, but the military forces on which it rested survive, at least in part. In this case we could speak of 'orphan' warlords, mostly former regional commanders of the central state army who faced with a political crisis at the centre opted to set up their own fiefdoms. A typical example of orphan warlordism might be White Russian generals after 1917.[54] There is historical evidence that while this is mostly a reactive phenomenon, would-be warlords motivated by some grievance against the central government, such as the fear of their impending dismissal, sometimes actively worked for the weakening of central state power. This most often takes the form of a claim to absolute power at the regional level. Recruiting private militias to deal with insurgencies is a practice that often found favour among rulers. There is evidence that this led to the formation of mafias and other similar 'interest groups', even in states normally perceived as quite strong, such as Turkey.[55] In some cases, where the state was not strong to start with, it may lead to the formation of warlordism or something close to it. The case of Sudan comes to mind here, both with reference to the war in the South[56] and to Darfur. Another example might include Tajikistan during and after its civil war.[57] Historical examples include post-Carolingian western Europe, the Byzantine Empire in the late tenth and the late Roman Empire. The rise of regional warlords may or may not lead to the collapse of the state, but the Afghan case is a fitting example of 'statecide' warlords.

Warlordism, on the other hand, is not always the direct outcome of an internal crisis of the state. It might be an indirect outcome, such as when non-state political organisations, such as armed movements, experience a weakening of the hold of the central leadership over its field commanders, who might then develop into warlords. A classic example of what could be described insurgent warlordism is Chad, where Frolinat, which started itself as a merger of different groups, disintegrated into multiple factions.[58] Liberia seems instead to represent a mixed process of warlord generation, with both 'orphan' former military officers and splintering commanders of the original insurgent force setting up their own groups. At least some of the actors in the Liberian civil war might better fit the definition of 'entrepreneurs'.[59] In the genesis of warlordism what we find is a problem of command and control of military organisations, faced by both central governments and ideological- or purpose-oriented non-state armed movements. Originating as fragments of the military structure of a state or of an insurgent organisation has important implications when we compare warlords to *entrepreneurs*. For example, it is often during their apprenticeship as officers or commanders within larger and politically more legitimate organisations that warlords earn their military legitimacy.

Warlordism is not necessarily the outcome of disintegration. It might equally result from the emergence of a charismatic leader out of a fragmented military class, as part of an 'attempt to re-establish stability within anarchy'.[60] From an anthropological perspective, the process starts with the formation of solidarity groups, characterised by strong personal relationships between the leaders and the members. This concept is akin to Ibn Khaldun's 'asabiyya' or 'group feeling':[61]

'Royal authority…(is) attained only through a group and 'asabiyya. This is because aggressive and defensive strength is obtained only through group feeling which means (mutual) affection and willingness to fight and die for each other'.

'Asabiyya 'gives protection and makes possible mutual defence…' and is centred around an individual who has 'superiority over the others in the matter of group feeling' and can 'act as a restraining influence and mediator [...] in order to keep its members from (fighting) with each other,' that is what we could nowadays a charismatic leader. Such solidarity or 'group feeling', with the 'energy and rapacious habits which go with it', can emerge only during 'desert life', that is in Afghan terms would be 'bandit' life in the mountains. The Bedouins of the desert are 'more disposed to courage' because 'they provide their own defence [...]. They always carry weapons. They watch carefully all sides of the road. [...] Fortitude has become a character quality of theirs.''The hamlets of the bedouins are defended against outside enemies by a tribal militia[...]' whose 'defence and protection are successful only if they are a closely knit group of common descent' or clients and allies who because of close contact with the master develop a strong relationship. When urban civilisation becomes weak and unable to dominate the 'Bedouins', an 'asabiyya can emerge to threaten the city, particularly if religion helps its members to mobilise for collective action.[62]

The consolidation of the solidarity groups into a military class is the second stage of the process leading to the emergence of warlordism. Where violence (using Ernest Gellner's formula) is 'pervasive, mandatory and normative',[63] warlords may represent an element of order, as opposed to the Hobbesian chaos where hundreds or even thousands of small military leaders all fight their own wars. Compared to the warlordism generated by the disintegration of a state, what I shall call evolutionary warlordism is likely to be a much longer process. From a historical perspective, warlords of this kind may be seen as part of a process of primitive accumulation of power, which ultimately might lead to the formation of a state once a 'critical mass of power' is achieved. If it is true that agrarian societies are characterised by the logic of the elimination of rival 'specialists in coercion',[64] warlords may represent a stage in this process. Examples of this type of warlords are relatively common in late antiquity and the early Middle Ages in Europe.[65]

Expansionist dynamics

From the discussion of the origins of warlordism, it derives that warlord polities often engage in expansionist drives. This is not necessarily simply the result of personal ambition, or of the manipulation of military legitimisation for political ends. The need to consolidate the fringes of their area of control or to pre-empt a threat from a rival polity might be genuinely dictated by political developments external to the warlords' own will. There might be an attempt to expand the revenue base, dictated by a desire of the military class to have more resources at its disposal, or by the need to finance a conflict and pay for a growing armed force. Expansionism might also be the result of the snowball effect of alliances with local leaders, who might involve the warlord in local conflicts and drag him beyond his existing area of influence through a complex web of relations (see chapter 10 for some examples from Afghanistan). Finally, the warlord might also be forced to intervene beyond his area of influence by the demands of external political allies, as happened to Dostum in Afghanistan after 1992.

Disintegrative dynamics

As hinted previously, feudal systems resemble some types of warlord polities, of which they are often an evolution. Scholars of feudalism have been trying to explain one of the main trends of feudal systems, towards fragmenting into many smaller and increasingly autonomous polities that differ widely in the way they are ruled. Because each vassal granted parts of his fief to a number of lower vassals (vavassors), there was no direct relationship between the lord and the vavassors. The low coherence of the system made control difficult. The lord was trying to reassure his vassals by gradually conceding hereditariness to the fiefs, with the result that in the medium and long term the power of the lord is minimised.[66]

This dynamic seems to be applicable with some explanatory value for 'orphan warlords'. However, as far as insurgent warlordism and evolutionary warlordism are concerned, Ibn Khaldun's theories might be of greater help. The Ibn Khaldunian cycle describes the dynamics of patrimonial politics. In his view, the key role in the formation of a new polity is a solidarity group ('asabiyya), as mentioned above. In the first period after the establishment of a polity,

'glory was the common (property) of the group, and all members of the group made an identical effort (to obtain glory), their aspirations to gain the upper hand over others and to defend their own possessions were expressed in exemplary unruliness and lack of restraint.'

'In this stage, the ruler serves as model to his people by the manner in which he acquires glory, collects taxes, defends property, and provides military protection. He does not claim anything exclusively for himself to the exclusion of (his people), because (such an attitude) is what is required by 'asabiyya, (and it was group feeling) that gave superiority (to the dynasty)'.[67]

Some time after having conquered power,

'(the rulers) will not need much 'asabiya to maintain their power' and [...] 'maintain their hold over the government and their own dynasty with the help, then, either of clients and followers who grew up in the shadow and power of the 'asabiya, or (with that) of tribal groups of a different descent who have become their clients'.

Moreover, '(royal authority), by its very nature, must claim all glory for itself.' Once the power of the ruler is consolidated, he

'claims all glory for himself, he treats the others severely and holds them in check. Further, he excludes them from possessing property and appropriates it for himself. People, thus, become too lazy to care for fame. They become dispirited and come to love humbleness and servitude'.

'When the dynasty continues in power and their rulers follow each other in succession, they become sophisticated'.

'Luxury will at first give additional strength to a dynasty', as 'a greater number of clients and followers is acquired'.

The result is the fragmentation of the original solidarity group and the over-taxation and over-exploitation of the subjects,[68] which may have disintegrative effects if not met by effective counter-measures.

Political economy of warlordism

If it is true that the model of the national state succeeded in becoming the dominant one because of its superior combination of elements of coercion and capital,[69] a similar combination might be crucial to the development of warlord polities too.

Even if, as argued earlier, political manipulation allows a polity to be run on the cheap and the warlord is not necessarily a *homo oeconomicus*, inevitably warlord polities too need revenue to function. In the early stages of state-making, i.e. where we find warlord polities, borrowing from rich capitalists, as in modern Europe, is not an option. The polity is too weak and freshly established to be considered as even remotely trustworthy by established creditors. Warlords may rely on whatever resources they can directly extract internally and on the patronage of external sponsors. More importantly in a Tillyan perspective, they may also team up with war profiteers and 'rogue capitalists' in order to develop their own shadow logistics and financial services. Contrary to established financial operators, these might be more inclined to lend financial support to warlords, in part for lack of alternative choice and in part for 'political (i.e. not strictly economic) considerations, such as consolidating a successful partnership developed within the realms of a war economy. Could a relationship of this kind represent an early form of the marriage of capital and coercion which in Tilly's interpretation 'made' Europe? For contemporary warlords it can be argued that the Tillyan model no longer applies because the process of state formation is overdetermined by international constraints.[70] As a result the relationship warlords might be able to build with rogue or shadow capitalists would be difficult to consolidate and legitimise, particularly in the long term. The financial cooperation between warlords and rogue capitalists tends therefore to be limited to war situations and the immediate post-conflict period. After that, warlords either turn into 'mafiosi' or are forced gradually to drop their dangerous liaisons and clean up their act if they want to reinvent themselves as politicians or statesmen. The rise and fall of Charles Taylor of Liberia is exemplary in this regard; his failure to clean up led to his quick downfall.

Another aspect hindering the formation of a long term relationship between warlords and rogue capitalists or war profiteers is the unstable character and unpredictability of internal conflict situations. War profiteers and rogue capitalists try to benefit personally financially from the conflict, exploiting the fact that war confers legitimacy on actions that otherwise would be seen as crimes. Because of this they have an interest in the prosecution of the conflict, but in my view their subjective interest is insufficient to make civil wars last indefinitely, as some authors have implied.[71] My hypothesis, which I will test throughout the book, is that once fortunes are accumulated, war and the uncertainty of outcome which characterise it become problematic. Too ruthless profiteering on the part of the warlord or his acolytes is likely to have a very destabilising effect on the fighters. The new rich become potential targets of enemies, as well of friends not endowed with such riches, and develop an interest in the stability and rule of law that peace could bring about. Those military leaders who have benefited economically from the war gradually lose interest in fighting and taking personal risks on the battlefield. Their interest in peace is at some point going to offset the interest in continuing war of other actors who have not yet succeeded in accumulating sufficiently large fortunes or who are not motivated by financial gain. Although the 'globalised' economy offers greater opportunities to safely invest away from the country in conflict,[72] therefore potentially removing one factor promoting the restoration of law and order, the war profiteer is unlikely to be able to use the conflict-ridden country solely as a source of revenue to be accumulated abroad. The real value of the services provided by profiteers is in the risk they assume, hence remote profiteering is not a real option. Moreover, the accumulation of capital through war is likely to stabilise after an initial rapid increase, as war is unlikely to generate a virtuous economic cycle capable of sustaining ever greater returns. In fact, the contrary is likely and diminishing returns from an increasingly devastated economy are to be expected. Peace (or at least 'a certain kind of peace') therefore becomes a more attractive option. I shall call this the peace cycle, which is in turn a combination of several trends:

- War may easily lead to unregulated predation due to the difficulty of exercising control over agents, in turn compromising the long-term economic bases of accumulation and starving the war factions of resources;
- Success in accumulation leads to the agent shaping his behaviour more closely according to the logic of the market and therefore shifting away from coercive accumulation to more capital intensive forms;[73]

INTRODUCTION

- The ability to mobilise for fighting erodes once accumulation starts bene-fiting members and leaders in disproportionate ways;[74]
- New factions or social groups might emerge in the wake of the conflict, which at some point might wield sufficient influence and power to forge new political coalitions in order to cut their transaction costs or facilitate their expansion in other ways;[75]
- Access to outside ideas or encouragement or even more so concrete help might provide the tools or have the mobilising effect among sections of the population which had hitherto been unable to organise for collective action.[76]

At different stages in Afghanistan peace cycles emerged during the series of conflicts which started in 1978 and some of these cycles will be described in detail in the book. None of these political economy cycles resulted in lasting peace. Why was this? *Empires of Mud* does not aim to provide a general answer as far as post-1978 Afghan history is concerned, but it will show which forces were at play that favoured the continuation of war over the establishment of peace in the case of the warlord polities of western and northern Afghanistan. Conflicts, including the Afghan one, cannot be reduced to political economy factors. Internal and international politics, as well as military factors, also have to be considered to understand Afghanistan's wars.

Cities and warlords

A key aspect of the dynamic of warlord polities is the role of urban centres. In a sense, the birth of the state has historically often been the result of the union of cities and 'territorial monarchs', even if the kind of cooperation which emerged in medieval Europe was of 'a very particular kind' and 'cul-minated in the rise of nation-states.'[77] Elsewhere the 'cooperation' might often have looked more like a 'forced marriage' or even a 'concubinate', as occurred several times in Afghanistan's history, but this need not prevent a state from emerging as a bastard child of the union. During the 1990s Afghan cities once again faced occupation by militarised 'solidarity groups' and were sometime forced into forceful marriages, sometime even 'raped'. In this regard too the model proposed by Ibn Khaldun can be useful. It focuses on the attraction exercised on the tribes by the city, but in my view it can be adapted to explain the relationship between cities and warlords. Not only is the city at the centre of a 'vortex' that leads to the creation of surplus-extracting struc-tures from the surrounding tribes or communities, but it draws the tribal leaders or warlords into the city, or towards the formation of coalitions trying to establish control over it. The leaders/warlords sometime capture the city, sometimes just move in, but are always attracted by the city because of its importance as a transport hub, as a financial and services centre and because of its prestige. The control of the city may prove a major competitive advan-tage against the leader's rivals, but over time in the Ibn-Khaldunian cycle the

21

leader or his descendants distance themselves from the solidarity group ('asa-biyya) which was their original power base, to the extent that they remain isolated and are easily overthrown.[78] This is why tribal states and unsophisti-cated warlord polities are both eminently unstable (see 'disintegrative dynam-ics' above). With the help of the resources of the city, warlord polities might potentially break the cycle by starting many of the institutionalisation and bureaucratisation processes described above. The city holds the keys to the specialisation and professionalism necessary to state-building.

The impact of the international system

It has been argued with good reason that the warlord must by definition be able to 'act financially and politically in the international system without interference from the state in which he is based'.[79] As argued above, in the 'Political economy of warlordism', this aspect should not be overesti-mated— in the existing international framework warlords will never rank as high as states in their ability to act beyond recognised national boundaries. Moreover, there is a tendency to overrate the widening of options made available to warlords by 'globalisation'.[80] The interaction of warlords with international crime networks, for example, certainly predates the 1990s, which is when globalisation is said to have taken off and the debate about it started. For example, it was already present in the case of the Chinese war-lords, at least in the form of relations with neighbouring countries and with international criminal networks.[81] The involvement of the Burmese warlords/druglords/insurgents with international criminal networks was also taking place long before the 1990s.[82]

There are more important ways in which the changing international sys-tem impacted on warlord polities during the last twenty to thirty years. The end of the Cold War and the so-called 'collapse of ideologies' might well have contributed to the proliferation of warlords through the (temporary?) dis-placement of ideological guerrillas, who lost the support of international powers.[83] This interpretation is useful but needs some qualification, for exter-nal support does not appear to be as crucial a factor as the strength of ideo-logical mobilisation itself. If there was a cycle of warlord marginalisation, it started with the Russian and Chinese civil wars of 1917–, when weakly resourced ideological movements defeated externally supported warlords. The exhaustion of a particular ideological cycle (communism) does not mean that others cannot follow, such as 'national liberation' in the 1950s-1970s or the current wave of Islamist movements. It is in the gap between ideological cycles that warlords found a ground free from strong competition. One has also to be careful about overstating the importance of the revival of warlord-ism during the 1990s, which might in part reflect a change of attitude among scholars trying to interpret what is happening in the world's civil wars, rather than a real change on the ground. In several studies of the wars of the Cold

War the term 'warlord' and the concept of warlordism were already being used, if sometimes only implicitly. The applicability of the 'warlord' label to the protagonists of the conflict in Lebanon is somewhat controversial, as this tends to be done rather indiscriminately, but it might be appropriate in the case of at least some protagonists of that civil war.[84] The politico-military actors of the civil war in Chad have also been extensively described as warlords in the scholarly literature.[85] Jonas Savimbi of UNITA is a perfect example[86] of some contradictions in the current usage of the concept of warlord. Having been a 'cold warrior' until 1992, he suddenly started being branded as a warlord the moment that Cuban and USSR support for the Angolan government ceased, without any obvious evidence that Savimbi himself changed his attitudes or his aims. His case shows well how warlords, as well as ideological movements, benefited from the support of foreign states during the Cold War.

Possibly the most important change in the international system to impact on warlordism has been the creation of international organisations after the Second World War and the rise of an 'international community' (as expressed in the formation of international organisations such as the United Nations), which has the ambition to prevent state collapse and the formation of new states (except for former colonies). Such attitudes were inevitably going to interfere and even prevent the state-making process out of warlordism from reproducing itself in the time-honoured pattern (see 'political economy of warlordism', above, and the literature cited there). In fact, the historical process of state formation had already been interrupted by the colonial era except in some of the most remote corners of the world or in peculiar circumstances. Even in the presence of an international community, it is not inconceivable that its demands might be sneakily eluded,[87] or that compromises might be made. If patrimonial polities can develop façades of bureaucratic processes in order to interact with the 'modern' world,[88] why should warlords not adopt similar tricks to develop their polities into states? They could, for example, use tactics such as institutional self-cooptation, described in the previous paragraph. The new international system, therefore, does not abolish the role of warlords in state-making; it merely modifies and constrains it.

Ideologisation (ideological contamination)

Warlords might not always be able fully to control the consequences of their own coalition-building with local communities and political organisations, as described in the previous sections. The possibility indeed exists that some contamination might take place and that ideologies and values might spread from those communities and organisations to the warlord's followers. While it might appear far fetched that ideologies of social justice might sound attractive to local military leaders, the same is certainly less true of nationalism, religious sectarianism and ethnicism. Sometimes, the warlord himself

23

might encourage such processes of ideologisation in order to strengthen his political legitimacy: in this case we have a convergence of representation-based legitimisation and ideologisation from below. In all cases the warlord risks losing control of his polity if he is not a careful and skilled manager. Ideologisation is at odds with the patrimonial character of warlordism and the ruler is likely to have sooner or later to rein it in, or accept that he will be sidelined. At that point a clash is likely, with potentially disastrous consequences.[89]

Peace-making and state rehabilitation

Since warlords flourish in the context of weak or disintegrated central states, perhaps the most obvious risk they can be subject to is the re-emergence or strengthening of the central state. This threat is a deadly one to any warlord polity: states, to the extent that they enjoy political legitimacy and have resources, are more than a match for warlords. As hinted when discussing the 'political economy of warlordism', with or without the intervention of the international community, with or without the warlord's own involvement, peace sometimes 'happens'. Even in the most anarchic or Hobbesian environment, war might not be sustainable without interruption and indefinitely. The 'explosion of peace' poses a number of problems for any ruler whose legitimacy derives from his role of military leader; usually it is only a matter of time before this legitimacy is eroded. Such a situation forces the warlord to choose between two extremes: return to war or accelerate a process of political legitimisation. Figures like Charles Taylor or Jonas Savimbi faced such a dilemma and made different choices. Even without peace, the re-emergence/ strengthening of the central state may still occur: international intervention or support for the central state (Congo DRC, Afghanistan), changing dynamics at the centre (Byzantium towards the end of tenth century), success in state-building by rival warlords or political movements, etc. Confronting such developments is likely to be too onerous for the warlord, who in order to avoid marginalisation is forced to adapt, renouncing in part his patrimonial power and adapting some of the institutionalisation and legitimisation strategies described in the previous section. Much of the story that follows in the coming chapters is exactly about how Afghanistan's warlords have coped with the demands of their environment and adapted to it. While it is useful to employ 'ideal-typical' constructions to impose a logic on a very chaotic subject, reality is very fluid, and the Afghan warlords analysed in *Empires of Mud* have experienced first hand most of the dynamics discussed in this introduction.

Notes

1. On this issue see also Ottaway/Lieven (2002).
2. 'Hurt', in *The man comes around*. I changed the original 'empire of dirt' to 'empires of mud' to implicitly refer to Afghanistan's typical mudbrick buildings (and to avoid offending any warlord in particular).

3. See for example Marten (2006/7): 'Warlordism plagues many weak and failed states, and the parochial and often brutal rule of warlords deprives countries of the chance for lasting security and economic growth.'
4. See Waldron (1991).
5. The literature on Chinese warlordism is quite abundant. On the warlords-gentry coalition see Ch'en (1979). See for a review McCord (1993).
6. Whittacker (1993).
7. See, for example, a pre-feudal example from European history in Smyth (1984). For post-feudal examples see Marten, who calls warlords the feudal lords of post-Carolingian Europe, Simms (1987) and Blaum (1994).
8. See for example Compagnon (1998) p. 83.
9. Service (1975), p. 195.
10. Claessen and Skalnik (1978), p. 626.
11. Adams (1975), p. 12.
12. Skalnik (1978), p. 615.
13. Skalnik (1978), p. 614–5.
14. On military legitimacy see below.
15. It is important to point out that what is being discussed is specifically *military* charisma, as distinct from *political* charisma. The term 'military charisma' or 'warrior charisma' was of course already used by Weber in opposition to other types of charisma.
16. Keen (1998). See also Adebajo and Keen (2000).
17. See for example Berdal and Malone (2000) and Collier and Hoeffler (2001). Mair (2003) refers more explicitly to warlords.
18. Berdal (2003).
19. See MacKinlay (2000), p 49; Roberts (1989), Riekenberg (1999) and Michael Bollig, 'Zur Ökonomie des Krieges: Die Gewalt und die Geschäfte der afrikanischen Warlords', *Frankfurter Rundschau*, 9 Jano. 2001.
20. Clapham (2002) and (1998).
21. Hsieh (1962), Lin (2002) and (2004).
22. The term was originally launched by Eide (1997). The quotation is from Eide (1998), p. 75.
23. On this see Compagnon (1998), p. 83.
24. See Olson (1993).
25. This point is also made by Marten (Winter 2006/07), pp. 41–73, as well as by Weber (1994), pp. 313–314).
26. See for example Menkhaus (2001); Hills (1997).
27. See Cramer (2006), ch. 4 on this.
28. Hawkins (nd.).
29. Gallant (1999), pp. 26–27; see also Peter Lock (2002), Chabal and Daloz (1999) p. 85
30. The greed of the lower ranks is eloquently shown in Keen (1998).
31. See DeVries (2001) and Anderson and Duffield (1998).
32. Jackson (2003), pp. 133–134. See also Battera, (2004) and Hills (1997).
33. All quotations are from *Il Principe* except where indicated.
34. G. Duby (1980).
35. Spruyt (1994), pp. 37–38
36. See Allen (1995).
37. The expression was previously used among others by Cohen *et al.* (1981) and Tilly (1990), paraphrasing economics.

38. Robinson and Scaglion (1987); Cyril D. Robinson et al. (1994).
39. NO. Machiavelli (1521), libro VI.
40. Strayer (1970), p. 6.
41. See Strayer (1970), p. 6–10.
42. Gallant (1999), p. 25.
43. Gellner (1996), p. 166.
44. Elias (1982), pp. 258ff. On the potential for the development of warlords into "democratic" players, see also Wantchekon (2004): 17–33 (www.nyu.edu/gsas/dept/politics/ faculty/wantchekon/research/warlord.pdf), who however fails to mention actual warlords.
45. Ibn-Khaldun, p. 126.
46. On the importance of 'control[ing] the symbols of legitimacy' in order to obtain social cohesion and loyalty, see Gellner (1995), pp. 165–6.
47. Geertz (1964), part V.
48. Ibid, part VI.
49. This distinction between weakly organised/bureaucratised polities and strongly organised ones is similar to that established by Duverger (1976) between committee-based parties and section- or cell-based parties (pp. 71–77).
50. Yarn (1991), p. 81.
51. The concept is derived from Gramsci and once expunged of class analysis can be so defined (paraphrasing Poulantzas (1973), 297–8): a contradictory unity of dominant groups, whose interests are antagonistic rather than monolithic, dominated internally by a hegemonic individual or group that politically polarizes the interests of the other components of the bloc in order to establish its own interests as the least common denominator in the political field and to make itself the representative of the general common interest of the power bloc.
52. See among other works Reno (2002). On the ambiguous relationship between warlords and central government in Afghanistan see Giustozzi (2003).
53. Spruyt (1994), ch. 5
54. See Pereira (1997); Bisher (2005).
55. See for example Karl Vick, 'In Kurdish Turkey, a New Enemy', *Washington Post*, 31 Oct. 2002.
56. See de Waal (1994) and Salih and Harir (1994), pp. 186–203.
57. See Dorenwendt (1997) and Nourzhanov (2005).
58. Azevedo (1998) and Buijtenhuijs (1987), pp. 320–325.
59. See Ellis (1999).
60. Jackson (2003), pp. 147.
61. See Aziz Al-Azmeh (1982), for a discussion of the term, pp. 32–5; Fuad Baali (1988), pp. 43ff.
62. Khaldun, pp. 123, 107, 95, 97–8, 120, 122.
63. Gellner (1996), p. 160.
64. Gellner (1996), p. 162.
65. See Coupland (1998), Smyth (1984) and Simms (1987) for examples.
66. Poggi (1978), pp. 25–31.
67. Khaldun, pp. 123–4, 133–4, 138, 141.
68. Khaldun, pp. 124, 133–4, 140, 230.
69. Tilly (1990).
70. See, with some caution, Herbst (1996–7); Leander (2003); Sørensen (2001).
71. Keen (1998) p. 12.
72. Jung (2003), p. 20.

73. See Volkov (2002). I am indebted to Jonathan Goodhand for pointing out this similarily in interpretation between the author and Volkov.
74. On the importance of links of reciprocity for the motivation of fighters see Gat (2006), pp. 298–9.
75. See Marten (2006).
76. See Marten (2006).
77. Fox (forthcoming).
78. Tapper (1983) and Glatzer (1983).
79. Duffield (1997).
80. The importance of globalisation and the ' chaos' deriving from it is stressed in Cerny (1998), pp. 36–64, and in Jackson (2003), pp. 133–134. Mackinlay (2002), pp. 15–29 is one of the few authors who illustrates in detail what trends might have favoured the emergence of warlordism and other criminalised insurgencies.
81. On the trade of weapons in warlord China see Chan (1982).
82. On Khun Sa see Lintner (1994) and Smith (1991), pp. 314–315.
83. The most interesting formulation of this process is to my knowledge found in Reno (2002), pp. 837–858.
84. See Picard (1996) and Dib (2004) for a description of a range of Lebanese 'warlords'.
85. Azevedo (1998) and Buijtenhuijs (1987), pp. 320–325.
86. Stuvoy (2002), Johnson (1999) and Bollig, op. cit.
87. A similar argument is developed in Roth (1968), pp. 194–206.
88. See Giustozzi (2008b) and (2008). See also Menkhaus' concept of 'paper states' (2003).
89. On the reaction of Chinese warlord Feng Yu-hsiang to the danger of the ideologisation of his organisation in the 1920s, see Sheridan (1966).

PART ONE

GESTATION, EMERGENCE AND CRISIS, 1978–2007

1

THE ROOTS OF WARLORDISM
IN AFGHAN SOCIETY

The warlords of the late twentieth and early twenty-first centuries were not the first to have emerged in Afghan history. Although historical evidence is often too sketchy to apply labels such as this with any precision, at least one famous example stands out. Ahmad Shah Abdali, the founder of the Durrani empire, started his political career as a former general, an orphan of the Persian Empire. He first of all succeeded in gathering the support of fellow Pashtun and Uzbek officers in the army of Nadir Shah, who all felt threatened by the disintegration of the Persian Empire after the assassination of the king. As he arrived in Kandahar in 1747 with his troops, he only had his military force and Nadir Shah's treasury as an asset, having been away from his home region for a long time and having been cut off from local tribal politics. Moreover, his Sadozai sub-tribe was weak and unable to compete with the main tribes of the region. The combination of the treasury and the superior skills of the former units of the Persian army that followed Ahmad Shah, which included a sizeable artillery contingent, gave him an edge over rival aspirants to the throne. Significantly, although the tradition has him elected on the advice of a holy man, the tribal jirga that formally selected him as king took place in the military base of Kandahar, where the influence of his armed force would be maximised. His very developed political instincts then allowed him to combine coercion and coalition-making rapidly to build a large empire.[1]

After Ahmad Shah, Afghanistan knew long periods of crisis alternated with attempts to re-establish central authority. Until the emergence of Abdur Rahman as a strong ruler in 1880–1900, it experienced an almost permanent state of crisis, with dynastic rivalries, loss of central control, foreign interference and intervention. It has been argued that the Afghan state was chronically under-funded due to lack of resources and so unable to stabilise its area of control, particularly once, surrounded by two much more more powerful neighbouring empires, it could no longer rely on external conquest as a means of rewarding the tribes.[2] Even able rulers like Dost Mohammad (1826–39; 1843–1863) faced immense difficulties in controlling the country and his sons fought a civil war against each other. British efforts to incorporate Afghanistan into the 'new international system' had succeeded by the end of the nineteenth century, not before two wars and much chaos. Abdur Rahman was the ultimate Afghan beneficiary of this development; his experience of the British and of the Russians gave him unprecedented diplomatic skills (by Afghan standards) and at the same time he had accumulated a detailed knowledge of the country through extensive travel and having served as governor in the provinces. Less of a charismatic military leader than Ahmad Shah, he proved to be a very effective if ruthless administrator and consolidator. Helped by British subsidies, he turned Afghanistan into an effectively unified polity, controlled by the centre and was even able to ensure that his son and successor Habibullah would still be able to keep the system running.

For a while, Abdur Rahman's effort at building a patrimonial state in Afghanistan had done away with all kinds of sub-state polities that had been proliferating until the 1880s. With the aforementioned exception of Ahmad Shah and his fellow former officers of the Persian army, warlords seem to have been rare in Afghanistan at that time, for reasons which will be made clearer below. Ahmad Shah's emergence as an 'orphan' warlord was the result of developments external to Afghanistan's society and political environment. This is not surprising, given the absence of a strong central state in Afghanistan at that time. Ahmad Shah's model, as we shall see, was emulated by Abdul Rashid Dostum in the 1990s. The same could be said of the insurgent warlordism of the 1980s and 1990s: the externally sponsored strong central state decisively provoked as a counter-reaction an insurgency serious enough to generate the dynamic processes leading to warlordism, such as the formation of a military class. Nonetheless, the Afghan environment still played a key role in shaping the polities which were created by the warlords. Moreover, Afghanistan experienced also evolutionary warlordism, in which external factors were less important. It is worth asking therefore whether a link exists between the Afghan environment and the emergence of warlords on the political scene. It might be tempting to see the geographical landscape and the limited accessibility of much of Afghanistan as a key contributory factor to warlordism. The evidence suggests otherwise: the two regions which in the 1980s and 1990s saw the strongest forms of warlordism to emerge (in the west and north) were in fact the flattest parts of the country. Of the two, only Herat was really remote from Kabul, while the north turned into the strategic backyard of the ruling party in the 1980s, who maintained its stockpiles of supplies there (see Map 1). The role of geography seems instead to have been that large warlord polities formed only where geography did not impede their control of the military class. In areas difficult to access, local military leaders felt sufficiently protected and had little incentive to surrender any of their autonomy to a larger polity. The case of Shura-i Nezar, which will be described in greater detail in chapter 22, is the exception which confirms the rule since it was not a warlord polity and relied to a greater extent on political legitimisation.

Map 1: Geographical constraints of the influence of warlords, 1990s

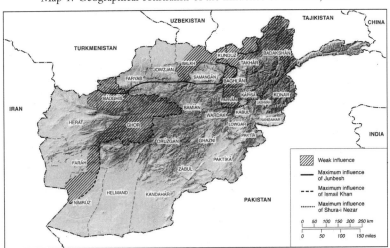

One aspect of warlordism, namely the regionalisation of military and political power, appears to derive from the slow and incomplete formation of nationwide social classes and groups. Fragmentation into local communities remained the norm in the 1970s. The closest thing to a national social group or class was in the 1970s the officers of the armed forces and police. Apart from that, only traders and sections of the intelligentsia were beginning to take the shape of classes and nationwide social groups and even these processes were not very advanced. The fragmentation of the intelligentsia into a multitude of political groups bears witness to this. The trading class, for its part, was still showing only modest levels of class consciousness as late as the twenty-first century. A sign of the ability of the business community to articulate common views is the formation of an organisation able to lobby in its behalf. The first such organisation to be formed in Afghanistan was the Afghan International Chamber of Commerce (AICC), established in Kabul in 2004. Its representativeness remained limited: by 2007 it had just 3,000 members, out of an estimated 30,000 medium and large entrepreneurs active in Afghanistan, suggesting low levels of mobilisation and interest. Even this poor level of support was achieved through the sponsorship and help of external actors, such as CIPE (Centre for International Private Enterprise, a non-profit organisation affiliated to the US Chamber of Commerce). American support magnified AICC's importance and transformed it into an unavoidable interlocutor for the government; it is likely that in its absence AICC might even have not formed at all.[3]

Afghanistan's social structures might be linked to the (re-)emergence of a military class in the 1980s, in turn a key precondition for the rise of evolutionary warlordism. The relatively strong presence of large landlords in certain areas (Herat, Kandahar, parts of the north) and of a strong stratum of local notables throughout much of Afghanistan was not the direct cause of the emergence of warlords and of the new military class. The Khans were the most important local leaders in pre-war Afghanistan, who had resources and recognised leadership skills to gather followers around them and therefore were able rapidly to mobilise people for political action.[4] In specific parts of Afghanistan (Hazarajat, Kandahar, Badakhshan) the Khans still had in the 1970s very well entrenched positions, which led one author to describe them as quasi-aristocratic.[5] However, although the 'old' Khan families had once initially established themselves as military leaders, at least in part, by the 1970s they had mainly lost the military role which they had had until at least the twenty-first century and rarely proved to have any military charisma when tested in the early days of the jihad.[6] The new military leaders who emerged in the 1980s were instead mostly new men, often from a humble family background. In the case of Herat, for example, landlords and notables played a direct role in the early phases of the insurgency, but during the war effective military leaders emerged from the ranks of former officers, political activists, former outlaws and only marginally rural notables.[7] It was mostly in remote areas, largely spared by the war, that the old Khan families maintained an important role throughout the 1980s and 1990s.[8]

Afghanistan's social and economic structures gradually allowed new military leaders to develop an autonomous economic and social base, as during the 1980s the military leaders turned into 'new Khans' or 'Islamic Khans', taking over the social and political role of the old notables. The title of Khan was in fact often given to military leaders in the earlier stages of the jihad. Often the new military class even took over the properties (land, houses) of the old Khans, later demanding payments from the farmers. The military class had somehow to support itself, particularly when external support was insufficient or non-existent. Even when the military leaders came from a politicised Islamist[9] background and had been active in the student movement, they rapidly became almost undistinguishable from the old Khans, indulging in 'personal feuds and revenge', 'competition for women', assassination of personal enemies, looting, bribe-taking… Younger fighters were expected to serve the older ones, while military leaders like the Khans distributed weapons and ammunitions, as well as cash and presents, often obeying not a logic of merit, but of patronage. The dependent villagers of Afghanistan seem to have found it easy to become the armed followers of new military leaders who took up the role, way of life and behaviour of the Khans. In part this pattern was also the result of a political culture of dependency of the rural population in many parts of Afghanistan, as the notables had often been the only link between the village and the external world; in the new context of the 1980s, military leaders were better placed to play this role of intermediary than the old notables.[10]

A counter-factual demonstration of the role of political culture and social structures can be sought in the regions where a military class did not emerge, or did not find strong roots. This is the case of the tribal areas of the Pashtun belt, running from the southern fringes of Herat province all the way to Kunar province. Until the early 1980s, Pashtun tribes were frequently described as an extreme example of a segmentary society, based on the research of such authors as Barth among the Swats of Pakistan and by Anderson among the Afghan Ghilhais.[11] The power of the tribal leaders, *maliks* and Khans, was described as limited and subject to the approval of tribal councils (*jirgas*). The tribes were seen as very egalitarian and their politics as very fluid, providing a type of political environment in which a military class could hardly consolidate its role and complex warlord polities hardly establish themselves. Generalisations based on the work of these two scholars failed to recognise that the Pashtun tribal system changed over time and varied from region to region and from tribe to tribe. In his work on the Pakistani tribal areas, Ahmad found that social differentiation could exist within Pashtun tribes. He described two types of social organisation among the Pashtun of Pakistan, the first was called *Nang* and corresponded to the egalitarian models discussed by other authors. In his definition, *Nang* are honour-bound Pashtuns, who still abide by the tribal code (*Pashtunwali*) in full and whose society is acephalous and segmentary. Yet he also found a second type of social organisation called *Galang*. This is characterised by a hierarchical social structure, where *Pashtunwali* plays a more modest role and where patron-client relations are dominant.[12] Soviet anthropologists, who intensified their work on the topic during the 1980s, developed Ahmad's argument further and went as far as talking of the feudalisation of some Pashtun tribes. This process was most advanced among the tribes living closer to the cities and towns and those closest to the monarchy, such as the Durranis. In these cases landlords used their ability to raise rent to turn into full time 'leaders', drawing on their resources to strengthen their influence and power. This trend was the result of the state co-opting tribal leaders and appointing them as local representatives, in charge of gathering taxes and duties from fellow tribesmen among other things.[13] Katkov distinguished three types of Pashtun tribes:

- *qaumi*—egalitarian, where the leader does not have real power and has to depend on the *jirga*;
- *rutbavi*—hierarchical, with a tendency towards feudalisation and usurpation of the power of the tribesmen by the leader; these leaders have the ability to influence the orientation of their followers, either directly or through their representatives, who allow the leader to maintain influence even if he resettles in the city;
- *kuchi*—nomadic and very egalitarian.

That leaders in many cases went far beyond the role attributed to them in the ideal of tribal 'tradition' is attested already in the nineteenth century. Elphinstone observed in 1815 that the tribes closest to the monarchy were the 'most obedient' to their *Khans*.[14] *Khans* have long been reported to be manipulating the election of *jirgas* so that their own people were selected. As the Afghan state started developing during the twentieth century, the leaders frequently and often successfully attempted to get their own relatives and friends into positions within the administration.[15] In the 1970s the scholarly literature reported a tendency towards a change in the role of tribal leaders away from lineage solidarity towards seeking individual or factional advantage even in areas previously unaffected. Some elements of this development seem to confirm the increasing reliance on dependent sharecroppers as a source of revenue and power.[16] Such a process, whether it is described as feudalisation or not, evidently creates a social environment more conducive to the consolidation of a military class, which was actually the original concern of the kings when they granted what essentially amounted to feudal titles to the aristocracy. It is in fact among the Durrani *rutbavi* tribes that signs of the emergence of an autonomous military class could be discerned during the 1980s, although the process rarely developed very far due to the weak involvement of the Durrani aristocracy in the conflict and the absence of strong military leaders, able to usurp its land. The failure of strong military leaders to emerge might be due to several factors, but certainly the disinclination of the Soviet military in Kandahar to engage in repeated large scale military operations must have been one. Anywhere else along the Pashtun belt, autonomous, relatively acephalous communities characterised by low or non-existent extraction of resources prevailed. This meant that military leaders were mostly unable to find an economic and social base that could have allowed them to turn into a stable military class. Exceptions were few and mostly limited to cases where the leader was able to find a reliable source of revenue. The most common pattern among Pashtun military leaders was either turning into bandits or retiring to private life. Signs of 'incipient warlordism' among southern Pashtuns will be discussed in chapters 2–4. However, because of the patterns just described, the focus of this volume is largely those parts of Afghanistan inhabited by non-Pashtuns and specifically Uzbeks and Tajiks (as mentioned earlier, for a series of reasons, warlordism did not feature prominently among Hazaras either).

Even some Tajik communities provided a poor social base for the rise of warlords. That acephalous communities incapable of extracting and accumulating significant resources represented a strong obstacle to the consolidation of a military class can indeed be confirmed by a comparison between the Tajiks of Kohistan (north of Kabul) and Badakhshan (north-east). The former had chiefs by the late eighteenth century, but these do not appear to have been powerful ones. According to Elphinstone, these chiefs (*Khans*) had few permanent armed followers and relied on community mobilisation to fight their enemies. They reportedly kept the villagers in 'imperfect subjection'. Although some local chiefs were allied to the monarchy, most of the Kohistani communities usually resisted royal rule and did not pay taxes to Kabul until the beginning of the nineteenth century. Even after the imposition of taxation, they several times rose against Kabul and tried to free themselves. In the absence of strong local leaders, the Tajiks of Kohistan differed a lot from the

Tajiks of Badakhshan, whose Khans had instead a much greater degree of control over the villagers. Both Kohistan and at least parts of Badakhshan (particularly in the region of Faizabad and along the road connecting that town to Teluqan and Kunduz) saw protracted warfare, but followed divergent patterns in the formation of political leadership, with Badakhshan ending up mostly dominated by the military class and Kohistan by party- and community-based militias (see chapter 22). Under the Rabbani government, the administration of Badakhshan was de facto subordinated to the military leaders, whom the local population called 'rulers', to the extent that the authority of the 'central government' was seen as merely symbolic. Forced recruitment was widely practised, at the discretion of each strongman. Military leaders could bypass the qazi and try people themselves, or in any case interfere in the execution of the sentence.[17]

If weak local leadership was an obstacle to the consolidation of a military class and hence of warlords, the contrary is not automatically true: strong local leadership did not necessarily lead to the formation of a stable military class as a dominant social force. This for example did not happen in the case of Hazarajat, the central region populated by Shiite Hazaras. On the surface, the social environment would seem to have favoured the emergence of an autonomous military class: the region was largely controlled by government-friendly Khans who often 'owned' whole valleys and had a stranglehold over the villagers. The mountainous geography of the region was not conductive to the formation of large warlord polities, as I have argued above, but could well have allowed the emergence of a strong military class. In fact, in 1979 several local strongmen emerged from among the ranks of the Khans, each running his autonomous military and administrative structure. They achieved their position by being selected by fellow Khans by virtue of their leadership and organisational skills. They usually relied on short-term conscription to organise their local militias, with subordinate commanders appointed to lead smaller groups, organised on a tribal or geographical base. The weak political leadership of Hazarajat, the Shura-i Ittefaq, was unable to exercise effective control from its HQ. As external threats to the region rapidly receded, never to resurface until the mid-1990s, conscription started being perceived as oppressive by the villagers. The fast rotation of the militiamen also prevented the formation of a base of followers personally loyal to the strongmen. The absence of armed conflict during the early years of the Shura government in Hazarajat and the initial good conditions of law and order were all factors militating against the formation of a military class, despite a propitious social structure. Interestingly, the only military leaders whose armed followers developed a strong loyalty towards them were all based on the fringes of Hazarajat, where fighting with government forces and rival groups was more intense and frequent.[18]

When a Hazarajat-wide military challenge finally arose in the early 1980s with the assault by the Khomeinist groups on Shura-ye Ettefaq, dominated by traditionalist clerics, the local military leaders were unprepared and were mostly swept away without having much of a chance to improve their skills or being replaced by more competent ones. By then the local military leaders of the Shura had already lost much legitimacy because of their exactions from the population. Lacking loyal and skilled armed followers, most of them disappeared from the scene. The main exceptions were those aforementioned military leaders who operated at the fringes of Hazarajat and had developed deeper roots, such as Sayyed Jaghlan of Ghazni, who continued to fight the Khomeinists for years. He and a few others were the only Hazaras to 'graduate' to the military class during the 1980s. Among the Khomeinists too local military leaders started becoming autonomous from the political leadership of the different pro-Iranian factions. By the second half of the 1980s they already represented an obstacle to intra-Hazara peace negotiations. However, these Khomeinist military leaders rarely succeed in consolidating as a military class, probably due to the relatively short length of the conflict and to the political domination of the clergy and of their strongly ideologised organisations. Once again only on the northern fringes of the Hazarajat did a Khomeinist military class emerge, and not before the 1990s, as a result of the intense conflicts characterising the region and of the weaker control exercised locally by the political and religious leadership.[19]

What the case of Hazarajat in comparison to other cases and particularly that of Badakhshan suggests is that the formation of a military class was the result of the combination of protracted warfare with the presence of social structures supporting strong local leadership. The insecurity spreading throughout the villages as a consequence of the withdrawal of the state gave the incentive to the villagers to arm and seek the protection of military leaders. Protracted warfare of an indecisive kind forged strong links among military leaders and between military leaders and their armed followers, leading to the formation of solidarity groups along Ibn Khaldun's 'asabiyya model (see Introduction). Then the existence of dependent farmers and villagers allowed the military class to consolidate itself by finding an economic and social base.

On top of all this, traditions of political leadership and organisation might have played a role in shaping the modes of political organisation which the new military class ended up adopting, by offering a ready mode of political organisation to an otherwise unskilled new generation of rulers. In northern Afghanistan, it is striking how the long-standing Uzbek tradition of highly devolved polities (usually known to scholars as the Chingizid appanage system) resurfaced in the 1990s (see chapter 6). The appanage system had been a somewhat effective way of organising territorial control in the absence of strong political organisation and of financial resources. In this system the sultan/ruler was merely a first among equals, whose right was limited to appointment and dismissal; he had no authority over the territory of the subrulers appointed to rule specific territories. Each sub-ruler further 'parcelledout' territory to military leaders called Amirs, who were then appointed as governors. The appointments to a specific territory were initially not hereditary, but the Amirs tended to come from the same families and over time appointments too became hereditary. There was also no centralised system of tax collection, while the inability of the ruler to intervene at the peripheral level made conflict among his regional Amirs common.[20] The appanage system had been wiped out by the Afghan conquest, completed in the late nineteenth century by Abdur Rahman, during which the old aristocracy was either physically eliminated or fled abroad. Thereafter tribal and clan leaders agreed to be subjected to the new Pashtun state.[21] Despite the similarities, there is no evidence that Dostum deliberately imitated the appanage system, and the resemblance with his own way of managing Junbesh might just be the consequence of the similar circumstances in which he operated.

With regard to Herat, while there might be a cultural component to the local desire for autonomy, for example having to do with the Heratis' sense of superiority over the rest of Afghanistan, there are more solid reasons too. The landed wealth of Herat's elites was the main source of their power and much of their effort to secure local autonomy might be explained by their desire to protect it from central taxation. The city had a tradition of rebelling against the dominant power, particularly when the local balance of power was being upset, and of demands for self-rule. This suggests that Herat's propensity for autonomy derived from the availability of internal resources sufficient to support a separate polity, a rather rare occurrence in Afghanistan.[22]

Rural-urban relations as they developed historically in Afghanistan might go further in explaining the rise of warlordism, or at least certain features which it adopted. In Afghanistan cities and towns have traditionally been identified with the bazaar, the centre of the administration and the large mosque. More recently cities also became the centres of advanced education (high schools and universities).[23]

Starting in the nineteenth century, with the spread of monetisation the bazaars played a key role in extracting surpluses from the rural population through unfavourable terms of trade. The hegemony of urban lifestyles led to rural notables and anybody who aspired to status buying imported products like china, kerosene, sugar and tea from urban traders at very high prices, while the rural economy stagnated. The monetisation of the economy also drew increasing numbers of landowners towards producing for the market and most importantly adopting capitalist methods of production, abandoning the reciprocity which had characterised patron-client relations. The result of these processes, driven by the urban economy, was to weaken the power and influence of the old Khans, who after all were still the main tool of social control by the state in the villages, while at the same time antagonising the rural population. Such antagonism was only exacerbated by direct state extraction. Although direct state taxation declined throughout the twentieth century, another important form of extraction of surplus from the countryside was the corruption of the administration, which was often institutionalised and more or less accepted, but also happened to be sometimes rapacious and out of control.[24]

Another key aspect of the antagonism between city and villages was the emergence in the 1970s of a new generation of 'intellectuals' educated in state schools and universities, who started challenging the influence and role of both the clergy and the rural notables, particularly if they were themselves of rural origins. As is well known, it was from the ranks of these 'intellectuals' that the revolutionaries of Khalq would emerge to turn their implicit challenge into outright aggression. In a sense, it could be argued that urban Afghanistan, which mostly identified itself with the central state, contributed to the rise of warlordism first by weakening the hold of the old elites on the villagers and second by creating an embryonic alternative rural elite (the intelligentsia), which tried to take over from the former, without success. The result was the unleashing of the accumulated frustration of the rural elites against not only Khalq but also the state as such. By severing the link between the state and the rural elites and therefore crucially weakening them, the Khalqis created the conditions for the drift of rural Afghanistan towards anarchy and chaos, an environment conductive to the rise of the warlords.[25]

Notes

1. I follow here Barfield's interpretation (p. 270), which looks more credible that the conventional one. See also Singh (1959), Misdaq (2006), pp. 42–3.
2. Rubin (1995), pp. 46–7.
3. Interviews with Chairman of AICC and selected members, Kabul, May 2005.
4. For discussions of the concept of Khan see Azoy (2002), pp. 27–32, Dorronsoro (2005), pp. 119–22.
5. Dorronsoro (2005), pp. 119–120.
6. On the military role of Uzbek Khans in the nineteenth century Century, see Harlan (1939), pp. 60–1; Ferrier (1857).
7. Interviews with former commanders and government officials, Herat, Sept.-Oct. 2005.
8. An example from Ghor is in Stewart (2004), p. 148–50.
9. The term Islamist is used here following Olivier Roy's definition, that is of Islam as a political ideology (see Roy (1990)).
10. Roy (1988), pp. 22–3; Roy (1989), p. 74; Roy (1994), p. 87; Roy (1995), pp. 107–8; Rubin (1995), pp. 257. On the dependent farmers see Grevemeyer (1980).
11. Barth (1959), Anderson (1978), pp. 119–149.
12. Ahmed (1983), pp. 196–7. See also Edwards (1998), p. 714.
13. Katkov (1989), pp. 54–55. Of course feudalisation is meant by Katkov in the Marxist sense and we too shall use it here with that meaning. See also TemirKhanov (1984), (1987). A critique of this use of the term is in Daoud (1982), p. 62, who argues that the lack of formal bounds of dependency prevents the use of the concept of feudalism. However, Soviet authors tend to describe the situation more in terms of a process leading to feudalism, rather than feudalism itself.
14. Elphinstone, (1815) p. 217, also quoted in Glatzer (2002).
15. Rasuly (1997), pp. 104–118.
16. Ewans-von Krbek (1977), pp. 276, 281–88, 301. A trend towards a more hierarchical system was also indentified by Anderson (1978), p 167–183.

17. Elphinstone (1815), pp. 314–5; C. Noelle (1997), pp. 30ff.; Grevemeyer (1982), pp. 108ff.; Dorronsoro (2005), p. 119; Roy (1990), pp. 189–90; UNSMA document, 11 May 2000, 13 June 2000 and 2 March 2001; UNSMA document, 11 July 2000.
18. Ibrahimi (2006), p. 12, 13
19. Ibrahimi (2006), p. 18; Ibrahimi (2008 forthcoming).
20. Lee (1996), pp. 32–34; McChesney (1983), pp. 33–70; Noelle (1997), pp. 66–71.
21. Khashimbekov (1994), p. 17–8.
22. Szuppe (1992), p. 67, 159–63; Tumanovich (1989), pp. 168ff.
23. Grötzbach (1986).
24. Centlivres and Centlivres-Demont (1988), p. 193ff., 243; Chaffetz (1981), p. 209; Anderson (1978); Tapper (1983);
25. On the reforms of the Khalqi regime and their impact, see Giustozzi (2000), pp. 3–6.

2

INSURGENT WARLORDISM

THE JIHAD MOVEMENT (1978–1992)

The jihad movement which started in 1978 was the result of the convergence of different factors and movements. Conservative elites were pushed towards armed opposition because they were targeted by the new government in Kabul. To most of the clergy, also antagonised by the new rulers, participating in the revolt was a way of furthering and expanding the role they had gained in Afghan politics for the first time during the Anglo-Afghan war of 1839–42. Rogue elements, such as bandits, saw the opportunity to recycle themselves in a noble movement. Local communities, whether antagonised by the new regime or not, saw it as a chance to expand their autonomy from the state.[1] The small Islamist armed groups which had had a presence in Afghanistan and Pakistan from the early 1970s saw the blunders of the new leftist regime in Kabul as an opportunity to find a wider constituency for its Islamic Revolution. Contrary to the other components of the jihad described above, the Islamists were in principle interested in organising a nationwide movement, centrally coordinated if not directed. However, in most of Afghanistan, the bulk of the jihadi movement was initially represented by local notables, naturally disinclined to accept the ideologisation of jihad as Islamic revolution, sponsored by the Islamists. Another factor complicating the task of the Islamists was the challenging geography of the country, which made command and control of insurgent groups difficult. Most of the few roads were under control of the pro-Soviet government, or were in any case patrolled by government and Soviet forces. While supplies could still enter the country in large quantities along caravan routes, despatching envoys from the party headquarters was rendered ineffective by the long travelling time. The introduction of long-range radios in the early 1980s allowed at least the headquarters of some parties to communicate with their local leaders, issue orders and gather information and reports from them. It did not make it any easier to ensure that orders were followed, or that the information provided was reliable. The only ways to maintain a degree of effective control would have been:

- establishing a system of 'political commissars' reporting directly to the head-quarters and not responding to the local leaders;
- creating a counter-intelligence system under the direct control of headquarters;
- to invest heavily in the ideologisation and indoctrination of the rank and file.

The establishment of such command and control systems was an option open only to those parties and groups that had sufficient numbers of edu-cated and ideologically motivated recruits in their ranks.

The existence of multiple anti-Soviet jihadi organisations was yet another major factor in making command and control from their Peshawar headquar-ters very difficult. Local military leaders always had the option of realigning their allegiance to a different group whenever they faced pressure to follow a particular behaviour or strategy. The jihadi movement was divided into a multitude of movements; even those officially recognised by either Iran or Pakistan numbered as many as seventeen at one point. Many former jihadi local leaders and sympathisers believe that the Pakistani government deliber-ately sought to divide the jihadi movement in order better to control and manipulate it. However neither Pakistani sources nor the CIA operatives who were working with the Pakistanis in running the insurgency subscribe to this view. Undoubtedly the Pakistanis imposed a ceiling on the number of parties allowed to be officially recognised in Peshawar and hence entitled to receive supplies, possible fearing that an excessively fragmented jihadi movement would have declined into insignificance. Initially the ceiling was established at six parties, but later, under Arab pressure, it was raised to seven to accom-modate Professor Sayyaf's Ittehad-i Islami.[2] The Iranians were the target of similar accusations, of trying to keep the Shiite jihadi movement divided, but there are alternative explanations, mainly having to do with Teheran's own internal divisions.[3] In any case, during the second half of the 1980s the Irani-ans played a key role in unifying the various strands of the Shiite jihadi armed groups, with only temporary success. To a large extent, the division in differ-ent parties seems to have been the consequence of the fragmentation of Afghan society.

Whatever the case, under pressure from both the Pakistani authorities and most likely from the Americans too, the main priority of the Peshawar-based parties seems to have been to increase the tempo of military operations as quickly as possible, without paying much attention to building solid structures inside the country. Each individual party was under pressure to follow such advice, as external support could always be easily shifted to a rival organisa-tion and indeed the more proactive groups were rewarded in terms of supply distribution. Since in 1978–79 these parties had a limited number of activists in their ranks,[4] the only viable option to expand their activities rapidly was to recruit individuals from other organisations, including existing local military leaders inside Afghanistan, who would be attracted by the offer of weapons and other supplies. In exchange, the new 'recruits' had to abide by certain 'rules', which varied from party to party, but which most parties had no way of enforcing.

Some of the jihadist organisations had greater potential than others to impart an ideological character to the movement. The so-called 'traditionalist' parties, Jabh-i Nejat-i Milli and Mahaz-i Milli, relied on Sufi networks as a unifying factor, but had no real organisation or chain of command to control their men in the field. Their main constituencies were tribal and as such made poor material for the formation of a permanent military class (see chapter 1).[5]

Another group, Harakat-i Enqelab-i Islami, often also described not very accurately as traditionalist, had a following mainly among the clergy, although it did not discriminate unduly and recruited local leaders into its ranks. While the fundamentalist-leaning clergy gave Harakat somewhat of an ideological line, its organisational weakness and the absence of 'modern educated' cadres from its ranks made it impossible for the leadership to have much control over what was going on in the field. At the beginning of the jihad, Harakat-i Enqelab was one of the two dominant parties, but it steadily lost support during the 1980s to groups which were better organised, more efficient and, as a consequence, increasingly better funded. The modest level of support that Harakat was able to provide made it difficult for the military leaders affiliated to it to mobilise and maintain large armed groups. Moreover, the strong presence of ulema in its ranks represented another obstacle to the consolidation of a military class within its ranks. In practice, these constraints meant that even when elements of the military class were forming within Harakat, they had the tendency to abandon Harakat-i Enqelab and join other groups or the pro-government militias.[6]

Abdul Rasul Sayyaf's Ittehad-i Islami was a mix of disgruntled Islamists and fundamentalists, who had left other parties, and of mercenary groups attracted by the abundance of Arab money on offer. Sayyaf was very much an ideologist, an Islamist with Wahabi leanings (hence his Saudi support), and kept the militias in his main stronghold in Paghman (Kabul province) under strict control, appointing trusted commanders to lead them. Outside Paghman, Sayyaf's following grew during the 1980s, but was fragmented and barely under the party's control. He had some support throughout most of the Pashtun belt and among the military class in Kunduz, Baghlan and Takhar, which was attracted to the party both by the cash and weapons on offer and by its relatively loose discipline, which gave them more freedom of manoeuvre than in other 'rich' parties. Some of these military leaders played a role in the emergence of warlordism, but the overall importance of Ittehad in this regard was marginal.[7]

The two strongest Islamist groups were Jami'at-i Islami and Hizb-i Islami, headquartered in Pakistan, while several Shiite groups were also operating out of Iran. These were the only parties that relied to some extent on the recruitment of ideologically motivated individuals outside the clergy, who could then potentially be moulded into cadres of a disciplined organisation, trained to respond to a direct chain of command linking the leadership and the individual mujahid through the field commanders. They too faced a major challenge in gathering a large following, given their small initial numbers. This was particularly the case of Jami'at, since Hizb and the Khomeinist groups had more educated individuals in their ranks. As explained in the previous chapter, warlordism did not develop in Hazarajat, except to a limited extent on its southern and northern fringes. The ulema leadership maintained sufficient leverage to impose (with strong Iranian support) a political solution to the civil war in Hazarajat, before the commanders became sufficiently autonomous.[8] Hizb-i Islami tried wherever it could to create a strong system of command and control, manned by educated activists. Often commanders too, particularly at the upper level, were educated activists with a strong ideological commitment. Given the scarcity of such activists, they were not always on hand. In the early 1980s Hizb-i Islami attracted a sizeable number of educated Afghans who were not particularly committed Islamists, but viewed the party as the best vehicle to wage jihad against the Soviet occupiers. Hizb-i Islami used them extensively, but at the price of diluting somewhat its ideological purity. The main compromise Hizb-i Islami had to make was accepting in its ranks a large number of uneducated, ideologically dubious military leaders in order to expand its numbers as much and as fast as possible. In its core areas, like Parwan and Kapisa, such military leaders were limited to a subordinate role. But the more remote from the party's core areas, the higher up the ranks such military leaders could be found. In the east, where Hizb-i Islami still had a strong following among the intelligentsia, it succeeded in maintaining control, but in the north-east and in the west several commanders gradually asserted their autonomy till they were beyond the control of the centre. On the whole, the direct contribution of Hizb-i Islami to the development of warlordism was modest, because it exercised strict control over the delivery of supplies and policed its commanders through a system of 'commissars' and its very developed intelligence service. Hence insubordinate military leaders would be cut off and forced to defect to the government or to other parties. To the extent that the party had influence in southern Afghanistan (in some parts of Helmand and Kandahar), it might in fact have stifled the development of local warlordism with its insistence on preventing the emergence of powerful local commanders. Hizb-i Islami was to pay a heavy price for its policy of tight control: its strength within the jihadi movement gradually declined from the early 1980s, when it was with Harakat by far the largest party, to the early 1990s, when Jami'at had reached almost an equivalent strength.[9]

Compared to Hizb-i Islami, the leadership of Jami'at was more inclined to absorb into its ranks many different non-ideological military leaders, with led to a much faster dilution of its ideological character. Relatively few Islamist activists had joined Jami'at as opposed to Hizb-i Islami, forcing Rabbani to accept a comparatively wide range of characters into the party. Moreover, Jami'at-i Islami's organisation was only marginally better than that of the other jihadi parties (apart from Hizb-i Islami). There was no attempt to create a system of party commissars, nor to create a counter-intelligence service reporting on the military leaders affiliated to the party. The attitude of its leader, Professor Rabbani, was based on extensive networking and weak organisational skills; this attitude had been one of the factors which drove him to split from the unified Islamist party in the 1970s.[10] While Hekmatyar actively sought to prevent the emergence of strong individual military leaders inside Afghanistan, Rabbani had no objection to this occurring. In fact, he actively encouraged the tendency by agreeing to recognise regional 'amirs' as responsible for the distribution of supplies to all the Jami'ati military leaders within the region of responsibility. Loose control and liberal supply and distribution policies were supplemented by a degree of ideological flexibility or even opportunism in his recruitment policy. Clerical figures were relatively common, making Jami'at the second most clerical Sunni party in the jihad (after Harakat). These likely played a role in constraining the growing autonomy of military leaders, several of whom also found their way into Jami'at, particularly in western Afghanistan. Moreover, the party's weak structures were unable to prevent or at least slow the transformation of even the more committed of its members into 'new Khans' first and later into increasingly autonomous military leaders.[11]

Another element favouring the formation of a military class during the jihad was the tendency of some of the original villagers fighting part time to turn into fulltime 'specialists in violence'. From the beginning of the jihad some fighters were involved in the war full-time, but their numbers grew as the economy was disrupted by the war and military needs dictated that military leaders have at least a few full-timers around them. If we consider that there were maybe 6,000 military leaders in Afghanistan by the end of the 1980s, each with a complement of full-time fighters ranging from four to hundreds, we can see how a sizeable class of 'specialists in violence' was emerging. This phenomenon of full time combatants was key to both the formation of a military class and the future 'political economy' of Afghanistan, as they would not smoothly re-integrate into society as the part-timers could. The climate of insecurity contributed to the consolidation of the military class as wealthy families were forced to seek the protection of military leaders due to rising insecurity, initially through cash payments and supplies to the jihadis and later through longer-term alliances, such as marriage strategies.[12] This was the first stage of a process that led to the emergence of the 'new Khans' (see chapter 1).

The abundance of external help (weapons and cash), which could even be said to have been excessive, slowed the 'evolution' of the jihad movement into something more effective, disciplined and capable. The 'natural selection' process through which weaker, less organised, less effective and badly led groups were weeded out in favour of the 'fittest' groups only operated to a limited extent. The Americans and Pakistanis in charge of distributing weapons and other supplies tried to favour the more efficient and combative groups, but no attention was paid to their capacity for political organisation and mobilisation. In fact, the over abundance of munitions may well have had the perverse effect of removing any incentive for the jihadis to develop their political organisation and set the trajectory of the movement towards warlordism at the expense of political legitimacy.[13]

The reduction in foreign aid to the jihadi movement after the Soviet withdrawal in 1989 came too late to remove the incentive to focus on the military aspects of the war. By then, many military leaders were already addicted to the plentiful resources that they had become accustomed to receiving, while the erosion of enemy military pressure was such that it could no longer affect the evolution of the jihadis. Quite the contrary, in fact: the Soviet withdrawal further weakened links between the jihadi's military leaders inside Afghanistan and the political leaderships in Peshawar. The military leaders were thus compelled to seek alternative sources of revenue, both internal and external. As Soviet patrolling of the highways ended and jihadi attacks on convoys declined commensurately, trade increased, which also provided sources of revenue to the military leaders through taxation. In principle, the latter claimed to be providing security in exchange for the taxes paid by traders, although the fragmentation of authority could often make guaranteeing security problematic or lead to over-taxation. In some cases, cash-hungry military leaders even established their own bazaars. Another revenue-raising strategy consisted in strengthening relations with Western and Islamic NGOs, which were taking supplies and sometimes even cash into Afghanistan directly, bypassing the political leadership in Pakistan. The rapid inflation that followed the Soviet withdrawal was caused by excessive printing of money by Kabul; this too prompted farmers to explore cash-generating activities, among which growing opium poppies was the most important.[14] The expansion of the cash and poppy economies in turn created another valuable local source of revenue for the military class. All these processes combined with the previously discussed transformation into 'new *Khans*' to allow the increasing autonomisation of the military class from political control.

This process was much more pronounced north of the Hindukush than south of it, but not totally unknown there either. The measures taken by the 'revolutionary' government established in 1978 further destabilised the tribal environment, creating a situation in which the old established *Khan* families lost much of their influence as security became the primary concern. The external patronage of the Peshawar-based opposition political organisations was another major factor in the emergence of a new generation of 'rougher' tribal/community leaders and strongmen, who were more likely to be proficient and ruthless in the handling of militias and armed groups and who exploited these new opportunities for raising revenue and establishing a following. They were mainly concerned with the policing of the communities rather than with any substantial military activity. At the same time tribal and ethnic affiliations reasserted themselves when the state started to collapse during the late 1970s and the centre gradually lost its authority over the periphery. The tribes stepped in to provide a modicum of security in the absence of the central state. The combination of the two processes resulted in many of these new and rougher leaders turning into 'tribal entrepreneurs', who claimed tribal leadership on the basis of a real or alleged unifying role within specific tribes or tribal segments.[15]

At the same time, while the Afghan tribes had still been able to teach careless British imperialists a lesson or two a century or more earlier, during the 1978–1989 war the military inadequacy of tribal warfare became obvious.[16] Although strongmen devoid of real military skills continued to control the larger part of the Pashtun tribes, in the areas of most intense fighting the demand for military leadership skills resulted both in the emergence of non-tribal, ideologically motivated groups,[17] and of the new generation of rougher strongmen who were more effective military leaders. A few of these even managed to develop an autonomous power base sufficient to consolidate them as members of the military class. In practice just three sources of revenue proved sufficient to provide such an autonomous base: drug money, control over the highways and government patronage. Esmatullah Muslim is an example of such a mix of military leadership skills, the exploitation of residual tribal identities, control over the highway and manipulation of government patronage (see chapter 3).

The Akhundzadas of Helmand are a similar example, but with drug money replacing road tax and government support. This family had played an important role since the outset of the jihad in the southwest and were originally based in Musa Qala district among a sub-tribe of the Alizais. It was first Mullah Mohammad Nasim Akhundzada who became a prominent commander of *Harakat-i-Inqilab-i-Islami*, led by Mohammad Nabi Mohammadi, the leading jihadi party in Helmand. A charismatic military leader with a large coterie of devoted fighters, he was seen as having led many successful battles against Russians and Afghan government forces, although the extent of his actual successes has probably been exaggerated given the limited interest of the Soviets in northern Helmand.[18] A talib with a very narrow understanding of Islamic dictates, he nonetheless engaged in fierce fighting against other jihadi parties, particularly Hikmatyar's *Hizb-i-Islami*, and his men were allegedly involved in atrocities against prisoners of war.[19] Like most other mullahs, his status within Pashtun society was quite modest. His rise to prominence was a by-product of the war, as he overtook the traditional *Khans* and accumulated much greater power than they themselves could muster. The secret to the resilience of the Akhundzadas was their exploitation of the narcotics business in Helmand. Starting from the time of jihad, but accelerating after the Soviet withdrawal, Nasim actively worked for its expansion. The poppies were a traditional culture in northern Helmand, but Nasim exported them to southern Helmand, a territory which he conquered once he had gained an edge over other commanders thanks to poppy revenue. The Akhundzadas never sought to build an organisation and always relied on tribal and clan networks to rule their territory. They never made any attempt to increase the level of sophistication of their armed force and their success was mainly due to their superior resources, which allowed them to mobilise thousands of men if need be The system created by the Akhundzadas was very resilient; it is remarkable that it survived Mullah Nasim's assassination and the death of his two successors, his brothers Mullah Mohammad Rasool and Mullah Abdul Ghaffar. After taking Lashkargah in 1993, Rasul Akhundzada became the governor of the province, a position which he kept until the arrival of the Taliban in 1994. Mullah Sher Mohammad, the son of Mohammad Rasul, became governor of the province in 2001 and a crucial ally of President Karzai.[20]

The growth of a largely autonomous military class can also be described as a process of gradual patrimonialisation of the jihadi movement; by the early 1990s such military classes were looking for modes of political organisation more suitable to their long-term interests. By relying on patronage, whether of their own initiative or because forced by circumstances, the political leadership of the jihad had planted the seeds of their post-1992 failure. Patronage marginalised ideological groups within the jihad movement. The Soviet withdrawal and the conciliating policies adopted by President Najibullah in Kabul were taking the steam out the jihad movement, which rapidly became deligitimised. To the extent that the military leaders inside Afghanistan had been committed to a superior cause, such commitment rapidly waned, contributing to weaken the link between them and the parties. The military leaders also lost any incentive to think in national or supra-local terms. Their attention turned to local, petty interests. Soviet sources reported that as soon as their troops left a location, Afghan armed groups started fighting over land, water sources, mountain passes. New, cross-factional alliances motivated by local and regional interests became possible. These emerging new networks played an important role in the formation of warlord polities when state power collapsed in 1992.[21]

Notes

1. Based on an extensive range of interviews in Herat, Faryab, Kunduz, Kabul, Jalalabad, Gardez and Kandahar, 2003–2007.
2. Interviews with former jihadi military leaders, Kabul, 2006–7; Adkin and Yussuf (1992); Bearden (2003).
3. Ibrahimi (2006).
4. Estimated at 1,100 in the late 1970s by Harrison (1989), p. 10.
5. Roy (1990), p. 114–5; Rubin (1990), pp. 203–11; Dorronsoro (2005), pp. 137ff.
6. Roy (1990), pp. 113–4, 127ff.; Dorronsoro 92005), pp. 137ff.; Rubin (1995), pp. 211–213.
7. Dorronsoro (2005), pp. 137ff.; Rubin (1995), pp. 220–1; Roy (1990), pp. 135–7.
8. Ibrahimi (2008 forthcoming).
9. Interviews with former commanders of Hizb-i Islami, Kabul, Jalalabad, London, Gardez, 2006–7.
10. For more details on the history of the Islamist movement in Afghanistan, see Giustozzi (forthcoming 2009a).

11. Interviews with former Jami'ati military leaders Herat, Teluqan, Kunduz, Faizabad, Kabul 2003–2007; Roy (1990), pp. 130–3; Dorronsoro (1990), pp. 137ff.; Rubin (1995), pp. 218–20.

12. Y. Gankovski, quoted in Kipp (1989), p. 393; Roy (1988), p. 24–7; Dorronsoro (1996), p. 154.

13. Rubin (1995), Coll (2004), Yusaf and Adkin (1992), Schroen (2005), p. 49; Bearden (2003), pp. 271–2.

14. Dorronsoro (1996); Rubin (2000), pp. 1792–3.

15. Based on an extensive range of interviews in Kandahar, Gardez and Jalalabad, 2005–7.

16. See on this point Roy (1988).

17. This is the argument developed by Roy (1989). Although ideologically motivated groups existed among the Pashtuns and during the 1990s they had an important role in altering the tribal patterns in politics and warfare, they existed and operated side by side with tribal warlords, often actually fighting them. In this study, I am trying to isolate 'tribal' society from the problem of ideological influences, in order to assess the role of warlords.

18. There was an undersized Soviet brigade based in Helmand with three battalions, which also covered Farah province (Urban (1990), p. 318).

19. Interview with Afghan notable from Helmand, London, June 2005; Giustozzi/ Noor Ullah (2006), pp. 9ff.

20. Rubin (1995), p. 263, 245; Giustozzi/Noor Ullah (2006), pp. 9ff.

21. ProKhanov (1988), p. 21; Dorronsoro/Lobato (1990); Majiruh quoted in Los Angeles Times, 30 April 1990; Danziger (1992), p. 200–1; Arney (1989), p. 198; Dorronsoro (1994), p. 459–464.

3

STATECIDE IN THE MAKING

GOVERNMENT MILITIAS AND WARLORDISM (1980–1992)

Their origins in the militia system

During the 1980s the pro-Soviet regime of Babrak Karmal started to rely increasingly on militias, given their difficulty in recruiting for the regular army. The main militia organisation (the Regional Forces) was officially sanctioned in March 1983 by a jirga in Kabul and a decree, establishing a framework for the conduct of such 'tribal units', was approved in December 1984. The aim was to utilise sectors of the rural population, which would otherwise have rejected service in the regular army, to control the countryside, to hamper the movement of rebel groups and to carry out recruitment. An elaborate framework was put in place to ensure that the militias did not acquire a patrimonial character. Theoretically commanders were chosen by the Ministry from a list of candidates presented by tribal notables and group commanders. The commanders of regular army units based in the area were supposedly in charge of militia recruitment and of the training of cadres. Regiment and battalion field commanders and regiment, battalion and company political officers, KhAD representatives, officers in logistics and other services were to be taken from the regular forces, while platoon and smaller unit commanders were selected by the selected leader of the armed group, that is the unit commander. In practice, it was always the group leader who was appointed and authorised to appoint military ranks in order to turn his armed group into a company, a battalion, a regiment or (later) a brigade and even a division. Political work was expected to transform former 'bandits' into real 'soldiers of the Revolution'. In some militias political work was actually carried out, like Dostum's, Pahlawan's, Jabbar Kahraman's and some others. At the same time great efforts were made to recruit HDK (Hizb-i Demokrati-i Khalq) members among the rank and file, but in most units their influence remained negligible.[1]

During the early years of the militias, the stress was on attempting to convince notables and the population to join the regime and then form militias or convince mujahidin group leaders to follow suit. By the time of the Soviet withdrawal, the focus had shifted towards directly bringing onto Kabul's side the armed groups, which in turn would guarantee control over the population. In this process one can discern an acknowledgement of the transformations caused by several years of war, in which the traditional notables had been supplanted by military leaders (the 'new Khans') throughout most of the country (see chapter 1). As a result former jihadis soon accounted for most of the regional forces: by later 1989 and early 1990, 100,000 former mujahidin had joined the various types of irregular armed formations.[2]

At the outset, the militias were expected to deal mainly with the control of villages and rural roads and paths, taking over part of the duties of the police. Because of the weaknesses of the regular forces, their military tasks gradually increased. From 1364 (1985/86) onward they were entrusted with recruitment in the countryside, which in fact became one of their main tasks. Particularly after the Soviet withdrawal, they were even requested to go beyond local defence and to participate in fighting throughout the country. High salaries played a fundamental role in the rise of the regional and border militias: even in 1987 a militiaman received a salary twice as high as that of a regular soldier. In the drive to expand the militias, some provinces abandoned recruitment for the army and even offered instead an enrolement prize of 20,000 Afs for those willing to join the militias. Najibullah himself not only offered exemption from military service to the tribal youth who agreed to form local self-defence units, but also declared his readiness to release from military service those already recruited. Furthermore prizes were available to militiamen for the capture of deserters, etc. Other advantages offered to communities joining the militias included electricity and televisions. Offers of military hardware turned out to be particularly seductive towards jihadi military leaders. From 1988 and particularly from 1989 even heavy weapons and armoured vehicles, including armoured transports (BTR) and tanks, were distributed in large quantities to trusted militias. Perhaps more importantly, military ranks were more and more generously distributed to former mujahidin commanders. By this time militias and government were clearly developing a symbiotic relationship. Although some militia groups deserted over the course of the war, the patronage relationship established with the government proved quite strong, based at is was mostly on mutual interest. Many jihadi military leaders may have approached the government just as an expedient source of revenue, but then became dependent on its patronage. If the jihadi groups were being trapped by the centre's patronage policies, the contrary was also true: by the early 1990s the Kabul government was effectively dependent on its militias. If we look at the balance of forces in Herat province in 1990, the 17th Infantry Div. in Herat counted 3,400 regular troops and 14,000 militiamen, while the 21st in Shindand had the same number of militiamen and 1,645 regular troops.[3]

Limitations of the militia system[4]

From Kabul's standpoint, the massive reliance on the militias created three problems. The first was the risk of full-scale rebellions, made all the greater by the fact that many militia commanders were developing peer-to-peer networks and even maintained contacts with the opposition parties. Although, as explained, the patronage link to the government was quite solid, should the financial resources at Kabul's disposal be reduced, the consequences would be explosive.

The second problem was that the priority given to the militias in recruitment further reduced the pool of recruitable manpower for the regular forces. Many in fact enrolled in the militias just to avoid being recruited to the army. The problem was exacerbated by the fact that even city-dwellers sometimes joined militias to avoid the draft. Najibullah himself even accused some regional units of sheltering deserters and draft dodgers and others of not doing much to implement the draft. A vicious cycle ensued, where the expansion of the militias led to the army being condemned to a perpetually weak role, in turn forcing an ever greater recourse to militias. As a result the militias' leverage was becoming ever stronger.

The third problem was the increasing autonomy and undisciplined behaviour of many militias. The task of 'protecting' the main roads was much desired by them, as it enabled them to raise much additional cash through 'taxing' drivers and travellers. All the most important militias were involved in the practice, including Dostum's and Esmatullah Muslim's. Often militia commanders had sufficient leverage to choose relatively freely where to deploy their men. The growing autonomy of the militias was not merely financial. The 1989 law on local autonomy stipulated that criminals would be brought to the qazi and, when condemned, delivered to government prisons. A military attorney followed the trials in the militia courts, but in fact the government accepted all verdicts without complaint. Only those prisoners charged with political crimes were tried by the National Security Court. This system was clearly drifting towards some sort of 'feudalism'. The autonomisation of the militias might have been further strengthened by the government's encouragement of the 'retribalisation' of the local communities, i.e. the rediscovery of tribal/ethnic links that had faded away, or had never been very important, in order to bolster their influence and legitimacy among the population.[5]

The growing autonomy of the militias reduced further their inclination to behave in a disciplined way. Far from spending their energy on 'forming party organizations', 'reactivating schools', doing 'work useful to the population' and reopening agricultural cooperatives, as Najibullah had wished in January 1988, after the Soviet withdrawal the abundance of militias led to a 'Wild West' atmosphere around the country, with dozens of wounded in their feuds being treated each month in just one Kabul hospital. It was widely reported that the government left the militias to their own devices and never complained about their transgressions. And even though regular army units indulged in various sorts of abuse, particularly in the first years of the conflict, militias went beyond that. Regular officers acknowledged that the militias were 'out of control' even in a town like Balkh and visitors were warned to leave the town by 4 pm. Unsurprisingly, the population was hostile to them. The growing arbitrariness of the violence exacted by the militias was damaging the reputation of the government, whose attempt to recover some legitimacy had huge political costs. The 'pacification' policy itself risked being affected, as the attractions of a peaceful life for the common man had been one of the main trump cards in Kabul's hands. The economy, already in a bad way, deteriorated further.

The Soviet withdrawal in early 1989 further tilted the balance of power massively in favour of the militias. The government tried to balance their rising power by deploying Guard Brigades in the North, where militias formed the great majority of the armed forces. Attempts were also made to force the militias to improve their discipline. A bill envisaging the introduction of military uniforms for tribal units was discussed in 1987, but it is not clear whether it was approved, as the militias continued to shun uniforms. In December 1989 the Supreme Army Command forcefully stated the need to instill the militias with discipline, with little impact. In 1990 Najibullah faced a crisis when he tried to speed up the incorporation of the militias into the regular army and had to backtrack. In any case, the transfer of militias to the regular forces was in itself no guarantee that a real change was in the making; certainly Dostum's 53rd Div. was widely reported to have continued to behave in the usual way after turning into a regular army unit: it did not even enforce the use of uniforms. Clearly the idea of exercising relatively strict monitoring, let alone direct control, over the tribal units was not realistic, given the geographical constraints and the persistent weakness and ineffectiveness of the regular forces. If the scarcity of trained cadres and political officers was also considered, any effort at reducing their autonomy was clearly bound to meet huge difficulties. It would seem that the relatively small numbers of regular officers sprinkled around the militia ranks ended up being absorbed by them, rather than shaping them according to government wishes.[6]

Given the patrimonial character of these militias, the personal characteristics of their leaders played a key role in determining the path taken after 1992. The following review of the most prominent militia commanders to emerge in the 1980s shows the diversity of patterns, but also important elements that they shared in common.

Dostum of Shiberghan

The most important militia commander of the 1980s-early 1990s was undoubtedly Abdur Rashid Dostum. Born in 1955 in a village near Shiberghan, from a peasant family, he later joined the HDK and entered the army as a paratrooper in 1973. He had risen to command an armoured unit at the time of the April 1978 Revolution. In 1978, after the expulsion from government of the Parcham wing of the HDK, to which he belonged, he travelled to Pakistan in search of contacts, part of a plan by Parcham to plan armed opposition against the Khalq regime. The heavily fundamentalist atmosphere of Peshawar and the wider failure of Parcham to organise discouraged Dostum, who rejoined the armed forces after the Soviet army invaded Afghanistan. He first commanded a local party militia near the gas fields in Shiberghan, but his good performance as a commander enabled him to lobby successfully for an appointment to lead militia battalion 734 of KhAD around 1982–83.[7]

Throughout 1982–1987 his militia grew in size due to an ever greater allocation of resources from KhAD, which allowed for the recruitment of more men into its ranks, and to his perennial success in luring opposition commanders to switch sides. By November 1987 Dostum was a major in charge of militia brigade of what was now called WAD (Wazirat-i Dawlat-i Amnyati) in Shiberghan (Jowzjan province). His 'Jowzyani militia' was already well known for its fighting discipline (which did not rule out looting at the end of the battle) and for its fierceness. With authorisation to form the 53rd Infantry Div. in 1988, his forces began to be increasingly active outside his home area. Not long thereafter he even became commander of the newly created 7th Army Corps, with responsibility for northern Afghanistan. The core of the militia was originally made up of relatively politicized troops, but many former mujahidin were gradually accepted into it. One of them, Lal Kumandan, eventually became his favourite. The importance of Dostum's forces to Najibullah's regime was demonstrated by his appointment to the Central Committee of the newly renamed Watan party, whose last plenum in June 1991 Dostum attended. 53rd Div. was defined by an analyst as 'the only real mobile reserve' of the regime, although this might be an exaggeration since some of the Herati and southern militias were also extensively used as mobile forces. By the early 1990s Dostum's total paper strength (presumably including all of 7th Corps) was 45,000 men, with most sources estimating the actual number of active troops at 20,000–25,000. Dostum himself admitted to be paying many men in the villages as 'ready reserves'.[8]

There are strong indications that even before the formation of 53rd Div. Dostum's actual power and influence went beyond that of the average 'Major'. He was reportedly given 40 million Afs. each month to build up his personal influence. In late 1987 a proposal to form four militia regiments from the ranks of Guruh-i Kar, a left-nationalist group which operated mainly in Faryab and Jowzjan provinces, had been approved by President Najibullah, probably at the insistence of his Soviet advisers, who felt that such a move would help to expand the social base of the regime and consolidated the collaboration between Guruh-i Kar and the government. However, the initiative would have endangered the incipient control of Jowzjan province by Dostum himself. The creation of the four regiments had been sponsored locally among others by the Shiberghan branch of the Ministry of Interior, which was dominated by adversaries of Dostum, presumably to create some counter-balance to his and WAD's power. As a result, Dostum intervened to prevent the formation of the regiments, voicing his strong opposition to the authorities and unleashing a wave of arrests of members of Guruh-i Kar, of whom at least one was killed. Because of Dostum's distinguished record on the battlefield, the central government could not afford to ignore him and had to backtrack: the regiments were never created.[9]

Dostum's behaviour in November 1987 already highlights concerns that went beyond what should have in theory been his role of military commander. He was keen on carving an exclusive sphere of influence within Jowzjan province, which at that time had no major regular army unit stationed there. With Dostum being the force to be reckoned with in WAD, the only challenge to his local influence was the Ministry of Interior, whose troops were mainly spread in small garrisons and ill-equipped for large scale confrontation. Possibly because of the incident with Guruh-i Kar, the central government started reconsidering its garrisoning policies and in 1988 a brigade of the newly established National Guard was deployed in Shiberghan. At the same time, in a complex balancing act Dostum was allowed to upgrade his military formation to a full division. His desire for something more than a purely military role emerged once again in 1990, when the central government replaced several key players in the security structure of northern Afghanistan. The new appointees were close associates of the military head of the northern region, Gen. Juma Asak, a central government loyalist and a centralist who disliked the ever growing power of the militias.[10] Even though Dostum did not act immediately, he resented the appointments and began to see the hand of the central government in a bid to limit his power.

In Dostum's, as in other militias, the regular army officers in charge of technical, political/ideological and communication issues were never more than a thin carapace over armed groups that remained exclusively loyal to their own leaders. As Dostum developed as a source of patronage rivalling Kabul, even regular army officers assigned at the head of the 53rd Div. rapidly developed personal relations with the former militia commanders (especially Dostum) and chose not to oppose the Dostum's revolt when it took place.[11] Structures external to the division in northern Afghanistan, like WAD itself and even the Ministry of Interior forces, either proved unable to control the militias, or were carried away with them when the insurrection occurred. Despite staffing the ranks of WAD with Najibullah loyalists, most of its northern sections aligned themselves with Dostum in 1992. A few figures showed their loyalty to President Najibullah by refusing to cooperate with Dostum and then promptly fled the region.

Rasul Pahlawan of Faryab

Rasul Pahlawan first emerged as a jihadi military leader of some importance in 1983, with the killing of Mawlawi Qara, a notorious and ruthless military leader who had expanded his control over the whole of Shirin Tagab district (Faryab) after militarily defeating other jihadis. His death caused what were previously his lieutenants to split again and start fighting each other. Among them, two rapidly established themselves as the dominant figures. Noor Mohammad took control over the southern part of the district, around Kohi Sayad, while Rasul Pahlawan occupied the northern part of Shirin Tagab, around his native town of Faizabad (see Map 2). Of the two, Rasul Pahlawan, scion of an important family of landowners, turned out to be the most charismatic field military leader and the most ruthless as well. Noor Mohammad was soon eliminated from the scene, but Noor Mohammad's allies in Jami'at-i Islami organised a large scale offensive against Rasul. The military pressure was so strong that there was no other option left for him but to join the central government. Since he was already a relatively powerful military leader, the centre appointed him to head a tribal regiment of 1,200 men. In his new guise he continued to wage war against the new ruler of Kohi Sayad, Haq Birdee. Rasul's relationship with the provincial and military authorities proved problematic and he defected back to the mujahidin. At that point it was Haq Birdee who joined the government and formed his own militia, soon outgunning Rasul, who by contrast was isolated from the jihadi parties, who no longer trusted him and refused to supply him with weapons. He tried to establish alternative sources of supply by joining a small Turkic nationalist party, Ittehadiya, opposed to the leftists in Kabul, led by Azad Beg. After his attempt to obtain arms deliveries from Azad Beg was frustrated, he turned to the good offices of his step-brother, Abdul Malik, a teacher and member of the ruling HDK, who brought him back on the government's side, after having granted Rasul an amnesty. As a hint of how far the militias manipulated the government, rather than vice-versa, it is worth mentioning how this time he was granted the command of a 4,800–strong brigade, with plenty of heavy weaponry. Now Haq Birdee and Rasul Pahlawan, who continued fighting each other over the control of Shirin Tagab district despite both being government militia commanders, had similar resources at their disposal. Once again Rasul proved to be the most effective military commander and forced Haq to seek refuge in Kabul, where he was later assassinated. Rasul Pahlawan was now the lord of Shirin Tagab district, after hundreds of deaths. His monopoly of violence was absolute, as was his centralised control of theft: even petty thieves were not allowed to operate in the area, while his family was very active in seizing land and other properties. The family in fact imposed its control over the local economy, with a monopoly over the transport of raisins, the main produce of the area. The district authorities held on to only nominal power and Rasul even managed to impose the transfer of the district administrative centre from Islam Qala to Faizabad, his home town.[12]

Rasul's career was far from having reached its peak. As shown in Map 2, his progression was remarkable. Some rivals he defeated in battle thanks to his superior firepower and charismatic military leadership. As his power and resources grew, he also began using them to lure or force military leaders of other districts of Faryab into subaltern coalition-building with his group. He sponsored relatively weak military leaders to challenge dominant players in their district, until they grew to control the area and then incorporated their militias under his own overall command. By 1992 he had acquired control of the central districts of Faryab. With the collapse of the regime in that year, Rasul also established control over the provincial capital Maimana and the surrounding villages. Apart from some marginal mountainous areas, only Pashtoon Kot district was still contested by other military leaders after 1989; Rasul expanded his control over most of this area too after 1992, even if some unfriendly military leaders continued to hold out.[13]

Rasul Pahlawan's success in expanding the area under his control was due to two main factors. While he was an uneducated man with little sympathy for intellectuals, his reputation for personal bravery established him as a charismatic military leader, who could command the loyalty, if not the love, of his soldiers. His effectiveness (and ruthlessness) on the battlefield gave rise to numerous stories about how his enemies used to flee or surrender just as they

Map 2: The 'career' of Rasul Pahlawan. Areas of control 1983–1992

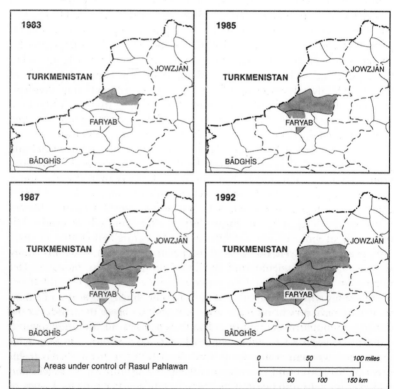

heard that Rasul was marching against them. Indeed, several surviving hostile commanders in his stronghold of Faryab surrendered to him during the 1990s.[14] The other factor was his ability to secure sources of support in terms of military hardware, first the Harakat-i Enqelab-i Islami party when he was a jihadi commander, then the communist government, and finally Gen. Dostum. Ultimately, however, the largesse which he received first from the government and later from Dostum was due to his valuable role as fearless military commander, a role which Harakat-i Enqelab failed to appreciate in the same measure. His gruesome reputation was not the reason why Harakat failed to support him adequately. After all, there were plenty of similar characters in the jihadi ranks in Faryab. The clerics who dominated the party might instead have disliked Rasul the ruthless scion of a landholding family. More importantly, Harakat had limited resources and tended to distribute them according to patronage criteria, hence it was not prepared to reward Rasul's military prowess.

Ghaffar Pahlawan of Sar-i Pul

Less of a charismatic leader than Rasul Pahlawan, Ghaffar Pahlawan started his military career as a militiaman under Khalq (1979). In early 1980 he defected, but rejoined the government in 1982, when he was put in charge of a pro-communist local militia. His influence among the inhabitants of some parts of Sar-i Pul province boosted his career, with appointments to the Loya Jirga (1985), to the Revolutionary Council of the Democratic Republic of Afghanistan (1986) and to the senate (1987). It was a sign of the times that after the fall of Najibullah his career took a turn back to the military, with his appointment as deputy commander of the 53rd Div. and, shortly later, as commander of the newly established 510th Div. and President of the Military Council of the Province of Sar-i Pul. Although he started off with some local influence of his own, ultimately he owed his growing power to support from the centre.[15]

Jaffar Naderi of Baghlan

The son of Sayyed Mansoor Naderi, leader of the Ismaili sect, Jaffar started forming a tribal regiment in 1984, which was later upgraded to brigade and eventually became the 80th Infantry Div. in 1988, with the incorporation of other, mainly non-Ismaili, units. In 1989 it numbered 13,000 men and 18,000 in 1992. Its capacity to conduct operations far away from its home area was limited, although small contingents were dispatched here and there, as for example to Jallalabad in 1989. The Naderis showed good diplomatic skills, helped by generous government funding, and even maintained good relationships with opposition forces, especially those of Ahmad Shah Massud, for example by letting their supplies through and offering economic help to those who did not attack government convoys along the main road. Naderi succeeded in pacifying large tracts of Samangan and most of Baghlan, gathering support even among non–co-religionists. Sayyed Mansoor was progressive by the standards of Afghanistan's local leaders. He allocated land to the peasants and was in favour of education for all, allowing mixed female-male classes till the 12th grade, while in Kabul at the time they did not go beyond the 6th. In Kayan, Mansour's personal residence, the government had built a hospital, a metal workshop, a repair garage and a veterinary centre. Under his control and with the cooperation of a strong local HDK structure, Pul-i-Khumri in the late '80s became the most 'normal' town in Afghanistan, with working administrative services, a health system, etc.[16]

Esmatullah Muslim of Kandahar

During his days as a jihadi commander in 1979 and in the early 1980s, Esmatullah Muslim refused to integrate into any of the existing parties based in Peshawar but formed his own group, which he called Fidayan-i Islam. This group of a few hundred followers had no discernible organisational structure and was essentially Esmatullah's private force. Until 1983 he was allegedly supported by the ISI (Pakistani military intelligence). He later developed differences with his patrons over supplies, with the ISI and fellow mujahidin accusing him of having stolen weapons and dealing with the Kabul government. He was also isolated from the old Durrani elites, who were hoping for an eventual restoration of the king and who held him in contempt for his lowly lineage.[17] Although he appears to have been close to President Karmal and after 1987 to have professed admiration for President Najibullah, he was keen to distance himself from the 'communist' government. In 1989 he was reported to have again offered his services to the ISI, who refused to hire him anew. Throughout the 1980s he maintained complete authority over his territory (the Spin Boldak district of Kandahar) and was seen by the government as an unruly character, an attitude strengthened by his fondness for alcohol and drugs. His militiamen were taxing not just private lorries on the highway, but also government ones.[18]

Esmatullah Muslim had been trained as an officer in Afghanistan and in the USSR, later serving as a major at the time of the Saur coup. Perhaps this is why he was more successful than others in organising a large militia, which was a comparatively proficient fighting force. His base in Spin Boldak district was very close to the supply lines of the mujahidin in Pakistan and exposed his group to constant military pressure. Yet it was only in 1988, after the Soviet withdrawal from Kandahar, that the mujahidin were able to defeat him, thanks to an onslaught coordinated by the ISI. Under the agreement with Kabul, Esmatullah was given the task of guarding all the Achekzai settlements and 130 km of the border with Pakistan, as well as the road connecting the important border post of Spin Boldak with Kandahar. A variety of sources recognise his high degree of activism against the mujahidin. He himself claimed to have successfully carried out twenty ambushes against mujahidin and to have captured six caravans loaded with weapons in the second half of 1985. Thanks to government resources and his own charisma, he was able to recruit extensively from among the unemployed youth, mainly his own Achekzais. He had the reputation of a brave commander and knew how to reward his fighters. Moreover many Achekzai smugglers, who had a fierce rivalry with Noorzai smugglers, also supported him for securing the lucrative smuggling route of Spin Boldak. By 1988 Gen. Esmatullah (he styled himself 'Marshal') could field at least 3,000 men (with some sources giving estimates as high as 6,000—10,000) equipped with armoured vehicles and heavy guns. Even after the loss in 1988 of his headquarters in Spin Boldak, he continued to fight alongside the Afghan Army around Kandahar, where he took part in a victorious counter-offensive in Tor Khowtal.[19]

Esmatullah had no realisation of the importance of maintaining a good image. He was widely rumoured to have personally killed hundreds of innocent people without reason, his victims allegedly including many tribal chiefs and travellers and even popular celebrities, such as the singer Ubaidullah Jan, a fact that magnified the impact of his abuses. He himself and his followers were repeatedly reported to have been involved in forced marriages, rape and torture and he boasted of having ten young wives and concubines. In November 1987 he was involved in a shootout in the Loya Jirga, to which he was a delegate, when the security services refused to let him enter while armed. At least fourteen people were killed in this incident and more bloodshed followed when he was placed under arrest in Kabul. One year later he was back in Kandahar. Once again he challenged the authorities, as demonstrated when he clashed with the Minister of Interior Gulabzoi, who had tried to stop him from taking a female singer hostage and forcing her to strip and dance for him. In another instance he was reported to have slapped the face of the head of Khad-i Nezami over a dispute. By the late 1980s he was refusing to talk directly to the government, using instead Soviet and WAD intermediaries. This attitude, although certainly related to his own character and bad habits, is likely to have had something to do with his acquired status of important leader. His role as the only militia commander in the border areas of Kandahar made him very precious to the government and thus there was no official pressure to get him to behave well. Significantly, when he died in 1991, in Moscow, where he was receiving treatment for cancer, in Afghanistan rumours spread that he had been poisoned by the government, who wanted rid of him without losing the support of his fellow tribesmen.[20]

A member of the Adozai branch of the Achakzai, he rapidly became influential within the tribe and claimed to lead 100,000 people, although more realistic estimates put the number at around 50,000.[21] Some sources claim that his original plan was to unify Durrani opposition to the communist regime, since the leaders of the other Pakistani-controlled parties were either Ghilzais or non-tribal. In any case, this project must have been soon dropped as a result his deteriorating relations with other mujahidin groups in Kandahar. Once he had firmly established himself as a leader of the Achakzais, he had little incentive or potential to try to expand beyond these limits. His military legitimacy was eroded somewhat during the second half of the 1980s, as he spent most of his time in Kabul rather than leading his men in the field. By then he had consolidated his tribal leadership thanks to his ability to secure patronage and favours for his fellow tribesmen. Partly because of this, he remained popular within his tribe even after his death, despite his record of abuses and the widespread loathing of almost everybody else. During the Taleban era his corpse was removed from the Khirka Sharif cemetery of Kandahar, but after the fall of the Taleban his tribesmen once again buried him in the same graveyard. A tribal militia under the leadership of his nephews joined the Barakzai strongman, Gul Agha Sherzai, in his fight against the Taleban in Kandahar in late 2001. After the fall of the Taleban, once again his men were appointed in Spin Boldak's border force, despite the fact that Gul Agha's father and Esmatullah had been bitter enemies during the time of jihad.[22]

The Khalqi militias of Lashkargah and Kandahar

Central Helmand is a relatively new settlement, where large tracts of land were reclaimed from the desert following an irrigation project sponsored by the US before the war started. Here the tribally mixed population became a fertile ground for the recruitment of party militias by Khalqis after the arrival of the Soviets. One such militia was that of Khano, the nickname of Khan Mohammad. He had migrated to Helmand from his original province of Farah. Because his elder brother was a member of HDK and closely associated to one of its leaders, Dr Saleh Mohammad Zerai, Khano became the commander of a small party militia. Since he proved to be a successful fighter, his value to the government gradually grew. He mainly recruited among the unemployed youth of the province, who were mostly not very ideologically committed. At the same time, they were not recruited through tribal networks either, contrary for example to the majority of Esmatullah's militia. The main factor driving recruitment was the rather generous pay and Khano's personal charisma as a commander. His militia was militarily effective, but Khano enhanced his position by developing an alliance with the other leading militia commander in Helmand, Allah Noor, and with a militia commander of Kandahar, Abdul Jabbar Kahraman.[23]

As a Barakzai from Nawa district, Allah Noor was an uprooted individual who had resided mostly in Iran before the war and who was involved in war profiteering. As with Khano, he became involved in the militias through a relative. He soon became the first chief driver in the transport department, where he managed to accumulate significant resources. He then organised a tribal militia during the Najibullah regime. This militia expanded considerably over time as Allah Noor's military successes brought increasing rewards and the financial resources to recruit more troops, as well as access to key personalities of the regime such as the Defence Minister. Given his attraction to material wealth, Allah Noor's decision to form a militia seems to have been motivated financially and in this sense he appears to have been some sort of military entrepreneur.[24]

Jabbar controlled Maiwand district in neighbouring Kandahar province and his force was so effective that in early 1992, after the beginning of troubles with Dostum, the government tried to transfer the latter's role of mobile reserve to him, but events took over. Maiwand too is a flat area, like central Hilmand, and populated by Rutbavi-type tribes, but Jabbar's militia was not tribal; instead it was relatively ideologised and political work was carried out within its ranks. He had an army background and became a General before the fall of Najibullah, even receiving an award as hero of the Democratic Republic.[25]

Militia commanders of Herat

The flatlands surrounding Herat in western Afghanistan also emerged as fertile ground for the development of militias. The first major militia commander to emerge was Daoud Ziarjom, a Noorzai jihadi military leader who operated in Zindajan and Enjil and joined the militias in 1985. His firepower increased rapidly and soon he would have 7,000 men under arms. By 1989, he had already earned the rank of General. As soon as his force started benefiting from Kabul's support, he started putting under increasing pressure on his traditional Alizai rival Sayyed Ahmad, Jami'at-i Islami's Amir of Guzara. The government assigned Guzara district to Daoud's militias and endorsed an offensive against Sayyid Ahmad, who was also on bad terms with the provincial leader of Jami'at, Ismail Khan. Soon Sayyid Ahmad decided that the only viable option left open was joining the militias. Two years after having joined the government, his force had trebled to 3,000. By the end of the war, they had grown to almost 8,000. Thanks to government patronage he could turn what had been a relatively narrow circle of full-time fighters supported by part-time village militias into a large permanent force. As an established militia leader who had proved himself, he began tutoring new defectors to the government side, using his government-provided patronage resources to absorb them into his structure. His operations soon encompassed neighbouring districts like Enjil and Pashtun Zarghoun, despite Ismail Khan's efforts to disrupt him. His dependence on government patronage emerged in 1988, when a big question mark was hanging over the fate of Najibullah's regime in the wake of the Soviet withdrawal. Ismail Khan offered him a chance of reintegrating in the jihadi ranks, but Sayyid Ahmad opted to cast his lot with Kabul once and for all.[26]

He first earned officer rank as a commander of a regiment, which was then upgraded twice. At the end of his life he was a General and was expecting a decree allowing him to form a division. He was also appointed to membership of Parliament. With the large amount of cash he received, the 'taxes' that his militiamen extracted from lorry drivers in exchange for their safe passage and his own resources (he was wealthy even before the war began), he bought a guesthouse in Kabul and a Mercedes. He was also allowed by the government to run business activities, which included the ownership of the only cement factory in the province. Disputes were regulated by him personally or by his second in command and he enjoyed virtually unlimited powers within his region. Although the government had conceded much to him, Sayyid Ahmad did his best to keep Kabul's influence at arms length. For instance he refused to allow political work to be carried out among his units and therefore his relationship with the regular troops was tense. On one occasion Ahmad was menaced with a pistol by a regular officer who wanted his bodyguards to deposit their weapons before entering Herat, as was stipulated in the regulations. Ahmad backed down, but some time afterwards the officer was assassinated by unknown assailants.[27]

Eroding the state from within

The militia commanders examined in this section came from different origins, some being former jihadis and others coming from the leftist party in power. Some were tribal leaders, others former military officers. Yet despite the fact that they mostly did not communicate with each other, the tactics and techniques that they used to expand their influence at the expense of the centre were remarkably similar. The extent of their success as increasingly autonomous military leaders always derived from similar sources:

- their charismatic military skills;
- their reputation as fearsome fighters;
- their ability to exercise 'restrained ruthlessness' and practise skilful brinkmanship; they did not balk at challenging the authorities, often even in extreme ways, but as long as they knew when it was time to make a deal they always managed literally to 'get away with murder';
- securing sources of revenue, such as control over highways;
- their ability to form networks with other military leaders.

Charismatic leadership allowed some of them to appeal more successfully than others to the fellow members of the emerging military class. Dostum excelled at luring other military leaders from different backgrounds to his side. Rasul Pahlawan, by contrast, relied more on coercion. The types of networks used varied: Esmatullah, Daoud Ziarjom and Sayyid Ahmad used tribal networks, which helped them in rapidly establishing their power base, but did allow them to progress much beyond that afterwards. Khano, Allah Noor and Jabbar relied mostly on individual recruitment, but also on a mix of Khalqi and tribal networks. Dostum and Rasul networked fellow military leaders. All however led armed groups at whose core was a solidarity group (Ibn Khaldin's 'asabiyya) forged in war by men who risked their lives together. All directed much of their efforts and brinkmanship throughout the 1980s and

1990s at carving out a patrimonial niche within the institutional framework of the state and, little by little, they succeeded. They tested the ground by gradually raising the stakes in their periodical confrontations with the authorities, eventually going as far as murdering government officials. In so doing, they laid the ground for the emergence of warlordism when the central state was fatally weakened by the loss of external support in 1991, following the demise of the Soviet Union. As charismatic leaders, they were in a sense forced to pursue their provocations to the extreme end, taking extreme gambles in order to demonstrate to their followers how brave and fearless they were. Eventually Dostum went the farthest, when he played a key role in bringing down the government of President Najibullah.

Notes

1. See Giustozzi (2000).
2. See Giustozzi (2000).
3. See Giustozzi (2000).
4. Except where otherwise stated this paragraph is based on Giustozzi (2000).
5. On artificial re-tribalisation through patronage see also Giustozzi (2006b).
6. Interview with former secretary of 53rd division, London, Nov. 2005.
7. Nabi Azimi (1998), p. 340.
8. Interview with former secretary of 53rd division, London, Nov. 2005; Giustozzi (2000), pp. 222–3; A. Davis, 'Makeover For A Warlord', *Time*, 3 June 2002.
9. Giustozzi (2000), pp. 209–10; Walwalji (1380), p. 33–34; Nabi Azimi (1998), p. 341.
10. Walwalji (1380), ch. 'The crisis in Khost as threshold of the rift between Dr Najibullah and Gen. Dostom'.
11. Interview with former secretary of 53rd division, London, Nov. 2005.
12. Interview with Turkmen intellectual and journalist, Kabul, May 2003; Hedoyat (nd.), passim.
13. Hedoyat (nd.), passim.
14. Interviews with members of Faryab's intelligentsia, Maimana, Nov. 2004 and London, Oct. 2002 and Aug. 2003.
15. Interviews with Uzbek intellectuals from Sar-i Pul and Faryab, Sar-i Pul, London and Kabul, 2003–2004.
16. Giustozzi (2000), p. 224.
17. The Barakzai elite, to which traditionally the Achazkais referred for leadership, was strongly pro-monarchy and had opted for a wait-and-see attitude, showing little interest for the war itself.
18. Urban (1990), p. 140; Dorronsoro (2005), p, 187; Anatol Lieven, 'Mujahidin fail to subdue the pirate turncoat', *The Times*, 26 Jan. 1989; Christopher Walker, 'Turncoats and eccentrics revel in intrigues of Kabul', *The Times*, 10 March 1989; Nabi Azimi (1998), p. 341. President Najibullah himself once described him in public as a drunkhard and an addict.
19. Urban (1990), p. 241; Lieven, 'Mujahidin fail...', op. cit.; Giustozzi (2000), p. 206.
20. Lieven, 'Mujahidin fail...', op. cit.; Giustozzi (2000), p. 230–1; Christopher Walker, 'Summit: Afghan dilemma—Kremlin looks for bloodless way to pull out of Kabul', *The Times*, 8 Dec. 1987; Interview with former KhAD official, London, Aug. 2005; Nabi Azimi (1998), p. 341; Giustozzi/Noor Ullah (2006), p. 8.

21. Giustozzi (2000), p. 206. There were certainly fewer then 100,000 Achakzais in Kandahar province, although Esmatullah might have meant to include in his claim some fellow Achakzais living in Pakistan.
22. Interview with UN sources, Kandahar, May 2005; Jeff B. Harmon, 'Toe-to-toe with Russians in Kandahar's holy war', *The Times*, 11 Aug. 1985.
23. Giustozzi/Noor Ullah (2006), pp. 15ff.
24. Giustozzi/Noor Ullah (2006), pp. 15ff.
25. Interview with former jihadi military leader from Kandahar province, Jan. 2006; Giustozzi (2000), p. 221.
26. Interviews with former militia commanders and government officials, Herat, Sept.-Oct. 2005; Giustozzi (2007e), pp. 6–7.
27. Giustozzi (2007e), pp. 7–8.

4

1992–2001

THE APOGEE AND CRISIS OF THE WARLORDS

The failure to re-establish an effective government

The fall of the President and of Afghanistan's pro-Soviet regime in April 1992 was, as is well known, largely the result of a combination of the mutiny of the northern militias and of a coup by elements of the regime hostile to Najibullah. The background cause of the collapse was, of course, the end of the Soviet Union and the cut off of external help to Kabul in 1991. Although by April 1992 supplies, particularly military ones, were still far from exhausted, the prospects for the regime were clearly dim and all the players knew that very well, including President Najibullah. Had his regime been more solid and the militias more loyal, there might have been a chance of getting the United Nations to broker a more favourable deal with the opposition. As it turned out, the northern militia commanders and some key military leaders negotiated their own deals with opposition groups, while the other key players of the regime either lost their lives (a few) or considered themselves lucky to escape alive and mostly resigned to fall into political insignificance.

The first president of post-Najibullah Afghanistan was Sebghatullah Mojaddidi, the elderly leader of Jabh-i Nejat-i Milli, who served for two months before handing over the post to Professor Rabbani, the leader of Jami'at, who was supposed to stay in the post for four months before handing over to a successor to be designated. Rabbani's later refusal to leave the post was one of the factors contributing to the slide towards civil war, which had already started for other reasons. The power-sharing formula devised in Peshawar in April failed to hold mainly because it proved difficult to establish a balance of power among the different factions. Each faction had its own views about the criteria to be used in determining the weight of the various groups within the new government and the agreement proved untenable in the absence of any acceptable external (international) brokering. The Pakistanis tried to play such a role, but were not considered neutral players as Islamabad was perceived as favouring some parties more than others. Many authors support the view that Pakistan sponsored Hizb-i Islami during the jihad and that such help continued after 1992. Massud and his aides repeatedly accused the Pakistanis of supporting Hekmatyar. Rabbani alleged that they helped supply Hekmatyar with privately printed Afghan cash. While Hizb-i Islami was receiving supplies from Pakistani territory, there is no evidence beyond rumours that these were directly provided by the Pakistani authorities; even Massud's and Rabbani's supporters could never produce any proof of that. Some analysts believe that Pakistan stopped directly supporting Hizb-i Islami at the end of 1991. In fact, there is some evidence that Hizb-i Islami was not well funded after 1992, even if it had stockpiled large quantities of weaponry and was therefore able to continue military operations. Hekmatyar was for example unable to pay the salaries of Shindand airport's air force officers, despite having announced with pride the creation of Hizb-i Islami's air arm after the capture of the airport. Increasingly some of his militias were imposing road taxation, another sign that external support, if it existed, was not plentiful. The most likely hypothesis is that Islamabad initially was intent on promoting a coalition government including Hizb-i Islami in a prominent role. In 1992, the Pakistani government offered $10 million to the Mojaddidi government, although it seems likely that the money was never delivered. It also appears that Pakistan put pressure on Hizb-i Islami to accept the Peshawar accords on power-sharing, contradicting Hekmatyar's original intention to reject them. The Islamabad accords of March 1993, which confirmed the power-sharing agreement of Peshawar, were also sponsored by Pakistan as well as by Saudi Arabia. Although these accords are seen as controversial, as Massud was to lose his position of defence minister, Islamabad showed its willingness to favour a compromise by inviting Dostum to the talks, even if at that time he was not yet allied with Hekmatyar and had been the object of most of the latter's verbal attacks. It was only once chances of a negotiated settlement in Hekmatyar's favour seemed to have evaporated that Islamabad declared Rabbani's government as illegitimate. During 1994 Islamabad enforced a blockade of Kabul-bound goods and its officials started openly expressing political support to Hizb-i Islami and its allies. Even then Islamabad seemed inclined to favour some compromise, as it re-opened its embassy in Kabul in that year. In sum, it is likely that Rabbani and Massud overstated the Pakistani role, in order to justify their inability to manage the situation and the strength of the opposition to their rule.[1]

What is certain is that Hekmatyar believed that in the Peshawar accords Hizb-i Islami had been given a far too small share of power, essentially limited to the premiership and some relatively unimportant ministerial posts. By contrast, its main rival for power, Massud of Jami'at-i Islami, had received the key position of Minister of Defence. After Mojaddidi's first two months, the presidency was also added to Jami'at-i Islami's positions. Another factor of irritation for Hekmatyar was Massud's efforts to recruit Hizbi commanders into Jami'at, particularly in the north-east but also in the northern part of Laghman. Already during the days of the occupation of Kabul, Jami'at and Hizb-i Islami had behaved as open rivals, each trying to outdo the other in order to secure the strongest negotiating position. The attempts to negotiate, whether sponsored by the Pakistanis or not, achieved little as the leaders of Jami'at felt that they were in a position of strength, being allied with a sizeable chunk of what had been the armed forces of Najibullah's regime and having been able to bring into Kabul substantial forces of their own. During the negotiations, the Jami'atis had steadfastly refused to give way to Hekmatyar's demands that key positions, including defence, be assigned to Hizb-i Islami and that the alliance with Najibullah's Generals be terminated. The Jami'atis believed, not without reason, that accepting even some of Hekmatyar's key demands would have given him the chance to make a bid for supremacy in Kabul. Soon the different sides were communicating through exchanges of gunfire. The first sign that the country was heading towards disintegration and civil war was in May 1992, when Hizb-i Islami launched a rocket attack on Kabul, which may have killed fifty people. Smaller clashes were occurring in the provinces almost every day. The Hizb-Jami'at rivalry was not the only one; by early June, fighting broke out between the unified Khomeinist front of Hizb-i Wahdat and the Sunni radicals of Ittehad in Kabul. Together with Hizb's August 1992 massive rocket attack, which may have 1,000 people, this event could be seen as the actual beginning of the civil war.[2]

It is not necessary for the purposes of this book to describe in detail the civil war, hence I will limit my analysis to the relationship between Kabul and the armed groups in the provinces. From the very beginning both the Mujaddidi and the Rabbani governments appeared very weak and unable to control Afghanistan, even if for the first few months the country was relatively quiet. A key step that contributed to the emergence of warlordism and to the onset of the civil war was Minister of Defence Massud's decision de facto to abandon the armed forces inherited from Najibullah. Gen. Safi, an influential General from the King's time, Gen. Nabi Azimi, commander of Kabul's garrison and deputy minister of defence under Najibullah, and Gen. Baigi, an Uzbek from the north-east, had all either privately advised Massud or publicly asked for the formation of a national army under Massud's orders as a preliminary condition to the takeover of Kabul by the jihadi political leaderships. Instead Massud accepted the advice of his circle that the 'old army' was no longer useful to him and allowed the leaders of the parties to enter Kabul and 'buy' their own chunks of the armed forces. Although the armed forces started losing personnel as soon as Najibullah was removed from power, the officers and the other professionals in the army had initially largely stayed in their place. Moreover forces of the Minister of Interior too did not immediately disband, and nor did the State Security. Although a big portion of the armed forces in the north had already been taken over by Dostum even before Massud entered Kabul, it would in principle have been possible to salvage elements of the military in order to counterbalance the centrifugal tendencies of the emerging warlords and of the different factions. It would appear that Massud's decision not to keep the army together was motivated by his self-confidence as a military leader, but also by the desire to eliminate a stratum of regular army officers who due to their residual *esprit du corps* could have represented a future rival power base in Kabul, or at least an obstacle to his full control of the Ministry of Defence. The result of his decision, combined with the pre-existing underlying tendency towards fragmentation, was that the remnants of the regular army declined rapidly. Although some units were officially kept in existence, they underwent a process of radical transformation which could well be described as 'de-modernisation' or 'de-bureaucratisation'. Without the support of a well funded central state, only Dostum's newly founded organisation, Junbesh-i Milli-ye Islami (National Islamic Front), and Massud had the capability to maintain these armed forces for at least some time. All the other factional forces could do no better than absorb a proportion of the personnel into their own militias, adopting the latter's structure and *modus operandi*. This was the case of the fragments which joined Hizb-i Islami or Hizb-i Wahdat, or were taken over by whatever local coalition had occupied the provincial centres. This rapid fragmentation was the result of the uncertain future of the military professionals, who were therefore hedging their bets by allying with the strongest local faction or with whoever they had managed to ally with. By default, what was left under the control of the central government was in practice absorbed into the military forces of Jami'at-i Islami under Massud's leadership, hence losing its national character. Moreover, Jami'at's and Junbesh's forces too would soon start degrading into irregular or semi-regular formations.[3]

The national air force too splintered into several small air forces, each with limited capabilities. Only Dostum's and Massud's air forces were substantial entities, while limited assets were also taken over by Ismail Khan in Herat and the shuras running Kandahar and Jalalabad. Hekmatyar briefly seized control of a small air force in Shindand, but he soon lost it to Ismail Khan. Most officers and specialists who needed to keep their jobs offered their services to whoever was willing to employ them and pay modest salaries.[4]

Regardless of any ill-feelings towards specific factions or groups, once the civil war between Jami'at and Hizb-i Islami had started both of the two largest groups needed to form alliances with other factions and military leaders in order to gain a competitive edge, or prevent the adversary from doing so. In 1992 and 1993 Junbesh and Wahdat were allied with Jami'at and at times Junbesh cooperated militarily with Massud against Hizb-i Islami, with a major impact in preventing Hizb-i Islami from making major gains in the capital. Hizb-i Islami was initially isolated, probably a result of both its over-confident expectation of being able easily to overcome its adversaries militarily and of the distrust with which the other groups viewed the party. Hizb-i Islami had been forming semi-regular military units during the last few years of jihad, in the expectation of using them in the battle for Kabul, and this might have contributed to the arrogance of its chiefs.[5]

However, the determination of Jami'at's leaders to centralise patronage and power in their hands weakened their ability to maintain allies, except for

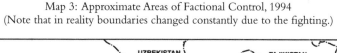

Map 3: Approximate Areas of Factional Control, 1994
(Note that in reality boundaries changed constantly due to the fighting.)

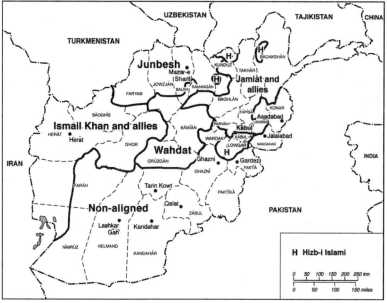

minor players like Harakat-i Islami and Ittehad-i Islami. The initial military containment of Hizb-i Islami had the combined effect of forcing its leadership to seek alliances and of convincing formally hostile potential allies that the threat of a bid by Hizb-i Islami for absolute power had receded, despite its continuing hegemonic ambitions. In December 1992 Massud, as part of his plans gradually to centralise power, moved to disarm the militias of Hizb-i Wahdat. As a reaction, in January 1993 Wahdat aligned with Hizb-i Islami in the civil war. Throughout 1993 the relationship between Jami'at and Junbesh too steadily deteriorated, as the latter's demand of formal recognition as a regional force in control of northern Afghanistan was continuously sidestepped by Jami'at and particularly by Massud. From January 1993 until May 1993 Junbesh refused to support Massud militarily, maintaining a de facto neutrality. Even after that its level of military support never reached previous levels. Towards the end of 1993 Massud and his local allies started intervening militarily to contain the expansion of Junbesh against Hizb-i Islami in the provinces. This convinced Dostum to move quickly towards a deal with Hizb-i Islami and Wahdat. In January 1994 the tripartite alliance of Hizb-i Islami, Wahdat and Junbesh was officially announced with an offensive by Junbesh in Kabul, which failed to achieve much success as Massud had been informed beforehand and Dostum's partners failed to support the offensive adequately. The three allies were clearly less than wholeheartedly committed

73

to the enterprise and manifested little coordination and cooperation even afterwards; they never came close to overthrowing the Rabbani-Massud government.[6] On the contrary, the civil war witnessed the slow erosion of the anti-Jami'at alliance in Kabul, while in the provinces the war continued without major successes on either side. The result of the inconclusive fighting was the complete collapse of whatever administration and law enforcement existed still in the provinces.

During 1993 Rabbani had tried to establish relations with the regional power-holders, with some modest success mainly based on the promise of reconstruction help and patronage once the conflict was over. When in early 1994 the civil war entered a new and even more violent phase, all the gains Rabbani had made on this front were quickly overturned. Jami'at-i Islami's victory in Kabul in 1995 finally allowed the government to consolidate its control over the capital during March-October of that year. Under unified control for the first time in three years, Kabul enjoyed a minor renaissance and aid agencies re-started their operations,[7] but the government had neither the strength nor the resources to expand its influence and control outside the capital. Its relationship with Ismail Khan in Herat reached its nadir in 1995, while the government's attempt to decisively defeat Wahdat by allying with its internal dissidents and bringing the war into Hazarajat only resulted in opening a new front in the civil war. Among Pashtuns the Rabbani government had very little support, as the supremacy of Shura-i Nezar was widely rejected; it was seen as unacceptable even by pragmatic figures such as the Arsala family of Nangarhar. During 1994 Rabbani and Massud encouraged the emergence of the Taliban as a potential ally in the Pashtun belt, particularly as they were sweeping away many of Hizb-i Islami's positions. As the Taliban came closer to Kabul, Rabbani and Massud's bluff was called and a coalition with Mullah Omar's seemed an impossibility. Soon the Rabbani government was at war with them. Under rising pressure from the Taliban, Rabbani managed to reach a deal with the increasingly weak Hizb-i Islami, hoping that this would consolidate his positions around Kabul. By then the influence and power base of Hizb-i Islami had evaporated and the agreement did little to prevent the final collapse of the Rabbani government in October.[8]

There are no reliable sources on the 1992–1996 period as far as the sources of funding of the Kabul government are concerned. What is certain is that it was badly cash-strapped, as were all the factions to some extent. Hizb-i Islami, which until 1991 had had good connections with sources of funding in the Arab Gulf States. lost most if not all of its support after it declared in 1991 its hostility to American intervention in the First Gulf War. Much funding was re-directed by Arab donors to supporting the refugees from the civil war in Tajikistan. Local taxes were pocketed by local military leaders, with no benefit for Kabul. Road taxes became increasingly popular among military leaders as the most cost-effective revenue collection system, given that no elaborate administrative structure was required, as it was in the collection of land taxes. By 1995 they had become a common feature throughout Afghanistan, but again little of this cash made it to Kabul's coffers. In the absence of a structure able to raise revenue at the local level, the centre had to rely on printing money, irrespective of funding that was coming from abroad or the 'private' revenue of the members of the ruling coalition, that is to say mainly Jami'at-i Islami (see chapter 22). The inflationary process which had started in the 1980s was dramatically accelerated. The Afghani, which was trading at 1,000 to the dollar in 1992, fell to 17,800 to the dollar by 1996.[9]

The military class in search of a future

While the new rulers in Kabul were proving unable to rebuild countrywide political structures, the military class and other provincial players sought to control local government structures. The actual formula varied widely from region to region. In the region where tribal structures had survived to a large extent, such as Nangarhar, Kunar, Laghman, Paktia, Khost, Ghazni and Paktika, local arrangements were made on the basis of creating regional or provincial councils integrating strongmen, community heads and military leaders. They seem to have worked reasonably well in maintaining a modicum of security and a balance of power among different players. In the cases of Nangarhar and Ghazni, the shuras even took over what was left of the old administration and of the police, as well as salvaging some units of the armed forces. As a rule in these provinces the transfer of power from the Najibullah regime to its successors was marred by looting to various degrees and by the distribution of the spoils of the state among different factions and groups, which later made it more difficult if not impossible to create some form of effective administration and the establishment of a monopoly of violence. As a result, these polities were extremely fragile because of their difficulties in raising armed forces to counter any external threat, often leaving them dependent on the goodwill of individual military or community leaders. They were all swept away by the Taliban with hardly any significant resistance. In this regard the contrast with Herat or Mazar was stark, not only because of the absence of looting, but also because of the far greater mobilising capability of the warlord polities.[10] It is precisely this difference that motivates *Empires of Mud*'s focus on the warlords.

The same type of shuras, incorporating the main players, failed miserably in Kandahar from the beginning, because tribal structures had largely disintegrated over the last couple of centuries. In Kandahar and the surrounding region, therefore, there was no effective governance structure. Although a military class emerged in this region, it had weak roots and lacked a charismatic figure able to bridge the gap between Khalqis and jihadis, allowing actors external to the region like Ismail Khan or newcomers like the Taliban to play a disproportionately important role. It also lacked the resources available to Dostum in the north or secure communication lines with sources of supply.

Where the military class existed and was strong, as in the west, north and north-east, it tried to consolidate its position through networking, coalition-building around the more resourceful players or deal-making with Rabbani and Massud in Kabul. In the chaotic and conflictual environment of post-Najib Afghanistan, different warlord-generating dynamics emerged in different parts of the country. The north, where the powerful 'statecide' militias of 1992 were located (see Map 4) and where strategic depots of military and other supplies were also available, was the most likely place to see military leaders seize political control, as long as they managed to establish some form of unity. This duly happened. Abdul Rashid Dostum played a key role as a charismatic military leader, able to earn the trust not only of other militia leaders in the region, but also of a majority of jihadi military leaders who had never gone over to the government of President Najibullah (see Part II for the details). This was a remarkable feat, although it was made possible or facilitated by Dostum's military superiority, with no force even remotely able to threaten him in the north-west (Jowzjan, Faryab, Sar-i Pul). It was also facilitated by Dostum's extensive networking with other key players in the region under Najibullah's regime, including Rasul Pahlawan. True to the political pragmatism of the military class, in the search for a patron many jihadi military leaders from different parties (Jami'at, Hizb-i Islami, Harakat-i Enqelab) joined Dostum in Junbesh, even if Kabul was trying to sponsor an alternative pole of aggregation around the regional leader of Jami'at, Ustad Atta. From this particular genesis, as well as from Dostum's particular attitudes and skills, derived the 'feudal' character of Junbesh, described in detail in the following chapters. The military class might have been discouraged from ally-ing with Kabul by its lukewarm or non-existent enthusiasm for any attempt to restore a strong central government, particularly if it had an ideological flavour. Thus the north was dominated by the dynamics of orphan warlord-ism, absorbing loose elements of the military class and preventing evolution-ary warlordism from playing much of a role.

Other former militia commanders were not as lucky or as skilful. The Kha-lqi militia commanders of Lashkargah and Maywand made their bid for orphan warlordism, but fell victim to a mostly hostile environment. Khano, Allah Noor and Jabbar were closely networked together. Through Allah Noor's residual tribal connections, they made a deal with a Barakzai strong-man from Jami'at and delivered Lashkargah town over to him. After two days of heavy fighting, the alliance of these four military leaders succeeded in defeating the attempt to take Lashkargah by the leading mujahid of Helmand, Nassim Akhundzada. The power-sharing agreement was endorsed by the Rabbani government in Kabul. Allah Noor took the position of division commander, Jabbar that of brigade commander and Khano that of chief of police. They had established good relations with Dostum in the north too and

Map 4: Location of Main Militia Units at the End of Najibullah's Regime

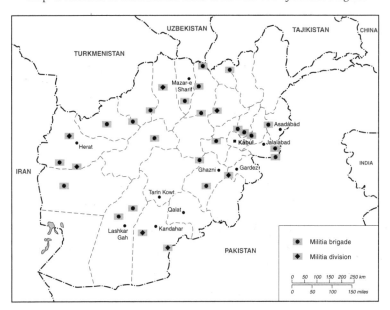

both Kabul and Mazar-i Sharif gave them cash and supplies. Rabbani even promoted both Allah Noor and Khano to the rank of General.[11]

The alliance could be described as an orphan warlords' polity, in that its existence rested largely on military strength. The political legitimisation deriving from the backing of Rabbani and Dostum was very weak, since neither of them had much support in the region. Compared to the real warlord polities of northern and western Afghanistan, it also lacked a strong charismatic leader as well as a powerful resource base. As Khano, Jabbar and Allah Noor were able to use only tribal networks as channels of communication, not as source of legitimisation, their position was bound to remain precarious despite their readiness to strike political deals. Beyond Lashkargah they were surrounded by uncompromising enemies: Akhundzada continued to control most of northern Helmand, but there was considerable hostility against the Lashkargah trio even among other military leaders of the region. The survival of the coalition rested on the inability of the surrounding strongmen and military leaders to join forces for collective action. Ismail Khan, the ruler of western Afghanistan, who was at that time trying to strengthen his jihadi credentials and well as his influence, approached the jihadi elements of Farah and Helmand and as a player external to the region managed to coalesce most of it around him in 1993. The Lashkargah forces were not strong enough to withstand such an onslaught.[12]

The dynamics of evolutionary warlordism were most evident in Herat, where the military class had developed much deeper roots than in the south. The militias of Herat had been developing a kind of self-consciousness and *esprit du corps*, based on shared interests, during the late 1980s and early 1990s. Although usually engaged in infighting, sometimes the militias formed coalitions. For example, in 1989, as Ismail Khan's forces probed the resistance of the militias in charge of protecting Herat by attacking two small detachments, most of the other militias rushed to their support and repelled the assault. While the formation of a warlord polity by the Herati militias after 1992 was a possibility, they too lacked a charismatic figure around whom to gather. This left the militias split in three rival networks, weakening what would otherwise have been their military superiority over Ismail Khan. Three alliances based on these rival networks emerged: one was led by Daoud Ziarjom's successor and allied to Ismail Khan, another was led by the successor of Sayyid Ahmad and aligned with the Jami'atis opposed to Ismail Khan,[13] while a third was led by former Hizb-i Islami commander Juma Gul. Faced with the gradual consolidation of Ismail Khan's Emirate, in October 1992 Juma Gul's and Sayyed Ahmad's coalitions coalesced together under the leadership of Hizb-i Islami and launched an attempt to chase Ismail Khan from power. As they outnumbered Ismail Khan's forces and could count on the silent complicity of several other military leaders, who were also wary of Ismail's consolidation of power, initially they succeeded in advancing towards the city from the surrounding districts. However, they lacked effective leadership, their combatants were not motivated and morale was low within the ranks. Soon their advance stalled and Ismail Khan's Hamza (see chapter 19), strengthened by what was left of the regular troops of the communist regime, easily beat them back. Some of the leaders of the anti-Ismail Khan opposition immediately fled abroad or to northern Afghanistan, others tried to resist in their own districts, but without success. In January 1993 a group of former militiamen, led by Khalif Sobhan, once again launched an incursion from Iran, but the chance had been lost in October and they could not mount a serious challenge to Ismail.[14] The defeat of alternative centres of power and influence in 1992–3 contributed decisively to the emerging centralised character of ismail Khan's Emirate, although as it will be shown in Part II the heavy Soviet military pressure around Herat in the 1980s and Ismail Khan's own autocratic tendencies were decisive factors too.

In sum, only the Dostum-led alliance of militias managed to survive beyond 1993 to emerge as one as the key players in Afghanistan. In the process, Dostum would have earned the unenviable title of Afghanistan's eponymous warlord. That that became possible was due to the inability of the jihadi political leadership which had taken over in Kabul to form an effective government and rule the country.

By the mid-1990s, the two survivors of all these attempts to create warlord polities, Ismail Khan's Emirate in the west and Dostum's Junbesh in the north, had emerged as key players in Afghan politics and appeared relatively solid.

Minister of Defence Massud in particular resented the habit of both Ismail Khan and to an even larger extent Dostum of ruling their regions with complete autonomy. Dostum's appointment of government officials, granting of military ranks and the formation of military units were all major irritants to Massud. Yet what was left of the 'central' government in Kabul to some extent resembled the two rival warlord polities and its area of control was hardly bigger than theirs either. Rabbani and Massud only controlled north-eastern Afghanistan and most of the Kabul region, with chunks of the eastern region (mainly in Laghman and Logar) (see Map 1, Shura-i Nezar), although they maintained more extensive contacts with provincial polities and individual players throughout Afghanistan than either Ismail Khan or Dostum. Sometimes these contacts were quite close, as in the case of Ghazni's governor Qari Baba. In other cases, as with the shuras of Nangarhar and Paktia, such authorities were in fact just maintaining a position of neutrality in the conflict and did not effectively recognise Rabbani as a legitimate president. Individual military leaders in various parts of the country maintained links with Kabul due mainly to party affiliation and patronage connections. In the north, some of the Jami'ati military leaders refused to join Junbesh and remained aligned with Kabul, although after 1994 they never managed to represent more than a nuisance for Junbesh. In Hazarajat, as already mentioned, Harakat and the faction of Wahdat led by Akbari supported Kabul, but their support among the population and the military leaders was limited.[15]

Not only was the territorial control of Rabbani and Massud hardly greater than that of the warlords; their administration too was barely more effective. They gathered resources along the same lines, levying whatever few taxes were not pocketed by the military leaders, relying on mining resources and printing money to make up for the difference. They also spent their funds in a similar way, that is to sustain the military effort, to buy support among local leaders and to pay their ineffective administration. The main purpose of maintaining a state administration at all was probably linked more to their claim to be the legitimate government rather than to anything else. Salaries were usually paid months late, if at all, particularly in Kabul. The military leaders appointed to run departments and offices sometime retaliated by suspending the distribution of even basic services, such as for example street lighting in Kabul. Many offices were closed to the public, probably contributing to further reduce the legitimacy of the government. Despite the 1993 decision to take sharia as the new basis for legislation, the authority of the Kabul-based government was not recognised even in judicial matters, not only in northern Afghanistan where Dostum kept the influence of sharia at a minimum, but also in areas controlled by fellow Islamists like Ismail Khan. Dostum, Ismail Khan and the Jalalabad shura all had fairly well funded separate judicial systems.[16]

It could indeed be argued that the most solid of these three polities was not Kabul but Ismail Khan's, who had a wider tax base by virtue of his control of the flourishing trade with Iran and did not need to print his own currency to fund expenditure, contrary to Rabbani and Dostum. He also carried out the reconstruction of Herat to a much larger degree than in Kabul, helped by the absence of large scale conflict in 1993–4 (except for some skirmishing at the border with Junbesh). His administration seems to have been somewhat more effective than Kabul's too. The main advantage enjoyed by the latter was international recognition, which it inherited from Mojaddidi's tenure in April–June 1992, when all the factions were still united in the immediate aftermath of the fall of Najibullah. As Rabbani violated the Peshawar agreement by staying in power longer than the originally agreed four months, he still carried with him international recognition, even if the advantage of enjoying it were limited because of the disregard in which the international community held Afghanistan after 1992. Even after Rabbani and Massud had consolidated control over Kabul in 1995, only a very small amount of aid was coming through the capital, playing a very modest role in making Kabul's 'central' government a more attractive option than self-rule or warlord. The main benefit of external aid to most Afghans was the free distribution of wheat, but while Najibullah's regime had been distributing 250,000 tonnes of wheat each year to the population through a system of coupons, during the Rabbani regime the UN were distributing just 120,000 and most importantly were doing so directly, without going through the government.[17]

The crises of 1995–2001

Apart from the activities of the warring factions aimed directly at undermining the economy of their adversaries, such as Hizb-i Islami's blockading of Kabul and its creation of a subsidised market south of Kabul to attract goods away from the besieged capital, economic and political mismanagement also contributed to weaken both Kabul's and the separate warlord polities' ability to control the situation. The new elites in power in Kabul and in the regions shared a lack of understanding and disregard for the advantages of bureaucratised systems of government. Although formally an administration was kept in place and so was an armed force, their nature changed radically during the months and years that followed the collapse of Najib's government. Recruitment was driven by nepotism and favouritism to a degree that surpassed by far even the dubious practices of the monarchical era, while efforts to supervise and discipline were largely abandoned.[18] As a result, the administration and often even the armed forces quickly went into a deep decline, accelerated by the impact of the high inflation rate on the purchasing power of staff members.

Particularly in Kabul and in Mazar-i Sharif, the phenomenon of 'ghost' soldiers was widespread: local military leaders, now appointed to command 'official' armed units, inflated the number of troops in their ranks and pocketed the difference in the salaries paid, burdening the coffers of the rulers with a massive military expenditure which did not even translate into real military strength. This was but one result of the administration's inability properly to supervise what was going on. The multiplication of road blocks (for the purpose of taxation) acted as a strong disincentive to trade and prevented the economy from recovering after the many years of war. Again, this was the result of the lack of proper policing, as police forces had been parcelled out to local commanders as a form of patronage with total disregard for effective law enforcement. Local police officers were now the protégés of the various rulers. Whatever the central administration might have been trying to do in terms of overseeing their activities and forcing them to improve the quality of law enforcement, this was counter-balanced by the ability of former local military leaders, now police officers, to appeal to their patrons.

The banking system was functioning arbitrarily and savers were unable to withdraw their deposits without paying bribes. The exodus of capital inevitably contributed to the rapid deterioration of the economy. The existence of different currencies in the north and in Kabul, as well as the refusal of Hizb-i Islami to recognise some of the notes issued by the Rabbani government, created an environment that made trade and economic activity of any sort even more troublesome. On top of all this the population and the business community had to deal with galloping inflation. At the same time, a new generation of businessmen also emerged out of the series of civil wars of 1992–2001. To use a classification proposed by Goodhand, they were a product of a war economy and developed their own 'shadow' economy while being instrumental to the war effort of the military factions. This is true especially of northern Afghanistan, although not only. The older generation of pre-war business families survived to some extent, but mostly with greatly reduced influence and power.[19]

The decline of the economy gradually reduced the already limited ability of the military class to raise revenue. The inability to enforce law and order also contributed to the loss of legitimacy of the new polities, particularly in Kabul and in the north. As the factions were locked in the confrontation without being able to emerge from it, they all gradually became more vulnerable. A peace cycle started gaining strength and an ever wider constituency inside Afghanistan. When the Taliban emerged in 1994, they were largely underestimated by the major players. Their initial expansion in southern Afghanistan did not worry Rabbani and Massud in Kabul, as they saw this movement of junior mullahs as a potential ally against Hizb-i Islami. In fact, Hizb-i Islami was the first victim of the Taliban, its military force being almost entirely crushed between 1994 and 1996. Some allies of Rabbani, such as the Ghazni Shura, were also swept away by the Taliban's advance, but that must have seemed a price worth paying. This success could be explained with Hizb-i Islami's exhaustion after a string of defeats and the failure to achieve any gains in three years of war, and appears to confirm that the party was not well funded. Many of the original fighters, more ideologically motivated, had left the ranks of the party and had been replaced by opportunists and bandits like Zardad in Sarobi, busy extracting taxes on the road and unwilling to offer serious resistance to the Taliban's advance.[20] When the Taliban turned on Herat and Kabul, they initially faced a tougher resistance, but it was only a matter of months before Ismail Khan's emirate collapsed; Kabul did not last much longer either.

How can this weakness be explained? These polities had been waging war on each other for years and their collapse in the face of the comparatively weak Taliban requires some explanation. Apart from mismanagement and ineffective, patronage-based administrations, another factor was that very much as the Junbesh-Wahdat-Hizb-i Islami alliance against Jami'at had failed effectively to coordinate and cooperate, the anti-Taliban front formed late and once formed was far from monolithic: its members kept subverting each other until after the fall of Kabul:

- Jami'at-i Islami's northern leader, Ustad Atta, kept trying to re-establish a presence in the north after his 1994 defeat and was still fighting Junbesh as the Taliban were closing on Kabul and Massud desperately needed Junbesh's support.[21]
- Even after the incorporation of Hizb-i Islami into the government in 1996, the different groups could not agree on the distribution of the ministries. They were still bickering as the Taliban took Jalalabad and were advancing in Sarobi.[22]
- After the fall of Kabul, Massud allegedly refused to transfer his planes from Bagram to Mazar-i Sharif under Dostum's control, preferring to let the Taliban seize control of them.[23]
- In November 1996 the Jami'atis finally agreed to elect Dostum Chairman of the Defence Council, but this was in fact a purely honorary position as all the field commanders were acting independently and were responsible for their own area.[24]
- In February 1998, despite the alliance against the Taliban, a coalition of Jami'at, Wahdat, Hizb-i Islami and Harakat-i Islami tried to capture Hayratan from Junbesh and eliminate it from Mazar-i Sharif, without much success, and again in April Jami'at tried to seize Tashqurghan from Junbesh.[25]
- When in June, under Iranian sponsorship, anti-Taliban groups agreed to mount an offensive against the Taliban in Qala-i Zal (Kunduz), the reciprocal suspicions still remained. The other parties feared that Junbesh might have exploited the opportunity to strengthen its control once again in Balkh and despite having agreed to supply large forces, despatched only small numbers to the frontline.[26]
- Even after the fall of the north to the Taliban in 1998, Massud would not accept Dostum's settling in Takhar to create an Uzbek front against the Taliban. Only by October of that year were some of Junbesh's commanders allowed to enter Takhar, but not Dostum himself or any of those very close to him.[27]

Explaining this ultimately suicidal behaviour is not easy. It might be speculated that the narrowing revenue base forced the different factions to compete even harder in order to grab as much as possible from their neighbours, despite the incumbent threat of the Taliban. It should also be considered that the horizons of many military leaders were quite narrow and their interests petty ones; in the absence of ideological commitment, none of them was willing to sacrifice his interests for a common cause. To local military rulers, the loss of their power base to a fellow military leader was as threatening as a takeover by the Taliban. The absence of an ideological glue and of an effective bureaucratised system also caused the three polities, as well as the smaller provincial shuras of the Pashtun belt, gradually to lose coherence and be weakened by centrifugal tendencies. As a result, the ability to mobilise the military class for collective action gradually declined in all three polities after 1992. The inability of anti-Taliban factions to cooperate effectively contributed to aggravate the other main cause of their failure to stem the tide of the Taliban, that is their weakening legitimacy. Already after 1989, as pointed out in chapter 2, the legitimacy of the jihadi organisations had been wearing out. After 1992, there was very little appetite among the population for yet another civil war. Recruitment of new combatants and maintaining old combatants in the ranks turned increasingly problematic, not least because of the inability to rely on strong organisational structures. The motivation to fight was in steep decline, which might explain why the militias faced each other off in mostly inconclusive fighting, with much reliance on the firepower inherited from Najib's regime, which caused casualties mainly among the civilians. The political and military leadership had increasingly to tolerate abuses by his militiamen, such as looting and rape, not only because of their inability to pay salaries but also as an incentive for them to keep fighting.[28] This in turn further undermined any political legitimacy they might have had. The absence of significant successes on the battlefield even weakened the military legitimacy of the leaders and made the prospect of shareable gains less and less credible. This was particularly important to the extent that looting and material rewards were becoming a key motivational factor for the fighters.

By 1998–2000 the peace cycle was nearing its peak, with opposition to the Taliban surviving in just a few pockets on the northern fringes of the Hindukush and in the north-eastern corner of the country, mainly in Badakhshan province. Even there what was left of Rabbani's 'state' was down to a very dysfunctional condition. He had no finance officer and was collecting tax revenue himself, or allowed the district governors to do it. The council of military leaders was the body authorised to take decisions, but never met regularly and had no formal procedures. The council showed little concern in relation to economic and social affairs, while officials were chosen on the basis of political affiliation, with no consideration for merit or skills. Because of the lack of institutionalisation, local military leaders only had loose arrangements with Rabbani, whose main concern was the distribution of patronage. His administration in Badakhshan employed 7,000 people, but without delivering much in terms of services to the population. He redistributed government land to relatives and supporters, upgraded alaqdaris (sub-districts) to woluswa-lis (districts) in order to create positions to fill, rewarding his loyalists, but without investing in the creation of anything resembling an effective admin-istration. In several districts, particularly the more remote ones of the north (Darwaz, Nusai and others) and of the south (Kuran-o Munjan), there was no administration to speak of. In the districts where it existed, all it provided was very basic health and education, the former in fact mostly coming from NGOs. Doctors had little incentive to stay as they were being paid just $20 a month in Faizabad and $2 in the districts. On the whole, only 30% of the population had access to any kind of health care. Patients were expected to pay $10 a day for hospitalisation. The inefficiency of the administrative system in Badakhshan made Jami'at rather unpopular there. In 2000, Rabbani had barely managed to repress an attempt by military leaders and clerics of the Ragh region and some other districts too to side with the Taliban, but the dissatisfaction was spreading to the villagers too. At the beginning of 2001, UN sources reported that community elders in Badakhshan expressed their support for sanctions not just again the Taleban, but also against Jami'at.[29]

Notes

1. John Jennings, 'Pakistan faces Afghan anger for rebel aid', *Washington Times*, 5 March 1994; Tarzi, (1993), pp. 172–3; Bearden (2003), p. 346–7; Atseer (2005), p. 71–2; Natasha Singh, 'Battle rages over Afghan capital despite mujahideen cease-fire', *United Press International*, 27 April 1992; Interviews with former members of Hizb-i Islami, Kabul, Feb., March and May 2007; Gelinas (1997), p. 60; Atseer (2005), p. 57; Atseer (2005), p. 66–8; Rais (1993), pp. 911–2; John Jennings, 'Paki-stan faces Afghan anger for rebel aid', *Washington Times*, 5 March 1994; Khalilzad, (1995), pp. 152; Gelinas (1997), p. 58.
2. Gelinas (1997), p. 57; Maley (2002); Gelinas (1997).
3. Ibid., p. 22; Nojumi (2002), p. 111; Baigi (2000), p. 40; Anthony Davis, 'The Afghan Army', *Jane's Intelligence Review*, March 1993.
4. Interview with former Afghan air force officer, Kandahar, Jan. 2006.
5. Interviews with former commanders of Hizb-i Islami, Kabul, Feb. and May 2006.
6. Baigi (2000), pp. 120
7. Maley (2002), pp. 206–7.
8. Ibid., pp. 215–6; Gelinas (1997), pp. 117–8.
9. Dorronsoro (1996), p. 169; Atseer (2005), p. 56; Maley (2002), p. 207; Rubin (2000), p. 1792–3.
10. Christensen (1995), p. 78, 81–2.
11. Giustozzi/Noor Ullah (2006).
12. Ibid. An alternative versions is that Rabbani actually encouraged Ismail Khan to organise his offensive as part of a wider plan to secure southern Afghanistan for Kabul (see Baigi (2000), pp. 104–5).
13. Both Daoud Ziarjom and Sayyid Ahmad had been assassinated by 1992.
14. *Radio Afghanistan* in Pashto, 1430 gmt, 21 Jan. 1993.
15. Baigi (2000), p. 63; interviews with Hazara intellectual, Kabul, April 2003; inter-view with MP from Ghazni, Kabul, March 2007.

16. Atseer (2005), p. 73; Christensen (1995), p. 102.
17. Christensen (1995), pp. 79, 77; Rubin (2000), p. 1793.
18. Dorronsoro (1996), p. 186; Atseer (2005), p. 119.
19. Atseer (2005), p. 55, 74; Dorronsoro (1996), p. 187; Goodhand (2004); Giustozzi (2007f).
20. Interviews with former commanders of Hizb-i Islami, Kabul, Feb. 2006.
21. Baigi (2000), passim.
22. Ibid., p. 255.
23. Ibid., p. 268.
24. Ibid.
25. Ibid., pp. 348–9, 372.
26. Ibid., p. 374.
27. Ibid., pp. 391, 393.
28. Interviews with former military leaders, Kabul, 2005–7.
29. Interviews with military leaders of Hizb-i Islami and Jami'at from Badakhshan, April and May 2007; UNSMA internal documents, 11 May 2000, 13 June 2000, 11 July 2000 and 2 March 2001.

5

THE EXPLOSION OF PEACE IN 2001

BRINGING THE WARLORDS BACK IN

By mid-2001 very little was left of the warlord polities that had emerged from 1992 (see Map 5). Ismail Khan was desperately trying to reclaim some influence in western Afghanistan from his Iranian hideout, without much success. Some of his former allies, such as the Nabizadah brothers, were somewhat more effective in the mountains of eastern Herat, Ghor and Baghdis, where they could count on some 600 fighters. Dostum was fighting for his life in Dara-ye Suf, where he had recently re-launched guerrilla attacks against the Taliban with a small group of loyal fighters, probably no more than 600 men before 9/11.[1] Some of Dostum's men were carrying out a low scale insurgency in the mountains of Faryab, Takhar and Sar-i Pul, while Mohaqqeq, the most prominent northern commander of Wahdat was also active in the northern fringes of Hazarajat with a few hundreds men. Other Wahdat commanders had several hundred more fighters in Yakaolang, a total of maybe 1,000 men under arms. Hazrat Ali, a Pashai military leader affiliated with Shura-i Nezar, also had a few hundred men in Dara-ye Noor. Only Massud still maintained a large force in the north-east, but was under heavy pressure from the Taliban. The main body of Shura-i Nezar was estimated to have 13–15,000 fighters before US money and Russian supplies allowed it to mobilise all its reserves and all available manpower. After leaving Kabul, Rabbani's and Massud's polity had mostly shrunk back to Massud's own Shura-i Nezar. Rabbani was completely marginalised and even in his home province of Badakhshan Massud was gradually imposing his own allies in the place of the President's cronies. Little was left of the patronage relationship which had been built with military leaders throughout much of Afghanistan, apart from some fugitive commanders from the Pashtun belt who did not want to surrender to the Taliban and who had joined Massud with a few hundred men and the residual followers of Professor Sayyaf, also with a similar number of fighters. For Shura-i Nezar the future prospects seemed dim as the territory under its control had been shrinking after 1996, despite some successful counter-offensives.[2]

The 9/11 attacks in New York and Washington were a blessing for the beleaguered opposition to the Taliban. Very rapidly contacts were established (or re-established) with the Americans, overshadowing the relationship with the Iranians and the Russians. Direct American help was essentially in the form of cash handouts, while the Russians intensified their deliveries of heavy military equipment to Massud's militias in exchange for cash payments. Junbesh, which was in no position immediately to operate large amounts of heavy equipment, received mainly cash. It is not clear whether Wahdat or Ismail Khan received American help, but it seems certain that they were aided by the Iranians.

The cash was mainly used to re-mobilise dormant or dispersed supporters and to buy off military leaders who had sided with the Taliban and had been turned into local militias by them. Such groups had been downsized by the new rulers and it was often necessary to prime them with weapons in order to restore them to a condition where they represented a significant military threat to the Taliban. The most interesting feature of the re-formation of warlord polities in Afghanistan from 2001 is the speed with which it took place. As pointed out above, at the beginning of military operations with the support of US Special Forces and of US air support, the three key players in northern Afghanistan (Dostum, Atta and Mohaqqeq) only had a few hundred men each.[3] During the last few months of 2001, the Americans delivered 767

Map 5: Areas Under the Control of Anti-Taliban Groups, Summer 2001

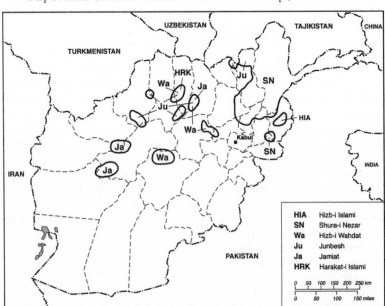

tonnes of supplies and $70 million, sufficient to equip and fund an estimated 50,000 militiamen to fight the Taliban throughout Afghanistan.[4] In just over two months each of them had expanded their forces to several thousand men under arms, including old and new fighters: Dostum had maybe 7,000 men, while Mohaqqeq and Atta too had a few thousand each. Shura-i Nezar as a whole had expanded its force to maybe as many as 50,000 by the end of 2001. Apart from US supplies, all sort of national and local power players sought to rearm themselves, by digging out hidden weapon caches or if necessary by purchasing new weapons on the black market. By early 2002 the number of militiamen in circulation had risen to a few hundred thousand.[5] Although it would have been impossible to defeat the Taliban in 2001 without the decisive contribution of the American air force, the very modest commitment of foreign troops to the occupation of Afghanistan made the anti-Taliban militias key players in the post-Taliban power game. ISAF had 4–5,000 men by the end of 2002, while Operation Enduring Freedom had 14,000 men in Afghanistan at that time, of which 9,000 were from the US Army.[6]

From the end of 2001 warlords, strongmen and political factions, which had all been part of the anti-Taliban front, became part of the ruling coalition. Under international sponsorship and with the approval of the armed groups, the 'central' government also included a core group of technocratic modernisers and 'aristocrats',[7] gathered around President Karzai.[8] This group included several Afghans educated abroad, mainly in the United States, and built its reformist credentials in large part on the promise either to 'civilise' or progressively reduce the power of warlords and strongmen in the provinces, as well as on a number of other projects aimed at rebuilding and modernising the Afghan state. Strongmen and warlords had been seriously weakened by the Taliban and in the early months of 2002 were still struggling to recover; they were convinced they could ill afford a confrontation with the American superpower.[9] Only Jami'at was really at the peak of its power and influence and was predominant in Kabul as Karzai took over the job from Rabbani, who had been acting as President for over a month in Kabul after the Taliban had fled. The capital was in fact under Jami'at-i Islami's military occupation. This made the 'technocratic' core of the government, which controlled the economic and financial ministries, very dependent on direct international support in order not to be overpowered by its own allies. Indeed, without such alliance and support, the technocrats would likely never have received a share of power in the first place. Because of the reluctance of the Bush administration, which feared getting bogged down in Afghanistan because of instability in the provinces, while it had bigger fish to fry in the Middle East,[10] confrontation with the regional military leaders was a weak or non-existent option in 2002, despite the weakness of most of them. This is why both technocrats and 'aristocrats' had for some time to agree to cooperating and sharing power with Jami'at and the regional forces. Although Defence Minister Fahim was seen during most of 2002 and 2003 as harbouring presidential ambitions, and despite repeated forecasts of the tension between

Fahim and Karzai escalating into open confrontation, the two managed to keep their differences within limits. In fact, Fahim helped Karzai on a number of occasions, offering the services of his cronies and allies to smooth Karzai's way through the two Loya Jirgas of 2002 and 2003.[11] Fahim also supported the policy of centralisation sponsored by the technocrats, the 'aristocrats' and Karzai himself, as long as he thought he could benefit from the process and use it against his factional rivals.[12]

The fact that Washington's chief concern in Afghanistan was short-term stability repeatedly led to political compromises which accommodated the interests of both Afghan and international partners by setting up 'façade' processes of institution-building reform, while allowing patrimonial processes of state seizure to take place unhindered. As a result, during the first three to four years of the post-Taliban era the development of bureaucratised and institutionalised security services proceeded very slowly, a fact that prevented the central state from sufficiently increasing its leverage on regional players.[13]

The original compromise seems to have been meant to result in something akin to the creation of a temporary and hybrid 'feudal state', which should have allowed to consolidate the centre, by building capacity in the ministries and creating new and loyal security services, while letting for the time being regional power holders run their fiefdoms with the blessing of Kabul. Once this consolidation had been achieved, the modernised and rebuilt core of the state could have started expanding towards the periphery, either by reining in and reforming the warlords/strongmen, or by replacing them and their acolytes. In reality, while technocrats and modernisers focused their efforts in some ministries such as Finance and Rural Development and Reconstruction, 'aristocrats' and Jami'atis used the remaining ministries and the presidency to compete against each other in the formation of extensive patronage networks among the country's local and regional power holders. During 2002–4, Defence Minister Fahim's efforts at expanding his patronage network were mainly focused on northern Afghanistan, where local Jami'atis were invoking his support against Junbesh. Karzai, by contrast, was focusing his own networking efforts on the south and south-eastern part of the country, in particular building solid connections through his brother Ahmad Wali with the strongmen in control of the provinces of Kandahar, Uruzgan and Helmand, some of whom even inter-married with the Karzai family.[14] In this way, the two avoided a direct clash.

The 'modernising' agenda was also negatively affected by the self-cooptation of many patrimonial leaders into the state structure, a result of the formation of the coalition government in 2002. As of early 2004, out of twenty-seven ministers, four were warlords, factional militia leaders or strongmen (Mohammad Fahim, Mohammad Mohaqeq, Sayyed Hussain Anwari, Gul Agha Shirzai) and at least three more (by a very conservative estimate) could be considered as deeply involved with the armed groups, one being the son of Ismail Khan, warlord of Herat (Mirwais Sadiq), and two close associates of Fahim (Yunus Qanuni and Abdullah Abdullah).[15] Fahim and his associates controlled among else Interior, Defence and Security, to an extent that it would be appropriate to speak of institutional seizure.

What was true of the central government was even truer of the local administration. Of the first group of thirty-two provincial governors appointed in 2002, at least twenty were leaders of armed groups and most of the remaining ones had links to the latter. Later the situation changed slightly, as some governors with a different background were appointed in a few provinces between the latter part of 2003 and the early months of 2004. However, the presence of governors with a background in the armed groups remained strong. The military class and the strongmen also populated the ranks of the district governors.[16] As they were themselves under very heavy pressure to reward their followers with jobs and positions of influence, and given that ministers, governors and chief of police had the power to make appointments in the structures which they were leading, the state administration was soon full of their clients.[17] Hence when the central government, under international pressure, set out to 're-educate' the military leaders, strongmen and patronage-oriented politicians who had been co-opted into the state structure, or sack them if they failed to comply, the task turned out to be much tougher than expected. In May 2003, for example, President Karzai tried to push a group of such governors, whom he had gathered in Kabul, to accept a set of policy guidelines, which would have restrained their freedom of action. Although they formally agreed to do so, once they returned to their provinces they mostly failed to comply.[18] The most obvious example of reform processes being manipulated and twisted to suit the interests of the military class was the Demobilisation, Disbandment and Reintegration (DDR) program, which resulted in the demolition of Fahim's patronage network within the structure of the MoD, but not in a significant reduction of the presence of armed groups in the rural areas. According to official estimates, which certainly overlooked many of the groups, there were 2,753 'illegal armed groups', numbering some 180,000 armed men, in 2006.[19]

The transition to electoral competition

Seen from the perspective of the military class, international intervention at the end of 2001 created nonetheless a new situation. None of the external patrons of armed groups in 2002 favoured re-starting the civil war. The prospect of presidential and parliamentary elections forced the leaders of armed groups to confront the problem of how to compete successfully in the new political scene. The armed groups were now compelled to organise as political parties or at least put together structures and networks that would allow them successfully to compete in elections.[20] The prospect of receiving an electoral legitimisation was the enticing aspect of the new situation. Other factors too contributed to facilitate the transition to electoral politics. Because of the experience of military stalemate in the period 1993–1996 and the exhaustion of the country, most of the factions had no objections to abandoning armed conflict (see chapter 4). Some of the politico-military groups, such as Junbesh and Wahdat, had consumed themselves in the military effort of the 1990s. This time, contrary to what had happened in the 1990s, not only the UN but also a number of countries, including the US, were ready to act as brokers among factions and guarantee that the latter would more or less respect the Bonn Agreement. The 'international community' also played a crucial role in maintaining a pluralistic political landscape. Pressure from the international community was much strengthened by the deployment of international troops as a (de facto) interposing force. ISAF secured Kabul against the threat of a coup against Karzai and the modernisers, while small contingents played the role of peacekeeping forces in the provinces. In northern Afghanistan, for example, British troops played a key role in preventing repeated rounds of factional violence from escalating into widespread conflict. Although the foreign military presence was modest, particularly until 2005, the different anti-Taliban factions had been impressed by the display of American air power and by its ability to tilt the balance of strength towards US allies. Several factions and individual strongmen would repeatedly use their informal, or pretended, alliance with the United States to bully local rivals, threatening to 'call in the B-52s'.[21]

While overt opposition to the transition to peace was discouraged by the international presence, the inclination towards compromise among non-Afghan partners in the process was meant to reassure the military class that their power base was not going to be dismantled anytime soon. As I have already discussed in the previous paragraph, DDR was more a façade than a substantial disarmament process. The same could be said of the banning of military leaders from the electoral process. While UNAMA had insisted on those clauses that banned the association of parties and candidates with armed groups to be included in the law on political parties and the elections law, the same rules were weakly and arbitrarily implemented by the Joint Electoral Management Body (JEMB), the UN-sponsored body in charge of the organization of the elections. During the 2005 parliamentary elections just thirty-two former military leaders were erased from the electoral lists for having failed to hand over weapons, out of more than 200 whose militia connections were established.[22] The armed groups mostly avoided overtly displaying weapons, and intimidation ceased in and around the towns. The façade of demilitarisation was saved while the military leaders were not altogether alienated.

Doubts about the aims of the international players and the inability of the UN and the US to negotiate a final settlement which was acceptable to all parties meant that the military class remained reluctant to play by the rules set by modernisers and the 'international community'. The Bonn Agreement did not provide for any institutionalized form of power-sharing, with the initial distribution of posts in the cabinet extending only to the Emergency Loya Jirga to be held six months later. This allowed the resurgence of factional rivalries over the composition of the cabinet after the Emergency Loya Jirga, thereby stoking distrust and giving the key players an incentive to maintain large armed militias. Particularly from 2003, as the original coalition gradually narrowed and the politico-military groups were one after the other de facto purged from government, doubts about future prospects of integration within the political system and about the neutrality of government security forces were rising among the ranks of the military class. The occasional flare up of local conflicts, particularly in northern Afghanistan until 2004, and the growing insurgency in the south after 2003 must also have advised caution. It was hardly surprising in these circumstances that the military class mostly maintained at least some connections with its old warlords and armed factions, which in turn were often happy to court their support. For example the political leadership of two of the parties that emerged from Jami'at, Nehzat-i Milli and Afghanistan-i Newin, advocated the strengthening of the role of the former military leaders in civilian life and the granting of special privileges to the jihadis.[23] Adding to the climate of uncertainty about the future, the military leaders had not yet been able fully to legitimise their role as 'new Khans' among an often hostile civilian population and competing elites, hence remaining dependent on their gunmen to protect their position.

Behind the façade of disarmament, military leaders mobilised their gunmen in 2002–5 to bolster their political allies' campaigns, as well as their own. Various forms of violence, ranging from intimidation to outright assassination, took place throughout Afghanistan during this period. The fact that all major candidates relied on the support of armed groups in order to be able to campaign outside Kabul, including incumbent and winner Hamid Karzai, added to the value of the military class and other leaders of armed groups, increasing their leverage and offering opportunities to establish precious direct contacts with Kabul. With the link between the military class and the big regional players only partially eroded until 2004–5, the position of the latter was boosted in the round of elections which took place in 2002–05: the two Loya Jirga 'elections' of 2002 and 2003, the presidential elections of 2004 and the parliamentary elections of 2005. Of these, the main test was the September 2005 elections for the Wolesi Jirga (Afghanistan's lower house of parliament). Party lists were not allowed by the terms of the electoral law, but many of those elected were affiliated to armed groups. The different factions of Jami'at elected about 20% of the MPs and Junbesh 9%, both of which could be described as satisfying outcomes. Electoral legitimisation had been achieved.[24]

These successes were not just the result of intimidation. The resources and energy invested by the different warlords and military leaders in the creation of electoral machines independent of the support of their gunmen varied as a result of of the incentives that they received and of their position in the post-2001 order. The more marginalised a group from central power and resources, the stronger the incentive to build an electoral base autonomous from the armed militias. For example, because of the early souring of relations between Junbesh and Kabul on the one hand, and its bad press on the other, this group was under particularly strong pressure to convince its military leaders to keep a low profile and develop political structures (see Part II). By contrast, the various Jami'ati groups were much better embedded in the state apparatus and as a result they openly retained a greater amount of weaponry, particularly in the Panjshir Valley; their incentive to build genuine political parties was modest and little effort was expended in that direction.[25]

Restoration: The Fragmentation of the Big Warlord Polities

Although as discussed above the military class initially remained behind the warlords, the explosion of peace was bound to have an impact on their relationship. The growing division within the leadership certainly contributed to weaken the allegiance of the military class. The principal cause of the split within Jami'at-i Islami was a generational conflict between the old leadership gathered around Professor Rabbani, and a new generation of 'Young Turks' that included the lieutenants of the late commander Massud. The conflict between these two groups originated in the 1980s, but only emerged as an open split in 2002. Unfortunately the new generation was not united either and later split into another two groups, with former presidential candidate Yunis Qanuni gathering the largest following (see chapter 22). The disintegration of Junbesh was a slower affair. Initially only Abdul Malik, who had tried to eliminate Dostum in a coup in 1997, set out to form his own Hizb-i Azadi. Malik never managed to gather more than a very limited number of followers, even if he seemed able for a few months during the summer of 2006 to expand his influence beyond central Faryab. In 2005 Majid Rowzi, who had long been a close associate of Dostum, also split, taking with him a small circle of Arab supporters. The 2006 crisis was far more serious and saw Junbesh lose some major bastions of support, including Ahmad Khan in Samangan and the majority of its key figures in Takhar.

The disintegration of the leadership was accompanied by an increasingly problematic relationship with the military class. A key passage was first the weakening and then the removal of Marshal Fahim from the Ministry of Defence. Fahim was initially mainly confronted by Minister of Finance, Ashraf Ghani, a protegé of Afghanistan's donors. Ghani played a key role in forcing the disbandment of official militias by threatening to stop transferring funds to the MoD by the deadlines set for the disarmament of the different units. As already mentioned, the disbandment, eventually completed in 2005, did not really eliminate the militias, which continued to exist underground, but deprived Fahim of a key source of patronage to maintain nationwide influence. Ghani's threat to resign the cabinet in the summer of 2004 appears to have played a role in forcing Karzai to end his alliance with Fahim and drop him from the presidential ticket. After much wrangling Karzai offered Fahim the vice-presidential post in the 2004 electoral ticket. When Fahim refused to resign from his ministerial post before registering as a candidate, as required by the electoral law, Karzai had a good excuse to drop him from the presidential ticket. Fahim was finally replaced as Minister of Defence in January 2005, after almost two years of rumours about his imminent replacement. Ghani was also instrumental in removing another key source of funding for the warlords and other regional players, by starting a process that led to the gradual reassertion of central control over provincial customs revenues.[26]

Another contributory factor to the disintegration of the warlord polities was the gradual loss of control over the Ministry of Interior by Fahim's allies and clients, a development which illustrated how institutional seizure is a risky strategy (see Introduction). Attempts to reform the MoI (Ministry of Interior) and turn it into an efficient and de-patrimonialised institution were far from successful. Yunis Qanuni, like Fahim a key player in Shura-i Nezar, was replaced after spending six months at the Ministry and after indulging in patronage on a massive scale. A new minister, Taj Mohammad, an Afghan-American and former governor under the king, was appointed in June 2002 with a mandate to undertake sweeping reforms. An elderly man who had little support within the ministry, he failed to change anything at the MoI. In January 2003 yet another new minister, Ahmad Jalali, who was aligned with the technocrats, in turn replaced Taj Mohammad. Jalali too promised to implement deep reforms, but his achievements during his first year in office were modest. In terms of its impact on the warlords, Jalali's most important reform was the abolition in 2002 of the zonal system, which had allowed warlords and strongmen to legitimise their control over multiple provinces by appointing themselves at the top of a zone.[27] Another potentially key move to curtail the power of the governors-strongmen took place in mid-2003, when they were forced to relinquish any role as military commanders, or else quit as governors. Jalali also tried to reclaim the direct control of the ministries over the provincial administrations. The role of the governors in 2002–2003 had grown much beyond what it used to be before 1978, especially in terms of influence over the administrative departments, which were once controlled directly by the ministries in Kabul.[28] Although the practice of provincial governors often appointing district governors without the approval of the MoI was curtailed during 2003, some of them, most notably Ismail Khan of Herat, were still indulging in it during 2004.[29] During the latter part of 2003 and 2004, the government also started to select provincial and district governors from outside the province of appointment, an old practice of the Afghan government abandoned in the 1980s.

Dostum, Ismail Khan and the north-eastern Jami'atis all tried to resist the pressure of the central government. Increasingly constrained in the use of armed force by the deployment of foreign troops in the provinces and by growing international scrutiny, they developed grassroots support structures which were used in public demonstrations and rioting, probably succeeding in slowing down their gradual marginalisation and achieving some legitimisation by participation. But they could not completely halt the process and Kabul's centralisation efforts certainly weakened the warlords. On the other hand, they did not necessarily strengthen the central government. Karzai and his tribal allies were not so much interested in institution-building as in the centralisation of patronage. Soon Karzai started to assert his views in front of Jalali the technocrat, who needed the President's approval for new appointments. Already by late 2003 and early 2004 the incisiveness of Jalali's actions appeared to be on the wane. This did not translate in a new wave of appointments favourable to the warlords, but increasingly in the direct cooptation of members of the military class by the central government, i.e. Karzai's circle, thereby bypassing the warlords. After the removal of Ismail Khan, many of his former collaborators seamlessly switched their loyalty to Kabul. In the north, military leaders had already started switching sides in 2004, but the process intensified as Junbesh grew weaker in 2006. In the north-east, Karzai used the parliamentary elections of 2005 to lure some of the military leaders onto his side and then boost their position with the support of state patronage. In the south, Karzai had established alliances with local strongmen in 2001, but by 2005 the Karzai family was strengthening its role in the coalition and reducing the autonomy of those more inclined to play their own game, who were forced into a junior role.[30]

From Military Networks to Mafias

The disintegration of the large warlord polities was underpinned by another aspect of the 'explosion of peace', that is the appearance of new opportunities to raise revenue. If not the warlords themselves, many within the ranks of the military class modified their priorities and started looking for ways to adapt to peace, both in terms of finding a new occupation for themselves and in terms of reaping benefits from it. I have already discussed the transformation into 'new Khans' (chapters 1 and 4), but their adaptation and efforts to consolidate their position in society took other shapes too. The regional 'shadow economies' came into their own, as the military class became more focused on opportunities for financial gains and hence active in business, although mostly via proxies. Those who had made substantial savings could now look to replenish their war coffers, as peace brought about a general economic recovery and offered new opportunities. Some likely viewed investment in Afghanistan as a way to consolidate their political and social influence: patronage and the distribution of benefits were often very important aspects of these businesses. As far as legal businesses were concerned, their competitive edge over real businessmen in fact derived from their political and military leverage and the consequent ability to carve out monopolies and privileges. In their new clothes of ministers and provincial governors, military leaders have also been known to have indulged in land graft, although mostly to distribute it to their supporters.[31] Another example of the constraints placed on businesses by the political concerns of the strongmen is that businesses associated with them would often receive requests to hand over cash to be used for political campaigning, a fact which could of course compromise business profitability and shows that profit-making was not always the priority.[32]

One exception might have been, according to available information, a major warlord who until 2004 was making so much money out of customs revenues that he might not have felt the need to get directly involved in business.[33] Other prominent figures developed powerful business interests. As a rule, they would refrain from directly exposing themselves as businessmen, mainly because of their ambition to occupy official positions within the state structure. There is some evidence (amid plenty of gossip) that they invested substantial resources in the business activities of fellow military leaders or of compliant businessmen. This indirect and non-official involvement in business activities rested on their perennial ability to intimidate their business partners against 'misbehaving' and on their capacity to punish whoever tried to violate their interests. Because their investments are not officially recorded, had they been unable to resort to intimidation there would have been little to prevent their business partners from walking away with the money. In this sense the partial conversion of Afghan military leaders into businessmen resembled in many ways the establishment of 'mafia' or organised crime networks, active both in the legal and the illegal economy and able to use force to protect their interests and possibly to expand. The building industry, larger-scale trading and fuel distribution, to name but three, appear to have been more extensively affected by attempts to enforce regional monopolies (fuel) or to favour friendly businessmen over others (construction) or again to force traders to move into newly built complexes where they would have to pay high rent and be easier to control (city markets). Starting from 2004, a decline in the pattern of abuses and intimidation began to be reported at least in the north,[34] although it is typical of all mafias once their system consolidates—resorting to violence rarely becomes necessary.

The involvement of the warlords in business did not significantly enhance their ability to keep most of the military class united around them. In part this was due to the failure of some of them to redistribute their gains, but there was also a growing divergence of interests between warlords-turned-politicians and the military class. For example, eager to play politics, the warlords appear to have compelled their men to remove most tax-collecting roadblocks between 2002 and 2003. The money thus raised was sticking to the hands of the gunmen without benefiting the big warlords. But probably the single most important factor contributing to the warlords' declining ability to maintain their leadership of the military class was the dramatic rise of the narcotics economy. Contrary to conventional wisdom, the warlords did not appear to be directly involved in promoting the cultivation of the poppies, nor were they making much money from the trade. As they had little direct territorial control and no permanently mobilised, centralised armed forces to control their vassals, it is difficult to see how Dostum or the leadership of Jami'at could have forced the military class in the districts to hand over part of the profits. In Dostum's case at least, allegations of his role in narcotics smuggling appears questionable, at least after 2003 when his influence over provincial authorities and police forces was waning rapidly. Moreover, judging from the amount of drugs seized in Uzbekistan or Turkmenistan compared to Tajikistan, it would seem that little of it crossed the border in the region under Dostum's effective control. Although the involvement of Jami'at in the smuggling of narcotics had been reported in the civil war of the 1990s, from 2005 the influence of Fahim and other leaders of Jami'at over local military leaders was also rapidly weakening; whatever their ability to extract part of the revenue in 2001–2004 might have been, it must have declined too. The available evidence points instead towards the involvement of local military leaders, who were in the first place well positioned to collect taxes from the poppy-growing farmers. According to UNODC such taxes were normally in cash and mostly amounted to 10% of the farmer's income, with peaks as high as 40%. More profitable seem to have been the provision of security to the narco-traders and involvement in the processing and smuggling of narcotics across Afghanistan's borders. In at least a few cases, vehicles belonging to such military leaders have been seized by Afghan police loaded with heroin or other narcotics.[35] In north-eastern Afghanistan cosy relations were reported between Afghan military leaders and border guards on the other side of the border.

As they increasingly achieved financial autonomy and even wealth, local military leaders had one more reason not to be dependent on the big warlords. Although Jami'at maintained a strong network of individuals linked to the party within the Ministry of Interior, it seemed to be changing its character and becoming increasingly depoliticised. Such networks appeared to be merging with once rival networks in southern Afghanistan in order to facilitate the movement of drugs across the country. Well entrenched in the central state, the merged networks hardly needed the protection of big warlords. The trap of the peace cycle thus seemed on the cusp of sidelining the increasingly redundant warlords. As of mid-2009, their fate seemed to hang on the end of this cycle and the start of a new cycle of war, thanks to the spread of insecurity due to the Neo-Taliban insurgency in the south.[36]

Notes

1. On Dostum see Berntsen (2005), p. 133–4; Walwalji (2007).
2. UNSMA internal documents, 11 May 2000, 13 June 2000 and 2 March 2001; Berntsen/Pezzullo (2005). p. 90.
3. A total of seven CIA teams were deployed in Afghanistan during Operation Enduring Freedom (Tenet (2007), p. 213), although only three of them seem to have played an important role distributing cash to fund the operation (see Crumpton (2005), p. 170); the one led by Gary Bertsen had $8 million with it (see Berntsen (2005), p. 106); Gary Schroen's had $3 million initially, to which another $10 million were soon added (Schroen (2007), p. 29, 94, 179). 12 Special Forces teams were also deployed, of which three were in the north and north-east (595, 555, 534); see

Boot (2006) and Dana Priest, 'Team 555' Shaped a New Way of War', *Washington Post*, 3 April 2002.

4. Schetter (2005), p. 114, citing UN sources; Tenet (2007), p. 210; Woodward (2002), p. 317.

5. See Giustozzi, KCL

6. http://www.whitehouse.gov/infocus/defense/enduringfreedom.html

7. The term is used here for brevity to indicate a group of genuine aristocrats, former state servants and their scions which had coalesced around the so-called 'Rome Group' in the wake of the negotiations for a future government in Bonn.

8. See John Lloyd, 'The crush of civilizations', *New Statesman*, 9 Sept. 2002; Pamela Constable, 'Karzai's Control Often Illusory', *Washington Post*, 25 Feb. 2002; http://www.export.gov/afghanistan/pdf/minister_bios.pdf.

9. Interview with an Afghan intellectual, Asadullah Walwalji, who met several of these leaders during 2002 (Kabul, May 2003).

10. See Woodward (2004); Hersh (2004), pp. 146–7 (quoting Richard A. Clarke); David Rohde and David E. Sanger, 'How a 'Good War' in Afghanistan Went Bad', *The New York Times*, 12 Aug. 2007.

11. At least one high ranking member of the MoD, Gen. Daoud, attended the Loya Jirga proceedings, contrary to the regulations, in the opinion of many with the purpose of intimidating the delegates through his presence.

12. Giustozzi (2004), pp. 6–7. For some of Fahim's pro-centralisation statements, see Rubin/Malikyar (2003), p. 40.

13. See Giustozzi (2007c) on army; Wilder (2007), Amnesty (2003) and ICG (2007) on police. For the example of the disarmament process, see Giustozzi (2008b).

14. The commando brigade of Kandahar was until 2003 under the command of Ahmad Wali Karzai, one of the President's brothers, and is composed of Karzai's fellow tribesmen. 15th Militia Div. of Kandahar is also made up of Popolzai tribesmen (Karzai's tribe) and is widely reckoned to be loyal to the president.

15. Gul Agha Shirzai was one of those strongmen who was constrained by the tribal nature of his base of support and cannot therefore be considered a true warlord. This type of strongmen is the most common throughout the 'Pashtun belt'. His military capabilities derived from some former members of Esmat Muslims militias and were not his own, hence he cannot be considered a member of the military class strictu sensu either.

16. Assessment carried out during fieldwork in Afghanistan.

17. See Giustozzi (2008b) for a description of the same process in the case of the army.

18. *Hewad*, 29 May 2003.

19. See Giustozzi (2008b).

20. See Giustozzi (2007a).

21. See for example 'Afghan Fighters Close in on Bin Laden, Squabble over Kandahar', *People's Daily*, 9 Dec., 2001.

22. 207 candidates were identified by the Electoral Commission as militia commanders, probably an underestimate (*The Economist*, 22 Sept. 2005).

23. See "Panjshiri With National Ambitions", *Afghan Recovery Report* No. 139, 6 Oct. 2004.

24. See Giustozzi (2007a) and Giustozzi (2007b).

25. See for example IRIN News, "Where the Gun Still Rules", 7 June 2006, http://www.irinnews.org/report.asp?ReportID=53768andSelectRegion=Asia

26. *UPI*, 27 July 2004; Giustozzi (2004), p. 8; Rubin/Malikyar (2003), pp. 30–33.
27. This was among others Dostum's case, who was head of the northern zone, and Ismail Khan's, head of the western zone.
28. See Rubin/Malikyar (2003), p. 10.
29. Interviews with members of the provincial administration, Herat, Nov. 2004.
30. See Giustozzi (2007b). On Kandahar province see Giustozzi/Noor Ullah (2007).
31. This is the case for example of Mohaqqeq in Mazar-i Sharif in 2005, according to one informer who used to work for one of his associates and who was interviewed by the author in May 2005.
32. Interview with collaborator of businessman linked to Mohaqqeq, Mazar-i Sharif, May 2005.
33. Author's interviews with Afghan businessmen and intellectuals, Herat, Nov. 2004.
34. See for example on northern Afghanistan Kate Clark, 'In the shadow of the gun', *BBC News*, 30 June 2005, accessed at http://news.bbc.co.uk/2/hi/south_asia/4118820.stm.
35. According to the author's personal communication with UN official in Kunduz, Oct. 2003, one such incident occurred in autumn 2003 to a military leader in Takhar, one of whose vehicles was seized in Salang. The leader was not in the vehicle at the time of seizure. Another example, concerning a general of the Ministry of Defence from eastern Afghanistan who was arrested with a truckload of heroin, is mentioned in Rubin (2004 road), p. 10.
36. Interviews with UN officials, Kabul, 2006–7; Giustozzi (2007d).

PART TWO

MODELS OF WARLORDISM

6

JUNBESH

ORIGINS AND GENERAL CHARACTERISTICS

In chapter 3 I examined the incubation of Junbesh-i Milli-ye Islami, the 'party' led by Gen. Dostum from 1992 onwards. Its actual emergence was due to a reaction against re-centralisation efforts by President Najibullah, starting from late 1991. The military and to a lesser extent the political leaders of northern Afghanistan had won a considerable degree of informal autonomy due to their role in fighting the insurgency against the communist regime in the 1980s. Efforts at pooling these discrete forces in northern Afghanistan started as early as 1990, in order to contrast what was perceived as an attempt by Pashtun nationalist circles around the President to re-establish their hegemony over the region. At that time Dostum began experiencing an increasingly difficult relationship with some Pashtuns both in the army and in the HDK/ Watan. He is reported to have stated, in July 1990 in Moscow, that Uzbeks and Turkmens in northern Afghanistan would not tolerate that Pashtuns should 'command everything' as in the past.[1] His refusal to accept the Pashtun General sent by President Najibullah in January 1992 to rein in the military commanders of Northern Afghanistan is a well-known story. It led to the alliance of a number of formerly pro-government military leaders, of whom Dostum was just the most prominent, with some of the jihadi factions. This alliance took the name of *Harakat-i Shamal* (the Movement of the North).

In their embryonic shape, Dostum's horizontal networks with fellow military leaders had emerged in the 1980s. At the time of the creation of 53rd Div. in 1988, Dostum displayed skills which he would often use in the future. He successfully liased with fellow militia leaders in the neighbouring provinces of Faryab (Rasul Pahlawan) and Sar-i Pul (Ghaffar Pahlawan and Habibullah Eshaqzai) and convinced them to form a lobby in favour of the creation of a larger militia unit under his leadership. They became brigade commanders under Dostum, within the 53rd Div… He also established close relations with other militias in the north, such as Naderi's Ismailis in Baghlan and Amanullah Gilamjan's brigade in Balkh, as well as with regular army officers: Gen.

Momin of 70th division (Hairatan), Gen. Hilal of the helicopter regiment based in the north, Gen. Nazimi of 18th Div. (Balkh). There is also evidence for the last few years of Najibullah's regime (1990–) that Dostum was dealing directly even with opposition military leaders and establishing personal connections with them, not always in order to encourage their defection to the government side. By the early 1990s if not earlier the contours of his future role of warlord were already beginning to take shape, as he intervened in the conflicts among military leaders and helped them to make peace. For example, in 1991 he reportedly acted as a broker between Nassim Mehdi, leader of Hizb-i Islami, and Hafiz Arbab, leader of Jami'at in Faryab, despite the fact that they were both still opposed to the regime. During 1991 Dostum started developing contacts with opposition military leaders not just in northern Afghanistan but as far as the north-eastern and central regions, first and foremost with Ahmad Shah Massud of Panjshir. Ultimately, these contacts would develop into the alliance that led the insurrection against President Najibullah in 1992.[2]

The expansion of Dostum's network of contacts and alliances was not accompanied by the establishment of a matching institutional framework, a key factor in explaining the future 'feudal' character of Dostum's leadership. In theory, the formation of 53rd Div. first and then of 7th Army Corps under Dostum's command offered such a framework. However, even within the 53rd Div. before 1992, when Dostum was an officially appointed General and his fellow militia leaders were theoretically his subordinates, Dostum was not able to command and demand obedience from them. They remained allies more than officers of a disciplined army. Both before and after April 1992, important decisions were always taken by consultation.[3] Military patrimonialism characterised Dostum's relationship with his force: contrary to what one would expect of the units of a regular army, 53rd Infantry Div. was virtually Dostum's personal property and the soldiers were personally loyal to him—there was no rotation of commanding officers. The same applied to the sub-units and their commanders. In other terms, despite having been incorporated into the regular army, the 53rd Div. maintained the typical features of the regional militias.

The first major step towards Dostum's effective 'coronation' as the leader of the north was his recognition as the representative of all the militias of the northern region during the 1992 insurrection. The other key players were:

- Gen. Momin, commander of 70th brigade in Hairatan;
- Amanullah Jilamjan, commander of 74th brigade in Shulgara (Balkh);
- Jaffar Naderi, commander of 80th Div. in Baghlan province;
- Rasul Pahlawan, commander of 510th brigade in Faryab;
- Ghaffar Pahlawan, commander of 511th brigade in Sar-i Pul.

They all had their own independent power bases, but were in fact quite a heterogeneous mix. Rasul Pahlawan, described above in chapter 3, was the eponymous self-made military leader. Momin was a trained army officer of

Tajik ethnicity, who had been given command of a militia unit, after he showed remarkable abilities in winning over members of the opposition. Amanullah, also a Tajik, nicknamed Jilamjan ('Uprooter') for his ferocity, was a former teacher whose family had been massacred by the mujahidin in early 1980 and was set on taking revenge. Like Dostum, he rapidly rose up the ladder after enlisting in 1980. Having started as a company commander, he was soon commanding a battalion and in 1990 was appointed commander of a brigade. By contrast Jaffar Naderi was a militarised community leader. He derived his authority from his father, Sayyed Mansoor Naderi and at the core of his force always remained a community militia. All those holding key positions in the Naderi's fief were family members: under Junbesh, Jaffar was commander of 6th Corps as well as governor, while the commanders of 54th and 80th divisions were Mansoor's sons in law. Many others in the administration and in the army were relatives, the only major exception being the chief of police of Baghlan.[4]

The next major step was the at least temporary acceptance of Dostum's leadership by all the mujahidin groups active in the North of Afghanistan. Among the regional mujahidin leaders who initially teamed up with Dostum the most prominent were:

- Ustad Atta, leader of Jami'at-i Islami in northern Afghanistan;
- Juma Khan Hamdard, leader of Hizb-i Islami in Balkh;
- Nassim Mehdi, leader of Hizb-i Islami in Darzab (Jowzjan);
- Azad Beg, leader of the Ittehadiya.

Although many military leaders of the mujahidin left soon, other stayed and merged within Junbesh. They were mostly concentrated in Jowzjan, northern Sar-i Pul, Baghlan, Kunduz and Faryab (see Map 6). Militarily, Atta was the most significant of the mujahidin leaders, while Azad Beg was mainly a political figure with just a modest fighting force. A large number of smaller players, sometimes loosely associated with the main figures mentioned above and sometimes not, also joined Harakat-i Shamal and later played a role in the nascent Junbesh. Each had his own demands in terms of status and recognition, as well as patronage resources. In consultation with the new power holders in Kabul, Dostum tried to handle the situation through the creation of a large number of military units, which both added a degree of legitimisation to the role that these previous military leaders of the mujahidin were playing anyway and at the same established some subordinate relationship with Dostum, who claimed the role of head of the northern region. The formal hierarchy was not playing a significant role in justifying Dostum's leadership over the former mujahidin. Since Dostum and his fellow militia leaders had easily seized control of huge depots of arms and supplies, he could now replace the political leaderships of the jihadi parties based abroad as a new and more generous dispenser of patronage. The army that Dostum and his fellow officers inherited in 1992 included five divisions, several independent brigades and militia formations, plus police and armed units belonging to the

Map 6: Military Leaders Incorporated Into Junbesh, 1992–3, by Party of Origin

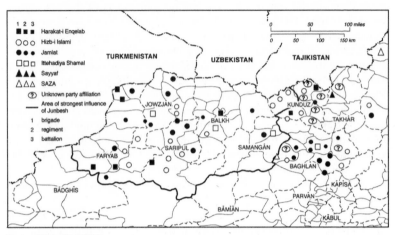

Sources: Walwalji (1378).

national security (WAD), to which a large number of former mujahidin groups should be added. On paper at least, this force counted 110,000 men, equipped with large amounts of armour and artillery and even an air force, spread across seven provinces, although the actual number of full-time troops was certainly much lower. Between 1992 and 1993 at least 72 new units, ranging from battalion to brigade, were formed in the northern and north-eastern provinces (Jowzjan, Faryab, Sar-i Pul, Balkh, Samangan, Baghlan, Kunduz, Takhar and Badakhshan).[5] On top of those, a number of units of the established militias were upgraded, from brigade to division, from regiment to brigade, etc. Dostum's generosity in supplying the newly formed units established their dependence on him, following a pattern already experienced during the previous regime (see chapter 3). As each military leader increased the number of his armed men, it became more difficult to secure adequate alternative sources of supplies. Even the Rabbani 'government' in Kabul found it difficult to compete, not only for lack of matching supplies, but also because of logistical reasons, as Dostum controlled the roads leading north.

After Jami'at-i Islami seized control of Kabul with the help of Dostum and other generals opposed to Najibullah, it only took a few months for the leadership of the Movement of the North to start feeling that it was being deliberately discriminated against. They were repeatedly told in Kabul that Harakat-i Shamal was not a political party and therefore not entitled to join the political discussions in Kabul.[6] There were at least two reasons for the cold reception in Kabul of the delegations sent by Harakat-i Shamal. First, Kabul saw its relationship with Harakat-i Shamal as a temporary alliance that gave the latter no legitimate claim to a share of power as such. Second, the dominant force within it was the former military and militia leaders of Najibullah's regime, which made it unpalatable to the jihadi leaders.

As a result of its lack of success in gaining acceptance as a permanent and legitimate player in Kabul, the leadership of Harakat-i Shamal, in particular the military leaders with the support of some but not all of the political components, established what could claim to be a party—Junbesh-i Milli-ye Islami—along the lines of Jami'at and other jihadi groups. The leadership was probably aware that creating a party would not have automatically provided the legitimisation that the leadership sought in Kabul, but the new party was expected to enhance the collective bargaining power of Harakat-i Shamal, as well as to consolidate the alliance of all the political forces of the north on a regionalist platform.[7] On 1 June 1992, the first congress formally established the party. Dostum was elected as the leader, but among the deputies we find Ustad Atta, the leader of Jami'at-i Islami in northern Afghanistan and a future enemy in many battles. At its core were the regular forces and the militias of Najibullah's regime,[8] but among the 31–strong membership of the Executive Council were representatives of all the parties of Northern Afghanistan. Ten were former members of HDK/Watan and other allied leftist parties, two were members of the Ismaili minority, who had supported Najibullah, and five were officers of the armed forces, mainly militia leaders. The remaining fourteen were military leaders and representatives of the mujahidin parties, such as Jami'at-i Islami, Hizb-i Islami, Ittehadiya Shamal, Hizb-i Wahdat, Harakat-i Enqelab and Harakat-Islami. Moreover, at least two of the militia leaders selected for membership were known for having maintained links to the jihad parties before the fall of President Najibullah.[9] On the whole, one could say that representation in the council had been roughly divided on a 50–50 basis between former supporters of Najibullah and the former jihadi opposition.

In these early stages in the life of Junbesh, there were several obvious obstacles to its consolidation. The desire to develop any type of structure was only half-hearted as far as the military leaders of Harakat-i Shamal were concerned. They wanted a tool that would legitimise them in the eyes of the international community and allow them access to political bargaining in Kabul. On the other hand, the single and rather tenuous unifying factor, that is shared northern interests, was hardly enough to offset tensions arising from the different interests represented within Junbesh. As a result of these conflicting aims and of its heterogeneous composition, during the first year or two of its existence, Junbesh was shaken by power struggles. The emergence of Abdur Rashid Dostum as the undisputed leader of Junbesh was not necessarily the obvious outcome to all the components of the organisation in the early days. Other jihadi figures had the ambition to lead the Movement of the North. This also explains why the leadership of Junbesh were to dedicate very little time to consolidating it.

The particular model of warlordism represented by Junbesh was centered on a charismatic military leader and a core group of advisers, mostly with a background in the Parcham faction of the old HDK. Of all Afghan warlords, Dostum was the closest to the 'orphan warlord'/statecide ideal type, because of his proud record in the regime's military. Dostum's martial reputation was well established by 1992. As the commander of the 53rd Div. he was known as a brave and decisive military leader who never gave up the opportunity for a fight and who would take to the battlefield with his troops, rather than observing the battle from some remote position, as most army generals would have done. In 2001 he personally took part in cavalry charges against Taliban defensive positions, although not among the first wave; and on at least one occasion he directly led an infantry team in an attack against a Taliban position. His tactical skills were never comparable to those of Massud, as he relied instead on instinct and ruthlessness. During the 2001 campaign against the Taliban, he confronted the enemy with old-fashioned charges, initially without even US air support. Although Dostum's fearsome reputation as a disciplinarian, who did not hesitate to have soldiers tortured or executed for their misdemeanours, might have been exaggerated, he tended to behave erratically under the influence of alcohol. In any case this aspect of his character did not prevent him from being popular with his men. Fighters, and in particular Afghans, tend to like this type of leader, who shares with them at least some of the dangers of the battlefield. Many of his fighters even tatooed his name on their chest and forearms in an expression of identification with him.[10]

His qualities as military leader, his martial legitimacy and credibility allowed Dostum to motivate and mobilise fellow military leaders, whom he managed through a quasi-'feudal' relationship. Without his personal charisma and ability to mobilise and motivate his military peers, Junbesh's strength as a system would have been virtually nil. At the same time, he needed diplomatic and intra-personal skills to keep his followers together. Control over key resources was another important aspect of Dostum's leadership.

In this model of warlordism, the 'feudal' warlord heads a hierarchy of networks, whose base is constituted of a large number of small military formations, normally no bigger that ten to fortymen, which operate at the village level. Sometimes these groups controlled more than a single village, and sometimes a number of groups shared the same village, but it would not be an oversimplification to describe their leaders as 'village military leaders', a term which I will be using from now onwards. From an analytical perspective, the most important components of the system are the middle ranks. One rung down after the big warlord are heads of networks of village military leaders, who rule over several districts and often over a whole province. When 'feudally' linked to the warlord, I refer to them as vassals. For a number of reasons, in a context of limited or primitive technology and more importantly of weak or absent bureaucratisation/institutionalisation, it is very difficult for a single individual directly to control a territory significantly larger than a province. Direct command and control, when based on personal (feudal) relations, reaches any degree of effectiveness only within a limited range, depending on the state of roads and the availability of communication systems. In most of Afghanistan, this 'law of decreasing effectiveness' makes a province the limit to the power of the average military leader. Another contributory factor

Graph 1: Model of Hierarchical Networking in the Context of Warlordism

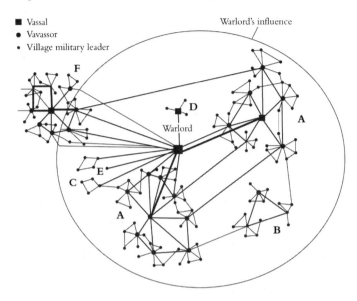

limiting areas of personal control by most military leaders to a single province is that many have a relatively important town or city at their centre, able to provide funding, services and support to a claimant to provincial leadership.

In this model, the 'feudal' warlord is unable to exercise tight control over the vassals. In a region like that Junbesh controlled in northern Afghanistan, encompassing five to seven provinces depending on the period, it would be impossible to exercise any form of direct control in the absence of a functioning bureaucratic structure and of a monopoly of armed force. While the 'feudal' warlord often controls part of the region himself, as in Dostum's case Jowzjan province and chunks of Balkh, he relied on a 'feudal' type relationship with provincial military leaders to maintain his influence over the larger area. Up to the provincial level, it is possible, if not always easy, for the vassal to exercise a certain degree of control over his domain. It is also feasible periodically to visit all the districts (up to ten to fifteen per province) and closely monitor the activities of all the main subordinate military leaders in the area. Even at this level however it is impossible to stay in close contact with each village military leader, of which there could be up to hundreds in each province. Another layer of power is therefore required between vassals and village military leaders. Sticking to feudal terminology, I shall call this layer vavassors, usually roughly corresponding to district military leaders, even if in practice some of these might control more then one district, and others might control less than a whole district, sometimes just a cluster of up to a few tens of villages each. Some district-size military leaders might be directly linked to the warlord and hence function like 'small vassals' (D). (See Maps 6–7 for an example of how this structure looked like in northern Afghanistan, with Map 8 including the 'vavassor'-level details.) Graph 1 shows a model of this type of hierarchical network, where the warlord is networked to the vassals, but sometimes also has direct links to vavassors and even some village military leaders. Vassals are at the centre of their own, subordinate networks, composed of vavassors but sometimes again even some village military leader (A). Vavassors and village military leaders are often connected by peer-to-peer networks (A, B). Even village military leaders can connect directly to the warlord (E), sometime belonging simultaneously to peer-to-peer networks (C). This structure is the result of the patrimonial, non-bureaucratised character of the system, which implies direct personal leadership at every level. The implicit limits to the capabilities of a single individual explain why it is not possible for the average 'vavassor' directly to control more than a few tens of village, district or provincial military leaders. Administration and policing by the Afghan state were based in the provincial and district centres and it is not surprising that in most cases these boundaries were also found to represent the limit of the area which military leaders were able to effectively control.

A complicating factor is the fact that such systems are usually not static, but highly dynamic. This might be due to both high turnover rates among the leadership ranks, to the instability caused by rival networks, but also to the fact that the control exercised by the warlord can be improved through a number of techniques, ranging from ruthlessness and deceit to technological or institutional development. These patterns will be shown in detail in the following chapters, but it is important to highlight the role of the city for Dostum and Junbesh. As already hinted in the introduction, cities are important to warlords for several reasons and Dostum was not immune to their

Map 7: Dostum and His 'Vassals', 1996

Map 8: Dostum and His 'Vassals' and 'Vavassors', 2003

attractions. He certainly viewed Mazar-i Sharif as a prestigious capital for Junbesh, able to enhance his claim to importance and his visibility, even if preferred to spend most of his time in the smaller town of Shiberghan. Mazar-i Sharif is also a major communications hub through which all the main roads of a region pass. Many in his entourage enjoyed the more comfortable life that Mazar had to offer compared to the villages where they had grown up. More importantly, no other urban centre of northern Afghanistan could even remotely be compared to Mazar in terms of its concentration of wealth, skills and services which would have been essential to Dostum to the extent that he wanted to increase the sophistication of his 'feudal' polity. Control over Mazar-i Sharif was not vital to Dostum, whose epicentre always remained Shiberghan, as Maps 6–7 show, but it was vital to Junbesh's long-term prospects as an organisation capable of developing beyond patrimonialism and warlordism.

Extensive patronage gave Dostum the leverage he needed to impose his recognition as regional leader and coopt the military class into Junbesh. As long as he was in control of the sources of supply, such leverage was enough to prevent (under normal circumstances) individual military leaders from defecting or siding with potential rivals. The exception was a group of Jami'ati military leaders, who with Kabul's support were hoping to overthrow Dostum altogether. Jami'at was at that time in control of Kabul's government, so that the local Jami'atis could reasonably hope to receive Kabul's help and eventually impose their leader, Atta, as the leader of the north. There was also an ideological component that precipitated confrontation with Atta, a committed Islamist who could not tolerate subordination to Dostum, the old 'communist' militia leader. Most (but not all) Jami'atis followed Atta, but he was defeated in an open conflict with Dostum in early 1994 and would not play an important role in the region again until 2001.[11]

111

What patronage could not do was force vassals and vavassors to act in a disciplined way and wage an effective military campaign (see chapter 11). This would have represented a key military weakness as soon as a serious military threat would emerge. Until 1997, such weakness prevented Junbesh from making significant inroads in Jami'at-i Islami's territory, despite wasting much material and human resources in various attempts. In 1997–98, as the Taliban started mounting determined efforts to conquer northern Afghanistan, this weakness proved fatal.

Notes

1. Kh. Khashimbekov, *Uzbeki severnogo Afganistana*, RAN (Institut Vostokovedeniya), Moscow, 1994, p. 38.
2. Walwalji (1380), p. 34–35; Baigi (2000), p. 12; Walwalji (1380), 'The crisis in Khost as threshold of the rift between Dr Najibullah and Gen. Dostom'; UN document, June 2004.
3. Walwalji (1380), 'The crisis in Khost as threshold of the rift between Dr Najibullah and Gen. Dostom'.
4. Interview with former official from Mazar-i Sharif, London, Sept. 2005; Baigi (2000), pp. 170–1.
5. Baigi (2000), 2000, p. 48; Walwalji (1378), pp. 27ff.
6. A. Walwalji (1378), Book 2, Part 1, p. 66.
7. The constitution of Junbesh states that "the Supreme Council of the Movement (...) is composed of representatives, with equal rights, of all the Jihadi organisations...". See Yunas (s.d.), p. 857.
8. For more details about the origins and development of these militias, see Giustozzi (2000), pp. 198–231.
9. Asadullah Walwalji (1378), book 2, part 2, pp. 4–6.
10. Gareev (1996), p. 309; Schroen (2007), p. 266–8; Jamie Doran, 'A drive to death in the desert', *Le Monde Diplomatique*, Sept. 2002; Schroen (2007), p. 260ff.; personal communications with UN officials, 2004–7; Nabi Azimi (1998), p. 340.
11. See Giustozzi (2005) for details about the Jami'at-Junbesh conflict in the north.

7

THE ROLE OF LEADERSHIP WITHIN JUNBESH

Apart from his patronage capabilities (see chapter 6), the source of Dostum's power was twofold. First was the ability to act as an interface between military leaders and foreign patrons, helping them indirectly to receive some form of international recognition. The lack of foreign relations was probably the biggest long-term weakness of local military leaders, although the larger vassals sometimes attempted to develop their own 'foreign policy', in an attempt to turn themselves into warlords too. Towards the end of his career (and life) Rasul Pahlawan attempted to establish direct links with Pakistan, both because Dostum kept monopolising links with Central Asia, Russia and Turkey, and because the rising star of the Taliban was giving a whole new importance to Pakistan's role in Afghanistan. He handled his 'foreign relations' quite clumsily, both because he failed to reach a deal with the Pakistan and because at the same time his efforts came to the attention of both Dostum's intelligence and his external patrons.[1]

Dostum was always very well aware of the importance of claiming a monopoly over foreign relations, as shown by his efforts to undermine Azad Beg's attempt to claim such a role for himself. Azad Beg clearly had the ambition of emerging as the political leader of the Turkic populations of Northern Afghanistan, and from the outset he sought to confine Dostum to a more military role. His movement had been awarded a strong representation within the Executive Council of Junbesh, where it had half a dozen members and sympathisers; but in terms of military strength Azad Beg was no match for Dostum. Azad Beg's strongest claim to legitimacy were his foreign contacts, especially in Pakistan and Turkey, but also Uzbekistan. In fact, his most noticeable activity was the lobbying of potential foreign supporters of Junbesh and particularly in Turkey. When in 1992 Ankara allegedly supplied Junbesh with US$10 million, US$6 were reported to have gone to Dostum and US$4 million to Azad Beg. Such foreign contacts, though useful, were not enough (quantitatively and qualitatively) to offset Dostum's influence among the military class and his patronage resources. Few of the other factions within Junbesh had much sympathy for Azad Beg, nor were they ready to endorse him as the leader of the movement. Azad Beg was not helped by his weak organisational structure either. That, together with Dostum's resources and military charisma, resulted in Dostum gradually attracting the loyalty of most of the military leaders affiliated with Azad Beg. By the time Dostum and Azad Beg finally broke their relationship in 1994, Azad Beg's claim to the leadership of Junbesh had long been defeated.[2]

The second source of Dostum's power was his charismatic ability to develop strong personal relations with military leaders, an ability which in a sense is the essence of 'feudal' leadership and is enhanced by the group solidarity that derives from military comradership (Ibn Khaldun's 'asabiyya). Undoubtedly, the strength of Dostum's leadership eroded over time. As far as it has been possible to establish, after the launch of Junbesh Dostum did not lead his troops in battle till September 1997, when he returned from his first, short exile. In 1992 he handed over the command of the 53rd Div. to Gen. Jura Beg. He relied instead on his former glories, but the charisma emanating from his past battlefield successes slowly wore out. The lacklustre battlefield performance of Junbesh from January 1994 and the rapid growth of the Taliban movement, which soon began to appear irresistible, both contributed to shake the faith in Dostum's ability to maintain the situation under control. Nonetheless, Dostum never completely lost his charismatic ability to gather the military class around him. In a sense Dostum's leadership could be described as based on his positioning at the centre of multiple networks of military leaders, thanks to both his charisma and his access to resources and to external support. The more networks Dostum was able to connect to his leadership, the more his leadership role was enhanced, hence as it will be shown later his constant preoccupation with expanding his contacts (chapter 10).

That Dostum's charismatic leadership remained crucial to Junbesh becomes very evident by looking at Abdul Malik's rule in northern Afghanistan, that is May-September 1997. The fact that Malik had unwisely invited the Taliban into northern Afghanistan was predictably seen by the many militiamen as an attempt to buy them off, although many civilians lauded what they considered an attempt to bring peace to northern Afghanistan. Cases were reported of Junbesh's military leaders refusing to fight against Dostum even after having joined Malik. Rumours abounded, especially outside his home province of Faryab, that Malik had staged the coup against Dostum after being bribed by the Pakistanis, rather than to avenge his brother or bring peace, as he claimed. He never had much charisma among the troops either, although his brother Gul-i Pahlawan made up for some of the gap. A city man educated at the Pedagogical Institute, Malik had no battlefield experience and never won the respect of the combatants, being perceived as a weak leader. Moreover, he had been educated to be a Pashtun, contrary to his step brothers Rasul and Gul, who were brought up as 'real Uzbeks', another fact that did not help him in the predominantly Uzbek environment of northern Afghanistan. Rumours circulated that while still in power he had moved his family and lots of gold and other valuables to Mashhad in Iran, strengthening the popular perception of Malik as a weak, uncertain and uncommitted leader. The complete break of relations with Uzbekistan might have had some positive aspects, helping his efforts to distance himself from Junbesh's roots in the previous regime, as Uzbekistan was still considered by Afghans as a communist state in those years. However, as the break implied distancing from Russia too, it deprived Malik of a major source of support. The declining internal revenues of Junbesh and the suspension of external support meant that he was soon completely unable to pay salaries and prebends to the vassals. He was even forced to send to Rabbani begging for economic support people like Ghaffar Pahlawan and Eshan-i Kamal, one of the businessmen whose fortunes rose with those of Junbesh. After only a few months Malik established a close link with Iran, too late to prevent the collapse of Junbesh's territorial control.[3] The revolt against the Taliban in May-June arose independently of Malik, it being a spontaneous upsurge, so his reputation was not enhanced by it. This was compounded by neglecting to boost his military credentials, by launching for example a campaign to clear a strategically threatening pocket in Kunduz, which had remained in Taliban hands after their withdrawal from the north.

Although most of the northern military class had initially supported him, his non-existent military legitimacy and weak leadership skills resulted in military leaders soon seeking contact with the exiled Dostum, as Malik's limitations started appearing obvious. He was forced to eliminate or marginalise any dissenter, was soon isolated and in the end could trust just two of Dostum's 'officers', Rowzi and Sher Arab.[4] As the end of his time in power approached, even these two had abandoned him and he was able to rely only on his own brothers. His weakening hold allowed other groups active in the north to become autonomous or re-emerge and challenge Junbesh's control over territory. Jami'at, Hizb-i Islami and Hizb-i Wahdat were soon all competing with Junbesh over the control of Mazar-i Sharif, effectively eliminating Junbesh's presence from its prestigious capital.[5]

On the contrary, Dostum, despite his humiliating flight in 1997, maintained a strong following within Junbesh and more widely among the northern military class, if not among northern Afghans. This is at least in part proven by the fact that when, later in 1997, the Taliban broke out of the Kunduz pocket to threaten the key logistical base of Hayratan, Hizb-i Wahdat appears to have insisted that he return to lead Junbesh in a more effective manner. With the support of the other main component of the newly established United Front, Jami'at, Wahdat eventually succeeded in forcing Malik to take Dostum back in September 1997. The Jami'atis, and in particular Massud, were also hoping that by letting Dostum back into Afghanistan, Junbesh would be permanently split into two factions, pro-Malik and pro-Dostum. Nonetheless, the fact that even the Jami'atis ended up asking Dostum back speaks volumes, given their hatred for the man. Important figures linked to Hizb-i Islami, like Juma Khan Hamdard, and others from Harakat-i Islami also welcomed Dostum back. Malik and Gul-i Pahlawan still tried to maintain control over Junbesh and minimise Dostum's role, putting pressure on the Jami'atis to keep recognising the brothers as the legitimate interlocutors. Massud tried to mediate between Dostum and Malik, but a diarchy within Junbesh proved impossible to sustain.[6]

In September 1997, as the Taliban were breaking out of their stronghold in Kunduz and advancing once again towards Mazar-i Sharif, Massud seemed to be succeeding with his alleged plan to break up Junbesh into virtually separate entities which would be strong enough to contain the Taliban but not to challenge Jami'at at a later date: Dostum and Malik reached a power-sharing agreement, which left Balkh to Wahdat and Jami'at, now temporarily allied, Jowzjan to Dostum, Faryab to Malik and Sar-i Pul to Gul-i Pahlawan, as Ghaffar Pahlawan had in the meanwhile fled to Iran.[7] However, Massud's plan underestimated Dostum's resourcefulness. Although Dostum's reputation was stained by his humiliation in May, his reappearance seems to have had a positive effect on Junbesh's militias, whose morale and battlefield effectiveness had been at their lowest ebb in early September 1997. Back in the battlefield with initially just fifty men, Dostum once again demonstrated his appeal to the military class and rapidly gathered a large following, leading his men to the recapture of Hayratan. The Taliban were beaten back and forced to withdraw to Kunduz once again. Dostum had no intentions of accepting his own reduction to the 'warlord of Jowzjan' and already immediately upon his arrival back in Afghanistan had started pumping money (of unknown origin) towards Mohaqqeq (the chief military leader of Wahdat), Majid Rowzi and Sher Arab, to boost them against Malik. In the meanwhile a new generation of military leaders had emerged from the chaos of northern Afghanistan to replace those who had been unable to stand up to the challenge. Among them, Ahmad Khan and Hashim Habibi were to emerge as key figures. Encouraged by his success, by November Dostum was feeling confident enough to seize complete control of Jowzjan from Malik's local allies and then attack Faryab. With the support of vavassors opposed to Rasul's brothers, he easily defeated Gul-i Pahlawan in Faryab and Sar-i Pul, forcing him and his brothers to flee. Hashim Habibi, one of Abdul Malik's vavassors, was promoted the new vassal of Faryab. As Samangan was falling under Ahmad Khan's control, the North was once again reunited under Dostum's influence, although not for long.[8]

One important aspect of Dostum's first 'resurrection' as a leader was that a different dynamic was at work compared to 1992. It was now the dynamics of evolutionary warlordism that pushed Dostum towards the top. This would not be the last time that Dostum returned to preeminence by riding a wave of support among the military class. The second collapse of Junbesh in 1998 and the second humiliation for Dostum in one year were again seen by many as the deathknell for Dostum's role as a leader.[9] His reputation was in part saved by the fact that he tried to drive the Taliban off before fleeing, leading the militias in the field.[10] Nonetheless, his status was clearly seriously weakened in 1998–2000 and his efforts to start a guerrilla campaign against the Taliban achieved only very modest results (see chapter 4). His willingness to deploy to northern Afghanistan in very precarious circumstances in April

2001 restored faith in his personal courage, as illustrated by his spectacular recovery in late 2001.

In 1999–2000, Dostum was only able to operate from exile with Iranian help, strengthening the last remaining pockets of Junbesh activity in Derzab, Balkhab, Sangcharak, Zari, Amrukh and Qaysar and establishing a new one in Dara-ye Suf, while Dasht-i Archi and Khwaja Ghar had been opened with Jami'at-i Islami's support (see Map 5). Dostum was acutely aware that he could ill afford to stay away from the battle front for too long, but only in April 2001 was he able to return to Afghanistan from Turkish exile, allied with Jami'at-i Islami and other parties within the United Front. Bearing testimony to the resilience of the system he had created and of the powerful dynamic of evolutionary warlordism, as rapidly as it had collapsed Dostum's leadership was resurrected for the second time, once favourable conditions matured. He and his revitalised Junbesh-i Milli played a crucial role in defeating the Taliban at the end of 2001 (see chapter 4). As soon as resources became available again, mainly in the form of American cash, the old network of personal relationships between Dostum and his former vassals was revived—the military class of the north was at one with him again. He was helped by the fact that some of those who had sided with the Taliban as they occupied northern Afghanistan, like Juma Khan Hamdard and others, had a difficult relationship with them and were keen to switch back to Dostum, who readily accepted them. Juma Khan Hamdard was even appointed commander of the 8th Army Corps in 2002. Others, like Hashim Habibi in Faryab province, switched back to Junbesh at the last minute, as the Taliban were collapsing. Dostum also re-established a good relationship with Hizb-i Wahdat and its military leaders in the North, mainly Mohaqqeq, despite the return within Junbesh's ranks of Juma Khan Hamdard, who had fought bitterly against Mohaqqeq.[11] A 'modern' bureaucratised polity, such as a state or a modern party, would not have been able to re-establish itself so quickly and indeed might not have been able to re-establish itself at all.

It is not easy to define the terms of Dostum's relations with the warlords and in particular how could these relationships survive splits and defections. There existed a subtle boundary which individuals were not supposed to trespass. The case of Hashim Habibi, who ruled Faryab province between 1998 and 2004, illustrates this well. He was nowhere as charismatic or capable a military leader as Dostum or Rasul Pahlawan and his rise up the ranks was due to Dostum's support against Rasul Pahlawan's brothers. He shifted his allegiance to the Taliban in 1998 and continued to serve them till the end as local militia commander in Faryab. He was not alone in doing this, but several other of Dostum's former vassals and vavassors had fallen out with the Taliban well before late 2001. What spoiled his relationship with Dostum was his reluctance to abandon the Taliban until the very end, waiting for them to leave Faryab rather then revolting against them and pushing them out of Faryab when Dostum asked him to do so in the autumn of 2001. Habibi had crossed what Dostum and his entourage considered the fine line between legitimate self-interest and betrayal. During the last days of the Taliban regime, Habibi even contacted Gen. Daoud of Shura-i Nezar, presumably to propose that he join that faction, but Dostum was informed of the move. Although Habibi was initially accepted back in Junbesh's ranks, his relationship with Dostum was never the same as in 1997 and throughout 2002–4 the two jostled for influence in Faryab, until Dostum eventually emerged as the winner (see chapter 8).[12]

Another good example of the importance of Dostum's personal leadership in keeping Junbesh together and making it work is provided by the very place where Junbesh failed to succeed during the 2001 comeback, that is Baghlan province. Here, Dostum had always relied on his alliance with Sayyed Mansoor Naderi and had never meddled with the running of Baghlan. Even in 2001, as Dostum was busy reconquering northern Afghanistan, he left to Naderi the task to seize Baghlan from the Taliban. Like Dostum, Naderi faced stiff competition from Jami'at, which had a keen interest in this strategic province and counted on the military power of its Andarabi military leaders to grab it. Contrary to Dostum, Naderi was unable to gather the local military class around him again, despite the extremely fragmented front put together by the Jami'atis. He was beaten by Jami'at in the race to Pul-i Khumri, the provincial capital. Naderi had already made several attempts to organise a comeback to Baghlan province, including one in 1999, even before Dostum reappeared in Afghanistan, but this did nothing to enhance his status among the military class. It is apparent that as a community leader Naderi maintained widespread support in Baghlan among the Ismaili and Hazara communities,[13] as many had benefited from his patronage in earlier years, but he failed to win over the military class at the crucial moment. During the 1980s and 1990s, he had gathered a substantial number of military leaders around himself through patronage, but this was not enough to emerge victorious from the cauldron of evolutionary warlordism. At the end of 2001 and again in early 2003 Naderi attempted to wrest back control of Pul-i Khumri from the Andarabi military leaders, even managing to bring the fight to the streets of the city, but was pushed back to Kayan valley, where a three month campaign by the Andarabi militias finally forced the family to flee once again after heavy loss of life.[14]

By contrast, Dostum had been much more successful than Naderi in building connections with local military leaders, even in Baghlan, where his efforts had been modest. He befriended Bashir Baghlani, who had been leader and governor of Hizb-i Islami during the civil war, and hosted him in Mazar for several months, even supporting his bid to recapture the northern part of Baghlan from the Andarabi and the renegade Hizbi military leaders associated with them. During 2003 Baghlani gathered together a militia (estimated at 1,000 men) in neighbouring Samangan, but never launched his assault, possibly following a direct intervention by Karzai or even by the US embassy, or the cooling of Dostum's support for the initiative. Typically Dostum even established good relations with some of the Andarabi military leaders aligned with Jami'at, who had been fighting on the regime's side before the fall of Najibullah, such as Mustafa Khan and Khalil Andarabi. He might even have discussed their support for a bid to overthrow the Jami'atis in Baghlan, a card that in any case he never decided to play. Finally, in part by playing the ethnic card, Dostum succeeded in making friends even among the Uzbek military leaders of Burka district, despite their formal allegiance to Jami'at. By early 2004 all had established open connections with Junbesh. The contrast between Naderi and Dostum could not be greater and reminds us once again that military charisma and leadership are not skills commonly found.[15]

The importance of charismatic leadership was not confined to Dostum's role, particularly when the dynamics of evolutionary warlordism were at play, as opposed to orphan warlordism. Because the system was based mainly on trust, those military leaders who evinced stubbornness and resilience were more likely to be accepted by other military leaders as 'lords'. Ahmad Khan of Samangan was in 2002 at the height of his power and reputation, by virtue of having stayed behind in Afghanistan in 1998–2001 and fought all that period in very difficult circumstances. This reputation was one of the factors that helped him to turn his 19th Div. into the most disciplined and best trained of Junbesh's army. By contrast several once influential military leaders, who failed to live up to their reputation as fearsome warriors, were all sidelined by 2002. After the first failed attempt by the Taliban to take over northern Afghanistan (1997), Rasul Pahlawan's brothers had even proven unable to manage their own fiefdom in Faryab. The supplies to the militiamen manning the frontline between Faryab and Herat/Baghdis had virtually dried up, while the new figures appointed to lead them were cronies of Abdul Malik rather then effective field military leaders. In such conditions, the Taliban offensive of September 1997 easily penetrated a crumbling system and only the return of Dostum saved the day, as explained above. By 2002 the Pahlawan family had very limited influence and could not even operate in Faryab, while Ghaffar Pahlawan was in exile in Iran.[16]

A key long-term weakness of Dostum as a leader is that he never developed a clear approach to succession, which could have reassured his constituency of the long term future of Junbesh. Like some other military leaders, Dostum took care of his son's education, who studied in Turkey, but there is no sign that he might have been grooming him as a successor. The creation of Junbesh and the resources invested in its strengthening in 2002–05 seem to suggest that the party might one day have been charged with selecting a successor, thereby de-patrimonialising the process. However, in the absence of any clear decision in this sense, the problem of succession was left unresolved. At the time of the 2006 crisis, many of the disagreements between the parties converged exactly on the problem of finding a successor to Dostum. No solution was found, except for those most unhappy with his leadership to leave Junbesh.

Notes

1. Interviews with members of the intelligentsia from Faryab, Maimana and London, 2002–4.
2. According to Asadullah Walwalji (1378), book 2, part 2, p. 31; on Azad Beg see Walwalji (1378), book 1, for details.
3. Interview with former NGO worker, London, Aug. 2005; 'Dar Maimana chegune saqut kard', *Salam* (Maimana), 27 Saratan 1377; Baigi ((2000), pp. 303, 320; Whitlock (2002), pp. 236.
4. Baigi (2000), pp. 308 for the case of Haidar Jowzjani, who was killed in Mazar in Aug. 1997.
5. Ibid., pp. 304.
6. Ibid., pp. 309–11, 320; http://www.afghanistan-seitende/afghanistan/bios_dostum.html#malik.
7. Baigi (2000), pp. 315, 322. Even if the plan seemed to have failed by Nov., Massud kept trying to eliminate Junbesh from Balkh province (p. 350).
8. Baigi (2000), pp. 317–9, 311, 320, 322–4; Griffin (2003), p. 150–151.
9. According to one source, after the Taliban broke the frontline outside Shiberghan, Dostum returned home and was seen weeping, maybe being prepared to see the end, but then accepted the advice to flee the country ('Dar Maimana chegune saqut kard', op. cit.).
10. 'Dar Maimana chegune saqut kard', op. cit.
11. Baigi (2000), pp. 395, 407, 409; personal communications with UN officials, Mazar-i Sharif, June-Sept. 2004.
12. Baigi (2000), pp. 332; interviews with UN officials, Mazar-i Sharif, June and July 2004.
13. Sources in Jami'at acknowledged in Dec. 2003 that his bid for election to the Constitutional Loya Jirgah would have attracted much support, had it not been for the riot organised in Kunduz (where the election was taking place) by Islamist elements belonging to Jami'at and Ittehad.
14. Pamela Constable, 'New Order Rises From Afghan Lair; Taliban Militia Reshapes Warlord's Luxury Base', *The Washington Post*, 21 May 1999; Rahimullah Samander and Danish Karokhel, 'Troubled Ismaili homecoming', *Afghan Recovery Report*, No. 45, Jano. 24, 2003; David Filipov, 'Another Deadly, Errant US Attack is Alleged', *Boston Globe*, 24 Dec. 2001.
15. Personal communications with UN officials, Kunduz, 2003–4.
16. Personal communication with UN official, Kabul, April 2003; Hedoyat (nd.).

8

JUNBESH'S POLITICAL DYNAMICS

Junbesh had the ability to resort to coercion from its early days, as it inherited the repressive apparatus of the previous regime. In the political climate of 1992, deploying it was not feasible, at least overtly. A large number of political assassinations of military leaders occurred in northern Afghanistan in 1992–1998 and rumours were widespread about the involvement of the structures which once belonged to Najibullah's WAD and had been taken over by Junbesh. While personal rivalries certainly accounted for quite a few of these killings, the security organs of Junbesh might also have responsible for a number of them. Even after 2001 Junbesh maintained control over the new Riasat-i Amniyat-i Milli (National Security Directorate), although it exercised such control with greater caution and avoided extreme violence. While it tolerated the activities of groups like Hizb-i Wahdat and Jami'at, with which it had a power-sharing agreement in the north, Junbesh's security apparatus repressed attempts by other parties to establish genuinely independent struc-tures, the more so if these were leftist parties, whom its leadership might have seen as the most dangerous competitors. As late as 2004 the structures of the police state were still being used to stifle political competition and to punish administrators who were felt to be disloyal to Junbesh.[1]

On the whole the bureaucratised 'police state' apparatus played a modest role within Junbesh in maintaining internal cohesion, mainly because it was itself fragmented among the vassals, as suggested by the fact that it proved unable to detect Abdul Malik's conspiracy in 1997. Moreover, most of the time Dostum and his vassals had to rely on various forms of coalition-build-ing to keep Junbesh going, where the weight of the coercive element varied from case to case but was rarely the key factor. The resulting complex web of coalitions, networks and power blocs was very dependent on charismatic leadership in order to function. At the centre of Junbesh, the system would hold together as long as Dostum maintained a balance among the different players (see chapter 7). His diplomatic skills were much needed there and the system was at risk of collapse every time that he was not able, for whatever reason, to fine tune it. As coalitions were most often built on shared hatred of

Map 9: Samangan Region in 1996 (left) and 1998 (right)

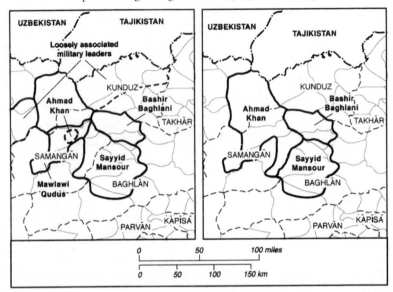

local rivals, managing this polity was difficult and often severely tested Dostum's skills.

Coalition-Building

When Dostum established good working relations with his vassals, genuine coalition-building could take place. A good example of this was Ahmad Khan of Samangan province, whom Dostum let run his province without known attempts to control, replace or weaken him until 2007, even if his policies sometimes diverged from Junbesh's. As he emerged in 1997 as the dominant figure in central Samangan, Ahmad Khan expanded his control over the territories north-east of the river, until then controlled by the Naderis of Baghlan. Then he occupied Khulm in 1997, emerging as one of the most effective military leaders within Junbesh, as well as as an able if autocratic administrator (see chapter 11 and Map 9).[2] After the end of the civil wars in 2001, Ahmad Khan maintained his patrimonial control at a time when Dostum was trying to sideline the military leaders elsewhere. He put forward his candidature to the parliament and did not allow other significant candidates of Junbesh to run in Samangan province for the elections of 2005. Other examples of high levels of autonomy in Junbesh's ranks include Haji Latif Ibrahimi of Imam Sahib (Kunduz), who kept running his affairs locally with little interference from Dostum. He too could not abide Dostum's policy of sidelining military leaders and got his brother (and armed wing of the family) Abdul Raouf elected to parliament in 2005.

Manipulative coalition-building

Simple coalition-building was however more the exception than the rule. Dostum faced the classical dilemma of every 'feudal' polity, that is how to maintain a balance in the distribution of power between the centre and the vassals. Any attempt to move away from the feudal model would have presented another dilemma, to wrest as much power as possible away from the vassals without wrecking the system in the process. Although Dostum was not a centraliser as such, the need to compete effectively with his external enemies often compelled him to seek ways to make the system more responsive. During his first period in power in 1992–8, he sought to escape the inherent contradiction between the long term aim to centralise power and patronage and the short term need to reward his vassals by replacing those most disloyal or unresponsive among them with new ones. In order to consolidate the network of alliances at the base of Junbesh and create stronger loyalties to himself, Dostum often resorted to exploiting local rivalries, or to creating them *ex novo*. Vassals and vavassors would do the same at the provincial and district levels. While this to some extent worked, it also resulted in a system that bred conflict. For example, Dostum initially supported Rasul Pahlawan's campaign against the Jami'atis of Faryab, in the hope of making Rasul dependent on his alliance with Dostum. Ahmad Khan's loyalty to Dostum in Samangan was also mainly due to his bitter opposition to his former party comrades of Jami'at, particularly after 1998. During the small scale guerrilla war against the Taliban in northern Afghanistan (1998–September 2001), Atta's Jami'atis were reportedly supplying information to the Taliban on Ahmad Khan's whereabouts in the mountains of Samangan. Across the north, Dostum also played on the rivalry between the military leaders of Hizb-i Islami (such as Juma Khan Hamdard) and the Jami'atis, binding the former to Junbesh but at the same time increasing the chances of a generalised conflict with Jami'at. Another problem with this tactic was that whenever Dostum moved to end one of the conflicts, which he had exploited to keep military leaders of disparate allegiance loyal to himself, the alliance with the military leaders could once again be called in to question. So once the peace deal with Jami'at-i Islami's leader Atta came into effect in the summer of 2004, it did not take long before both Juma Khan Hamdard and Ahmad Khan quit Junbesh. Already in 2004 Juma Khan was openly supporting Karzai's presidential bid, while Ahmad Khan 'defected' in 2006.[3]

Dostum did not just resort to the manipulation of rival factional networks, but also to the destruction of networks which he found difficult to manipulate, by fostering personal rivalries. Dostum used this tactic in the early days of Junbesh to prevent the formation of alternative poles of influence that could rival his role at the centre of Junbesh. In this way he succeeded in dissolving the network of military leaders associated with Azad Beg's Ittehadiya, behind which initially there was considerable political momentum due to the way Harakat-i Shamal had come into existence. Ittehadiya had always focused on advocating the cause of the Turkic populations of northern Afghanistan (and Central Asia), but its structure on the ground did not go beyond a collection of local military and tribal leaders, ridden by rivalries caused by the competition for resources and territory. Dostum found it relatively easy to absorb many of the military leaders of Ittehadiya within his ranks, by virtue of his superior resources. The strongest among them were in a position to maintain a greater degree of autonomy and proved more resilient. The leaders of Junbesh, including Dostum himself, soon started exploiting those rivalries, promoting lesser military leaders at the expense of the larger ones. The earliest example of this pattern was Ashoor Pahlawan, the strongest military leader associated with Ittehadiya, based in the north of Jawzjan province. In early 1993 Dostum granted another local notable associated with Ittehadiya, Manaan Makhmood, the right to form a brigade within the territory controlled by Ashoor, setting in motion a rivalry between the two. Ashoor was then assassinated later in the year due to a personal feud. As a result of these tactics, Azad Beg lost his military base and was rapidly sidelined. Little was heard of him after 1993, until he was enlisted by the Taliban to take part in the 'liberation' of northern Afghanistan.[4]

Dostum often used these manipulative tactics even when trying to expand his influence and counter-balance the power of the provincial warlords. Typically, he would establish direct links with smaller military leaders, typically vavassors of some of his vassals (see Graph 1 in chapter 6). Dostum used this system expansively especially in Faryab province, where Rasul Pahlawan and his brothers were growing increasingly reluctant to accept their role of vassals. An obvious drawback of this practice of manipulation was that often the vassals tended to react violently (see chapter 11). Dostum continued to use this tactic even after the fall of the Taliban. While Hashim Habibi was the 'vassal' running Faryab province and the commander of the local 200th Div., Dostum maintained direct contacts with a number of vavassors who were purposely given independent units outside 200th Div. to limit Hashim's control over them. Dostum's concern with the rising power of Habibi was due to his distrust for him (see chapter 7). Initially, Dostum's manipulations badly misfired. His concern about Habibi was so great that throughout most of 2003 he even flirted with Farouq, the chief military leader of Jami'at in Faryab, hoping to use him to counter-balance Habibi's power. Dostum acted to strengthen Farouq at the expense of Hashim Habibi. When it emerged that Farouq's loyalty was quite solidly with Jami'at, Dostum's manoeuvre ended in a blind alley. The split within Junbesh allowed Jami'at to grow relatively unchallenged for several months, fed by strong financial support coming from its headquarters in Mazar and Kabul. Finally Dostum had to build up Habibi's strength once more in order to prevent a takeover of Faryab by Jami'at.[5]

Once Farouq was eliminated from the scene, Dostum resumed his support for the anti-Habibi networks in Faryab. This tactic probably accelerated Hashim Habibi's drift towards the central government, especially after a new governor, Enyatullah Henoyat, was appointed in 2003. By early 2004 Habibi had developed a solid relationship with Henoyat and was ready to announce that he took orders only from Kabul and not from Dostum. Like the Pahlawan brothers before him, he also responded to Dostum's penetration of his fiefdom with repressive measures. He started a purge of pro-Dostum military leaders within Faryab, forcing them to flee to Dostum's court in Jowzjan. The re-establisment of an internationally-sponsored central government in Kabul had changed the dynamics of power in Faryab and Dostum had to innovate in his tactics in order to achieve his aim. In April 2004 a combination of street demonstrations against Habibi and Henoyat, sponsored by Junbesh, and of a pronunciamento of several of the remaining vavassors of Faryab finally succeeded in forcing Habibi and Henoyat out.[6]

The example above shows how a key problem with Dostum's tactic was that it tended to damage the bond of trust between Dostum and his vassals. This in turn lead to a growing trend among their ranks to maximise short term benefits at the expense of long-term ones, in the expectation that one day Dostum might get rid of them. Habibi himself seems to have entertained doubts about Dostum's commitment to him already in his early days in power. When he took charge of Faryab in 1998 following the killing of Rasul Pahlawan and the defeat of his brothers by Dostum, he had just witnessed a long chain of turmoil and betrayal and seems to have been convinced that he would not stay in his position for too long. Most of the money earmarked to provide logistical support and supplies to the troops never reached them, while individual military leaders were left operating without effective leadership. A renewed Taliban attack found a completely disorganised and corrupt system, which again failed to hold the line.[7]

An additional consequence of the increasingly worn bond of trust within Junbesh's 'feudal' system was that it gave the vassals the incentive increasingly to shift towards pre-emptive violence. For example, in Sar-i Pul province, after the fall of the Taliban a reasonable balance of power seemed to exist. The province's head of NSD, Osman Khan, represented Dostum's interests and guaranteed a degree of control.[8] At the same time the 'vassal' Kamal Khan and his brother Haji Payenda maintained a large degree of autonomy, with little sign of Dostum trying to interfere. The two brothers still seem to have felt insecure about Dostum's future intentions and to have expected a move to alter the balance of power at their expense. In 2002, when Junbesh's former governor of Sar-i Pul in the 1990s was returning home from exile in Germany, gunmen stopped him on the road and killed him. His family alleged who the culprits were, presumably fearing that Dostum might have used him to strengthen an alternative pole of influence.[9]

Coercive coalition-building

As mentioned earlier, Dostum's ruthless and cunning tactics were mirrored by what the vassals practised within their domains. The different vassals adopted

125

Table 1: Turnover of Top Military Leaders of Faryab

Area		Military Leader
Dawlatabad		Awraz Zabet
		Abdul Malik
		Taliban commander
		Aurat Zabet
Shirin Tagab		small military leaders
	Kohi Sayad	Mawlawi Qara
		Noor Mohammad
		Rasul Pahlawan
		Haq Birdee
		Rasul Pahlawan
		Abdul Malik
		Taliban
Khwaja Sabz Posh	Sahra Qala	Ghulam Shakee
	Aslam	Komandan Zahir
	Sahra Qala	Sayyed Amin
	Sahra Qala	Rasul Bik
	Sahra Qala	Sharabudin Bik
Almar		Abdul Rahman Pahlawan
		Abdul Hafiz Manqa
		Bazar Boy
		Hafiz Arbab
		[Rasul's 'vassal', name unknown]
Qaisar	Mobasher	[name unknown]
	Tawakle	[name unknown]
	Fazel Haq	Abdul Raouf Sawri
		Abdul Raouf Sawri
Gurziwan	road to Maimana	Ghaibullah
		Qaree Ghulam
		Mawlawi Seraj
	Sarchakan/Gurziwan	Aman Pahlawan
		Amer Kareen
	Shar-i Qala	Kumandan Tela
Bilchiragh		Kafeel Ghasaudin
		Majeed Brot
		Majeed Kal
Pashtoon Kot		Ghulam Nabi Jij
		Haji Skander
		Aqmorad Arbab
	Sar-i Howz	Rais Abdul Rahman
	Dahandara	Haji Qamar
	Chartoot	Meerzad
	Sar-i Howz	Rais Abdul Rahman
	Sar-i Howz	Aman Pahlawan
	Sar-i Howz	Mawalawi Abdul Rahman Teelani
	Sar-i Howz	Eil Aman
	Sar-i Howz	Amir Chopan
	Sar-i Howz	Ghulam Qader

Fate	by whom	when
forced to flee	Rasul Pahlawan	1983–84?
forced to flee	Taliban	1998
forced to flee	Awraz Zabet	2001
removed	Dostum	2004
defeated in battle	Mawlawi Qara	1981?
killed		1984
assassinated	Rasul Pahlawan	1984
forced to flee	Hafiz Arbab	1984
forced to flee	Rasul Pahlawan	1985
assassinated	?	1996
forced to flee	Taliban	1998
forced to flee		2001
killed	?	1983?
killed	?	1984
assassinated	?	
forced to flee	?	
killed	?	
killed	?	
forced to flee	Bazar Boy?	
killed	Rasul Pahlawan	
killed	Rasul Pahlawan	1995
forced to flee	Taliban	
defeated	Abdul Raouf Sawri	early 80s
defeated	Abdul Raouf Sawri	early 80s
forced to flee	Hafiz Arbab	
assassinated	Rasul Pahlawan	1995
defeated	Hashim Habibi	
defeated	Hashim Habibi	
defeated	Hashim Habibi	
defeated	Hashim Habibi	
defeated	Hashim Habibi	
assassinated	?	
defeated	Hashim Habibi	
defeated	Hashim Habibi	
defeated	Hashim Habibi	
killed	Soviets	early 1980s
killed	Soviets	early 1980s
killed	Soviets	early 1980s
forced to flee	Mawalawi Qara	
killed	?	
forced to flee	Rayees Abdul Rahman	
forced to flee	Yarmala, Amir Chopan	
forced to flee	Yarmala, Amir Chopan	
killed	?	
killed	?	
forced to flee	Rasul Pahlawan	
forced to flee	Rasul Pahlawan	

Sources: Walwalji, Hedoyat.

different mixes of violence, diplomacy and incentives, depending on their personal inclinations and skills.[10] Rasul Pahlawan, for example, had been operating in an extremely violent and instable environment from the early 1980s. During the jihad and civil war periods (1980–2001), the eight 'core' districts[11] of Faryab province all witnessed several violent changes of their military leaders. Power changed hand on average almost six times for each district (see Table 1). Of these forty-seven transfers of power, seventeen saw the existing 'vavassor' or military leader being forced to flee following a military offensive against him, eighteen saw him being killed (mostly assassinated) and eleven saw him defeated in battle and forced to hand over control. Only in one case was the military leader in charge removed peacefully. The environment only stabilised when a strongman asserted his control over the whole eight districts and imposed his *pax*. Rasul Pahlawan was the first such leader.

In the absence of a bureaucratised and institutionalised system and of a monopoly of violence, even the coercing of military leaders into a coalition could only be temporary. The warlord or the 'vassal' ultimately still had to allow fellow military leaders to retain an autonomous power base; hence they could at any time decide to oppose him or switch sides. The comparison between Dostum's and Rasul's coalition management shows that the stronger the component of trust and the weaker the components of coercion and manipulation in coalition-building, the more viable and stable the system. Essentially, the viability of the system rested on mutual trust and interdependence between the warlord and the vassals, or between vassals and vavassors and vavassors and village military leaders. Rasul tried to implement a degree of control hardly compatible with his resources and the absence of bureaucratised structures on which he could rely. Once Rasul had embarked on his violent drive, it became self-perpetuating. Whenever he feared that his subaltern allies were not trustworthy, the only viable option was preventive action. Dostum relied less on violence and coercion, but still extensively recurred to manipulation.

On the other hand, as we have already seen, trust was not sufficient to infuse in the system a sufficient degree of discipline and responsiveness to the 'orders' of the warlord. During the limited time span of Junbesh's existence, other techniques were tried to resolve this dilemma. Among them was the appointment of relatives in positions of power. Dostum only rarely used this practice, probably due to the limited human resources of his clan. Rasul Pahlawan by contrast largely indulged to a much greater extent and brought into his 511th Div. and other security establishments two brothers, a father in law, a nephew, a brother in law and some other more distant relatives. There are drawbacks even in the use of nepotism, of course, and Rasul's over-indulgence in the long run isolated the family. Examples of vavassors who remained isolated because of their nepotistic practices include Awraz Zabet and Hashim Astana in Faryab, both of whom were unable to gather support when facing a move against them.[12]

Networks and coalition making

As discussed earlier, much of the power of both Dostum and his vassals derived from their unique positions at the centre of multiple networks of military leaders. Yet their control of these networks and ability to manipulate them was far from complete. One factor complicating the task of controlling the networks was that they were often rivals. Another factor was that warlord, vassals and vavassors could only successfully operate as network managers to the extent that they were trusted by the members of the networks. As I have shown, military and political vicissitudes made sure that this was not always the case. An example of how the networks might be difficult to control comes from turbulent Faryab. In 1996, when Rasul Pahlawan's power had reached its peak and he had eliminated all non-Junbesh military leaders from the region, an alliance of military leaders formed against him within Junbesh, among whom the most prominent were Abdul Qader and Abdul Raouf Sawri. Dostum's efforts to patronize the new network were contained by Rasul and then beaten back by his brothers (see chapter 11).[13]

Often the networks were able decisively to constrain the choices and policies of the 'lords'. Once again a good example was found in Faryab, where, after October 2003, Jami'at-i Islami's challenge to Junbesh having just been utterly and definitely defeated, vavassors started forming rival groups within Junbesh. Initially, the tension within Junbesh formed along a pro- or anti-Hashim Habibi (the ruling 'vassal') axis. A large anti-Habibi grouping was formed including most vavassors, such as Hashim Astana, Rahmat Rais, Fataullah, Awraz Zabet, Salam Pahlawan and Qadir. Things got more complicated after Habibi's ejection from Faryab in April 2004 (see above). A number of military leaders of doubtful loyalty to Junbesh were active in Faryab, among whom the most prominent were Salam Pahlawan and Ghulam Qader. But this was not in any sense a confrontation between loyalists and more tepid supporters of Junbesh. The complex web of personal rivalries and power struggles led to the formation of a first group, very close to Dostum, and centered around Hashim Astana and Rahmat Rais (see Graph 2). Another powerful group developed around Fataullah, who was not so close to Dostum but still reputedly loyal to him. This group was on bad terms with Astana, as the two leaders were vying for provincial 'vassalage'. Fataullah also maitained relations with the two vavassors of doubtful loyalty to Junbesh, Salam Pahlawan and Ghulam Qader. Finally, a smaller group formed around vavassors who did not have good relations with either Astana or Fataullah and included Abdul Rahim Pahlawan and Ghafour. The junior members of each network often choose one over the other on the basis of local rivalries. For example, Najibullah and Abdul Rahim Pahlawan were competing over the control of Gurziwan district, hence they joined rival networks. When Dostum choose Fataullah as Hashim Habibi's successor, he was not choosing the vavassor closest to him, but the best networked and hence most influential one.[14]

In part Junbesh's internal instability was the result of the competition among networks and their internal fluidity. Once again kin relations were mobilised by players within Junbesh as an obvious means of strengthening networks and alliances. Inter-marriage among the families of different military leaders was common, while marrying into local communities was also widely practised. Such a strategy seems to have been much more effective than nepotism (see 'coercive coalition-building' in this chapter): after 2001, the most resilient military leaders of Faryab, like Fataullah, Rahmat Rais and Ghulam Qadir, were also well linked into the local communities with a web of marriages and succeeded in stabilising Faryab to a hitherto unprecedented extent.[15]

Graph 2: Networking Among Military Leaders in Faryab Province, 2004

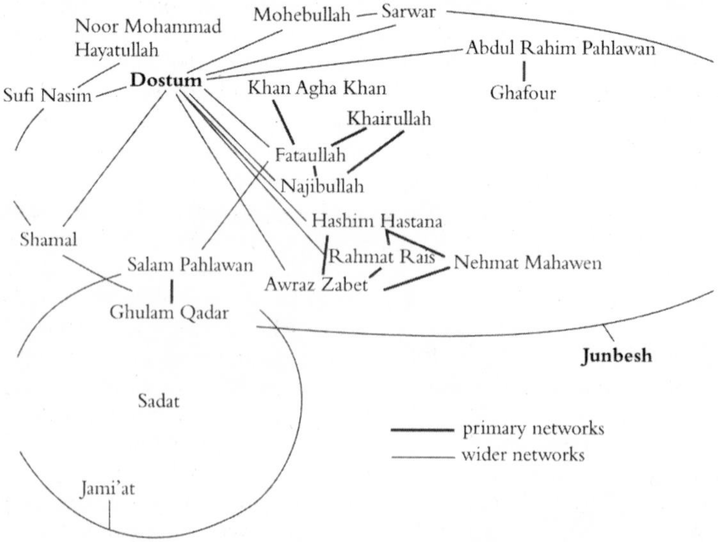

Source: Based on interviews with UN officials, intellectuals and factional members in Mazar-i Sharif, Maymana, Shirin Tagab, Dawlatabad, Qaisar and Almar, June–September 2004.

Notes

1. Personal communications with political activists, Mazar-i Sharif, July 2004.
2. Hedoyat (nd.), pp. 158ff.
3. Walwalji (1378), Hedoyat (nd.); Personal observation, Mazar-i Sharif, summer 2004.
4. Asadullah Walwalji (nd.), pp. 55–58; Baigi (2000), pp. 101. Azad Beg died in an aircraft crash before getting actually involved.
5. Interviews with UN officials, Mazar, June–July 2004.
6. Government media initially reported an invasion of Faryab by Junbesh forces, which however a UNAMA investigation found to have never happened (UNAMA internal documents, April–May 2004).
7. Hedoyat (nd.).

8. The local NSD was considered one of the best staffed and efficient of the north in 2004.
9. Interview with two informants from Sayyad district (Sar-i Pul), Mazar, Aug. 2004.
10. This section is based on interviews with Homayun Sorkhabi in London and with officials working for international organisations in Faryab and Mazar-i Sharif, as well as on Hedoyat (nd.).
11. This excludes Greater Andkhoy and Kohistan district, which were outside the area of influence of Rasul Pahwalan and his brothers. Greater Andkhoy was also given authonomy in the 1980s and was provisorily transferred to Jowzjan province in 2003.
12. UN source, June 2004. Zabet never recovered his previous influence and afterwards lived in 'exile' in Jowzjan, hosted by Dostum. With the latter's support, Hastana was able to recover his fiefdom in Faryab after the ousting of his nemesis, Hashim Haibi.
13. 'Dar Maimana chegune saqut kard', op. cit.
14. Personal communication with UN official, Maimana, Nov. 2004.
15. UN source, June 2004.

9

JUNBESH'S POLITICAL ECONOMY

Internal resources

As of 1992 Dostum had plenty of weaponry, ammunition, spare parts and other supplies in store, due to the fact that most of the strategic depots of the now defunct Afghan armed forces were located in northern Afghanistan. The problem remained of how to pay his troops, one compounded by the need to pay salaries to thousands in Junbesh's civilian administration and by a range of other expenses. Dostum could not rely on the new government in Kabul, dominated by Jami'at-i Islami, to pay the troops, first because it lacked resources itself and second because it had no interest in contributing to maintain such a large military establishment, over which it had no direct control.

Although precise statistics are unavailable, many observers and commentators might have overestimated the level of internal revenue on which Dostum was able to rely. Given that centralised direct taxation had long fallen into disuse, no means of enforcing it was available. The 'jihad taxes' that existed before 1992 were maintained after the end of the jihad and the influx of former mujahidin into Junbesh might have led to this type of taxation becoming more widespread, but the actual revenue would have been modest—even if all villages were taxed, not exceeding a few million dollars every year. Moreover, this revenue would not accrue to Dostum's coffers, but rather stay in the hands of local military leaders who collected it. The same was true of road taxes (see Table 2).

The gas fields of Shiberghan had stopped producing for export after the Soviet withdrawal, although small quantities of gas continued to be extracted for internal consumption. The single largest source of revenue appears to have been customs. Custom fees must not have been too high, if reportedly books and medicines were cheaper in Mazar than in Tashkent and goods in general were relatively plentiful. In sum, it is extremely unlikely that the border posts along the northern frontier would have netted more than some few million dollars a year, far too little compared to the needs of Junbesh. According to Baigi, customs revenue covered about half of the cost of maintaining Junbesh's army.[7]

Table 2: Junbesh's Revenues, 1990s

Sources	Size	Notes
Gas	8 million cubic feet annually, sold cheaply to the public[1]	
Electricity		Low profitability
Oil from Angot (Sar-i Pul)	300–500 barrels per day[2]	Refined in small private refineries around the area
Customs revenue (Hairatan)	levied on few tens of million $ annually	In 1996, total official external trade for Afghanistan reached just US$230 million (both imports and exports), of which only a minor part went through Hairatan
Customs revenue Andkhoy	Levied on $7.7 million in 1997	
Kod-u Barq fertiliser factory	US$20–30 million annual turnover, though normally not working at full capacity.[3]	Probably not very profitable.
Dawlatabad salt mine	Profits of no more then a hundred thousand dollars annually.[4]	
zakat, ushr and kalla-pulli	Locally levied and not transferred to Junbesh's leadership.[5]	
Road taxes	Locally levied and not transferred to Junbesh's leadership[6]	

After 2001 the sources of revenue were similar, although customs must have been more profitable as the country started recovering from war. The small custom post of Andkhoy (on the border with Turkmenistan), earned for example $3.38 million in 2005. However after 2001 it became necessary to share the revenue accruing from Hayratan and Khod-i Barq with both Jami'at and Wahdat, because of the shared control over Balkh province. In fact, Jami'at by 2003 was reportedly getting the higher share of customs from Hayratan (50%), as opposed to 37% for Junbesh and the rest for Mohaqqeq. During 2004 the total internal revenue of Junbesh was estimated at US$7 million a year, of which each vassal ('division commanders') pocketed $240,000–600,000. Even by 2007 most of this much reduced revenue base had gone, with the customs, Khod-i Barq and Dawlatabad salt mine now under the control of the central government.[8]

External support

Claims concerning foreign support are more difficult to investigate, although direct US backing for Junbesh waned as soon as the campaign against the

Taliban regime was over. It is often alleged that Russia supported Dostum, at least in the early years of the existence of Junbesh, but the extent of its aid is unclear. Russia seems to have at times sponsored the delivery of weaponry to Junbesh, but, according to one of Dostum's leading lieutenants, until after the fall of Kabul that was on payment of cash by Junbesh. In spring 1997 however Russian authorities, worried about the rise of the Taliban, promised the free delivery of military equipment, including 5 Su-22 planes and ammunition; at least part of these were effectively delivered. There are some other indications that it delivered material supplies, mainly military equipment, until at least 1997 and then again in 2000, but there is no indication of any cash payments being made. These are of course much more difficult to detect, but given Junbesh's weak finances it can be assumed that big amounts of cash were not forthcoming. Even some of the claims of deliveries of military equipment appear wild exaggerations. The allegation that Russia printed the Junbeshi Afghani, the currency that Dostum used to pay his men, is also doubtful. Certainly by the end of 1995 Dostum was actively seeking help in printing banknotes as far away as the United Kingdom. Whoever was printing banknotes for Dostum, this might have been the greatest source of help to the embattled Junbesh. As discussed in chapter 4, printing money certainly helped him a great deal in the short term, as it allowed Dostum to pay his troops. The gap between actual resources and expenditure financed by money print-ing must have been a large one since strong inflationary tendencies emerged after 1992 in the northern region. The devaluation of the Junbeshi Afghani was even faster than that of the Afghani of the Kabul government and by 2002 it was worth about half of the latter.[9]

If Russian help likely never amounted to much most of the time, Iran stepped in after the emergence of the Taliban as a major threat to its national interests. Officials of Junbesh are reported to have acknowledged in 1999 that they had received help from Teheran.[10] By 1996, the level of Iranian support to anti-Taliban factions was certainly exceeding that of Russia, but the main beneficiary of this help was Jami'at-i Islami and not Junbesh. Moreover, from the end of 1997 Iran started viewing Dostum with suspicion. In part this was due to the fact that they were hosting Dostum's nemesis, the fugitive Abdul Malik, but also to the widespread feeling that Dostum was being encouraged by the Americans to sign a deal with the Taliban. Dostum's publicising of the massacres of Taliban in the north during Malik's short reign and his release of Taliban prisoners was likely motivated by his desire of discrediting the rival as a butcher, as Malik had been trying to sell himself as a peacemaker to the population of northern Afghanistan. Dostum's public relations exercise was perceived by many in Afghanistan and in the wider region as a prelude to a deal with the Taliban. Iran's worries were revived when in April 1998 an American delegation led by the US representative at the UN arrived in Shi-berghan for talks. An Iranian delegation landed there immediately afterwards and promised a cessation of hostilities against Junbesh from its client party, Hizb-i Wahdat (see 'Peace cycles' in this chapter). They also invited Dostum to an official visit to Iran. At the end of April he did indeed visit Teheran and received promises of 'material and moral' support—some of which it seems to have been delivered. In June 1998 for example the Iranians agreed to pay for the ammunition needed by all member groups of the United Front to mount an offensive in Qala-i Zal against the Taliban.[11]

Iranian help arrived too late and in insufficient quantities to stem the tide. After the fall of the north to the Taliban, the Iranians for some time paid little attention to Dostum, as they seem to have shared Massud's and many others' view that Dostum was finished. However, by March 1999 the failure to re-open the northern front by either Jami'at or Wahdat had convinced the Iranians and the leadership of Wahdat that Dostum had to be involved. He was invited again to Iran and offered financial support and supplies, which he took to Afghanistan with his single Termez-based transport plane (AN-32), landing on a small strip in a pocket of territory controlled by Wahdat. After his return to Afghanistan, Dostum settled in the remote mountain district of Balkhab, where Wahdat was also operating. Iranian support was delivered through an officer of the Pasdaran posted there. Sources close to the leader of Junbesh report that the Iranians were paying Dostum $500,000 a month. Iranian support through Pasdaran liaison officers continued after he moved to a more secure location in Dara-ye Suf and until the Americans arrived shortly after 9/11. Once American support replaced the Iranian, relations between Iran and Dostum deteriorated again. In October 2001 a CIA team was deployed with Dostum, the first such in Afghanistan. The priority accorded to him was the result of contacts between Dostum's representatives in Tashkent and the Agency, which had been going on already some months prior to the 9/11 attacks. By 2005 or 2006 the Iranians were so irritated by Dostum's insistence on seeking Turkish and American political support that they seem to have started backing financially Abdul Malik, at that time busy trying to re-establish a presence in north-western Afghanistan. Their pressure, combined with Dostum's disappointment at growing American indifference and Turkish criticism, appears to have succeeded to some extent in forcing a re-alignment of Junbesh, as shown in Dostum's willingness to enter the Iran-sponsored Jabh-i Muttahed-i Milli in March 2006, if only half-heartedly. Such a move was unlikely to please his former American patrons even if Dostum did not try to raise his profile within the Front.[12]

Uzbekistan, for a while Dostum's keenest supporter, certainly helped Junbesh until at least 1997 and then again in 2000–2001, but probably did not hand over any cash. If it did, it would not have amounted to much, given Uzbekistan's own strained finances. On the other hand, it is virtually certain that Uzbekistan helped Dostum with arms, ammunition, spare parts and supplies for tanks, armoured personnel carriers and other mechanised vehicles. It also serviced combat aircraft at Termez airport. Non-military supplies included wheat, electricity and occasionally fuel.[13] Starting from 1997, the relationship between Dostum and Uzbekistan became very strained and almost all aid was cut off. The Uzbek regime appears to have lost faith in

Dostum's and Junbesh's ability to keep northern Afghanistan stable and under control and became more concerned about not upsetting its new neighbour, the Taliban. Uzbekistan's only help between 1997 and 2000 consisted in permitting some of Dostum's men to move across its territory and in allowing his last remaining AN-32 transport plane to be based in Termez. Only in the second half of 2000 did Uzbekistan resume its assistance to Junbesh and even that at the insistence of Russia and Turkey. The relationship warmed up again after 9/11, when there were even unproven allegations that Uzbek army troops assisted Junbesh against the Taliban. In 2002, Tashkent opened its first consulate, not in Kabul, but in Mazar-i Sharif, and Uzbekistan was the only country still supporting Dostum during the 2006 crisis within Junbesh.[14] Financial support however remained puny if indeed there were any.

Although the Turkish government only officially recognised having provided 'humanitarian help' to Junbesh between 1992 and 1998, there is some evidence that it provided cash to Dostum both before and after 2001. Cash might have been favoured if anything else because of geographical and logistical constraints made the dispatch of help in kind difficult. The amount of such assistance is unknown, but it is likely to have been modest, given Turkey's limited financial resources and its relative remoteness from Afghanistan. An initial delivery of US$10 million reportedly took place in 1992, after which others might have followed. In 1993–4 Turkey shied away from Dostum following the sidelining of Azad Beg, who had contacts among Ankara's nationalist circles. That episode was soon forgotten and Turkey moved closer to Dostum after his relations with Uzbekistan worsened from 1997, not least because of the much more generous treatment which Dostum received from the former. In early 2002, as American financial support evaporated following the fall of the Taliban regime, Dostum visited Turkey, enlisting that country's support for his role in Afghanistan. As a result Turkey seems to have emerged as Junbesh's foremost financial backer, not only openly supporting AINA TV but also reportedly providing covert funds too.[15]

While Junbesh's resources might have seemed quite substantial compared to most other Afghan factions, they were quite modest once its comparatively large military and administrative structure is taken into account. That Dostum was not able to accumulate large reserves of cash abroad is confirmed by his conditions when he was forced to flee the country for the second time, in 1998. For two years he lived very modestly in Turkey, unable to re-establish a presence in Afghanistan. The Iranians suspended their support a few months after northern Afghanistan fell to the Taliban and did not restore it until the capture of Massud's headquarter in Taluqan in north-eastern Afghanistan. At that point Massud agreed to allow him back into Afghanistan, opening the way to Iranian support for Junbesh. Only at this point was Dostum able to relaunch Junbesh. His main funds at that point consisted of Afghanis privately printed in England, which the Uzbek government safe-kept in Termez, but which were of no use outside Afghanistan. These he gave to Massud to sweeten his attitude towards Dostum's return on the scene. Again in the summer of 2006, when the Turks suspended their financial support, Dostum was soon unable to pay Junbesh's running costs or hand out cash to his vassals, implying that he had not accumulated large resources. In 2007, when Junbesh was trying to organise its third congress, Dostum was unable to fund it and had to sell his house in Tashkent to raise money.[16]

Cheating by military leaders compounded the problem. It appears that a significant share of what was supposed to be spent on rank and file salaries was pocketed by the officers, who often claimed to have many more soldiers on their payroll than was actually the case. Such practices were not new and Dostum himself had been accused by Soviet advisers of receiving cash to pay 45,000 men, whereas he only had 25,000 full time soldiers, but after April 1992 Junbesh could ill afford them. Now Dostum was in the same position as the Soviets had been before, unhappy about such corruption, but unable to confront his generals in order to enforce greater accountability. As a result, both civilian and military employees were normally paid months late. If feeding and paying the troops adequately was a problem, delivering services to the civilian population soon became impossible.[17]

The war economy

As the war continued into the 1990s, new opportunities for economic profiteering emerged in addition to extracting revenue from the few enterprises still active and collecting tax and customs dues. The most extreme form included forced labour, which a leading warlord used extensively, compelling farmers to work as labourers for his family or to look after his sheep.[18] The most common type of accumulation of or transfer of resources generated by the increasingly lawless environment were land grabs. Land (re-) distribution was widespread throughout northern Afghanistan (as well as elsewhere in the country) (see Table 3), yet it appears to have been mainly a form of patronage to reward followers. While there are no statistics concerning private land, figures do exist for state landholding, although their reliability is uncertain. They reveal how land distribution seemed to go hand in hand with factional conflict: it was much more widespread in provinces where local factional conflict was perpetual (Baghlan, Sar-i Pul) or factional control fluid (Balkh). Where factional control was solid (Jowzjan, Faryab, Samangan) or conflict more exogenous in nature (Kunduz), little distribution took place.

Land grabs aside, the heavily factionalised environment of northern Afghanistan led to various aspects of life, including business, being largely absorbed into the factional system. The result was that few if any entrepreneurs or traders could get by without some form of relationship with the main factions, especially Junbesh. In the case of Mazar-i Sharif, by far the most important centre of the region, previously dominant business families, like the Barats, were marginalised, while a new generation of businessmen emerged on the strength of their factional connections. Most of them were

Table 3: Land Grabs in the Northern Provinces

Province	Land Seized Including Arable and Some Range Land (Jeribs)	Government (or Non-Private) Arable Land (Jeribs)	Estimated Total Cultivated Agriculture Land-1990s (Jeribs)
Baghlan	375,082	78,719	1,700,000
Balkh	401,420	305,008	2,556,000
Jowzjan	27,221	37,327	2,000,000
Faryab	30,773	114,824	3,000,000
Samangan	1,940	36,847	1,480,975
Sari Pul	500,000		
Kunduz	3,731	98,684	1,300,000
Total	2,567,729	2,357,541	33,025,000

Source: Department of Land Management & Distribution of the AMLAK, (2005).

Uzbek or Turkmen, a fact probably linked with the importance of trade with Central Asia and later with Turkey too, and were associated with Junbesh. In comparison, the business profile of other northern factions was very modest. Although many of them were not from Mazar-i Sharif, they were typically attracted to it and established their headquarters there, playing a key role as an interface between Junbesh's rural militias and the traders of the city, slowly favouring the forging of a symbiosis between the two.

The leading business 'partners' of Junbesh included Ghulam Haidar Jowz-jani, Khudai Qol, Nabizadah, Kamgar, Eshan-i Kamal and Mullah Ghafour.[19] The trajectory of their rise to riches shows remarkable similarities. Privileged access to Central Asian markets was a key factor. Nabizadah, for example, was a simple employee in the Khod-i Barq fertiliser factory during the Soviet occupation. He developed connections with Russian advisers and sometimes helped them, thereby enabling him to get a visa, which he used to start a business with Russia after the fall of President Najibullah. During the 1990s he developed excellent relations with the Uzbek authorities, to the extent that the notoriously suspicious Uzbek border guards reportedly would not even check his vehicles or his passport when he crossed the frontier. Another example was that of Kamgar, who would launch the Kam Air airline after 2001. He used to be the coach of the police volleyball team in the 1980s. He slowly built up working relations with the Russians, managed to get a visa, started travelling north often, especially to Uzbekistan. After the fall of Naji-bullah he started exporting goods that were in scarce supply in Uzbekistan. At that time he became close to Dostum, rapidly turning into one of his unofficial partners. He too was reported to be able to cross the border easily, without checks, due to his closeness to people in the high ranks of the government.

Another factor was the protection that Dostum and other top figures in Junbesh were able to afford to these businessmen. One of the most obvious examples is that of Mullah Ghafoor, who built his business through his close relationship with Dostum. Where most other businessmen were afraid of investing, he felt protected by Dostum and took the risk. After the fall of Najibullah he built Kefayat market in Mazar-i Sharif and transformed it into a very profitable venture, with Dostum's help, relocating the money-changers there and establishing control over them.

It is not clear what direct financial benefits Dostum and Junbesh derived from these business cronies, apart from logistical services and access to otherwise scarce goods. In northern Afghanistan allegations are widespread that some self-proclaimed businessmen were in fact smugglers of goods, including narcotics, across the border, and that they paid a cut to key characters within Junbesh. If this is the case, it is unlikely that much of this cash made it to Junbesh' coffers and stayed instead in the pockets of local military leaders. The relationship was not always an easy one, a fact that bears witness to how Junbesh's share of the profits in this partnership might not have been very big.

Peace cycles

Junbesh's model of warmaking had been under pressure from the civilian population even as it was taking shape in Najib's time. Dostum's style of military operations, essentially based on daring (or ruthless) frontal assaults, was expensive in terms of human casualties. Intellectuals and politicians from Jowzjan had openly complained about this between the late 1980s and early 1990s. Dostum had tried to appease them by excluding from military service many young Uzbeks, especially those from powerful families, engineering a 'system' where they were reported to have served with the central authorities. This brought little relief for the households whose youth continued to be drafted into the militias.[20] Eventually the heavy casualties contributed to the emergence of a peace cycle by driving many households to accept the Taliban in 1997–8 as a better alternative to never-ending warfare.

The burden of the system on the civilian population gradually intensified. In 1992–6, a degree of order had existed in northern Afghanistan, with a working police force, a security service and some disciplined army units to counter-balance the presence of unruly militias. Road blocks to extract taxes from the travellers were already a plague which could not be prevented despite many negotiations. Travellers reported that road blocks in northern part of the country were among the worst in all Afghanistan, likely a result of the particularly high density of armed men in the region. In some cases military operations were organised to clear the worst rogue military leaders, who were making travel and trade unsafe, but armed escorts often had to be provided for civilian vehicles along many roads. Still for the first couple of years, trading and economic activities continued with limited hindrance and salaries of officials were being paid. Junbesh's authorities were even able to assist the population with reasonable efficiency in the event of natural disasters, such as in the case of a big landslide in Sar-i Pul. However, by the first months of 1994 Junbesh lost the ability to pay salaries to troops and civil servants, due both to the high cost of continuous warfare and the gradual exhaustion of Hayratan's reserves, which made it necessary to purchase growing amounts of equipment and supplies on the market.[21]

After Abdul Malik's failed coup against Dostum (1997), the rapid degeneration of Junbesh's already weak command and control led to a chaotic situation. The breakdown in relations caused by Malik's coup were major factors in causing a deterioration of law and order. That part of the local population who had no links to military leaders or directly to Dostum had already been exposed to the depredations of his troops, but in 1997–1998 nobody was safe from the militias anymore as these started targeting even rural communities and towns which were previously integrated in Dostum's 'system'. The fighting caused a decline in trade with the neighbouring countries, a major source of income for the militias, which in turn increased exponentially its extortion from the rural population. As the looting was going on, alienating much support, all Dostum could or would do was to preach good behaviour to his troops. After his return to Afghanistan in 1998, Dostum had been unable to reassert his control over Mazar-i Sharif. During much of 1997, the city was theatre of fighting between Abdul Malik's militias and different factions of Hizb-i Wahdat, with the latter eventually succeeding in seizing control over the city. The arrival of undisciplined Wahdat units from Bamyan in 1997 also contributed to the mayhem in Mazar and Hayratan. In 1998 there were even popular demonstrations against the exactions of Wahdat's militias in Mazar. The process of emergence of a symbiosis between Junbesh and the urban world of Mazar-i Sharif was thus abruptly interrupted. Especially when the news began to filter through that the Taliban had put an end to the abuses of the warlords in other parts of Afghanistan, the deal 'peace and security at the price of dominance of the warlords', which had earned Dostum much support especially in the cities, started breaking down. By 1998 even the urban population and not just in Mazar began to complain of the hoarding of food by the armed groups and of the increased looting carried out by the troops, who were rumoured to be selling the booty on the Central Asian markets.[22]

The crisis of command and control which derived from Junbesh's internal strife in 1997–8 was not the only factor accelerating the decay of Junbesh as viable polity. Undoubtedly, a number of Dostum's vassals developed a very strong appetite for personal enrichment during the civil wars, to the extent of relinquishing their military role. The existence of a peace cycle is best shown by the example of Ghaffar Pahlawan, who by 1995 had reportedly turned into the most corrupt of the vassals. Not content with having relinquished his combat duties, he developed a habit of embezzling the pay of his troops and invest the cash in the building industry. Dostum had to replace him with Ghaffar's own son Qahaar as commander of 510th Div., in order to prevent or limit the extent of the embezzlement. After Qahaar's killing, Dostum opted to appoint another of Ghaffar's sons, Satar. He had to be supported by one of Dostum's key aides, Gen. Fawzi, because of his limited abilities. Ghaffar Pahlawan however moved against Fawzi after a couple of months, presumably in order to recover full control over the division and its finances. Ghaffar succeeded in lobbying Dostum to remove Fawzi, but as soon as that happened, Satar tried to start a purge in 510th Div., to eliminate the officers who had showed too much familiarity with Fawzi. The officers responded with a mutiny against Satar, which developed into a major crisis within Junbesh. Dostum tried to mediate between Satar, Ghaffar and the officers, who had seized full control of the garrison of Suzma Qala. Rasul Pahlawan lobbied heavily in favour of Ghaffar Pahlawan, asking Dostum threateningly 'if tomorrow the same situation comes upon me, will you sit there and watch [...] my trial?' Among Junbesh's heavyweights, some sided with Rasul like Majid Rowzi, but Dostum was aware of Ghaffar's wrongdoing and was worried about the possible defection of several military leaders of Sar-i Pul. The tension was not resolved, as the assassination of Rasul Pahlawan followed shortly and a resurgence of fighting contributed to distract the attention. Later Ghaffar liased with Abdul Malik and Gul-i Pahlawan and played an important role in pushing them towards the 1997 coup, apparently thinking erroneously that the Taliban would bring peace and allow him to maintain the accumulated wealth and offer him status and honour.[23]

Ghaffar Pahlawan's case was however far from unique. Gen. Baigi once reported to Dostum that his vassals and vavassors

were no longer his old commanders who would be interested in fighting, and in fighting for him and for his Junbesh because all of them had become rich; and all of them now had multiple wives, Buzkashi horses, multi-storied houses and nice apartments. They were not concerned about the welfare of their soldiers and many of their personnel were [...] brought to the front by force. Their soldiers had not undergone any training; they could not recognise their commanders and did not care about the orders from their commanders [...]. All commanders were engaged in pleasure-seeking activities and would not go to the front line.[24]

By the summer of 1995, Junbesh's logistics were already out of control and its army was no longer able to allocate resources efficiently. On some fronts supplies would virtually dry up, hijacked by other, politically more powerful, vassals operating in areas of lesser strategic importance. By 1997, when Malik's coup was ongoing and Dostum and a few loyalists were trying to summon support, the decay had reached the point where almost nobody among the dignitaries of Junbesh turned out to be willing to fight. The middle rank military leaders had mostly been arrested treacherously by Malik, but those who were remained showed a greater willingness to resist than the top leaders, particularly in parts of Faryab, Sozma Qala and Balkh. War profiteering turned out to be incompatible with effective war-making and a major source of weakness within Junbesh's ranks. Already in January 1997 warning signs were visible, like the wild fluctuations of the local currency. It appears that Junbesh's Generals and other prominent figures in the North were trying to convert as much local currency as possible into dollars. For want of better alternatives, the generation of a peace cycle in 1996–1998 happened to play decisively in favour of the Taliban, who were presenting themselves as peace-makers and were promising enticing settlements to many key players within Junbesh. Whether or not any deals were signed between the latter and the Taliban, such offers weakened the will to resist within Junbesh's ranks.[25]

Even after the fall of the Taliban, Dostum's militias, like those of Jami'at and the other parties, had hardly changed their patterns of behaviour towards civilians. Raping and kidnapping did not appear to be as common has they had been in 1997–1998, but looting and stealing certainly were, particularly in 2001–2. Villages suspected of having supported the Taliban occupation were particularly targeted. Armed clashes with other militias also reappeared as a regular occurrence in 2002–4. This time Dostum made a more deter-mined effort to push his military leaders towards enforcing better discipline among their troops, although much of what he did was still mere lecturing. There are examples which show that at least occasionally Dostum's personal intervention led to an improvement of the lot of local communities. For example, in 2002 Turkmen villagers in Balkh complained to minister Qarqin of looting and stealing of sheep carried out by the militiamen of Majid Rowzi and others. Qarqin turned to Dostum and the theft of cattle stopped, with some of the stolen sheep even being returned.[26] Looting and stealing became rare after the initial wave that followed the 'reconquista' of the north and was replaced by a more systematic but less arbitrary system of taxation. Road blocks too, which had been widespread in 2001–2, were mostly removed. After seizing the North back in 2001, Dostum's hard won awareness of the need to restrain military leaders and their men intensified his personal supervision and encouraged him to develop stronger contacts with notables and intellectuals, a choice which highlights his strong inclination towards continued patrimonial rule rather than institutionalisation. Moreover, by 2002 the slow re-establishment of a central state in Afghanistan meant that compe-tition for legitimate control over the northern provinces would soon intensify (see chapter 10).

Notes

1. http://www.eia.doe.gov/emeu/world/country/cntry_AF.html.
2. EIA, *Afghanistan country analysis brief*, Oct. 2002; *Petroleum Economist*, 17 Dec. 2002.
3. The $200,000 a day quoted by *AFP*, 28 May 2003, would imply profits of $73 mil-lion a year, which seems far too much given the context. At prices of $270 per ton (FAO/WFP (1997), even at its maximum production of 105,000 tons per year the factory should not have exceeded a turnover of $28.4 million. Profits, therefore, should have been in the range of $0–4 million at the most, which was then shared between Junbesh and other parties. Most Afghan factories were running at a loss in the 1970s and 1980s, so it is quite possible that profits might have been lower than that or even non-existent.

4. Interview with the managing director of salt mine, Dawlatabad, Sept. 2004.
5. According to Eckart Schiewek of UNAMA, in 2002 throughout Afghanistan the value of 'taxation' by private militias was in the range of $2–2.5 per head per year. Even if all villagers in the North had been taxed by Junbesh, the revenue would therefore not have exceeded $3–4 million.
6. Whitlock (2002), p. 224–225.
7. Baigi (2000), p. 93.
8. 'Customs Revenues', *Islah* (Kabul), 31 Jano. 2007; Malikyar/Rubin (2002), p. 33; personal communication with Eckart Schiewek (UNAMA), Mazar-i Sharif, Aug. 2004.
9. Baigi (2000), pp. 116, 283, 240; 'Afghanistan gets new currency', *Reuters*, 7 Oct. 2002.
10. According to Human Rights Watch (2001), p. 37, although footnote 163 does not indicate any specific source for Junbesh.
11. Baigi (2000), pp. 327–8, 358–9, 372.
12. Ibid., pp. 392, 394–5; Walwalji (2007); Schroen (2007), p. 190; Makia Monir, 'Former strongmen forms political alliance', *Pajhwok Afghan News*, 13 March 2006; personal communication with UN officials, Kabul, April 2006.
13. According to Human Rights Watch (2001), pp. 46–47, citing Uzbek journalists and western diplomats, and Whitlock (2002), p. 308. See also Dorronsoro (2005), p. 262.
14. Baigi (2000), pp. 394; Anthony Shadid, 'Old divisions persist in 'new' Afghanistan', *Boston Globe*, 16 Jano. 2002; Walwalji (2007).
15. 'Turkey Vows To Help Pro-Dostum Forces', *Hurriyet*, 31 Oct. 1996; Walwalji (s.d.), p. 31; Baigi (2000), pp. 360–1; Walwalji (2007).
16. Walwalji (2007); Personal communicaton with UN officials, Kabul and Mazar-i Sharif, Oct. 2007.
17. A. Davis, 'Makeover For A Warlord', *Time*, 3 June 2002; Christensen (1995), p. 79.
18. Interview with member of the intelligentsia from Faryab, 2004.
19. Baigi (2000), p. 46. This paragraph is based on interviews carried out in Mazar-i Sharif in May 2005, involving businessmen, intellectuals and officials of international organisations.
20. Walwalji (1380), ch. Khust Crisis the threshold of rift between Dr Najibullah and Gen. Dostom.
21. Elmi (1997), p. 212–3; Baigi (2000), pp. 49, 92–3, 171, 53, 155–6, 179.
22. Baigi (2000), pp. 305, 137, 314, 321, 338, 346–7, 349, 353; John F. Burns, 'As Foes Splinter, Afghan Islamic Victors Press On', *New York Times*, 16 Feb. 1997; Baigi (2000), p. 321.
23. Baigi (2000), pp. 240ff, 285.
24. Ibid., pp. 282.
25. Ibid., pp. 223–4, 291, 289; Griffin (2003), p. 87–88.
26. Alden Wily (2004), pp. 15–6; interview with Noor Mohammad Qarqin, Kabul, May 2003.

10

JUNBESH'S EXTERNAL DYNAMICS

Expansionism

Throughout its existence, the leadership of Junbesh rarely took any clear decision to militarily expand beyond its existing area of control. The two exceptions are the occupation of Baghdis in 1995 and repeated attempts to occupy Kunduz in 1994–5, both being attempts to consolidate its borders rather than genuinely aggressive moves. Nonetheless, Junbesh was often driven towards expansion by the role which networks of military leaders played within it. As shown in Graph 1, some of the latter could occasionally be tempted to fight for a particular faction through new or old links with its members (F). Gradually this could lead to the whole network being dragged away from one faction towards another, obviously a highly conflictual process. Initially most of the networks only partially included in Junbesh were mainly composed of former militiamen of the Najibullah regime and leftist groups, significant chunks of which had been left out of Junbesh in 1992 because of geographical or logistical considerations. During 1992–3 such 'lost' branches of the militia networks often invoked the help of their colleagues inside Junbesh and ultimately of Dostum himself, in order to have a better chance of surviving in an environment populated with hostile mujahidin. Examples include the Khalqi militias of Helmand and Kandahar (see chapter 4), which had established a link with Junbesh despite their geographical separation, until they were defeated by Ismail Khan in July 1993. Dostum tried to send supplies to Khano and Jabbar, but they arrived too late. Another case is that of militiamen once linked to the SAMA group and based in the Shomali region, who in April 1993 tried to establish a link with Junbesh. Some sources allege that Massud's intelligence section, aware of the negotiations between the two and wary of Junbesh establishing itself in a region of strategic importance for Jami'at, promptly eliminated the leaders of the SAMA group. A third example was that of the militiamen of Takhar, who had been expelled from their province in 1991 and tried to re-establish their presence with Dostum's help after 1992. In Ghor, too, former militiamen established contact with Junbesh and dragged it into a province where initially it had nothing at stake (see Map 11). A final example is that of the former militiamen of Herat who, once defeated by Ismail Khan, appealed to Rasul Pahlawan for help and received his support to deploy in Baghdis against the Amir of Herat.[1] By the second half of 1993 the remnants of Najib's militias had all been incorporated in Junbesh or had disappeared from the scene. Different networks continued to follow a similar dynamic afterwards.

Sometimes, whole networks that had not previously been linked to Junbesh approached Dostum for support, particularly when their relationship with their old 'lord' was in crisis. For example after Massud had imprisoned, disarmed or killed a number of his own vassals from Parwan, including among others Agha Shirin Salangi, Karim Qarabagh and Anwar Dangar, their village military leaders approached Dostum towards the end of 1994. An even more important example is that of the jihadi military leaders of northern Takhar, whom Dostum assiduously courted after 1992. While Dostum failed to achieve much through his sponsoring of the former Takhari militia leaders, dealing with their former enemies in the long term allowed Junbesh to expand its influence to Takhar. A number of mujahidin military leaders like Pir Mohammad, Qayum Bey, Hazrat, Pahlawan Ibrahim and Haji Agha Gul established relations with Dostum. In this case Uzbek ethnicity was explicitly used as a recruitment theme, exploiting the rising tensions between the Uzbeks, organised in their own relatively independent network, and their Tajik rivals, who were affiliated with Jami'at-i Islami, the dominant force in those areas. The fruits of what had been sowed in the 1990s were harvested from 2001. In that year, after the re-launch of the alliance with Jami'at within the framework of the United Front, Junbesh's representatives were allowed to travel freely throughout north-eastern Afghanistan, which had previously been hostile territory. Although the purpose of the agreement was mainly to allow them better to organise their efforts to resist the Taliban, such representatives exploited the opportunity to re-establish links with the military leaders operating in these regions. Even in remote Badakhshan they were actually welcomed by many military leaders, especially Uzbeks, who were beginning to feel sidelined by the Jami'at-i Islami, a party dominated by Tajiks. Traditionally, Uzbek military leaders in Badakhashan divided their loyalties between Hizb-i Islami and Jami'at, but power was concentrated in the hands of Tajiks. As a result, Junbesh was able to recruit several Uzbeks in the districts of Keshm, Argu, Baharak and Doraim. A similar process appears to have taken place in Takhar and Kunduz provinces. The consolidation of Junbesh's influence encountered an obstacle not just in Jami'at-i Islami's reaction, but also in the inability of Junbesh's cadres, with their urban-leftist background, to merge with the conservative mujahidin of the Northeast. At least in the case of Badakhshan, it was the cadres who decided to leave before being chased away by Jami'at.[2]

Ultimately, the cultural gap between Junbesh's cadres and the local military leaders, as well as the distance and Jami'at-i Islami's superior financial resources, prevented Junbesh from establishing a firm foothold among Uzbek military leaders in Badakhshan, who were bought away from Junbesh by Professor Rabbani of Jami'at in a matter of a few months. In this case Dostum was unable to exercise his irreplaceable role as Junbesh's charismatic leader and networker. However, as freedom of movement was restored to Afghanistan in 2001, various sources confirmed that most Uzbek military leaders and many notables, not just in Badakhshan, but also in Baghdis, Kunduz, Baghlan and especially Takhar developed or maintained close links with Dostum, even if they formally still belong to Jami'at or other mujahidin parties.[3] One of Takhar's leading Uzbek military leaders, Motalleb Beg, had participated in Junbesh's Second Congress in June 2002 (see chapter 13), the first step of a process which would bring the network of Uzbek military leaders of Tahkar openly to switch their support to Junbesh in late 2003.

As pointed out already, network-driven expansion was not without its risks. Often some vassal would drag the whole of Junbesh into a new conflict as a result of having formed a local alliance with a military leader in search of protection. One such example is provided by the struggle for Ghormach district (Baghdis), which, starting from September 1993, saw a local military leader, Tur Longatai, offering his services as a new vavassor to Rasul Pahlawan and enlisting his help against the forces of Ismail Khan, helping to touch off a conflict which was to last years. The role of cross-boundary networks in breeding conflict among factions worked the other way round too. For example, military leaders of Jami'at-i Islami in Faryab, but also former Pashtun militiamen of Qaysar, were working to get Ismail Khan involved in their fight against Rasul.[4]

Dostum and his vassals were particularly keen to answer the call of military leaders networked with them, despite the risks involved, because their power and influence was largely based on being at the centre of as many networks as possible (see chapters 6, 7 and 8). Another reason for this almost compulsive expansionism was the micro political economy of warlordism. The village military leaders, and through them the vavassors, were largely dependent for their income on direct control over the villages. Hence they were naturally inclined to expand their area of control. A third factor driving Junbesh's expansionism, at least in specific stages of its existence, was Dostum's desire to increase his leverage in negotiations with Kabul. Yet another factor was likely the desire to secure Junbesh's vulnerable borders, particularly in the east. While in the west it was Rasul Pahlawan who was driving Junbesh's expansionism towards Baghdis and Ghor, the greatest effort in terms of resources was thrown towards the military leaders of the north-eastern provinces of Kunduz, Takhar, Badakhshan and Baghlan, from where access to the north was easiest. Dostum was so keen to ensure their friendship and cooperation that he kept presenting them with fuel, money and even cars. The Jami'at-led alliance misinterpreted Dostum's efforts as an aggressive move and reacted in 1993 by attacking these military leaders, in the end effectively pushing them into Dostum's arms and consolidating their relationship with Junbesh.[5]

Towards the end of Junbesh's first period (1992–8), Dostum seems to have tried new approaches towards securing his borderlands, possibly disillusioned by the lack of lasting results from his investment in the existing networks of military leaders east and west. In Baghdis he attempted to create what in Carolingian terminology would have been called a '*marche*', by choosing a military leader on the basis of personal trust and providing him with support so that he would attract other military leaders or recruit more followers, until he would finally be able to eliminate rivals from the territory. His chosen man was Mullah Malang, a former military leader of Hizb-i Islami who had first allied and then broken with the Taliban and had approached Dostum in 1998. Dostum welcomed him and invested all his hopes for Baghdis in Malang, believing that he could turn him into his vassal in that province.[6] This type of expansion could be described as feudalisation, but the collapse of Junbesh shortly thereafter put an end to the experiment.

In expanding his influence, Dostum relied also on the good offices of grand notables. In establishing contacts within Badakhshan he used one of his closest associates, Gen. Fawzi, an Uzbek from Faryab who has been governor of the province under Najib, while in Baghdis Dostum deployed Maulana Abdur Raouf, an Uzbek notable who had been a member of parliament at the time of President Daoud.[7]

Networking among military leaders knew high and lows, but it impacted positively on Dostum's influence and even popularity. The pattern of voting in the 2004 Presidential elections shows how increased political support for Dostum matched the strength of networking among the military class beyond the northern region. During the presidential elections of 2004, Dostum received 39.5% of the vote in Takhar, 7.8% in Baghlan, 5.7% of the vote in Badakhshan and 2% in Baghdis (see Map 10).

Managing external challenges

Just as Dostum used networks of military leaders as the main avenue for expanding his influence in his rivals' territories, he too was vulnerable to other warlords using the same tactic against him. In chapter 9 I illustrated how the peace cycle precipitated disintegrative pressures within Junbesh in 1997–8. Another factor endangering Junbesh's internal cohesiveness and solidity was the encouragement that local opposition was receiving from other warlords or the central government openly to challenge Dostum. The existence in northern Afghanistan of an active network of Jami'ati military leaders centered around Ustad Atta was initially the main threat. After his party colleagues had taken Kabul, Atta had likely stayed in the Harakat-i Shamal only to facilitate his fight for hegemony in the north. During 1993, the early manifestations of the conflict between the two leaders led to the northern branch of Jami'at effectively quitting Junbesh, even if quite a few Jami'ati military leaders stayed behind and sided with Dostum. Jami'at had

Map 10: Matching Between Areas of Military Control by Junbesh and Dostum's Share of the Vote in the 2004 Presidential Elections

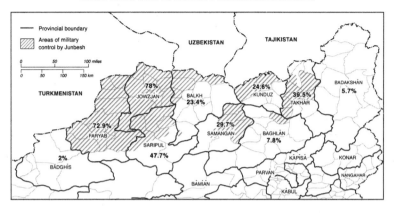

Map 11: Expansion and Contraction of Junbesh, 1992–2007

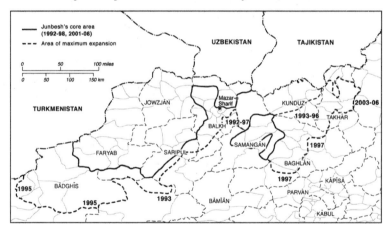

been well represented in the Executive Council of Junbesh, with half a dozen members, while Atta himself had been appointed deputy. Core Jami'atis had strong ideological reservations about leaving northern Afghanistan de facto under the control of their former enemies. Immediately after the Lashkargah incident in 1993 (see chapter 4), Massud authorised the military leader of Jami'at in northern Afghanistan, Ustad Atta, to form a new Army Corps, which would have responded directly to Kabul and not to Dostum, and provided him with a sum of money. Immediately Ustad Atta established a Jihad Council and set out to recruit former mujahidin military leaders into it, explicitly presenting this organisation as in alternative and in opposition to Junbesh's politico-military structure.[8] This development can be seen as mark-

149

ing the formal separation of Jami'at-i Islami from Junbesh in northern Afghanistan and was a clear sign of Jami'at-i Islami's medium and long-term ambitions in the North. The Jami'ati challenge only took an explicit military form in 1994, when it was utterly crushed by Dostum through the successful mobilisation of his military resources.

Dostum's ability to respond militarily to hostile networking inside his ranks was severely constrained in post-2001 Afghanistan. As a result, Dostum was often on the defensive against the more resourceful Jami'at. Already in 2002 Jami'at was competing hard against Junbesh in its core areas, especially in Balkh province, where traditionally Jami'at had some important strongholds. In part Jami'at-i Islami's expansion was achieved by military means, as the battle of Khulm in early 2002 shows. Exploiting its control of key positions within the transitional government, Jami'at was able in 2002–4 to behave aggressively without incurring Kabul's wrath. Junbesh never tried to wrest back control of this largely Tajik district. The sneaking, virtually bloodless seizure of Mazar-i Sharif by Jami'at during 2002 was also due to a display of military muscle and possibly Junbesh's fear of not having the resources to administer the city without Kabul's help. The despatch of troops and armour from Kabul to Mazar in April 2002, officially meant to celebrate the anniversary of the fall of Najibullah's regime, might have been a warning to Dostum, that the MoD was ready to support Atta if Dostum did not bow to him. During 2003 rumours abounded in northern Afghanistan that a civil war between the two parties was about to start and that Ustad Atta, the leader of Jami'at, was gathering strength while waiting for the opportunity to make a strategic move. He invested a significant amount of cash in order to have his fleet of Soviet vintage tanks overhauled by Russian engineers.[9] In fact Atta was more likely trying to put psychological pressure on Dostum, to force him to make concessions in terms of territorial control.

Jami'at put its greatest effort into buying off military leaders, targeting several networks and areas, among which were:

- A network of Pashtun military leaders based along the road between Mazar and Shiberghan, who after having cooperated with the Taliban had placed themselves under the protection of Junbesh;
- Arab and Turkmen military leaders in Faizabad and Mordyan districts of Jowzjan;
- Uzbek military leaders in the southern and central parts of Faryab province;
- Village military leaders in Shulgara district of Balkh province (see Map 12).

The example of Faryab illustrates well the odds faced by Dostum. After late 2001–early 2002, Dostum lost the ability to create new units and appoint officers to lead them, due to the monopolisation of the MoD by the Jami'atis, who wasted no time in exploiting his weak position. At the end of 2002 the Ministry of Defence, headed by a Jami'ati, Marshal Fahim, established a new division in Faryab, the 24th, and gave it funds to recruit new troops, with the

Map 12: Targeted Recruitment Areas Identified by Ustad Atta/Jami'at-i Islami, 2002–

purpose of using patronage to coalesce mainly Uzbek military leaders around Jami'at. The move looked initially successful and by mid-2003 Jami'at was already staking a strong claim to 50% of official positions in Faryab province, one of the key strongholds of Junbesh.

Dostum had to demonstrate considerable brinkmanship skills in fending off Atta's threat. As far as the buying off of military leaders went, Dostum waited for Atta to overstretch himself and then moved in, buying back as many as possible of them. For example in Shulgara by the summer of 2002 Atta had managed to buy off almost all military leaders there, but he subsequently run out of cash and Dostum quickly purchased the loyalty of many of them. On the military side Dostum had to show restraint, but still managed to demonstrate Jami'at-i Islami's continuing military inferiority. Dostum also showed some good brinkmanship management at the beginning of May 2002, when his men decisively defeated Jami'at in Sar-i Pul town, tempering Jami'at-i Islami's assertiveness but without starting an all-out conflict. The decisive test of Dostum's brinkmanship was in October 2003, when quick and decisive military offensives wiped out Jami'at-i Islami's presence in eastern Jowzjan and Faryab. At the same time, Dostum also confronted Jami'at in Mazar; even if the intervention of British peacekeepers and UN diplomats prevented him from finishing Atta off, he convincingly demonstrated his military superiority by outmanoeuvring Atta's armour and seizing all the key positions around Mazar. Apart from clawing back everything that Jami'at had gained throughout 2003, Dostum delivered a clear message: that he would not be marginalised without a serious fight. Dostum also succeeded in convincing Atta that no easy victory was there for the taking and that the Uzbek warlord would not be intimidated.[10]

The enmity between Ismail Khan and Junbesh was to a great extent due to Rasul Pahlawan and Ismail Khan being dragged into a conflict by the lobbying of local military leaders (see above).[11] With the disappearance from the scene of Rasul and his brothers, Dostum stabilised the western border of Junbesh by greatly improving his relations with Ismail Khan, who in turn began tilting towards Dostum.[12] After having been betrayed to the Taliban by Abdul Malik, Ismail Khan probably renewed his appreciation of Dostum, especially as the latter had been smart enough to take care of Ismail Khan's family when the latter was in Taliban captivity, winning his gratitude, although some rivalry remained.[13] The two warlords seemed to have reached a modus vivendi and after 2001 there was no further clashes around the borders of Faryab province. When Ismail Khan was attacked by a coalition of his estranged military leaders in August 2004, Dostum even expressed his solidarity to him and ventilated, rather unrealistically, the hypothesis of sending military help. What he did send was a delegation to help negotiate a settlement between Ismail Khan and Zahir Nabizadah, one of the leaders of the anti-Dostum coalition, who had some connection with Dostum.[14]

Jami'at was not the only source of hostile networking inside Junbesh's heartland. The surviving Pahlawan brothers created Junbesh-i Islami (Islamic Front), an alternative Junbesh that by early 2003 had some presence in the Shirin Tagab and Faizabad districts of Faryab province. Later in 2003 Malik replaced this organisation with another party, Hizb-i Azadi. Another threat emerged in the shape of a network of former Hizb-i Islami military leaders of Uzbek background, some of whom, like Nasim Mehdi, had joined Junbesh in 1992. The network constituted itself as a political party under the name of Shura-i Adolat and tried to attract more military leaders to its ranks, particularly in Takhar where many Uzbeks had also been in Hizb-i Islami. Rumours abounded that these anti-Dostum players had received funds or at least encouragement from Jami'at and Kabul to create their own parties and compete with Junbesh among the Uzbek population. Dostum once again tried to react with 'cautious ruthlessness'. He let Shura-i Adolat collapse under the weight of its own contradictions, which happened quite rapidly. Against the Pahlawans, he tried to use limited force to scare them from Faryab. Although Gul-i Pahlawan was forced to flee the province not long after having returned there, Dostum's ability to control the militias affiliated to him had eroded after their official disbandment. The result was that the central districts of Faryab became the theatre of continuous skirmishing between military leaders affiliated to Junbesh and Azadi, hardly an outcome in Dostum's interest. The fighting peaked in 2006, coinciding with Junbesh's internal crisis, and even though Junbesh partially recovered some strength in 2007 it could not wipe out Azadi's threat in that area. Under international pressure in October 2007 it even had to agreed to the arrest of the military leaders involved in the fighting.[15]

Centre-periphery relations

The contrast between a regionalist force like Junbesh and a central government in Kabul, which remained committed to an ideal of a centralised

Afghanistan, was inevitably bound to complicate relations between Junbesh and Kabul from 1992. Moreover, Junbesh's insistence on power-sharing in Kabul did not help to ease relations with Massud in particular, whose position of Defence Minister was demanded by Dostum. Massud seems to have believed that Junbesh was too heterogeneous to survive for long and opted to wait for its collapse, possibly deliberately trying to accelerate it by denying recognition. To the extent that Junbesh was showing its staying power, Massud seems to have seen it as a threat to his attempt to expand his hegemony over as much of Afghanistan as possible.[16] Rabbani was more inclined to discuss Junbesh's demands, which also included participation in the Shora-ye-Ahl-i-Hal wa Aqd, but Massud and others continued to deny any political legitimacy to Junbesh. Rabbani's greater acquiescence won him Junbesh's support for an extension of his mandate by two years in the Shura, where many of the 916 votes he received came from Junbesh's delegates (of 1360). This resolved the tension between Kabul and Mazar-i Sharif hardly at all, since Rabbani failed to follow up on his promise to Dostum of appointing him in Kabul. Rabbani and most of all Massud's centralising instinct and the inability of different factions to agree on power sharing were among the causes of the impending civil war, but were compounded in Dostum's case by ideological differences and by the difficulty of both sides to manage local allies. Even before Dostum joined Hizb-i Islami and Hizb-i Wahdat in the battlefield against Jami'at-i Islami in January 1994, Junbesh and Jami'at had the opportunity to confront each other. The first opportunity was the aforementioned indirect involvement of Dostum with the Khalqi militias in Lashkargah (see the first paragraph of this chapter). Even if formally the Khalqis were not part of Junbesh, the incident did not strengthen the trust and understanding between the latter and Jami'at. At this point it was already obvious that Jami'at intended to contain Junbesh, and Dostum started reconsidering the prospects of the alliance with Jami'at. It appears that shortly afterwards, in the summer of 1993, Dostum struck the first agreement with Mazari and Hekmatyar, probably concerning his neutrality in the conflict. Discussions continued and eventually led to Junbesh fully aligning with the opposition to Jami'at.[17]

The second opportunity for a confrontation was provided by the events of September–November 1993 in Kunduz province, which seem to have determined Dostum's final decision to switch sides. This was the first direct armed clash between Junbesh and the forces under Massud's command. Meaning to prevent an attack by Gen. Dostum against the town of Kunduz, which apparently Dostum was not actually planning, Massud ordered an operation against Junbesh's easternmost position in Kunduz province, Sher Khan Bander. Not well defended, the town easily fell to the Jami'atis. Junbesh launched a counter-offensive, which before the enforcement of a Rabbani-sponsored truce won back other areas that Jami'at-i Islami's allies had gone on occupying, but not Sher Khan Bander, which remained under the control of Jami'at-i Islami's allies. It is known that representatives of Junbesh, Hezb-i Islami and Wahdat met in Azerbaijan in December 1993, to define the details of the participation of Junbesh in the battle against Jami'at and the divisions of the spoils in the event of victory.[18]

In dealing with Junbesh, Jami'at exploited one of Junbesh's key political weaknesses, that is its regionalist platform. By refusing to take a separatist stand and at the same time implicitly abstaining from becoming a country-wide force in its own right, Junbesh was structurally in a position to have to bargain with Kabul, whoever might have been in control of it. Hence Junbesh's military campaigns could only have limited objectives—there was no final victory to be achieved. As a result, Junbesh was in a position of per-petual strategic inferiority. Its only real option was to ally with the weaker factions hoping to force the centre to a compromise that was never likely to be implemented. The same weakness was repeatedly exploited by the Taliban too. When they emerged as a major force in Afghan politics, like other Afghan factions, Dostum did not initially take them too seriously. In fact he saw their emergence as a strategic advantage for him, particularly during the last few months of 1995 and throughout 1996. Until the fall of Herat in September 1995 he did not even share a border with them, although the mauling inflicted by them on Dostum's ally Hizb-i Islami weakened Junbesh's strategic position. Strategically speaking, at this point it made perfect sense for Dostum to strengthen the Taliban, as they would have put pressure on his enemies, such as Ismail Khan and Ahmad Shah Massud. In the summer of 1995 he contacted the Taliban and reached an agreement with them, which later resulted in the intervention of his air force in support of their operations against Ismail Khan, as well as in the availability of his technicians to maintain their air arm, although according to some sources in this latter case he demanded to be paid in cash.[19]

By early September the Pakistanis, also keen to exploit the weaknesses of Junbesh's regionalism, were actively lobbying for the formation of a full alli-ance between Junbesh and the Taliban and against any rapprochement between Junbesh and Jami'at, while the Iranians were lobbying in the oppo-site direction. By December there were even promises of military supplies from Pakistan to entice Dostum into an alliance. Shortly later Dostum was even invited to talk to the Taliban's High Council in Kandahar, which he declined to do. At this time he was still fighting with Massud on the Kabul/ Baghlan fronts and probably could not have imagined that the Taliban would effectively defeat Ismail Khan very soon and take Herat, therefore becoming his neighbours. When Herat actually fell, Dostum moved quickly to take Baghdis province and other parts of Ghor from Ismail Khan, possibly as part of an arrangement with the Taliban. The move was likely also dictated by the need to consolidate his western border and was welcomed by many former local allies of Ismail Khan, who were also fearful of a further expansion of the Taliban.[20]

After the fall of Herat, Dostum effectively stopped all active cooperation with the Taliban, in part because he was worried by the implications of their and the Pakistanis' steadfast refusal openly to recognise Junbesh's role in the

Taliban's recent military advances. Increasingly suspicious of their genuine willingness to strike a deal with him, by January 1996 he was talking to the Rabbani government about peace terms, although he waited until October before re-opening the Salang pass, a step finally heralding a new alliance with Massud. If this was delayed, it was in part due to the opposition of Rasul Sayyaf, a key ally of the Jami'atis, but also to Massud's opposition to Dostum's demand that he be appointed Minister of Defence.[21] As Dostum's relationship with the Taliban and the Pakistanis cooled, Islamabad turned to Rasul Pahlawan, whom it courted throughout the first half of 1996 if not earlier. It is likely that the Pakistanis were trying to convince him to organise a coup against Dostum. There is no evidence that the assassination of Rasul Pahlawan in June was organised by Dostum, Russia or Uzbekistan, but nonetheless it seemed to suggest to the Pakistanis that immediate alternatives to a direct deal with Dostum were not viable.

With the fall of Kabul, the Taliban were beginning to be seen as likely winners of the civil war and dealing with them was no longer a matter of strategic opportunism. The logic of Junbesh's regionalism once again forced Dostum to seek an accommodation. A disconcerted Dostum restarted negotiations with the Taliban, with the Pakistanis pushing him towards a resumption of the war against Massud, almost succeeding in getting him to sign a truce with them on Pakistan's terms. Eventually, however, Dostum's instinct warned him not to trust the Pakistanis and he backed down from the agreement.[22]

As I discussed in chapter 4, the relations between Dostum and the Rabbani-Massud axis remained largely dysfunctional after the fall of Kabul to the Taliban. This is also true of the period following the fall of the north in 1998. Despite his near desperate situation in 2000, Massud continued to resist Dostum's return within the framework of the United Front. When finally Massud gave way under pressure from his foreign supporters (Iran, Russia and India) and Dostum was allowed to return to Afghanistan, Massud still did his best to prevent him from re-establishing himself in the north. He steadfastly refused to support Dostum's plans to start operations among the north-eastern Uzbeks, which would have allowed him to have his rearguard covered by Massud's forces. Instead, he insisted that Dostum deploy to north-western Afghanistan, in his traditional strongholds, where he would have been isolated among the Taliban. In the end, Dostum was forced to do Massud's bidding and deployed by helicopter with a handful of men in Balkhab, having been promised plentiful supplies. Even then, Massud delivered almost no munitions to Dostum, who was unable to use Iranian money effectively to purchase weapons from such a remote location. He would later claim to have been about to succumb to the Taliban in 2001 and to have been 'saved' by the 9/11 attacks on New York.[23]

As a result of Junbesh's regionalist platform, its position vis-à-vis Kabul remained weak even after 2001. Among the Jami'atis, who in 2001–2005 were again the real power in Kabul, Dostum's relations were worst with

Fahim, who seemed intent on following Massud's path in this regard. In order to circumvent Fahim's enmity, Dostum tried to befriend Jami'atis and members of Shura-i Nezar who did not like Fahim either, such as Professor Rabbani and Ahmad Wali Massud. During 2004, as Kabul's pressure was mounting, Dostum even managed to improve his relations with his archenemy in the north, Ustad Atta, whose efforts to weaken Junbesh were clearly encouraged by Fahim. As early as May 2002 he agreed to hold periodical meetings with Atta to prevent factional infighting, following negotiations sponsored by the UN, although for another two years periodic outburst of serious fighting with Atta's men kept taking place. In fact the nadir in the relations between the two was reached in March 2003, when Dostum obtained the authorisation from Karzai to disband Atta's 7th Corps. In protest Atta resigned from the position of deputy head of the Leadership Council of the northern provinces of Afghanistan, led by Dostum himself, which had been an attempt to institutionalise a power-sharing deal in the north. In October of that year a civil war nearly broke out in the north and was only prevented by the quick intervention of a British peacekeeping force. The real breakthrough in the summer of 2004 was the consequence of none too subtle attempts by the central government to strengthen its positions in the north at the expense of both Dostum and Atta. Dostum convinced Atta that a power-sharing deal was necessary if they were both to avoid being weakened by Kabul. As a result, Atta abandoned any attempt to challenge Dostum's supremacy in the north-west, while Mazar-i Sharif and much of Balkh province was conceded to Atta by Dostum. Although Dostum and Atta were never able fully to discipline their men in the different parts of the north, localised factional conflict declined markedly after their deal, reducing the opportunities for the central government to penetrate the north. In Shulgara district, the continued fighting led to the two leaders authorising the arrest of their military leaders by the central authorities and ISAF troops.[24]

After Jami'at-i Islami's positions in Kabul started being seriously eroded at the end of 2005, the main opposition to any appeasement with Dostum came from Karzai's own circle. Karzai's own distate for Dostum was compounded by the hostility of Pashtun nationalist elements within the administration towards what they saw as an ethnic minority leader. Junbesh was still being starved of appointments in the provinces, almost wiping out Dostum's ability to rewards his followers. Gradually, Kabul became more assertive and even started encouraging officials to take on Junbesh. In Shiberghan itself, governor Juma Khan Hamdard pressured Junbesh to return buildings owned by the government to his control and replacing middle rank officials still loyal to Junbesh in the administration. In May 2007 the attempt by a weakened and tamed Dostum to use the brinkmanship card failed to impress his adversaries in Shiberghan and in Kabul and street demonstrations in the city resulted in loss of life without any appreciable wider political impact, although his popularity in Jowzjan rebounded as a result.[25]

Notes

1. Walwalji (1378), p. 43; Walwalji (s.d.), p. 39; personal communication witn UN official, Herat, April 2004; Dorronsoro (2005), p. 261); Dorronsoro (1993–1994).
2. Baigi (2000), pp. 177; 79; Walwalji (2007); interview with Ismail Akbar, Kabul, May 2003.
3. Interviews with Ismail Akbar, Kabul, May 2003; Ahmad Shaker Kargar, Kabul May 2003; Anders Fange, Kabul May 2003; Aziz Saheb Khizry, Kabul May 2003; Homayoun Fourkhabi, London Oct. 2002.
4. Hedoyat (nd); Dorronsoro (1993–1994).
5. Baigi (2000), p. 360; Dorronsoro (2005), pp. 264–5.
6. Baigi (2000), p. 367.
7. Interview with Uzbek intellectual from Faryab, London, 19 Oct. 2002; interview with Mr Homayoun Fourkhabi, London Oct. 2002.
8. Walwalji (1378), book 1, p. 61; Walwalji (s.d.), pp. 60–61. See also Giustozzi (2004), p. 15.
9. Interviews with UN official, Mazar, July 2004; UN political officer, May 2003; UN official, Kabul, April 2003.
10. Personal communication with UN officials, Mazar-i Sharif, July 2004.
11. G. Dorronsoro argues in "La Révolution Afghane" (p. 253) that Ismail aimed at defeating Junbesh, whom he even refused to meet in Kabul in June 1994.
12. See an interview with Ismail Khan, http://membres.lycos.fr/afghanainfo/IsmailKhan_inter.htm, where he recognises that 'Dostum is respected by the Uzbeks'.
13. In May 2003, for example, Ismail accused Dostum of hoarding a greater amount of custom revenues than himself, trying to re-direct the unwelcome attention of the central government towards his old rival (*AFP* 28 May 2003).
14. Personal communication with UN official, Herat, May 2004; personal communication with UN officials in Kabul, Sept. 2005.
15. Personal communications with UN officials, Kabul, Oct. 2006 and Mazar-i Sharif, July 2004; interviews with representatives of Junbesh, Maimana, Nov. 2004; interview with Uzbek intellectual from the north, Kabul, Oct. 2006; personal communication with diplomatic and UN officials, Mazar-i Sharif and Kabul, Oct. 2007.
16. This is the image which emerges from Walwalji (1378).
17. Baigi (2000), pp. 80–2, 116.
18. Ibid., pp. 110–1, 115–6; see also Walwalji (1378).
19. Ibid., pp. 211, 219; Rashid (2000), p. 39.
20. Baigi (2000), pp. 226, 233, 238, 219; interview with former military leaders of Ismail Khan and Zahir Nabizadah in Baghdis, Herat, Oct. 2005.
21. Ibid., pp. 234; Griffin (2003), p. 45; Holl (2002), p. 60, 71.
22. Ibid., pp. 135–143; Baigi (2000), pp. 256–8.
23. Interview with Indian diplomat, London, June 2006.
24. Walwalji (2007); Personal communication with UN officials, Mazar-i Sharif, Sept. 2004.
25. Personal communication with UN official, Sept. 2007.

11

JUNBESH'S MILITARY DYNAMICS

The 'demodernisation' of the army

The military force inherited by Junbesh in 1992 had included a fair percentage of regular troops, centered around 18th Div. based in Balkh province, 20th Div. based in Baghlan and a number of National Guard brigades (72nd, 76th, 73rd) based in Mazar-i Sharif and Shiberghan.[1] They had played an important role before the 1992 coup, acting as a counter-balance to the power of the militias, and could have served a similar purpose under Dostum, increasing his leverage in dealing with often recalcitrant vassals. Moreover, the militia units had been progressively transformed into hybrid units, with a large presence of regular army officers and specialists in their ranks. Bureaucracies cost money, and Dostum's perennial lack of cash led to a progressive erosion of the role played by regular troops in his army and their slow but steady replacement by semi-regular and irregular militias, who responded only to their direct leaders. The regular units were affected by the shortage of cash to a much greater extent than militias and mujahidin units, which at least knew how to live off the ground, having done so for years. The militia units had lived off salary, looting and road taxing, whereas the mujahidin groups had relied on jihad taxes imposed on the villagers as well as road taxing and looting. It is quite possible that some regular units might have gradually adopted the 'way of life' of the semi-regular and irregular formations, but they were mostly garrisoned in urban areas and often lacked the same opportunities, as Dostum was keener on maintaining order and discipline in the cities and towns. To the extent that they did adopt the way of life of their semi-regular colleagues, their discipline soon degraded and rapidly they became indistinguishable from the militias.[2]

Although Junbesh centrally distributed supplies and salaries, its military leaders were responsible to their own men. They would top up their salaries with land and road taxes and organise looting to make up for any shortcoming in supplies. Most importantly, any residual element of bureaucratic supervision within the army was done away with, as trained officers lost their authority vis-à-vis patrimonial military leaders, whose role was fully recognised by Dostum as such. This allowed Dostum to save money by doing away with bureaucratic structures, that were needed to enforce the military discipline, recruitment and training typical of a modern army. From his point of view, making military leaders responsible for recruiting and paying the troops might have looked more cost-effective. The result was the gradual 'demodernisation' of his army.[3]

Attracting new soldiers for the regular army must have proved difficult in these conditions, especially since the more comfortable alternative of joining the militias was readily available. In the militias, a recruit would still spend most of his time in their own village rather than in the barracks or in remote deployments. Forced recruitment was not a viable option for regular army units that had little territorial control. Often officers themselves were not too keen to recruit, preferring to pocket the salaries of ghost soldiers.[4]

The feeble efforts to train new troops made maintaining regular units even more difficult. The failure to create or maintain proper institutions for the training of new officers and specialists can only be imputed to Dostum. His collaborators with a regular army background would often remind him of the importance of training and discipline. In 1992 a training regiment was established under the orders of Col. Qayum, but in practice only 3,000 men of the Guards Brigade were undergoing serious training. In September 1992 the launch of a training session for Junbesh's forces was celebrated with great fanfare, then training structures were established and officers assigned to train the different units, but the military leaders resisted the introduction of such training. Apart from the Guards, the army soon adopted the way of the militias and chose not to stay in barracks, but in the villages and had to be called up for each operation, a time-consuming practice which greatly reduce the operational effectiveness of the units and opportunities for training. Dostum probably had in mind the weak performance of the regular army in the 1980s when he decided to invest few resources in training. Irregular and semi-regular fighters had proved to be more motivated on the battlefield and more apt at engaging forces of a similar type.[5] Dostum and his vassals were also hostile to the creation of a strongly hierarchic and impersonal structure of command, preferring to remain the key players in the battlefield and the only leaders with real authority, confident as they were of their charismatic powers. One of Dostum's favourite sentences was 'the commanders and the soldiers will never retreat in my presence'. They however failed to consider the shortage of charismatic military leaders to lead irregular forces successfully against the enemy. Few were the men of the stature of Dostum or Rasul Pahlawan who could enforce discipline among military leaders and prevent them from retreating at the slightest difficulty. Moreover, by early 1995 however the discipline of Junbesh's forces had already deteriorated to the point that not even the fear of Rasul Pahlawan's raging outbursts could stop a disastrous retreat. Dostum himself was by the second half of the 1990s no longer feared enough as in his new political role he had shown leniency towards his military leaders on a number of occasions.[6] The resulting lack of discipline greatly reduced the ability of Junbesh's armed force to manoeuvre in the field and paved the way for looting and harassment of civilians.[7]

During 1992 and 1993, Junbesh's military units based in Kabul, which were mostly from the regular army, performed well on the battlefield, playing a key role in defeating the attempt of Hizb-i Islami to take over the city. By late 1993 the quality of these units had already been significantly degraded, in part due to the corruption and carelessness of their commanding officers and in part to the declining number of enlisted troops. After a year and a half of little or no recruiting, some units had more officers than privates in their ranks. It comes as no surprise then that the attempted coup against Massud in January 1994 failed, resulting in the start of yet another phase of an inconclusive civil war, which contributed to the final destruction of much of Kabul. Junbesh's contingent in the capital was estimated to number 5,000 of its best troops at the beginning of 1994. Its attrition through constant fighting resulted in the loss of many officers and experienced soldiers, as did that caused by the state of continuing warfare on several fronts throughout the 1992–1998 period. Dostum himself claimed in July 2003 that the Taliban alone had killed 20,000 of his troops, 1,500 of which during Operation Enduring Freedom, although these could be overstatements. Internal conflicts within Junbesh also caused loss of life and the disgrace of several former regular army officers. The final blow to the existence of regular units within Junbesh came with the fall of northern Afghanistan to the Taliban in 1998. Some former mujahidin military leaders, like Ahmad Khan, refused to flee or surrender and continued to fight in remote areas of the countryside. In contrast, the surviving regular army officers could not tolerate the life of a guerrilla and opted for flight, losing most of whatever credibility they had left.[8]

As a result of all these trends, while initially regular army units represented a key part of Junbesh's order of battle, soon the role of former militia and mujahidin military leaders began to expand, at the expense of army officers, who were largely relegated to merely representative or advisory positions. Only the security and intelligence service continued to be manned by professionals. In 1992, of the leaders of the major military units under Dostum's orders five were officers from the regular army (including Dostum himself), four were militia leaders and only one had a mujahid background, Rasul Pahlawan. Even the latter, had joined the militia years earlier, in 1987. The picture looked completely different ten years later. As can be seen in Table 4, not a single regular army officer was left among the leaders of major units. Two of them had a background in the militia, in at least one case after having been in the ranks of the mujahidin, while the remaining four had been mujahidin until 1992. Those former army officers who continued to be active in the field were relegated to relatively small units. Gen. Majid Rowzi, for example, who had been one of the officers closest to Dostum, was in charge of the 1st Assault Unit, only a few hundred strong. Most of the regular army officers who made it to 2002 in the ranks of Junbesh occupied ceremonial and advisory positions, deprived of any real power, being in charge of training or working as deputies of military leaders with a background in the jihad movements. Four of them were military deputies of Dostum. Their selection had been carefully balanced ethnically, to show how Junbesh was a multi-ethnic regional party, aiming to represent all ethnic groups of northern Afghanistan: Gen. Azizi (a Pashtun), Gen. Rowzi (an Arab), Gen. Fawzi (an Uzbek) and Gen. Shahzada (a Tajik). Their role was evidently more political than military. Gen. Rowzi appears to have been a candidate for the command of the 18th Div., but his candidature was blocked by the Ministry of Defence and a former mujahid, Haji Habib, was preferred to him.[9]

Table 4: Commanders of the Main Military Units of Junbesh-i Melli and their background, 1992/2002

	1992	2002
53rd Div.	Rashid Dostum (militia, RA)	Lal Mohammad (M, militia)
2nd Border Div.	Zeeni Pahlawan (militia or M)	[disbanded]
70th Div.	Gen. Abdul Momen (RA)	Wali Mohammad Khel (M)
18th Div.	Jura Beg (RA)	Haji Habib (M)
511th Div.	Rasul Pahlawan (M, militia)	[replaced by 200th]
200th Div.	−	Hashim Habibi (M)
80th Div.	Gen. Sayed Zahir (militia)	[disbanded]
82nd Div.	−	Kamal Khan (militia)
19th Div.	Abdul Qudus Rahmani (M)	Ahmad Khan (M)
20th Div.	Abdul Wahab (RA)	[taken over by Shura-i Nezar]
54th Div.	Sayyid Shahbuddin (militia)	[taken over by Shura-i Nezar]
6th Army Corps	Sayyid Jaffar Naderi (militia)	[taken over by Shura-i Nezar]
510th Div.	Abdul Ghaffar Pahlawan (militia)	[disbanded]
Guards Div.	Gen. Mohammad Homayun Fawzi (RA)	[disbanded]
8th Army Corps	−	Juma Khan Hamdard (M)

Note: M = former mujahid, RA = former regular army officer.
Compiled from a variety of sources.

Dostum never relied much on regular army units to counter-balance the power of the vassals. Nonetheless, as his 'central army' gradually decayed, his leverage towards his vassals also gradually declined during the 1990s. The expansion of Dostum's own militias in Jowzjan could not match that of some of the vassals and particularly of Rasul Pahlwan's, if for no other reason than the greater demographic weight of Faryab. The weakening of the centre of Junbesh to the advantage of its periphery explains at least in part its declining strength after 1992.

Command and control

One of the consequences of the demodernisation of Junbesh's army was its growing difficulties in exercising command and control. Although Dostum's charisma allowed him to resolve or contain a number of weaknesses in the functioning of his polity, others were beyond his abilities. Similarly to feudal systems in general, one of the weaknesses of Junbesh's structure lay in the difficulty to control and mobilise the potential military resources of his allies/ vassals. Despite his military charisma, the military leaders would often ignore Dostum's decisions, making the pursuit of a coherent strategy highly problematic. This is true for example of Rasul Pahlawan, who was a sworn enemy of Jami'at-i Islami and in particular of Ismail Khan. After the conflict between Dostum and Jami'at-i Islami's Massud in Kabul and north-eastern Afghanistan had broken out, Dostum's efforts to mobilise all the military potential of Junbesh-i Milli against Massud were hampered because Rasul Pahlawan remained locked in a conflict against Ismail Khan and considered that his first priority. After the Taliban had become a threat in 1996, Rasul opposed the reconciliation efforts between Dostum and Jami'at-i Islami, which could have proved crucial to the long-term future of Junbesh. The Jami'atis, like many others, alleged that at this point Dostum had Rasul Pahlawan assassinated to facilitate the brokering of an agreement, although there is no evidence of a plot ordained by Dostum. The modalities of the killing too seem to point to a personal rivalry rather than to a political plot.[10] Dostum himself accused the Jami'atis of the job, pointing to the simultaneous onset of a Jami'ati offensive in Faryab as evidence. A number of other assassinations were also widely attributed to Dostum, rightly or wrongly, including that of Gen. Momin, who died in a mysterious helicopter crash just as he seemed to be considering switching sides to Massud in early 1994. The widespread allegations that Dostum's followers may have been involved in such assassinations clearly show the hallmarks of 'feudal' politics.

It tells us much about 'feudal' politics that even after the demise of Rasul Pahlawan, Dostum proved unable or unwilling to seize direct control over his fiefdom, the province of Faryab. Dostum endorsed the succession of Rasul's brother, Gul-i Pahlawan, as commander of the 510th Div. and appointed his half-brother Abdur Malik as provincial governor of Faryab. Dostum might have endorsed the brothers in an attempt to make virtue out of necessity, probably accepting the fact that he would not be able directly to control Faryab anyway, at least in the short term, due to the absence of a credible substitute. His attempts to exercise some influence in Faryab independently of Rasul and his brothers were usually based on establishing direct relations with one or more of their vavassors or some other locally influential figure. During Rasul's rule, for example, he tried to retain Abdur Rahman, one of his allies, as provincial governor, despite Rasul's hostility towards him. Abdur Rahman's role was probably also to moderate Rasul's arbitrariness and penchant for violence. Dostum also had relations with the network of military leaders opposed to Rasul Pahlawan and led by Abdul Qader and Abdul Raouf Sawri. Other beneficiaries of Dostum's attention were two of the key frontline military leaders, holding the line against the Taliban in 1996, Sharaf Bek and Moallem Abdul Rahim. Such tactics created friction between Dostum and Rasul, who like some other key players in Junbesh appears to have been increasingly fearful of Dostum's inclination to allying with vavassors at the expense of the great vassals like himself (see also chapters 8 and 9). It is probably because of this that Rasul started talks with the Pakistanis, fearing a move to replace him. After Rasul's death, Dostum was indeed seen by many as building up the status and power of Sharaf Bek, the vavassor of Juma Bazar (Shirin Tagab district), as the future vassal of Faryab. Certainly Rasul's cohorts were of this opinion and considered Sharaf Bek as a potential rival. They reacted brutally, launching a campaign of extermination against Dostum's loyalists in Faryab: Abdur Rahman, Sharaf Bek, Abdul Qader, Abdul Raouf Sawri and Moallem Abdul Rahim were all killed. After Rasul's death in 1996, his brothers Abdul Malik and Gul-i Pahlawan continued to oppose any reconciliation with Jami'at and also inherited Rasul's fear of Dostum's plans. As may already have been the case with Rasul, they were driven by that opposition and fears for their own safety towards a deal with the Taliban, manipulated by the Pakistanis with great skill.[11]

In less dramatic circumstances, Dostum's other main vassals too, such as Gen. Momin, Gen. Baba Jan and Sayyed Mansoor Naderi, maintained their own private agendas toward other factions, severely disrupting Junbesh's ability to operate as a coherent organisation. Naderi's military leaders would often openly disregard the orders and recommendations of Junbesh's leadership, particularly when the latter was trying to force upon them an alliance with either of the two other main forces in Baghlan, Hizb-i Islami and Jami'at. Although the leader of Hizb-i Islami, Bashir Baghlani, was allied to Dostum after 1993, he would never be fully integrated into Junbesh due to his disagreement with Naderi. As the two fought each other regularly, Dostum could do nothing else but send supplies to both of them. Dostum appointed a new chief of police (Haji Nawab) thinking that he would be well positioned to mediate between the two, but he was soon assassinated. The Naderis had also problems with Mawlawi Qudus, Dostum's vassal in Samangan, as they controlled the part of Samangan north of the river, which Qudus also claimed. Repeated skirmishes took place and this intra-Junbesh rivalry immobilised significant forces that could not be deployed elsewhere. Dostum always refused any appeal to intervene and resolve the dispute, fearful to alienate either of his key allies. In 1998, after the death of Qudus, the new 'vassal' of Samangan, Ahmad Khan, seized that part of the province under the Naderis by force. The Naderis did not accept the fait accompli, but were never able to counter-attack due to the military pressure of the Taliban pocket in Kunduz and other conflicts in Baghlan.[12]

Gen. Momin, who controlled the 70th Div. in Hairatan but also had troops in Kabul, and Gen. Baba Jan, who commanded a brigade in Kabul, were the most prominent among those Tajik officers who had sided with Dostum in April 1992. While Uzbek officers were more inclined to stick close to Dostum, possibly because of a fear of being otherwise marginalised, Tajik officers were more assertive as they maintained good relations with Massud too. Gen.

Momen had already displayed signs of independence in 1993, when he was creating new military units on his own initiative, evidently with the aim of expanding his influence. Their constraint on Dostum's decision-making was the exact opposite of Rasul Pahlawan's: they fiercely supported the alliance with Jami'at and opposed switching sides to Hizb-i Islami. The tension between Dostum and some of his Tajik officers escalated as the conflict with Jami'at approached. As came out in the open in January 1994, Baba Jan immediately went over to Ahmed Shah Massud. Gen. Momen too appears to have opposed Dostum's alliance with Hizb-i Islami, but died in a helicopter 'accident' on 5 January 1994 before his position was fully clarified. His troops were mostly incorporated into the central forces of Junbesh, but a minority based in Kabul went over to Jami'at-i Islami.[13]

The problem of command and control was not just Dostum's; it was reproduced at the next level of authority within Junbesh. After Rasul's death, Gul-i Pahlawan could not match his charisma and authority; even less so Abdul Malik, who had no charisma as military leader. They used the allegations against Dostum concerning the death of Rasul to mobilise the Faryab troops behind them, succeeding to some extent in winning their loyalty, at least temporarily. However their difficulty in controlling the vavassors emerges from the fact that they rapidly lost control over the military leaders of Baghdis, some of whom rapidly started drifting towards the Taliban despite all the efforts to rein them in. When in 1997 Abdul Malik allied with the Taliban and organised a putsch against Dostum, most of the other vassals and of the vavassors followed him, but there was also open opposition within Faryab's military class, which would have been unconceivable under Rasul. Similarly, Ghaffar Pahlawan faced resistance in Sozma Qala of Sar-i Pul when he co-organised Malik's coup. A question which arises is whether, given the context and the resources, it would have been possible for Junbesh to adopt a different, more centralised politico-military system, rather then the feudal one adopted by Dostum. In fact, a different model was adopted in practice in Samangan, where Ahmad Khan refused to decentralise his power to vavassors in the districts when he rose to power in 1998, and in Sar-i Pul from 2001, where Kamal Khan maintained direct relations with the village military leaders without relying on vavassors. Ahmad Khan's authoritarian approach was effective in securing his nearly total control over the central districts of Samangan, where looting and harassment of the population ceased, making him quite popular among the locals. But he lacked sufficient resources to expand his direct control beyond the core Uzbek districts of Samangan and this constrained his ability to exercise control and influence over the southern districts and the northern district of Khulm,[14] mainly populated by Tajiks and Hazaras. It is doubtful whether Ahmad Khan would have been able to apply his system of direct control over a significantly larger area without developing a bureaucratic structure. The example of Khulm illustrates this well. Even though Ahmad Khan seized the district from Jami'at in 1998, his hold on the district was always precarious because he did not have a local 'vavassor'. In

2002, after Ahmad Khan had re-established his hold on Samangan, all he had in Khulm was just a couple of village military leaders having posts around the town. When the Jami'atis attacked, it proved easy to expel Ahmad Khan's allies. Similarly Kamal Khan could directly control the northern districts of Sar-i Pul, but it is doubtful that he would have been able to do the same over a significantly larger territory. The logical conclusion seems to be that that while Ahmad Khan's and Kamal Khan's centralising approach maximised control, Dostum's 'feudal' approach maximised influence.[15]

The implications of such a weak system of command and control were huge in terms of battlefield performance. A good example of this is the battle of Kunduz in February 1994. Under the leadership of Gen. Abdul Rauf Bigi, the troops of Junbesh managed to occupy Kunduz, but then he lacked the authority to restrain them as they indulged in the looting of parts of the town. As a result, the local groups affiliated to Hizb-i Islami, who had sided with Junbesh during the offensive, revolted against it and caused the Kunduz operation to end in a rout. Another important and in the long term potentially fatal consequence of Junbesh's inefficient command and control was its inability to mount a real strategic challenge against its rivals, whether they were Jami'at or the Taliban. In order to mount operations beyond its strongholds, Junbesh usually needed to assemble a composite force, with contingents from the different vassals and vavassors. Because of the autonomous power of the military leaders, commanding such a mix in battle required diplomatic skills as much as charisma. Another example shows this clearly. At the end of 1996 Dostum replaced Gen. Baigi, who was such a diplomat, with Lal Kumandan, who was not, to command the Parwan front where Junbesh was trying to save Massud's forces from total rout against the Taliban. Soon the military leaders started refusing to obey Lal's orders and the front collapsed. Even under the command of a skilled 'diplomat', Junbesh's armies used to fall apart in a matter of weeks if not days. In practice only Dostum and Rasul Pahlawan were able to lead armies effectively and they could not be everywhere all the time. As a result Junbesh was mostly on the defensive strategically.[16]

Limited mobilisation capabilities

Another consequence of Junbesh's power structure was a limited mobilisation capacity. In theory, the strength of Dostum's army in 1992–1997 reached up to 110,000 men, but in practice the actual number he could field was much lower. This was in part because of the logistical and financial difficulties that such a large force would have implied, but also because of the unwillingness of his vassals to cooperate fully. For example, during his 1993–94 campaign against Massud in Kabul, one of the most important he ever fought, Dostum never fielded more than 5,000 men, mostly from what was left of the regular units. As a whole, including the troops employed on all fronts, Dostum never fielded more than 20,000 men at the same time.[17] Dostum's ability to mobilise his vassals depended on several factors, including their perception of the chances of success and risk versus benefits calculations, which were often far from accurate given their lack of education, information and the relative isolation. Changes in the situation and the spread of gossip could have an impact out of all proportion with real events and cause dramatic falls in the morale of the militiamen. It appears that radio reports (BBC, VOA, RFE) of the fighting in the north in 1997, which described Dostum as finished long before the military situation was effectively compromised, played a major role in bringing about the collapse of the frontline: from a strictly military point of view, the Taliban did not have enough men in the north at that time to defeat Dostum's loyalists if they had put up stiff resistance.[18]

His vassals had a very limited interest in providing troops for expansionist moves organised by the centre (i.e. Dostum), if their personal reward was unclear. Most military leaders were reluctant to participate also because they did not like to fight under somebody else's command. The limitations of Junbesh's military structure, like those of other warlord armies in Afghanistan, were compounded by the fact the feudal relationship between Dostum and his vassals was reproduced at the next level, between the vassals and the vavassors, and the bottom of the hierarchy too, between vavassors and village military leaders. Just as Dostum relied on a central military force under his direct command to ensure some ability to intervene directly throughout the region and outside it, the vassals maintained their own central force, which could in part be used to contribute to expeditions organised by Dostum for either defensive or offensive purposes. The difficulties that Dostum met in mobilising the resources of his vassals were mirrored by the limited extent to which they could mobilise the resources of their vavassors. The offensives of the Army of the North were mostly patchy enterprises, with a number of warlords contributing a few hundred men or even a few tens of men each. To assemble a force of just several hundreds, Dostum needed to get contingents from a number of vassals and vavassors, as well as whatever could be scratched from the waning regular units. In the battle for Sher Khan Bander (November 1993), the 300 regular soldiers that Junbesh fielded were commanded by six generals, including a political commissar and an intelligence officer. The 860 militiamen deployed for the operation followed five military leaders, of which four were generals. One of Dostum's leading generals, Abdul Rauf Baigi, was dispatched to command the whole force. These eleven generals could not muster together much generalship, as they lost the battle very easily. It appears that here, at the fringes of Junbesh's area of control, patrimonial military leaders and officers with a regular army background were all busy doing anything else but training and organising their troops. In addition to having succumbed to the need or desire to increase their income, the 'generals' were not able to establish a clear chain of command and responsibility.[19] Sher Khan Bander is also a clear example of the process of degeneration and corruption that was affecting the old regular units even at this relatively early stage.

Junbesh was better at mustering its components for collective action only when defending and the threat was primarily military in nature. His vassals would then be forced to fight, the likely alternative being their own demise. This was the case during the battle of Mazar-i Sharif in January 1994. As Dostum became aware that Ustad Atta, the leader of Jami'at-i Islami in northern Afghanistan, was campaigning against him among the former mujahidin military leaders and that Atta was getting ready to launch a large-scale military offensive to seize control of Mazar-i Sharif, he rapidly mobilised a large military force, estimated at 10,000 men, from the whole region under his control. The battle for Mazar-i Sharif ended rapidly in Atta's total defeat and many of the military leaders associated with him being captured, although he himself managed to escape.[20] The military structure of Junbesh, despite the clear signs of corrosion, was still able to work well under pressure. Ustad Atta to some extent realised that he had to offer military leaders a way out of Junbesh if he wanted to take on Dostum, but during his 1994 campaign he had naively thought that offering them participation in an Islamist-leaning ideological alliance would have been sufficient. He learnt his lessons and during his subsequent major campaign to replace Dostum as the leader of the north in 2002–4, he more effectively enticed military leaders with offers of financial and status rewards, in the end at least in forcing Dostum to a compromise over territorial control (see chapter 10).

By 2002 of course the latter was well aware of the limitations of his old 'feudal' approach. In early 2002 he sought to consolidate his control over his recently re-established militias, rapidly developing a mixed system of full time and part time militias numbering around 20,000 men,[21] a much smaller force than it existed until 1998 although still fairly substantial. Although his anti-Taliban alliance with Jami'at-i Islami was rapidly breaking up, the leverage gained with his participation in the fight against the Taliban meant that at the end of 2001 he was granted full control of 8th Army Corps, where most of his militias were concentrated and registered with the MoD. The only exception was the 19th Div., commanded by Ahmad Khan, which was incorporated into the 7th Army Corps, apparently mainly for geographical reasons. In Samangan and Sar-i Pul Ahmad Khan's and Kamal Khan's centralised systems were their own creation and Dostum was not involved (see also chapter 8), but in Jowzjan, Andkhoy and Balkh Dostum had considerable room of manoeuvre. Like the other northern militias, post-2001 Junbesh relied on a mix of volunteers and forced recruits. An estimated half of the militiamen serving at any given time were forced recruits, mobilised from the villages mostly with some form of cooperation from local elders, serving for a period of three months before being replaced by fellow villagers. The system had several advantages, apart from expanding Junbesh's ranks:

- It provided some training to young villagers;
- It forcefully created a link between villages and Junbesh;
- It established a reserve of at least partially trained men to be mobilised in times of need.[22]

Judging from instances of fighting in 2002–4, the new system was more efficient and quicker at mobilising combatants. Such improvements were the result not of an increase in institutionalisation, but rather of the replacement of the most reluctant or incompetent military leaders with a new generation of military leaders who had proven themselves in difficult conditions. This was the case of Fataullah in Faryab, Ahmad Khan of Samangan, Lal Kumandan of Jowzjan and others, most of whom had taken part in the guerrilla war against the Taliban in 1998–2001.

Notes

1. A. Davis, The Afghan Army, op. cit.
2. Walwalji (1378), Baigi (2000), Hedoyat (nd.), passim
3. Ibid.
4. Ibid.
5. On the limits of regular armies fighting irregulars see van Creveld (1991), pp. 216–217.
6. Baigi (2000), pp. 335–6.
7. Ibid., pp. 48–9, 61, 71–3, 185, 405–6.
8. Walwalji (1378), passim; *Jowzjan TV*, Sheberghan, in Dari 1655 gmt, 19 July 2003; Brian Glyn Williams, 'Rashid Dostum: America's Secular Ally In The War On Terror', *Terrorism Monitor*, no. 6, 20 Nov. 2003.
9. Personal communication with Eckart Schiewek (UNAMA), Sept. 2003.
10. Baigi (2000), pp. 248–9.
11. Baigi (2000), p. 284, 250; 'Dar Maimana chegune saqut kard', op. cit.; Malik claimed once to have agreed the removal of Dostum from power as early as summer 1994 with Rabbani and Massud (Baigi (2000), p. 308); it is not clear when he turned against Jami'at.
12. Giustozzi (2004); Baigi (2000), pp. 85–6, 101, 170–1, 364–6.
13. In spring 1993 he authorised Muawin Sher Ahmad to form a new brigade in Khulm (Walwalji (nd), p. 40); Walwalji (nd), p. 71.
14. Khulm was transferred to Balkh province in 2002.
15. Baigi (2000), pp. 250, 289, 285, 288, 364–6; interview with UN official, Mazar, July 2004.
16. Walwalji (s.d.), pp. 166–167; Baigi (2000), pp. 130ff., 272–5.
17. Estimates based on Baigi (2000), p. 288.
18. 'Dar Maimana chegune saqut kard', op. cit.
19. Asadullah Walwalji (s.d.), pp. 68–75; Baigi (2000), pp. 111ff.
20. Baigi (2000), pp. 141ff.
21. Personal communication with UN officials, Mazar, Aug. 2004.
22. Personal communication with UN official, Mazar, April 2004.

12

JUNBESH'S FAILED DE-PATRIMONIALISATION

International Recognition

Given the obvious limitations of Junbesh as a patrimonial organisation, as I described in previous chapters, and the precariousness of its role in post-1992 Afghanistan, it would not be surprising if its leadership was attracted by certain forms of institutionalisation. I shall start from that unique form of institutionalisation which is the true hallmark of the state in the twentieth and twenty-first centuries, international recognition. As already noted, Dostum was extremely keen to maintain his hold on the foreign policy of Junbesh (see chapter 7). Increasing his credibility towards his vassals was only one of the reasons pushing him in that direction. He was also seeking international recognition in order to find a more stable place for himself in the regional environment. Dostum's concern for his international image was such that he invested considerable resources in the building of a luxurious guesthouse for foreign guests. He was often criticised for this 'indulgence', but it was probably one of his smartest investments. During 1992–1998, he tried to cultivate the support of neighbouring countries and often travelled abroad, sometimes on official state visits (Turkey, where he met both President and Prime Minister, Saudi Arabia, Turkmenistan). He hosted in his guesthouse Mahmud Mestiri and Norbert Holl of the UN in Mazar in 1996–7, a delegation of US Congressmen (August 1996), a representative of the US Department of State (March 1997), as well as Iranian, Saudi, French, Russian, Pakistani, Turkish, Italian and German diplomats. He opened overseas offices of Junbesh in a number of countries, including Iran and the United Kingdom. Iran, Uzbekistan, Pakistan, Turkmenistan, Russian and Turkey opened or re-opened consulates in Mazar-i Sharif in 1992–4. As pointed out in the introduction, the chances of warlords receiving formal international recognition in the age of the 'international community' are virtually nil and Dostum was well aware of that. Indeed none of the countries mentioned above could or wanted to recognise Dostum in an official role, but at least Turkey and Uzbekistan appear to have informally recognised Junbesh as their counterpart in northern Afghanistan. Having defeated the attempts of both Azad Beg and Abdul Malik to become the darlings of the Turkish political establishment, Dostum was eventually recognised as Turkey's interlocutor in Afghanistan, although for years he faced many complaints in Turkey for his bad treatment of Azad Beg. After 2001, Afghan students seeking to travel to Turkey for study had to obtain Junbesh's endorsement before being granted a visa from Turkey's consulate in Mazar-i Sharif. Associates of Junbesh also seem to have exercised some degree of control over trade with Turkey. The relationship with Turkey only deteriorated in summer 2006, when during the rebellion of Junbesh's parliamentary group against Dostum the Turkish authorities sided with the MPs and cut off their support to Dostum. By the end of the summer, he had re-established some link to Turkey, after attempts to find an alternative leader of Junbesh had collapsed. Although far short of formal recognition, these relationships added somewhat to Dostum's diplomatic power and ultimately to his resilience. Indeed the restoration of the link with Turkey at the end of the summer of 2006 also spelt the end of the internal revolt against his leadership, although not before many defections.[1]

Dostum's diplomatic efforts in 1992–1998 turned out to be insufficient to save Junbesh, mainy because of the relatively low calibre of his interlocutors. After his return on the political scene in 2001, Dostum paid greater attention to securing international support from the key players of the day. In particular, he invested heavily in his relations with the US, by then the foremost international actor in Afghanistan, so that these were in 2001–2 unquestionably better than those of his rivals of Jami'at. Some aspects of his cultivation of American support were almost kitsch, such as the memorial he built to Michael Spann, the CIA agent killed in Qala-i Jangi in November 2001 by mutinous Taliban prisoners. However, he did much more than that and often at significant cost. Already in October 2001, faced with the impasse between Shura-i Nezar and the Americans over the support that he was receiving (see chapter 5), Dostum volunteered to share the support he was receiving with Atta as well as to split the CIA team that accompanied him. The Americans were favourably impressed, even if they continued to consider him a 'classic warlord' and a 'true opportunist'. During 2002–5, in order to maintain a good relationship with the Bush administration, Dostum repeatedly bowed to US pressure to comply with the demands of the Karzai government, even when the immediate benefits were dubious:

- in 2003 he embarked on a serious effort to eradicate the poppy fields in the areas under his control;[4]
- in June 2003 he handed over to the government the custom post of Hairatan, which as a result later stopped turning custom revenue to Junbesh and other local factions;[5]
- in late 2004 he agreed to end the threat of boycotting the presidential elections;[6]
- during 2004 he showed a greater willingness to demobilise his troops compared to Jami'at (see 'public relations' in chapter 13);[7]

- in April 2005 his campaign to be appointed to a prestigious position in Kabul ended with him accepting a mainly honorific post; the position of 'chief of staff of the commander of the armed forces'[8] was empty of any relevance unless President Karzai declared a state of war;
- on that occasion he even initially accepted Karzai's request that he move to Kabul 'permanently' in order to take up the post, clearly a ruse to keep him away from Junbesh and in northern Afghanistan.[9]

Dostum knew that the allegiance of the military leaders was to a great extent dependent on his claim to be their interface with the outside world and he boasted of his direct contacts with the US embassy.[10] Although the actual rewards of Dostum's attitude to US demands were meagre, being perceived as a friend of the US was certainly strengthening his credibility. His naïve rhetoric stressed his past and potentially future role in fighting 'international terrorism'. In March 2006 he suggested that he might be appointed as head of a special task force in charge of dealing with the insurgency in the south, in a clumsy attempt to remind the Americans of his effectiveness in October 2001. It is not clear whether he realised that the reason why the Americans continued to treat him as an interlocutor had more to do with their apprehension that he might otherwise have helped to destabilise Afghanistan, than with the old alliance against the Taliban. By 2007 there were indications that the Americans were avoiding contact with Dostum, even as far as officials dispatched to the provinces were concerned.[11]

In general Dostum was careful to maintain good relations with the UN and any international actor turning up in northern Afghanistan. Even in these cases every occasion to re-claim the old role of 'warrior against international terrorism' would be exploited. For example, in Faryab province, after 2002, his men were routinely claiming that the Taliban were once again becoming active in the area, probably among other reasons in order to justify their role and make their own cooperation with the coalition and the local PRTs worth more.[12]

Institutional self-cooptation

As discussed in chapters 4 and 10, Dostum's aspiration in his dealings with Kabul throughout the post-Najibullah period (1992 onwards) was a position of prestige and power in the government, which would have institutionalised and strengthened his role in the north. Junbesh as a movement aspired to be recognised and accepted as a national player and stakeholder. From the point of view of Dostum and his entourage, they had served the central governments faithfully until 1991 (Najibullah) and in 1992–3 (Rabbani-Massud), but still had not received full recognition of their political interests. In a sense, both Najibullah and Rabbani/Massud showed that they were only willing to accept Dostum and his militias as a military partner, not as a political one. Although Kabul could claim that Dostum lacked political legitimacy, the

argument was a thin one, since neither Najibullah nor Rabbani were particularly legitimate leaders either. The situation that Dostum had faced in 1992
was reproduced after the fall of the Taliban regime. During the campaign to
oust the Taliban regime in late 2001, Shura-i Nezar's leaders tried repeatedly
to prevent the Americans from directly supporting him and exerted great
pressure to force them to switch their support to Ustad Atta. At the time of
negotiating the Bonn Agreement, the Jami'atis and more specifically the
Shura-i Nezar group, were not particularly keen to concede a major role to
Junbesh and allegations surfaced that they made a major effort to claim exclusive representation of the United Front, trying to exclude Dostum's representatives from the negotiations. The situation was complicated by Dostum's
own hesitation in choosing his representatives, with the Uzbek nationalist
intelligentsia pressuring him to appoint one of their own. Dostum in the end
despatched three representatives to Bonn, only one of whom was finally
grudgingly admitted to the talks. Unsurprisingly, the weight of Junbesh in the
first provisional cabinet was almost negligible. Having demanded the Foreign
Ministry for himself, he was initially offered the appointment of his representatives to the Ministries of Agriculture and Mines and Industries. Dostum
complained vociferously and even threatened to boycott the new government. In the end Junbesh was given two junior ministerial positions and
Dostum was appointed Deputy Minister of Defence in December 2001—
significantly, the same position he had been granted by the jihadi governments of 1992–1993. Shaker Kargar, an Uzbek technocrat very close to
Junbesh, was appointed as Minister of Water and Electricity, while Alem
Razm, an Aimaq with a personal connection to Dostum, was appointed Minister of Mines and Industries.[13]

Dostum continued his lobbying within the diplomatic corps, allegedly
receiving (according to those close to him) a 'promise' by US ambassador
Khalilzad of being appointed Minister of Interior at the time of the Emer-
gency Loya Jirga of 2002; he was also 'promised' that his associate Enyatullah
Nazary would be appointed to the prestigious position of Minister of Justice.
In the end all he achieved was a slightly better share of ministerial posts for
Junbesh in the transitional cabinet that took charge in June 2002. Noor
Mohammad Qarqin, a Turkmen who had been among the founders of
Junbesh, was appointed Minister of Labor and Social Affairs, although at the
same time Razm was transferred to the Ministry of Light Industries, something of a demotion. Shaker Kargar was confirmed in his post. The three
ministers had been proposed by Dostum himself, who wanted to project a
better image of Junbesh by keeping military leaders away from the front
benches. Neither of the three had much power. Moreover, two of them soon
distanced themselves from Junbesh and Dostum, in order to improve their
own personal influence among his Turkmen ethnic group (Qarqin) or personal connections in Kabul (Razm).[14]

The relationship with Kabul remained problematic, not least because
Dostum's appointment as Deputy Minister did not translate into any real

power. Dostum was not consulted once while in post and there is no record of any contribution he was requested to make, except for the occasional trip abroad, such as Ankara in January 2002. Nor was he confirmed as Deputy Minister in the successive administrations formed by Karzai. The issue of his role remained open, with the US embassy attempting to mediate between him and Kabul. His greatest, if short-lived, success came with his appointment in March 2003 as special adviser on security and military affairs, with instructions to dismantle Army Corps No. 7, commanded by Atta, who refused to comply, transforming Dostum's new job into yet another merely ceremonial appointment. The move had been conceived in Kabul as a divide and rule tactic to foster the hostility between the two northern rivals and weaken them vis-à-vis the central government. After that, Kabul began befriending Atta and moving towards a policy of confrontation with Dostum, challenging his hold over northern Afghanistan through the appointment of local officials belonging to factions opposed to Junbesh. During 2004 barely a single supporter of Junbesh was appointed in any official position in the north, a development which drove Dostum again towards a more proactive and oppositional role. The end result was his candidacy to the presidential elections of October 2004, which among several aims was also meant to demonstrate his strength in the core provinces of the north and make Karzai's re-election more troublesome.[15]

It was a successful gamble and with 10% of the total votes he strengthened his position vis-à-vis Kabul. A new round of negotiations ensued, where Dostum insistently demanded the post of Chief of Staff of the MoD, which he could not get due to the opposition among others of the Shura-i Nezar group, still well entrenched in the ministry despite the replacement of Fahim as minister. The US Embassy was once again instrumental in negotiating a deal, which yet again turned out to be at Dostum's cost. He was appointed Chief of Staff of the Commander of the Armed Forces, a position that he was led to believe would imply supervisory powers over the MoD and MoI. As it turned out the position was merely ceremonial and held no real power. Sources close to Dostum expressed his disappointment, the more so since he had been required to resign as leader of Junbesh in order to take up the post. In sum, similarly to what had happened in Rabbani's time, Dostum failed either to force or convince the central government to grant him a suitable position. There were several reasons for this, including personal hostility towards him and what he was supposed to represent. President Karzai himself and a number of other key players in government were said to strongly dislike Dostum. The underlying reason however was Junbesh's weak leverage as a regionalist force, unable to compete for power in Kabul. In this regard his confrontation with Jami'at/Shura-i Nezar weakened his position vis-à-vis the central government, as it did with Jami'at-i Islami's, but Jami'at was initially unwilling to come to terms with Dostum, hoping instead to preserve its own strong position in Kabul indefinitely.[16]

After Shura-i Nezar started losing ground in Kabul and first the MoD and then the MoI began a purge of elements associated with it in 2005–7, the

relationship between them and Dostum showed signs of improvement. The
negotiations to agree on a common candidate to face Karzai in the presidential elections failed to produce an agreement, probably because under US
pressure Dostum was still more inclined to negotiate his own deal with Kabul
rather than form a common anti-Kabul front. The fact that Qanuni, the candidate of the Shura-i Nezar group, also entertained negotiations with Karzai
must have represented an additional reason why neither of them trusted the
prospects of a common front. Significantly, when in 2005 a National Reconciliation Front was established under Qanuni's leadership to contest the parliamentary election as an alliance of several anti-Karzai groups, Junbesh stayed
out of it.[17]

Dostum was not the only one in Junbesh keen to be appointed to an official position of status and resources. It is testament to the attraction of cooptation into state institutions that most military leaders, big and small, wanted
to be a piece of the action. Even Rasul Pahlawan, the most ruthless of Dostum's
vassals, had been keen to relinquish his role of a non-state actor. There are
pictures portraying Rasul in the uniform of the armed forces of Afghanistan
and he appears to revel in it (compare for example the pictures on page 178).
Before 2001, and particularly before 1992, military leaders mainly aspired to
military ranks, if for no other reason than the leftist governments would not
allow them to enter high level politics except as members of parliament. After
the outbreak of peace in 2001, positions in the ministries and local administrations were in high demand. However, because of their weak relationship
with a slowly resurgent central state, by 2004 Junbesh's military leaders found
all paths to self-cooptation closed. During 2004–2005 most of them lost their
existing institutional role, as their militia units, previously incorporated within
the MoD, were officially disbanded and their officers' ranks abolished. The
reduction of Junbesh's direct control over the provincial administration
between 2003 and 2004 was very significant, closing the main alternative
avenue to self-cooptation too. Of thirteen positions identified as key ones in
the provincial administration of Faryab, in November 2004 only two were
clearly held by Junbesh loyalists, while several other important members of
the administration maintained an ambiguous relationship with Junbesh and a
few were openly hostile to it. This picture was quite different from that of
mid-2002, when at least five of the thirteen top officials were Junbesh men.
At the district level, the influence of Junbesh was still more visible, as five out
of nine governors belonged to it in November 2004. Of the nine governors
two were Jami'atis and two were independents. In 2002, all the district governors were from Junbesh, with the exception of Kohistan, where no governor could take up his position due to the opposition of Sadat, the local
military leader of Jami'at.[18]

The figure of Fataullah, vavassor of Qaysar (Faryab) until 2004 and then
vassal of Faryab, epitomises the ambiguous position of these military leaders.
Since it became clear that his institutional role as commander of the 200th
Div. would not last, as the unit was scheduled for disbandment and probably

he was hoping to be coopted into some other institutional role, he had for some time carefully built up his position as a 'reasonable' military leader, acting like a 'real Khan'. While there were many reports of his abuses against the population in early 2002, by 2004 he had cleaned up his act and officials of international organisations in the area described him as 'a man you can talk to'. He even removed some of his more notorious local associates. The most noteworthy case was that of Salam Pahlawan, 'vavassor' of Almar district, who was involved in a number of abuses and was confronted by the hostility of the local population. After some hesitation, Fataullah authorised his arrest, contributing to an unprecedented weakening of the power of the militias in Almar. Salam's militia was disarmed and by the end of 2004 Almar was the only district of Faryab genuinely free of any militia presence. Especially after he and his fellow military leaders had taken action in April 2004 to remove governor Enoyat and his ally Hashim Habibi, and Fataullah had been endorsed by Dostum as a new vassal, there was an effort on their side to appoint district governors only loosely connected to Junbesh and with little military background, a sign of their willingness to improve their image and not to antagonise Kabul. By the end of 2004 it was plain that, far from causing trouble, the military leaders and their militias were playing a key role in maintaining law and order in Faryab, given the police's lack of resources, who were unable even to patrol rural roads. In most of Faryab, security was remarkably good given the poor effectiveness of the police, likely a consequence of the commitment of the military leaders to establish their good name. Roads in particular appeared to be quite safe. Tax collection had ceased in most of Faryab, although it is not clear whether this is due to the drought, which had been affecting the region, or whether this is a long term measure, as the local authorities claimed. In areas where the influence of Fataullah and his allies was weaker, such as the southern and south-eastern districts of Kohistan, Gurziwan and Belcheragh, tax collection continued.[19] Although Fataullah never got the appointment he hoped for, he reaped the benefits of his campaign to clean up Faryab when he was elected to parliament in 2005.

Seizing the state administration

Revitalising and occupying the remnants of the old state bureaucracy was the easiest option for Junbesh in terms of establishing an institutional framework, since it inherited both the state administration and the security services in 1992. It also involved several conflicts of interest from Junbesh's perspective. The necessary alliance with sectors of the urban strata, such as the intelligentsia and the educated, would have constrained primitive accumulation of power by military leaders. As long as these elements were uncertain about their future because of the war and their own lack of legitimacy, they were likely to maximise the opportunities for quick, dangerous and short term accumulation over slower, safer but longer term options. Moreover, institu-

Rasul Pahlawan as mujahid

Rasul Pahlawan after joining the pro-government militia

tional seizure would have also re-established a structure liable to be reclaimed by the central state once it recovered strength. Yet another risky aspect of institutional seizure resides in the assumption of responsibility for the functioning of the state structure, particularly when complete control of the state is not possible. Inevitably this creates expensive expectations both among employees and the public, which if disappointed may facilitate the reassertion of a central authority.[20] Hence warlords were inclined to seize state institutions and use them mainly for legitimising their rule, but without showing much interest in consolidating and strengthening them. In many cases existing institutions were allowed to decay. In the case of Faryab, until the fall of Najibullah, in the areas under Rasul Pahlawan's control, provincial and district authorities continued to function or were re-established after having been wiped out in the insurrections of 1980, although they had little power in matters of any substantial importance, such as policing and the administration of law. Until 1992, the central government kept trying to exercise some control over its surviving infrastructure, in order to forestall an outright seizure of power by Rasul and other military leaders. After the fall of Najibullah, Rasul seized complete control of these local authorities, appointing them directly and endowing them with even less power then before. His arbitrary actions continued and intensified. It is doubtful whether Rasul had the ability successfully to manage relatively complex political organisations if he had seized them, but he could have called on the help of his allies in Khalq[21] and Guruh-i Kar, similar to how Dostum had acted with the Parchamis. The fact that he did not shows how he rejected institutions as a brake on his ability arbitrarily to dispose of his enemies, real and perceived, and to exploit the population, while offering him little short-term advantage.

Rasul's attitude might have to do with his position as the rising star of Afghan warlordism. Unwilling as he was to accept subordination, he was compelled to expand his power as much as possible, trying to reach the critical mass needed to become a major player himself. His intermediate position in 1993–6 was extremely precarious: he depended on Dostum for arms and ammunition, but his relations with him were deteriorating and at the same time he was considered with hostility by the factions in control of Kabul and their allies. Hence he sought ruthlessly to accumulate as much power and to expand as far as possible, a task which political institutionalisation would have hampered. He was probably trying to reach the critical mass that would have transformed him into an autonomous regional warlord in his own right. Interestingly, Rasul was reported to be hoarding as many supplies as possible in his stronghold of Faryab, where stockpiles were said to be at record levels.[22]

Although Rasul Pahlwan enjoyed a particularly gruesome reputation, his attitude towards institutionalisation was exceptional but not unique. In 1998 an intellectual with a background in Guruh-i Kar, Enyatullah Hedoyat, was appointed by Dostum as governor of Faryab, with a mandate to reform the administration. He set off to recruit educated people in the administration, but faced strong opposition even among core Junbesh players like Gen. Fawzi, who were probably coming under pressure from their own constituencies within the military class. Even after 2001 local military leaders maintained an ambiguous relationship with any attempt to re-institutionalise local administrations in the provinces. Often they could barely tolerate the activity of administrators close to Junbesh, but were unwilling to yield to their demands because they were intent on playing their institutional role. It was not uncommon to see district governors forced to flee by military leaders. One particularly unruly military leader of Pashtun Kot district of Faryab, Shamal, was reported in November 2004 to have arrested two judges who had criticised him and the governor had a hard time trying to convince him to release them.[23]

In Faryab, as late as 2004, Junbesh's military leaders were still nostalgic for the days when their crony Saleh Zari (governor in 2001–2002) ran the province. Although his fellow colleagues in the administration were later to recall how he was quite ineffective and showed little concern with running the administration, military leaders still preferred him by far to people like his successor Enyatollah Henoyat, who was instead described as having been a more honest and efficient administrator, but who insisted on placing educated people in key administrative positions. From July 2004, given the now nearly non-existent ability of Junbesh to seize institutions, Junbesh attempted to work through allies like Faryab's governor Amir Latif, who was more pliable to Junbesh's demand of maintaining a degree of control over the local administration. The military leaders were not particularly bothered by the fact that Latif was not an official member of Junbesh, as he had maintained a good connection with it since the 1990s, especially through his brother, Abdur Raouf.[24] He tried to position himself as a neutral administrator, who could legitimise Junbesh's hold on the province and at the same time sell to Kabul the acceptable face of Junbesh in the form of reasonably skilled administrators. He spent his early months in office trying to get appointment letters for the district governors and other key members of the administration, after having replaced a few of them, who looked too factionally aligned or too much of some military leader's cronies. Among his new appointees a good example was Maimana's new mayor, Khair Mohammad, a former Parchami with a background in KhAD and the police, but who cooperated with the mujahidin after 1992. He appeared to have been chosen as somebody who could communicate with (almost) everybody but at the same time still maintain some loyalty to Junbesh.[25]

Due to lack of interest in Kabul in any form of compromise with Junbesh, Latif's success had been by November 2004 rather limited: just one of his proposed appointments, the district governor of Pashtun Kot district, had been formally endorsed by the Ministry of Interior. Moreover, this man belonged to Jami'at and, despite being recognised as a moderate, his appointment caused some uneasiness in Junbesh's ranks, within which a number of aspirants to official positions were becoming increasingly restless.[26]

The gradual erosion of Junbesh's presence in the state administration and in the armed forces from 2003 exposed the risks of institutionalisation by seizure: the central government was slowly reclaiming its space. Throughout 2004–07 Junbesh was increasingly forced to accept unfriendly governors and chiefs of police in its own strongholds. In the summer of 2007 Junbesh even had to accept the humiliation of returning to the state authorities the building that it had been using in Shiberghan. The influence of Junbesh and of its military leaders was now reverting to a more informal procedure. Despite the impact of DDR, the military leaders maintained a considerable degree of influence, not least because they were known to have at their disposal large unofficial militias, which could be mobilised quickly. In Faryab, the governor still had to negotiate any appointment with them. Their influence could be seen in many events that had an impact in the province. For example, in the summer of 2004, following the decision of the Ministry of Mines and Industries to commandeer all the production of the Dawlatabad salt mine and have it delivered to iodine-enriching factories in Shiberghan and Mazar-i Sharif, rather than to the local market, a protest erupted by traders and elders in the towns of the province. A delegation appealed to Fataullah, at that time leader of 200th Div. in the process of being demobilised, asking him to get the salt delivered again to the local shops. Fataullah intervened and forced the director of the mine to request Kabul for an authorisation to deliver at least part of the salt directly to the local market.[27]

As the prospect of controlling existing institutions appeared weaker and weaker, the temptation to 'go rogue' was always present. In early 2005 Fataullah had to succumb to pressure from his vavassors, who were seeking a more direct control over the local institutions, and 'appoint' one of them chief of police in Maimana. At the same time, reports started to emerge that Fataullah himself had started again to tax the population and quite heavily so, probably as a result of Dostum's rising difficulties in funding his vassals.[28]

Institution-building

The most obvious alternative to the revitalisation/seizure of state institutions was for Junbesh the creation of a strong party organisation, which could then have in part worked as a party-state. Such an option would have avoided some of the problems linked to institutional seizure, particularly any chance of reclaim by the central state, but nonetheless it still required the establishment of good relations with at least some sectors of the urban educated class. Although the provincial organisations of HDK/Watan had collapsed at the time of the revolt against Najibullah, many of their members were absorbed into Junbesh, if anything else for reasons of survival and social status. Those who accepted an official position within Junbesh's administrative structures were promised a house, a car and other benefits, in exchange for political support, and the majority did not refuse. Some small leftist parties had also joined Junbesh. Although Jami'at and the Ittehadiya broke off fairly quickly from Junbesh and Hizb-i Islami stayed in Junbesh but did not have much of an organisation in the north, there still was sufficient support to move quickly

towards establishing an organised party. From the early days of Junbesh there
was a strong lobby within it arguing in favour of the creation of strong party
structures along the model of the defunct HDK/Watan. The supporters of
this option were inevitably former members of HDK, in particular of the
Parcham faction. In the words of one of them, 'educated people need help, it
is not possible to operate without the support of a militia. We hope to change
Junbesh's way'. The leader of HDK until 1986, Babrak Karmal, was based near
Hairatan for some time after the fall of Najibullah. He was alleged to have made
some attempts to establish his own 'new' party or to have encouraged his followers to join Junbesh. It is not clear how much influence Karmal had over
Dostum. Some sources argue that Dostum, who definitely had been an admirer
of Karmal in earlier years, was under Karmal's spell, but there is little evidence
of this. Those who met Karmal came away with the impression that the man
had drifted away from politics, living in isolation in a village away from Hayratan. More likely, the influence of Karmal on Dostum was indirect, through
some of his former associates who went on to advise the Uzbek warlord.[29]

Whatever Karmal's role might have been, even if Dostum continued to
privilege his military organisation throughout 1992–1998, a serious effort
went for some time towards re-establishing and maintaining a party-state
inspired by the HDK model. As resources were limited and constraints great,
only certain elements of the party-state model could be implemented. Following the holding of the first congress in June 1992, the election of a Con-
sultative Congress, an Executive Council and a number of other councils
took place. However, as Junbesh entered a full state of war in January 1994,
the structures created originally, like the Executive Council and others, hardly
played any role any more. What was needed now was first of all an organisational structure to support the military effort and only secondarily to legitimise the leadership among the population through the provision of services.
Even more then in the case of the HDK, Junbesh's activities thereafter focused
on maintaining administrative structures. With the obvious exception of army,
police and security officers, the role of former leftists was in practice limited
to manning the bureaucracy of the proto-state set up by Junbesh and providing
advice to the leadership and local administrators, whose educational levels often
left much to be desired. None of the civilian ex-members of the HDK figured
prominently among the leaders. In this sense, it could be said that between
1992 and 1998 Junbesh functioned mainly as a tool of social control. Other
functions of the party-state, like the selection of the elites and the recruitment
and training of the new generations, were never activated.[30] The party had no
real autonomy from its patrimonial leaders. When Malik forcefully seized
control in 1997, he smoothly obtained the endorsement of the Executive
Council as the new leader of Junbesh, without significant opposition.

Even with these limited functions, Junbesh the party faced serious problems in trying to operate outside the main northern cities. This was for example the case of Faryab, where the remnants of Parcham, with whom local
warlord Rasul Pahlawan had always had poor relations, enjoyed even less

influence than elsewhere. Other political factions and cliques within Junbesh were also treated badly. Guruh-i Kar, who had his main stronghold among the Faryabi intelligentsia, maintained an uneasy relationship with Rasul in the early years of Junbesh, mainly for the sake of the common cause of northern regionalism, but split from him after Rasul's involvement in the assassination of a number of their members, whose attempts to interfere in the administration he resented. Rasul was as ruthless with the mujahidin, especially the Jami'atis. Not only did he remain bent on exterminating those Jami'ati military leaders who had refused to accept his leadership, but he remained unfriendly even with those who had sided with Junbesh. For example, he steadfastly refused to allow Karim Zary, a former Jami'ati appointed governor of Jowzjan by Dostum, to enter Faryab province.[31] The source of Rasul's hostility to political organisations was likely related to himself being an illiterate man, suspicious of the intelligentsia who represented the backbone of the leftist parties and, together with sections of the clergy, of Jami'at-i Islami. He must have perceived that he would not have been able to compete with them in terms of administrative capabilities and had no interest in the establishment of a principle of elite selection based on any criteria other than military force.

In sum, up to 2001 there was no serious move towards the symbiosis of Junbesh's rural militias and the urban-educated class. However, over time the leadership of Junbesh found better ways to exploit the leftists' skills for the development of a political organisation to legitimise Junbesh by pursuing some specific political goals. In 2002 plans to create a fully fledged party organisation re-emerged with renewed energy (see also chapter 13). Although in no way it can be argued that Junbesh rapidly became a de-patrimonialised organisation, compared to its Afghan competitors it had moved further down that road. By 2003 Junbesh was the only military-political organisation which could claim to have produced a party program and internal regulations. During 2002 and 2003, Junbesh demonstrated an ability to put forward detailed proposals on the major issues of the day and maintain a remarkable discipline in defending them. Its delegations to the Loya Jirgas (2002 and 2003) stood out as the most disciplined ones. There were occasional problems caused by some maverick figures within its ranks, but such individuals were relentlessly purged. This was for example the case of Akbar Bay, who in September 2004 issued a bellicose declaration not in line with the party policy and was immediately sacked. The de-patrimonialisation of Junbesh, however, was bound to conflict with Dostum's role at the centre of it. By 2006 the development of Junbesh as a party had reached the point where its parliamentary delegation started clamouring for a role in determining the party's policies, a major factor in unleashing the summer 2006 crisis (see next chapter).[32]

Notes

1. Khashimbekov (1998), pp. 53ff; Baigi (2000), pp. 77, 94–5, 161, 94; 'Dar Maimana chegune saqut kard', op. cit.; interviews with Afghan traders in Mazar-i Sharif, May

2005; interview with Afghan student seeking Visa to Turkey, May 2005; personal communication with northern intellectuals, Kabul, Oct. 2006. Azad Beg's house in Mazar-i Sharif was plundered by Junbesh's militiamen after he left the city.

2. Brian Glyn Williams, 'Traveling beyond the blackboard', University of Massachussets alumnus article (www.umassd.edu/alumni/commconn/travelingbb.pdf)
3. Schroen (2007), pp. 238–9, 190.
4. Personal communication with UN political officer, Kabul, May 2003.
5. *AFP*, 3 June 2003.
6. *Reuters*, 13 Oct., 2004.
7. Personal communication with UNAMA and ANBP officials, Mazar-i Sharif and Kabul, June-Sept. 2004.
8. This position is not to be confused with that of Chief of Staff of the Armed Forces, which continued to be held by Bismiallh Khan of Shura-i Nezar.
9. Interview with officials of international organisations, Kabul, March 2005.
10. See for example the interview with Eurasianet, 24 April 2002.
11. Sayed Yaqub Ibrahimi, 'The General and the Taliban, *Afghan Recovery Report*, No. 208, 27 March 2006; personal communication with diplomatic official, Kabul, Oct. 2007.
12. UN source, June 2004.
13. Schroen (2007), p. 191–2, 238; Brian Whitmore, 'Fighting Terror / The Military and The Future Bonn; Afghan Delegates Jockeying For Seats At Talks, *The Boston Globe*, Nov. 27, 2001; Walwalji (2007); Key Afghan warlords reject Bonn deal', *BBC News*, 6 Dec. 2001.
14. Walwalji (2007); interview with Qarqin, April 2003.
15. Personal communication with UN official, Mazar-i Sharif, Nov. 2003; interview with UN official, Kabul, Aug. 2004; Interviews with UN officials, Mazar-i Sharif, June 2004.
16. Interview with UN officials, Kabul, July and Aug. 2005; 'Afghanistan: Powerful Commander Gets High-Ranking Military Post', *RFE/RL*, 2 March 2005; Wahidullah Amani, Concern at Dostum's appointment, *Afghanistan Recovery Report*, No. 165, 18 March 2005; Interview with UN official, Kabul, Aug. 2005.
17. Personal communication with UN officials, Kabul, Sept. 2004.
18. Figures based on field research carried out in Faryab in Nov. 2004.
19. Personal communication with Afghan officials, Maimana, Nov. 2004.
20. See for example Edward Cody, 'In Afghanistan, Most Politics Is Still Local', *Washington Post*, 16 Jano. 2002.
21. According to the sources, Rasul Pahlawan had a good relationship with Gulabzoi, Minister of Interior in the 1980s and leading Khalqi. He later employed quite a few Khalqis in his militias (interview with UN officials, Mazar and Amimana, June-Aug. 2004).
22. 'Dar Maimana chegune saqut kard', op. cit.
23. Interview with UN official, Maimana, Aug. 2004; interview with UN official, Maimana, Nov. 2004; IRIN, 'Trial of strength as governors take on warlords', 23 Dec. 2004.
24. Interview with UN official, Kunduz, Oct. 2003; Baigi (2000), p. 64. Amir Latif had been governor of Kunduz in 2002–2003.
25. Interviews with members of the provincial administration, Maimana, Nov. 2004; interviews with UN officials, Maimana, Nov. 2004.
26. Personal communication with UN official, Maimana, Nov. 2004.

27. Sayed Yaqub Ibrahimi, 'Playing with Fire in Afghanistan's North', *Afghanistan Recovery Report* No. 256, 8 June 2007; 'State-Owned Properties Returned In Jawzjan', *Killid* (Kabul), 14 July 2007; interview with officials working at the salt mine, Dawlatabad, Aug. 2004.
28. Interview with UN official, Kabul, Feb. 2005.
29. Interview with Uzbek intellectual from Sar-i Pul, Kabul, 19 May 2003; interview with former member of HDK, who then joined Junbesh, Teluqan, March 2004; interviews with former members of HDK, 2003–2004; Elmi (1997).
30. Interviews with former HDK members in Junbesh, Kabul, Sept. 2004 and Mazar-i Sharif, Aug. 2004.
31. Interview with supporter of Junbesh from Maimana, London, Oct. 2002.
32. Personal communication with UN official, Kabul, April 2003 and Sept. 2004; personal communication with UN official, Kabul, Sept. 2004; 'Party Official Blames President for "Conspiracies" Against the North', *Thabat* (Kabul), 10 April 2004.

13

EFFORTS TO LEGITIMISE JUNBESH

Legitimisation by cooptation

Perhaps unsurprisingly at this point, Junbesh's leadership consistently privileged ways to seek legitimisation which were most easily compatible with patrimonial rulership. Dostum's efforts to build up direct relationships with local notables in Northern Afghanistan started in Najibullah's time. By 1994 such efforts had entered a new stage, in which Dostum was no longer handling the relationship with local notables personally, but was coopting grandnotables to positions of prestige (governor, etc.) so that they could manage it for him. In part the relationship with the notables was needed to take the pulse of the mood among the population, but it also served the purpose of containing the brutal character of the militias' domination of the countryside by institutionalising a relationship between Junbesh and local elites. The policy of wooing local and grand notables did not disappear with the end of the civil wars. In October 2001, when Dostum was struggling to re-establish his network, he was reported to be spending 12–16 hours a day meeting people. During 2002 and 2003 Dostum maintained extensive contacts with traditional notables, clerics and intellectuals throughout northern Afghanistan and beyond it, including northeastern provinces like Takhar. These notables would in turn help him mediate with the local population. A generous supply of American dollars helped him in the early post-Taliban days and at least for some time afterwards. During his presidential campaign of 2004, Dostum was once again busy all day meeting notables, who travelled from all over Afghanistan to be his guests in Shiberghan.[1]

The same tactic was used at the local level by vassals and vavassors, again sometimes with attempts to institutionalise a role for the local notables. After 2001 for example it became a widespread practice of military leaders to appoint local shuras, including a mix of genuine notables and cronies. Thus after Hashim Habibi was chased out of Maimana in April 2004, his rival military leaders challenged him in his strongholds of Bilchiragh and Gurziwan. After taking Bilchiragh, they appointed a council to lead the district. Of the fourteen members, four were directly linked to the military leaders, but the remaining ten were genuine local notables. In Gurziwan, a thirteen-member council was appointed, among whom none was an associate of the military leaders. Six were notables, two government employees and four members of the intelligentsia, including two former security officers.[2]

In terms of national politics, legitimisation by cooptation often targeted intellectuals and other prominent figures. During the 1990s a number of well-known Uzbek, Turkmen and Arab intellectuals agreed to cooperate with Junbesh or maintained a relatively close relationship with it, like Ismail Akbar, Enyatullah Hedoyat or Asadullah Walwalji. This however proved to be an unreliable way to expand Junbesh's influence. Unhappy about the constraints they faced, most intellectuals increasingly distanced themselves from Dostum and started to criticise him openly. Again between 2002 and 2003 Dostum managed to woo several relatively high profile individuals, not as often linked to leftist groups as before. They were mainly intellectuals living abroad like Dr Azam Dodfar, Dr Mohammad Akbar, Enyatullah Shahrani and others. But once again Dostum's relationship with the intellectuals proved troublesome. By the end of 2004 Dodfar had already switched to Karzai's side.[3]

Customary legitimisation

Customary legitimisation was another option, easily compatible with patri-monialism, that Dostum resorted to, occasionally turning himself into a sort of grand notable following the model of historical leaders. Possibly to pay homage to Uzbek traditions of strong leaders, for a while he adopted the title of Pasha and being cast as the 'new Tamerlane Pasha'. An interesting anecdote in this regard is his readiness to sponsor the production of a movie on the life of Tamerlane. According to Uzbekistani film director Ali Khamraev, Dostum promised him '20,000 soldiers and 5,000 horses' for the shooting. Dostum built up his image of first among the grand notables by lavishly distributing money, weapons and other supplies to all those who approached him during 1992–7, including in 1992–3 even the Rabbani government. His concern for his image as grand benefactor was such that he rejected any advice to be more prudent in managing his resources and continued to hand them out without much regard for how they were used or how rapidly his reserves were drying up. After 2001 the resources at his disposal were much more modest, but the principle remained the same: a journalist accompanying him in early 2003 noticed how Dostum was distributing cash among local com-munities as a way to get them to listen and to comply with his requests. The impact of Dostum's use of customary legitimisation was greatly enhanced by the launch of Aina TV at the beginning of 2004, which provided a forum for casting his image of 'traditionally styled' leader of the Uzbeks wider, without having to travel extensively. About $1 million were initially invested in the TV station, which broadcast in Dari, Pashtun, Turkmen and Uzbek and received funding from the Turkish government.[4]

His vassals were similarly making large use of customary legitimisation. Coming from a wealthy landowning family of Faizabad (Shirin Tagab), Rasul Pahlawan was well schooled in the use of the established patterns of influence and forms of legitimisation. He privileged the redistribution of wealth as a way to build up support. While there is some controversy about how much popular support his patronage earned him and his family, it was significant. Even a hostile source conceded that as late as 2004 his family still had the support of 20% of the population of Shirin Tagab. While the strength of support declined the farther he went from Faizabad, he spread his search for influence as far as the neighbouring provinces of Baghdis and Ghor. In Baghdis, as we have seen, he focused his patronage on local military leaders, while in Ghor he also had a link with a popular Pir.[5]

Public relations

During the civil war years little attention could have been paid to improving Junbesh's image. The fact that quite a few of Dostum's vassals believed that it is better to be feared than loved did not help in this regard. This was certainly the case of Rasul Pahlawan. In a context of civil war or highly competitive politics, this might well be true, as pointed out by Machiavelli. As I have shown, it was in fact not his own personal involvement in the mistreatment of civilians, ranging from rape to murder, which brought him down. Behaviour such as having a rival assassinated after inviting him for negotiations, which he did in on at least one occasion, must have been particularly damaging for his credibility as coalition-builder.[6]

Junbesh's public relations became much more prominent after the 'explosion of peace' at the end of 2001. The early hopes to have Junbesh fully incorporated into the post-Taliban government and therefore enjoy a full share of state resources like Jami'at and some other factions had already been disappointed in Bonn in late 2001 (see above, 'institutional self-cooptation', in chapter 12). The subsequent disappointment probably raised the awareness of Junbesh's need to improve its image in order to compete more effectively in the political arena. The first clear sign of heightened interest in 'public relations' was Dostum's exchange of his military fatigues for a suit in early 2002, apparently on the advice of some Americans within his entourage. Later, he would often be seen dressing in the traditional Afghan garb when receiving Afghan guests in his residence. His statements began to reflect the need to appear as a man of peace, or rather the successful warrior who wants to hang the uniform to the wall and engage in reconstruction. Starting from 2002 his statements began to include constant references to his war-weariness and his desire to invest his energies in reconstruction, in order to make northern

Afghanistan an example for the rest of the country. He was repeatedly stress-ing the importance of expanding the educational opportunities for young northeners, especially Uzbeks. In 2003–4 Junbesh actually started offering training courses in English and computing for the youth of several northern and north-eastern towns. In a clear attempt to appeal to new or disaffected constituencies, he even criticised his own role in the civil war. His party cad-res were keen to point out in interviews and speeches that better conditions prevailed in the North compared to most of Afghanistan.[7]

An important message that the 'new' Junbesh was keen to send out as early as June 2002 (Second Junbesh Congress) was that the presence of military leaders within the Executive Council was being significantly reduced, with top generals like Lal Mohammad and Ahmad Khan being excluded. At the same time, the presence of educated people and intellectuals was greatly increased, in part through the mobilisation of sympathisers of Junbesh within the Afghan diaspora abroad, but also with a return on the scene of many former HDK members and other leftists. Overall, military leaders and officers were down to a third of delegates in 2002. Similarly, Junbesh tried to keep its military leaders away from the electoral lists for the 2005 parliamentary cam-paign, although it only succeeded in doing so in Jowzjan and even that after tension within the ranks. In Takhar, where military leaders were particularly weakly integrated, the contrast between the political and military wings wrecked Junbesh. The military leader of Rustaq, Piram Qul, was the first to quit, deciding to run as an independent on a conservative platform. The more moderate Mahmoor Hassan supported the candidature of his son. Over the next several months most of the military leaders of Takhar quit, despite hav-ing aligned with Junbesh as recently as 2003.[8]

Junbesh's participation in the Karzai transitional administration also illus-trates well the new image-conscious approach. While the other organizations that emerged out of the civil wars stuffed the cabinet of ministers with their leaders and warlords, Dostum chose to send more presentable characters, who could not be mistaken for warlords. Alim Razm, despite his past as a general, never played much of a role in the civil war and was described by those who met him as 'a nice man', while Ahmed Shaker Kargar was an educated indi-vidual with no army background. Neither of them could boast of much regional support and their presence in government was meant to appeal to foreign observers and the educated middle class, as well as to the war-weary Afghan 'man in the street'. Nur Mohammad Qarqin had not been involved in the civil wars either (see chapter 10).[9]

Junbesh exploited the opportunity offered by its Second Congress in 2002 and the attention it attracted in order to improve its image among potential constituencies. For example, care was taken to point out that women made up 6% of the delegates and 4% of central committee members, not such modest figures by Afghan standards. During the presidential campaign of 2004, a decision was taken very early to nominate a woman as one of the two vice-presidential candidates. The choice fell on Shafiqa Habibi, a well known radio journalist. While promoting women's rights during the civil war could only have been counter-productive, it must have been thought that at the time of elections there were obvious rewards to be reaped. The party leadership was also increasingly keen to stress the increasingly national character of Junbesh, proudly announcing to have members in provinces as far away from the north as Paktia, Ghazni and Uruzgan. It also boasted of publishing the only Afghan papers printed simultaneously in Dari, Pashto, Uzbek and Turkmen.[10]

The biggest problem associated with Dostum's image, that is being a man of war and leader of unruly militias, proved difficult to shake off and did much political damage to Junbesh during 2002 and early 2003. He was conscious that merely cosmetic changes would not have sufficed to distance himself from his past as a warlord. During 2002 Dostum stopped justifying the behaviour of his militias as he had done in the past[11] and tried by contrast to appear intent on restraining them, especially with regard to their attacks against Pashtun communities in northern Afghanistan. These attacks had been given much publicity in the media after a detailed report by Human Rights Watch was published. In May 2002 he had the report read to an assembly of military leaders from both Junbesh and other parties and then advised them to behave, lest the 'dangerous men' from HRW took them to an international court of justice. Attacks against Pashtuns in the North nearly stopped afterwards, although it could by no means be said that militias, including Junbesh's, had stopped all abusive behaviour towards the civilian population.[12]

Dostum's public relations campaign took a major turn in July 2003, when he broke ranks with his reluctant fellow warlords and militia leaders and launched a major new initiative on disarmament. In June, during the consultations on the constitutional process, the provinces influenced or controlled by Junbesh had been expressing their opposition to the establishment of a national army, asking to maintain regional militias instead. On this point, all the other regional leaders and warlords agreed at that time. After testing the water with American policymakers and other international players, he surprised many by declaring himself ready to start the demobilisation of the militias even earlier than the rest of the country and expressing support for the new national army being trained in Kabul. He even invited on the radio his generals to start sending recruits to the new army. Many regarded his move on demobilisation as merely propagandistic and did not expect to see it implemented. In fact, despite being far more advanced than anything Ismail Khan or Fahim seemed willing to accept, in its original version his proposed demobilisation still fell short of what the UN was pushing for, as it maintained some role for the militias after a restructuring and downsizing. Moreover, Dostum's demobilisation initiative stalled during 2004, when it became apparent that the central government was not interested in appointing him to a high status job in Kabul and Junbesh was increasingly discriminated against in the local appointments. However, after he decided to run in the Presidential elections, the demobilisation campaign was re-launched. Dostum first committed himself to sever the link between militias and Junbesh and then agreed to process his whole militia force through the DDR program. By the end of 2004 his militia had formally been disbanded and his heavy weapons handed over, the first factional militia to complete demobilisation. This was a significant achievement in terms of image, even if the militias continued to exist underground—as did those of other parties. Dostum even engaged in a well-publicised campaign to 'sell' demobilisation to his military leaders: he would first offer some money, then threaten to call in the B-52s, then 'invite' the reluctant ones to his mansion and threaten to keep them there until they agreed to comply.[13]

Some of the positions which he took during the campaign to improve his image were actually self-serving, as for example when he called for non-factional police units to be sent to Mazar-i Sharif from Kabul and for a deployment of international troops.[14] Some real attempts to rein in the worst rogues in Junbesh's ranks were indeed implemented, as in the case of Aurat Zabet, a district military leader in Dawlatabad in Faryab province who had been very close to Dostum, but had an extremely bad reputation among the population. In January 2004 he attempted to re-establish his power in Dawalatabad, from which he had been hounded by Hashim Habibi (the vassal of Faryab) before his defection to the government, but faced Dostum's opposition and had to accept 'exile' in Shiberghan.[15] Other examples of initiatives taken in response to complaints from the population include:

- in spring 2004 the district governor of Shirin Tagab was replaced because he was not popular among the population;[16]
- in October 2004, following Dostum's peace deal with Ustad Atta in mid-2004, for the first time the two warlords consented to joint military-police operations to arrest rogue military leaders belonging to both factions;[17]
- in 2005 came the offer of a peace deal with the Pashtun tribal notables of northern Afghanistan.[18]

Despite these efforts, enough abuse remained to prevent Junbesh from building a better image.[19] Some of the worst behaved military leaders had gone, but enough of them were still around to represent a continuing liability to Junbesh's image. Given the situation prevailing throughout Afghanistan, Junbesh remained in any case dependent on the militias to carry out political activities. As late as summer 2004, in a province like Kunduz, where Junbesh had no overt military presence, local representatives of Junbesh were open about the fact that they had started public activities only because they felt safer after the appointment of a chief of police linked to Junbesh, Motalleb Beg. In Khwaja Ghar district of Takhar province, local military leaders opened the Junbesh office. Disciplining the militias or genuinely disbanding them was still a largely unfulfilled task throughout Afghanistan, a fact which would in any case have prevented Junbesh from taking a firm stand against its own armed groups. These difficulties highlight the main dilemma in the transition from warlordism to legitimate political leadership under international scrutiny: how to restrain or eliminate the military leaders and their men without using ruthless and illegal means, which in turn would again have a deligitimising and possible destabilising impact? To the extent that Dostum had the means and the willingness to discipline his subordinate military leaders or vassals without using violence, he would have been prevented from making full use of them by the interference of competing warlords and of the central government, always too keen to recruit his military leaders on their side, and of the international community, always ready to criticise the recourse to violence. Intervention from abroad thwarted their accumulation of power by freezing the status quo in late 2001. Preventing Afghanistan from falling into a new civil war also blocked the accumulation of power and the consolidation of a working political order. To the extent that coercion, deceit and ruthlessness are essential prerequisites for the achievement of the primitive accumulation of power, which in turn is a key pre-condition to the establishment of legitimate political leadership (see introduction), Dostum was after 2001 effectively in limbo, trapped between full scale war and peaceful/inclusive state-building. The transition away from warlordism towards a transformation of armed organisations into political parties might have had some chance of working in the presence of a cooperative central government. Kabul could have helped the transition away from warlordism by rewarding those who did better at disciplining or dismantling their militias and punishing those who did worse. The Karzai administration did exactly the contrary, most probably in the attempt to prevent the emergence of a political pole of attraction independent of the central government.[20]

Delivery-based legitimisation

Helped by having inherited the administration of the previous regime, as well as the loyalty of many of the people who staffed it, Junbesh made extensive efforts to deliver services, even during the civil war years. Educational investment stood out in a country where nobody else was doing much in this regard. During its first period (1992–1998) in power, Junbesh funded the establishment of Baghlan University (1994), the upgrading of several professional institutes to university level, the building of students' dormitories in Balkh University and the despatch of hundreds of students to Turkey for education. Such investments were of particular significance as they opened up higher education to many, particularly Uzbeks and Hazaras (in Baghlan), who could otherwise have hardly afforded access to it. Extensive public works were also carried out, including bringing natural gas to Mazar-i Sharif, the renewal of the gas pipelines in Shiberghan city and two districts, the improvement of roads in Faryab, Shiberghan and Sar-i Pol, the asphalting of some roads in Mazar and Shiberghan, the building of apartments in the main cities, the digging of wells and the building of a power line to Samangan, the starting of the Shiberghan-Andkhoy highway (which was never completed). In Shiberghan in particular the city master plan of the 1980s was finally implemented under Junbesh, leading to the widening and asphalting of roads and house construction. Service delivery appears to have been mainly the concern of the Parchami circles around Dostum and in Junbesh's administration, affecting therefore mainly Jowzjan and Balkh. This bears out the fact that urban elements were playing a far from negligible role within Junbesh, and that vassals in the provinces showed much less interest. Rasul Pahlawan, for example, tried only half-heartedly at best to deliver any public works that would benefit the general population. His main achievement was the repairing of the Maimana-Dawlatabad road, which also served his own purposes, facilitating control over that district and his economic activities there. He also tried to deliver electricity to Shirin Tagab, but the project remained incomplete at the time of his death in 1996.[21]

Service delivery remained a concern of Junbesh's leadership after 2001. The scale of their efforts was smaller, in part because the presence of an internationally supported central government in theory exempted Junbesh from such initiatives. The focus this time was on re-establishing a relatively good level of public services in the cities it controlled, mainly gas and electricity supplies. Throughout northern Afghanistan examples abound of efforts to demonstrate to the population that Junbesh was able and keen to provide services and indeed better at that than the central government. In a highly publicised move, in October 2003 Dostum donated US$800,000 towards education and the rehabilitation of Faryab province. The results could be seen a year later. In Juma Khan, for example, a school had been re-built with this money and the local district governor was keen to stress that the central government had built none. Even one of Dostum's notoriously most autocratic vassals, like Kamal Khan in Sar-i Pul, could claim to have built a road. Dostum's 'public relations' was also well aware of the importance of religious feelings and, much like his competing warlords, he spent money on well-publicised initiatives such as the rewiring of a sixteenth-century mosque in Mazar and the replanting of the gardens surrounding it. Maybe as a reminder of Kabul's shirking of its duties, in Shiberghan Junbesh paid for the renovation of the stadium, leaving to their fate roads and electricity supply, both of which were in urgent need of repair.[22]

On the whole, Junbesh's policy of delivering services was one of its most successful initiatives and appears to have been instrumental to gaining a degree of support among the urban population which benefited from them. Certainly this appears to be what the leadership of Junbesh itself thought. As soon as a deal was made with Ustad Atta in summer 2004, one of the first decisions to be trumpeted was the re-establishment of gas delivery to Mazar-i Sharif,[23] which had been suspended once Atta marginalised Junbesh in Mazar.

Participation and indoctrination

During the first phase of its existence (1992–1998), Junbesh showed little interest in involving potential supporters in its activities and remained largely a hollow structure beyond its military organization and civilian administration. The predominance of military leaders, the almost perpetual state of war, and its composite character all militated against favouring a larger participation as a means of fostering identification with the party. The left-wingers dominated the administration and the regular armed forces, but irregular forces and militias controlled large tracts of the countryside and were an essential part of Junbesh's power structure, not to speak of the fact that any hint of leftism would have left Junbesh even more dangerously isolated in Afghanistan. Any activity carried out by the former leftists was highly suspect, whether advocating leftist positions or not. The members of Hizb-i Islami were among the former mujahidin who tended to be more scornful of their erstwhile HDK members, especially in private,[24] but the general climate was strongly hostile. This contributed to dampen any interest that the leadership of Junbesh might have had in grassroots politics of any kind, and while there are no clear signs that such activity was banned or discouraged by the leadership, certainly nothing was done to encourage it either. Whatever little grassroots activity took place was occasional in character and limited to the urban centres, chiefly Mazar-i Sharif. As a result, the influence of the Karmalists and the other leftists was mainly expressed in terms of committing Junbesh to a set of minimal policies, formerly part of the leftist agenda, such as secularism and women's rights.[25] They also played a key role in whatever efforts Junbesh made to consolidate its organisation. Significantly, after the congress Junbesh started distributing membership cards, a rare hint of interest in grassroots politics. However, with the onset of full scale civil war, in January 1994, any concern about legitimising Junbesh through the creation of a credible political structure evaporated and the organisation shrank back to its core function of party-state (see chapter 12).

Things changed after 2001, when the newly found peace and the expectation of having to compete in elections led to a change of attitude towards grassroot participation. The II Congress of Junbesh (June 2002), which gathered almost 2,000 members and sympathisers, was already an achievement of sorts, given that at that stage Junbesh was still mostly a patronage-based and 'feudal' network maintained by Dostum and a few other leaders. Twelve months later Junbesh had not yet reintroduced party cards, possibly also a sign that many were reluctant to commit wholeheartedly to Junbesh as long as the political situation remained uncertain. In organizational terms the real take off only occurred in mid-2003. Until that date Junbesh had just opened offices in a few provinces outside its core region, including in Kabul. By early 2004 instead the party was already busy creating a network of offices at the district level and by the end of that year efforts to create village councils was well under way in the northwestern region (Faryab, Jowzjan). In some districts of Faryab as many as 80% of the villages had shuras by June 2004.[26]

This effort was an attempt to mobilise new sectors of the population. In particular, Junbesh started investing considerable resources in mobilising the youth, through the creation of Jawanan-i Junbesh, a youth organisation which enjoyed a considerable degree of autonomy from Junbesh itself and acted as the 'vanguard' of the party, no doubt upsetting quite a few members of the old guard. The first steps towards the formation of the Jawanan were taken in 2002, when it held its first plenum in Maimana. Even in 2003 Jawanan-i Junbesh was able to interfere in the activities of the military leaders. In March of that year it organised a large demonstration (by Maimana's standards) to stop a round of fighting between the Junbesh-affiliated 200th Div. and the Jami'at-i Islami's 24th Div… Hostilities actually ceased and the two headquarters were relocated outside the city, although the exact role of Jawanan in determining this outcome is difficult to establish. During the summer of 2004, complaints against Jawanan were widely reported among the Junbesh military leaders of Faryab province, not without reason. In April of that year, Jawanan played a key role in organising the demonstrations which led to the ousting of Hashim Habibi and Enyatullah Henoyat from Maimana. In autumn 2005 Jawanan's demonstrations forced Gul-i Pahlawan to flee Faizabad, after he had tried to oppose its establishment in that district. The rise of Jawanan's power elicited various reactions from the military leaders. In at least one case (Dawlatabad), one of Junbesh's military leaders, Wadud, forcefully replaced the elected village heads of Jawanan-i Junbesh with his own cronies, giving rise to a conflict between the two wings of Junbesh, military and political.[27]

By 2004 Jawanan covered all districts in Faryab, if unevenly. It also established its organisation in Jowzjan, Takhar, where it arrived in 2003, Kunduz, Badakhshan, Sar-i Pul, Baghlan, Samangan and Balkh.[28] Outside its strongholds in the north-west, core membership was modest. Based on attendance at the Balkh provincial meeting which chose the leadership in August 2004, the core membership of the Jawanan in August 2004 must have been around 200 in this heavily populated province. Throughout Afghanistan, the group probably counted a few thousand active members, but the organisation seemed to have some genuine life: it did not look as if the election of its heads of provincial councils were being staged. For example in Mazar the delegates were reported to have enjoyed genuine freedom of choice and opted for the most educated among the candidates.[29]

Establishing Jawanan-i Junbesh as a counter-weight to the military leaders was an effective but expensive strategy. Its cadres were paid $100 a month and its recruitment strategy was in part based on the provision of subsidised language and computing courses, in great demand in the Afghan provinces. The creation of Jawanan and other aspects of Junbesh's grassroot activities were a significant burden on Dostum's stretched finances. According to sources close to Junbesh, during 2003–4 Dostum was transferring $100,000 a month just to Takhar, to fund the establishment of party structures there, including the establishment of a weekly newspaper, as well as smooth the recruitment of local military leaders. Jawanan's activities peaked in 2004–5, in coincidence with the electoral season, but declined afterwards as less and less funding was made available from Dostum. By 2007, it was estimated that funding to Jawanan was down 85% from its peak and its activities declined correspondingly.[30]

Electoral legitimisation

The leadership of Junbesh demonstrated a keen awareness of the importance of electoral sanction as a source of legitimisation after 2001, but the party-state heritage showed in the early attitude displayed during electoral processes. During the Loya Jirga election process of May-June 2002, Junbesh demonstrated its unwillingness to take risks. On the one hand, Dostum more than any other leader of politico-military organisations was quick to accept the Loya Jirga process and he sent emissaries to the various districts to campaign for Junbesh. On the other hand, he tried to get as organised as possible in order to seize control over the selection of participants. The tools utilised to ensure the success of Junbesh were still mainly military ones, similarly to those that Jami'at and other mujahidin groups were mobilising at the same time. Junbesh's ability to bring 140 delegates from northern Afghanistan to the Jirga was therefore also due to its success in enforcing a pre-selection of candidates to the Loya Jirga, which were then acclaimed as winners without any real competition. Nonetheless, many delegates seem to have been genuinely elected. For example, Junbesh succeeded in getting some candidates elected even in areas it did not control militarily, like Takhar province, where at least two were elected, including one, Nurullah Taleqani, who was a technocrat and not a military leader. The election of about ninety independent candidates in northern Afghanistan also showed that the political climate was changing and that intimidation was no longer enough to prevent elements of pluralism from surfacing. The fact that just above half of a total of 270 delegates elected in the northern provinces were associated with Junbesh is indicative of the party's control over those provinces. In comparison, throughout northern Afghanistan Jami'at elected just about thirty and Hizb-i Wahdat ten, despite similar efforts to rule out competition.[31]

Junbesh's attitude towards the electoral process evolved over time. Perhaps having gained in confidence after the success of the first Loya Jirga, by the time of the Constitutional Loya Jirga of November 2003, Junbesh's interference in the elections was much more constrained and indirect. This resulted in a modest reduction in the share of representatives won in the five northern provinces, which was still sufficient to confirm in the eyes of the leaders that they could compete successfully, even without excessively obvious manipulations of the process. Moreover, the losses in the north were offset by increased representation from the provinces of the north-east, so that overall the share taken by Junbesh was about the same: 65 out of 500.[32]

The zenith of this conversion to 'electoralism' was the 10% share of popular vote obtained by Dostum in the presidential elections of October 2004, which was widely seen as a success. Although intimidation and manipulation still played a role, Junbesh had by now learnt to be discreet. The role of military leaders was undoubtedly smaller, but it was still far from being marginal. Their existence, however carefully ordered, was still essential if the party were to control northern Afghanistan, but it was in part replaced by the expenditure of cash. A source close to Dostum claimed that $80,000 was given by Dostum just to Fataullah for Faryab. The instinct of many middle-ranks 'appa-ratchiks' was still to rely on the security services to deal with political chal-lenges, although there were signs that security officials were becoming less and less responsive to 'illegal' requests to arrest political rivals. In one such example in Shiberghan province in 2004, the Head of the Provincial Council of Junbesh allegedly requested the NSD to arrest three local leaders of a leftist party, but the security officer refused to comply on the grounds that such a request was illegal.[33]

Dostum's satisfying result in the 2004 Presidential elections was confirmed in the parliamentary elections of 2005. His financial resources were insuffi-cient to conduct a large campaign for all Junbesh's candidates and only a limited number were well supported. Some others paid for their own cam-paign. Twenty-three MPs associated with Junbesh made it to the elected Wolesi Jirga, out of a total of 249. The charismatic character of Junbesh's lead-ership played out rather negatively in the electoral context, with an excessive concentration of votes on such figures as Dostum in Jowzjan and Ahmad Khan in Samangan. Because of the electoral system, if the votes had been bet-ter distributed Junbesh would easily have brought to parliament a few more people. The actual group of MPs elected was a mixed bag of military leaders, former party and security services functionaries and notables (see Map 13). This success was to become a major source of internal conflict in Junbesh, due to the entrenched incompatibility of electoral legitimisation with an organisation which still remained patrimonial at its core. In the summer of 2006 a rift developed over issues of leadership between the majority of the MPs and Dostum himself. Set off by the alleged beating by Dostum of one of his front bench MPs, it soon grew into a debate over Dostum's role as a cred-ible leader and his inability to control his behaviour, particularly when under the influence of alcohol. Apart from endangering Junbesh's foreign relations too (see chapter 9), at one point the rift saw two thirds of the MPs even refusing to talk to Dostum. As the MPs tried to push him to withdraw from active political life, they failed to identify a credible alternative leader. By the beginning of the autumn, as Dostum had recovered at least some external support and was buying back the support of his military leaders, some of the rebel MPs opted to make peace with him. Several definitely broke with Junbesh and proclaimed their autonomy. Junbesh's efforts to form its own parliamentary group, requiring at least 21 MPs, had already been repeatedly frustrated by the rivals' ability to purchase the support of a few of its MPs for other parliamentary groups. With the defections of summer 2006, the chance of Junbesh having its own group appeared definitely dead. The contradiction between patrimonialism and electoral legitimisation was highlighted by the different attitude shown towards Dostum by the MPs, depending on who had paid their electoral campaign. Those whose electoral campaign had been paid by Dostum/Junbesh eventually remained loyal, while the others split.[34]

Map 13: Junbesh's Elected MPs by Background (2005)

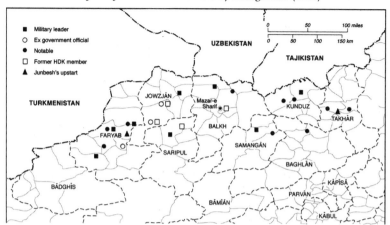

Representation: secularism

As has been mentioned above, the presence of many urban leftists within Junbesh's ranks gave them a certain influence, or at least allowed the formation of a constituency pushing for certain issues to be promoted by Junbesh. While such a constituency failed to push for a wider leftist agenda, it was instrumental in convincing the leadership to adopt secularism as a means of situating Junbesh within the Afghan political landscape. Even secularism, which could be seen as a remnant of the former leftism, was not so easy to market in the Afghanistan of 1992–2001. Initially, it is likely that Dostum and his circle supported secularism mainly in order to give an incentive to the leftists to stay, which in turn was necessary if they wanted the administration to keep running and prevent the regular armed forces from disintegrating. There was however more to Junbesh's commitment to secularism. In northern Afghanistan Junbesh's commitment had a strong legitimising effect among educated strata and the majority of the urban population. In terms of Junbesh's national role, by contrast, the secularist choice had obvious drawbacks and it might have contributed in precipitating the conflict with the Kabul.

Even at the regional level it proved controversial. Junbesh's leadership was keen on keeping the religious lobby on board too and even allowed it to leave a mark on the Constitution of Junbesh, which stated its opposition to any political set-up 'which is against Islamic beliefs'. The lobby included former mujahidin as well as mullahs and ulema, some of whom even were the beneficiaries of important positions in Junbesh's administration. Even if the majority of the ulema who supported Junbesh were 'modernists' trained under the communist regime, a number of conservatives, mainly from Hizb-i Islami and Jami'at-i Islami, were found in its ranks. However, in the war of the lobbies the Islamists lost out to the secularists. This led to the gradual departure of much of the religious lobby, but most of the former mujahidin were surprisingly at ease with Junbesh's secularism. A jihadi party whose northern membership was largely absorbed smoothlessly into Junbesh was the Harakat-i Enqelab-i Islami of Nabi Mohammedi, but Hizbis and Jami'atis were found in large numbers too. It might be that north-western clerical networks were not as conservative as in other parts of Afghanistan. By the time it had reached its peak in 1996 Junbesh had succeeded in merging the majority of former mujahidin military leaders and giving them a new Junbeshi identity.[35]

It is not entirely clear to what extent the secularist agenda was somehow forced on a Dostum fearful of compromising his alliances with the jihadis, or whether he eagerly endorsed it, which is what he claimed in later years. Whatever the case, a number of developments led to the strengthening of Junbesh's secularism over time. A key one was the influx of many former supporters of the HDK regime from Kabul, Herat and other places to Dostum's capital of Mazar-i Sharif. These migrants belonged to different ethnic groups, including many Pashtuns, who could not adapt to life under the mujahidin and feared for their safety. Another factor was the progressive alienation of Islamist groups within Junbesh's original framework, which allowed the former leftists to expand their role further. The Taliban occupation of northern Afghanistan reinforced the hostility to Islamic fundamentalism of Junbesh's rank and file and by 2002 secularism was firmly entrenched as one of the main pillars of Junbesh's identity, to the extent that any such identity existed. By 2002, moreover, Junbesh's caution about secularism had largely evaporated, because of the end to the civil war and of international intervention, and also because it was beginning to compete openly with the jihadi parties for a political space. Far from being the liability it used to be in terms of relating to other Afghan factions, secularism began to be seen by the leadership as a way to conquer a political space.

Ethnicisation[36]

The main limitation of secularism as a legitimising ideology was that it only appealed to limited segments of the population, mostly parts of the urban population. Given the way Junbesh had come into being, the acquaintance of its leadership with the Soviet model, and the presence within it of three different ethnic groups, the potential of ethnic politics in terms of mobilising support must have been clear to Dostum and his inner circle. The actual composition of Junbesh was however an obstacle to any moves in this direction. Although Uzbeks represented a plurality of Junbesh's political and military leadership, they were only modestly over-represented compared to the Uzbeks' share of the population. Many Tajiks, Turkmen and even several Pashtuns were found in the early Junbesh. Pashtuns were under-represented, but this is not surprising, given that Harakat-i Shamal had started in response to a perceived attempt to 'Pashtunise' the upper ranks of the northern zone's military. Given the ethnic heterogeneity of Junbesh in its early days, its leadership tried to shape the organisation around an idea of northern regionalism which could gather the support of all northern ethnic groups. During 1992–3 Dostum behaved as if regional autonomy had already been acquired, creating a whole range of regional institutions which were supposed to run the northern provinces as a single entity. The Rabbani government ignored these developments, if for no other reason than it would have been unable to do much.[37] Northern regionalism had obvious limitations as a political program or ideology to mobilise support. In the presence of a very weak central government, the different groups of the north were hardly motivated to create a common front against Kabul, giving instead priority to local infighting. Moreover, regionalism was a weak source of identity and even in the presence of a stronger challenge from Kabul, as happened during the Taliban's spell in power or after 2001, the northerners were more likely to split between those who sided with Kabul and those who opposed it. Indeed the regionalist option was dealt a series of internal blows with the breakaways of Jami'at, Ittehadiya and a number of smaller groups, which although beneficial in terms of Junbesh's cohesiveness, strongly deligitimised Junbesh's claim to represent the whole north. Then, with the start of the civil war in January 1994 northern regionalism became completely outdated because it would have cast any advance in enemy territory as an occupation by the north.

The need for a stronger ideological legitimisation slowly pushed Junbesh towards ethnic politics. Groups characterised by an ideological view of ethnicity were present in Junbesh at the beginning, such as Azad Beg's Ittehadiya, SAZA and Guruh-i Kar, but their influence was always modest and they soon started leaving Junbesh. They were not an important source of Junbesh's drift towards ethnicism. Dostum's efforts to secure exclusive control over ethnic constituencies and his attention to ethnic representation suggest that he and his entourage did think ethnically, but mainly in terms of analysing the political environment, rather than in ideological terms. As long as military means were sufficient to maintain control over the Turkic heartland, an openly ethnicist discourse was not needed to mobilise support.

Junbesh's gradual ethnicisation was instead a response to a set of changing circumstances. Pashtuns were mostly out of Junbesh because of the way it had emerged and because of local ethnic conflicts, particularly in Faryab, having to do with the expropriation of Uzbeks landlords under the monarchy. Hazaras were attracted towards the existing de facto ethnic party (Wahdat) before the appearance of Junbesh and had no incentive to join Junbesh in significant numbers. Tajiks were numerous within Junbesh's ranks initially, but they gradually drifted away from it. In 1992 Junbesh and Jami'at were the two only real poles of attraction in northern Afghanistan (no other groups had any resources). The leadership of the two groups was predominantly Uzbek and Tajik respectively, but the dividing line was not ethnic as much as ideological. However, local military leaders hostile to Jami'at had little choice but to join

Junbesh and vice versa, bringing with them their hostility. Much of the hostility originated in local conflicts where an ethnic element was present. Local military leaders gathered support among their own kin and solidarity group, which tended therefore to belong to the same ethnic group. Further recruitment took place at the local level through personal networks; chances were once again that recruiters and recruited belonged to the same ethnic group, although this was not a prerequisite, especially in the early stages of the ethnicisation of Junbesh and Jami'at. Alliances among military leaders and links between them and party/faction leaders were also based on personal networks, thus favouring the formation of relatively homogeneous ethnic clusters. The growing Uzbek or Tajik majorities within Junbesh and Jami'at had a catalysing effect, drawing greater and greater numbers of military leaders towards their respective ethnic groups.[38]

Until after 2001 Junbesh remained to some extent multi-ethnic. It was after that date that the changed Afghan political landscape dramatically accelerated the process of ethnicisation. The post-2001 electoral campaigns meant that Junbesh had now to appeal to 'masses' of small communities and individual voters. Finding an effective glue to hold together a movement mainly created on the basis of Dostum's military charisma, and at the same time appealing to the electorate, became an obvious problem for Junbesh. Even if the 'northern region' rhetoric was never completely abandoned, ethnic nationalist arguments were increasingly used to mobilise Turkic feelings among the population. The rising credibility of Dostum's claim to be a leader of Afghan Uzbeks could be seen already a few months into the post-Taliban era, when he received the endorsement of one of Uzbekistan's opposition parties, Birlik, which in July 2002 published a favourable report on its website, not to mention the enthusiasm that Dostum aroused in some Turkish politicians. Although there was little sense for Uzbek ethnicity in Afghanistan before the war, during the 1990s there were signs that this might be changing even outside educated circles. For example, the term *qawm*, originally meant to indicate one's own tribe or subtribe, by the beginning of the twenty-first century was increasingly being used to indicate all Afghan Uzbeks. Membership of a particular tribe or subtribe appeared to be losing importance. While this trend had much deeper causes than Junbesh's propaganda, it might well have contributed to it too. One key development in this regard might have been the gradual expansion of AINA TV's coverage to most areas where Uzbeks and Turkmen were living.[39] Looking at the outcome of the presidential elections of October 2004, when Dostum obtained 10% of the votes, it could be argued that his efforts to be seen as a candidate of the Turkic minority had been successful. Since Uzbeks and Turkmens account for about 9–10% of Afghanistan population, it appears obvious that Dostum gathered sweeping majorities among them. A province-by-province analysis of the vote confirms this (see Map 10), and his success came about despite the hostility of a large part of the northern intelligentsia. In the parliamentary elections of 2005, eighteen of the twenty-three Uzbeks elected (78%) were linked to Junbesh, two more had been so in the past. The same was true of half of the four Turk-men MPs elected.[40]

As in the case of electoral legitimisation, ethnicisation is a powerful tool of legitimisation but it is not necessarily compatible with patrimonial politics. The summer 2006 revolt within the ranks of Junbesh's parliamentary group was mainly led by the more ethnic nationalist-minded elements. The same ethnic nationalist predominated among those who excluded themselves from Junbesh afterwards.[41] By pursuing a path of ethnicisation of his political plat-form, Dostum had effectively surrendered much of his room for manoeuvre as a patrimonial leader and had aroused unfulfilled expectations. Unable or unwilling to transcend his patrimonial leadership, he had unwittingly set up Junbesh for an internal crisis.

Notes

1. Robert Young Pelton, 'Warlords, Future, More', National Geographic News/ National Geographic Adventure Magazine, 15 Feb. 2002; *Balkh Radio*, Mazar-e Sharif, in Dari 1551 GMT, 19 May 2002; Woodward (2002), p. 248; personal communication with UN official, Mazar-i Sharif, Sept. 2004.
2. UN source, Mazar-i Sharif, June 2004.
3. Interviews with Uzbek intellectuals, Shiberghan, Mazar-i Sharif and Kabul, 2003–2006.
4. See http://www.angelfire.com/ny/Chapandaz/WARLORDSORLEADER.htm, a site maintained by supporters of Junbesh. See also John F. Burns, 'Afghan Fights Islamic Tide: As a Savior or a Conqueror?', *New York Times*, 14 Oct. 1997; Sanobar Shermatova, 'Mini-Tamerlanes All Around', *Moskovskie Novosti*, 2 Nov. 2005; Hedoyat (nd.), p. 12; Baigi (2000), pp. 45–6; p. Grangereau, *Libération*, 10 Jan. 2003; Parwin Faiz and Noor Ahmad Ghafori, 'New Options on the Airwaves', *Afghan Recovery Report*, No. 105, 18 Feb. 2004; interviews with Uzbek intellectuals, Kabul, Oct. 2006.
5. Personal communication with UN official, Mazar-i Sharif, Aug. 2004; interviews with members of Junbesh from Faryab, Maimana, Nov. 2004 and London, Oct. 2002.
6. The leader of Jami'at-i Islami for Almar district, Hafiz Arbab, was killed in Oct. 1992 in Maimana while negotiating with Rasul his rallying to Junbesh.
7. Pelton, Warlords, Future…', op. cit.; Personal observation, Teluqan, March 2004; Speech in *Balkh Radio*, Mazar-e Sharif, in Dari 1551 gmt, 19 May 2002.
8. 'An American writes on NIMA', 5 Aug. 2002, www.junbish.org; personal com-munication with UN official, Kabul, Nov. 2005; interviews with UN official, Kabul, May and Oct. 2005.
9. Personal communication with BBC journalists in Kabul, April 2003.
10. 'An American writes on NIMA', op. cit.; Interview with official representative on Junbesh in Mazar-i Sharif, Aug. 2004.
11. See *Le Monde*, 29 May 1992.
12. Human Rights Watch (2002c); Ilene R. Prusher, 'Battling warlords try civility', *Christian Science Monitor* 9 May 2002.
13. *Balkh TV*, Mazar-e Sharif, in Dari 1530 gmt, 17 May 2003; 'Afghan Security Adviser Begins Disarming His Own Troops', *RFE/RL Newsline*, 1 Aug. 2003;

'Afghanistan: Dostum Defends Delays On Disarmament; Proposes New Force', *RFE/RL*, 22 Jano. 2004; personal observation, Maimana, Nov. 2004; *Libération*, 10 Jano. 2003.

14. *Balkh TV*, Mazar-e Sharif, in Dari 1650 gmt, 25 May 2003. His rival, ustad Atta, had predominant control over the city police, so that the deployment of non-factional police would have damaged him more than Dostum.
15. UN sources, June 2004.
16. Ibid.
17. *AP* Oct. 27, 2004
18. Personal communication with Farouq Azam, London, July 2003.
19. See for example Sayed Yaqub Ibrahimi, 'Villagers Flee Intimidation', *Afghan Recovery Report*, No. 157, 14 Jano. 2005.
20. UN source, Aug. 2004; UN source, Sept. 2004; Giustozzi (2007a).
21. Hedoyat (nd.), Baigi (2000), p. 402; interview with former secretary of 53rd division, London, Nov. 2005; personal communication with UN official, Maimana, Nov. 2004.
22. *Jowzjan TV*, Sheberghan, in Dari 1420 gmt, 14 Oct. 2003; M. Ignatieff, 'Nation-Building Lite', *New York Times*, July 28, 2002; Ann Marlowe, 'The Afghan Model', *National Review*, 19 March 2003.
23. Interview with UN official, Mazar, Aug. 2004.
24. Walwalji (s.d.), pp. 80–81.
25. The first official statement to the international press referred to the 'chauvinistic sovereignty of one nationality' as a cause of the revolt. See Yunas (s.d.), p. 852.
26. Personal communication with member of Junbesh, May 2003; personal communication with official representative of Junbesh in Maimana, Nov. 2004.
27. Walwalji (2007); interview with UN source, Aug. 2004; interview with Afghan police source, Aug. 2004.
28. Walwalji (2007).
29. Several of the delegates professed to have attended the meeting only out of boredom and because of the meals provided (UN official, Mazar-i Sharif, Aug. 2004).
30. Walwalji (2007).
31. Giustozzi (2007b); interview with Asadullah Walwalji, Kabul, May 2003; interview with Ismail Akbar, Kabul, May 2003.
32. Interview with Mahmoor Hassan, representative of Junbesh in Takhar, March 2004.
33. Sayed Yaqub Ibrahimi, 'Villagers Flee Intimidation', *Afghan Recovery Report*, No. 157, 14 Jan. 2005; 'Parliamentary Candidates, Voters Complain About Local Commander In Faryab', in *Erada* cited in *Afghan Press Monitor*, 17 Aug. 2005; Walwalji (2007); interview with left wing party activist, Mazar-i Sharif (5 Sept. 2004).
34. Carlotta Gall, 'Ethnic Uzbek Legislator Beaten, Afghans Confirm', *The New York Times*, 30 June 2006; Abdul Rauf Liwal, 'MP thrashed in Jawzjan', *Pajhwok Afghan News*, 31 July 2006; Interview with northern Afghan intellectual, Oct. 2006; personal communication with UN official, Kabul, May 2007; personal communication with foreign diplomat, May 2007; personal communication with Asadullah Walwalji, Oct. 2006.
35. Yunas (s.d.), p. 856; interviews with members of Junbesh, Maimana, Mazar and London, 2002–2004.
36. This paragraph is based on Giustozzi (2005 ethnicicy).

37. Giustozzi (2005 ethnicity).
38. Interviews with local notables and military leaders, Mazari Sharif, Sar-i Pul and Shiberghan, June-Sept. 2004; Walwalji (s.d.); Hedoyat (s.d.).
39. AINA also announced its intention to start covering eastern Afghanistan as well (Nangarhar), a region inhabited by Pashtuns.
40. 'World Media Reports About Afghan Uzbeks Biased', BBC Monitoring, 13 July 2002; personal communication with Dr Umit Cizre, Geneva, July 2004; Rasuly-Paleczek (1998), pp. 221–222; *AINA TV*, 6 Feb. 2005; personal communication with UN, NGO and embassy staff in Kabul, Nov.-Dec. 2005.
41. Walwalji (2007).

14

THE EMIRATE OF HERAT

ORIGINS AND GENERAL CHARACTERISTICS

A captain of the Afghan army and a Tajik from Shindand district, Mohammad Ismail Khan started his career as an insurgent when he participated in the Herat revolt of March 1979. The city garrison (17th Infantry Div.) mutinied, killed two Soviet military advisers[1] and joined the rural rebels, with the exception of a minority of soldiers, officers and party activists, who established themselves in the city's blue mosque. After the revolt was ruthlessly repressed by army reinforcements from Kandahar, the leaders of the officers' group, Sardar Jagran and Rasul Baloch,[2] went on to form an 'officers' front' with maybe sixty insurgents in an area remote from Herat. The group included Ismail Khan. His initial role was far more modest than his supporters would later claim.[3] Due to their remoteness, none of these officers played much of a role in the first year of the insurgency. The officers' group disintegrated after Rasul Baloch, who had taken them to his home area, was killed in an accident and differences emerged between Ismail Khan and Arbab Mohammad, another of the leading figures. At this point Ismail Khan withdrew to Iran for some time. Ismail Khan returned to Afghanistan from Iran in 1979, after having established contact with the growing Jami'ati network in the region, setting up a small group of fifteen cavalry guerrillas in Gulran district, not far from the border. The fighting in Gulran was not intense, as the government presence was weak and its attention rather more focused around the city of Herat and along the main road connecting Herat to the northern border and to Shindand and Farah province, as well along the road from Islam Qala on the Iranian border to Herat. Ismail Khan could not muster any additional support in Gulran, as the environment was very tribal and the local military leaders were mainly concerned with the self-defence of their communities rather than challenging the government or, after December 1979, the Soviet army. Moreover, there was little fighting among military leaders either, which made the situation very stable and offered few opportunities to an outsider like Ismail. By early 1980 Ismail Khan had moved from

Gulran. He approached other military leaders, asking them to allow him and his small band of fifteen to operate in their areas. Military leaders from Enjil, an area of comparatively intense anti-government fighting, allowed him to establish his base in Telab village.[4]

Ismail Khan's career really started to take off when he was selected as provincial leader of Jami'at-i Islami. The dominant dynamics of Ismail Khan's rise pertain therefore to insurgent warlordism. In 1981–82 the leader (Amir) of Jami'at in Herat was Mir Ali Khan Jamju, who had been chosen because of his reputation as a brave military leader and because he led one of the largest groups (numbering a few hundred men). He was coming under growing pressure as his obvious limitations as a leader in terms of organisational and management skills became apparent, as well as in terms of upgrading the tactical skills of the insurgents facing the Soviet Army. He asked to be replaced and offered the post to a member of the old group of mutinous officers, Alauddin Khan, who refused it. He then offered it to the other prominent former officer in the Jami'at-i Islami's ranks, Ismail Khan. Ismail Khan refused his offer too, arguing that with just fifteen men under his command, he would have been unable to exercise real authority. At this point Ali Khan promised to place his own men under Ismail Khan's direct authority and Ismail Khan accepted the post, becoming Amir. From this point onwards Ismail Khan's strength grew significantly. An important step was Ali Khan's death, who was assassinated in 1985. Ali Khan's brother switched to the government side after the assassination, but most of Ali Khan's men remained under Ismail Khan's exclusive control and for the first time he was leading a relatively large group of mujahidin.[5]

Not long after having been appointed Amir, Ismail Khan set out to form something resembling a proper military organization, as opposed to the anarchy large or small armed bands which were proving ineffective against the Soviet army and its Afghan clients. Because the main roads ran mostly through flat terrain, the opportunities for an ambush based guerrilla warfare against supply convoys were limited. The argument in favour of the new system was that if the jihad were to hurt the Soviets and the government, it had to bring the war to the outskirts of Herat and fight with determination. He used his experience as an army officer as model. He tried to build a system based on centrally imposed discipline (as opposed to the locally enforced discipline characteristic of guerrilla movements), complemented by some elements of a civilian administration to support the military effort (see following chapters).

For all his interest in establishing a civilian administration, Ismail Khan always remained committed to an extreme patrimonialist model, never showing any sympathy towards the intelligentsia of any colour. One of his most famous statements runs 'one obedient non-educated person is better than 100 disobedient intellectuals'.[6] Consequently, his relationship with the city of Herat was bereft of contacts with the local intelligentsia, even if he built relations with the business community and greatly appreciated the importance of

Herat as a prestigious 'capital'. This would be reflected in the weak profes-sionalisation of the administration (and of the army) once Ismail Khan became effectively ruler of Herat from 1992. He had weak roots in Herat city itself, to the extent that he preferred to employ people from regions remote from Herat as advisers and lieutenants.[7]

He relied on discipline to a much greater extent than Dostum, whose approach was based on personally wooing military leaders to join him as loosely subordinated vassals and vavassors and treated them as peers or 'friends' rather than as subjects. Ismail Khan lacked such charismatic features and was not at all inclined towards establishing a feudal-type relationship with the military leaders of Herat. Moreover, contrary to Dostum, Ismail Khan opposed the government in the 1980s and had to compete with the Afghan state to gain the support of the military class. To develop the leverage neces-sary to gather the local military class around him, he opted to rely on coer-cion and on the ideology of jihad. One of his first steps was to resort to creating a strong military organisation with himself at the centre.

Throughout the 1980s, Khan faced strong competition from a number of sources and his emergence as the undisputed warlord of Herat was far from a foregone conclusion. Hizb-i Islami controlled large pockets of territory in Shindand, east of Herat city and near the border with Turkmenistan. Jami'ati groups hostile to Ismail Khan, such as the Niazi and the Afzali fronts, had commanders scattered throughout the region. Mahaz-i Milli had tribal back-ing in areas populated by Pashtuns, while Haraqat-i Enqelab had considerable support among the clergy. Shiite groups were receiving help from Iran and operated along the border and around Herat city. Moreover, from the mid-1980s onwards a growing slice of territory around Herat city was under the control of pro-government militias. On the fringes of the region Ismail Khan faced potential competitors for influence and even potential enemies. In Faryab, Rasul Pahlawan was a powerful military leader with thousands of men at his disposal. Worst of all, even military leaders formally under Ismail Khan's orders often cooperated with him only reluctantly.[8] There was in Ismail Khan's rise a strong element of evolutionary warlordism too, in combination with insurgent warlordism.

The challenges faced by Ismail Khan when he started expanding his influ-ence beyond Herat province were even greater. The military leaders of the province of Baghdis, even when in theory aligned with him, had not been effectively incorporated into the Emirate and were far from dependable. Khan's control over Nimruz and Farah was even more patchy. The mostly tribal (Pashtun or Baluch) strongmen operating in these two provinces were very fragmented politically and especially in Farah only a minority had any-thing to do with the Emirate. This failure to develop durable relationships with the military class appears to have been related to Ismail Khan's rejection of a feudal model and his insistence in imposing a disciplined and centralised system, which limited the role of the military class to obeying orders. Another key attitude of Ismail Khan was his reluctance to establish relations with the central government. While this was easy to explain until 1992, even after his conquest of Herat Ismail opted to keep Kabul very much at arm's length... This was a major weakness on Ismail's side, a strategical cul de sac, except in the unrealistic case of a total and unrecoverable collapse of the Afghan state. His position in this regard was even weaker than Junbesh's regionalism, as the latter at least formulated a hypothetical solution, such as the federalist reform of the state, however slim the chances of this being adopted may have been.

A possible explanation for Ismail Khan's lack of any strategy aimed at reconciling his power in Herat with the national set-up could be that at the back of his mind he planned to use his Herat base to become a key national player. His first attempt to raise his profile nationally was launched in the mid-1980s as a from of major public relations campaign, which culminated in July 1987 in the convocation of a meeting in Ghor province of military leaders from all of Afghanistan. The twelve day long meeting saw an attendance of 1,200 and effectively launched Ismail Khan for the first time as a national figure, although it changed little in his relationship with local military leaders. Later, he tried again to raise his profile with the 1993 expedition to smash the militias of Lashkargah and by organising the Ghazni meeting in April 1994, where he tried to claim a key role in mobilising a jihad against the Junbesh-Wahdat-Hizb-i Islami alliance.[9] The remote location of Ismail Khan's power base compared to Kabul meant that, in the absence of a strategy of alliance with players in the capital's politics, his chances of becoming a national player were doomed from the beginning.

Paradoxal as it may seem, the dynamics of orphan warlordism too played a role in the rise of Ismail Khan, as a result of a dramatic and unforeseen change in the international environment. By 1991 he was on the verge of defeat, with most of the province's mujahidin having crossed over to the government. Officials serving in Herat at that time estimate that at least 40,000 militiamen were actually fighting on the government side, a figure confirmed by sources close to Ismail Khan and Russian sources too (see also chapter 3). These militias had the upper hand in the area around Herat city and the main highways (see Map 14). By contrast, at its peak Ismail Khan's organisation had no more than 2,000 core fighters, plus as many as another 13,000 more loosely connected to it. Moreover, these were spread much wider than the militias. Only about 6,000 were based around the city.[10]

In May 1991 the leftist regime mobilised its resources in the province and launched a major offensive under the leadership of Gen. Raouf Baigi against Ismail Khan's main remaining stronghold around Herat, the district of Zindajan. The pro-government forces succeeded in inflicting severe casualties on the mujahidin and surrounded Ismail Khan. Then, for the following ten months, they besieged him in Zendajan, as the militias halted their advance and formed a perimeter around the besieged areas, having laid minefields for self-protection. Finally, at the beginning of 1992, the siege was lifted and Ismail Khan could claim his greatest victory, even if little fighting had occurred at all after the first few weeks. The outcome of the offensive was

Map 14: Spread of the Militias at Their Peak, 1991

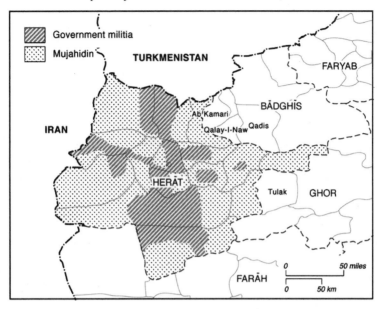

likely connected to changes taking place in the Soviet Union, which was approaching its deathknell. As Russian president Boris Yeltsin manoeuvred to sideline Soviet president Gorbachev, he also moved to take over foreign policy, appointing vice-president and Afghan veteran Alexander Rutskoi to manage Afghan policy. Regarding Najibullah as a creature of the KGB and wanting to mark a difference from the Gorbachev era, the Yeltsin team moved to find new partners both within the Watan party and the mujahidin. Although the actual impact of these changes on Herat remains fully to be assessed, it may well be that an informal coalition was formed at that time between elements in Kabul and Ismail Khan, with Moscow's intercession. Gen. Baigi was replaced as the Zindajan offensive was still going on by Gen. Asif Delaware, who would later emerge as a key ally of Ahmad Shah Massud and Rabbani in Kabul. With Delaware in charge, the offensive stopped and ended in the siege being lifted.[11]

The battle of Zindajan was of crucial importance because it gave Ismail Khan the military legitimacy that he had never really enjoyed before. He was able to present it as the result of his military skills, rather than as the result of negotiations and of a changing international environment. As a result, he could gather around himself most of the military leaders of Herat, at least for a certain time. Perhaps more importantly, the same factors which saved him in 1991 continued to operate in April 1992, when Najibullah's regime collapsed. In 1992, HDK officials in the city who had contacts with Ismail Khan opted to hand power over to him rather than to a coalition of Hizb-i Islami and militias that had support from some other elements within the HDK in Kabul. In this sense Ismail Khan's position in 1992 resembled that of orphan warlord Dostum in northern Afghanistan, having inherited much of the state structure in Herat.[12]

Notes

1. Kraznaya Zvezda, 18 Nov. 1989. According to the official record of Soviet casualties in Afghanistan, released after the war, a total of five advisers were killed in Afghanistan in 1979 (see Lyakhovski (1995), appendix 14), but it is not clear whether the figure includes civilian advisers or not. A number of family members might also have perished in the revolt. According to Cpt. Mohammad Omar Zarif, who was in Herat at that time, three or four advisers were killed together with their wives (Nabi Azimi (1998), p. 190). According to Rodric Braithwaite, the former Soviet officers 'in a position to know' whom he interviewed tend to support Omar's view (personal communication, Dec. 2007).
2. They might correspond to Sardar Khan and Ghulam Rasul Khan, identified as the leaders of the uprising by Gilles Dorronsoro, although the ranks do not correspond. See Dorronsoro (2005), p. 99.
3. This description of the revolt of Herat is based on Dorronsoro (2005) and interviews carried in Herat, Sept.–Oct. 2005.
4. Interviews with former mujahidin military leaders, militia commanders, members of the intelligentsia and government officials, Herat province, Sept.–Oct. 2005.
5. Interviews with former mujahidin military leaders, militia commanders, members of the intelligentsia and government officials, Herat province, Sept.–Oct. 2005; Dorronsoro (2005), p. 126.
6. Interview with Zahir Azimi, Kabul, Oct. 2005.
7. Dorronsoro (2005), p. 127.
8. See Giustozzi (2007e).
9. Baigi (2000), p. 147.
10. Interview with former official of HDK in charge of recruiting militias, Herat, Oct. 2005; Oleg Kulakov (2003), p. 83; Lyakhovskii (1995), p. 221; interview with former member of the Azfali front, Herat, Oct. 2005; Grachev (1998). Ismail Khan himself has been reported to have estimated the number of militiamen in Herat at 20,000 as early as 1987–1988. See Nojumi (2002), p. 76.
11. Interviews with former government officials, Herat, Sept.–Oct. 2005.
12. Interviews with former comamnders, Herat, Sept.–Oct. 2005; interview with notable from Obeh, Herat Oct. 2005.

15

ISMAIL KHAN'S LEADERSHIP ROLE

The role of Ismail Khan within the Emirate was evidently crucial, to an even greater extent than Dostum was to northern warlordism. Ismail Khan shaped the Emirate in his own image, allowing little space to collaborators and allies and giving it an administrative structure long before the conquest of Herat. The pronounced patrimonial character of the Emirate was the result of Ismail's own personality and desire to exercise control over every minute aspect of the functioning of its machinery, as well as a consequence of a political culture which did not put much store by the role of political organisations. During the jihad, his ability to control remote parts of the region under his influence was limited and he was forced to delegate power, but once it ended his centralising and patrimonial attitude emerged with greater strength.

One of the most common complaints against Ismail Khan from military leaders who were part of the Emirate during the jihad is that he was hoarding supplies and only distributed a comparatively small proportion of them. Before Ismail Khan received from Jami'at the monopoly over supplies, other leaders who had weapons to distribute, like Saifullah Afzali and several others who would receive weapons from Pakistan and Iran, had been distributing them on a basis of a more or less equal basis. Ismail, on the other hand, in part using the justification of having to cater for the 'crack troops' of his 'regular army' (the Hamza, see below), kept a much larger share for himself than the number of mujahidin under his direct command would have warranted. Rather than buy the friendship of fellow military leaders by giving them a fair share of what he had and incorporate them in a 'feudal' system, Ismail opted for a strategy of centralisation of patronage, using the targeted distribution of supplies in order to impose his own control on them. Military leaders who did not obey Ismail's orders would be starved of supplies and, over time, be marginalised from the jihad. The supplies withheld from 'bad *kumandanha*' could then be used to reward the 'good' (or complying) ones. Moreover, by hoarding supplies Ismail Khan was able to divert them to areas of particularly intense fighting or particular strategic concern, although this does not seem to have been his primary concern.[1]

It remains a matter of discussion whether Ismail Khan was primarily concerned to prosecute the jihad more effectively, or increase his own personal power. It is likely that in his mind the two aims were intertwined. In any case, he could convincingly argue that the early model of fighting jihad, with a large number of independent military leaders operating without any coordination, would not have been able to inflict significant casualties on the enemy once the Soviet army had become a major player. Furthermore, while Ismail Khan's autocratic tendencies were alienating the military class, there are clear indications that his system enjoyed a degree of popularity with the population at large, because it implied a higher degree of discipline and better behaviour of the part of the militiamen. In this sense, Ismail Khan was able to develop some degree of political legitimacy (see chapter 16).

Ismail Khan's habit of controlling public revenues is probably the most obvious example of his patrimonial attitude during the post-1992 period. His insistence on concentrating both civilian and military power in his own hands is another clear indicator. In general the entire system of the Emirate was structured to be entirely dependent on Ismail even from a formal standpoint. Particularly after 2001, he even seemed intent on establishing a succession line, grooming his son Mirwais as future leader. One of the consequences of his strongly patrimonial approach was that much more than in Dostum's case, Ismail Khan's preference for a completely loyal administration resulted in it being staffed almost entirely by his closest followers. This had a number of implications in terms of representativeness and inclusiveness, as not only did most political, sectarian and ethnic groups feel excluded, but the military class itself felt in large part marginalised.

Under Ismail virtually the entire administration comprised Sunni Tajiks from rural backgrounds. Among the few exceptions were (in 2002–4) a handful of Shiites: the head of the water department, the head of the traffic department (who was then replaced) and the commander of the Border Forces. Hardly any Pashtuns served in it, but neither did Aimaqs, despite the latter having mostly supported Jami'at during the jihad. In fact, even the different Tajik sections of the population were not fairly represented as almost all the members of the administration came from a few communities which had provided many supporters to Ismail Khan during the jihad: Mir, Khoja, Sayyed, Agha and Hazrat. Another consequence was a shortage of qualified administrators. One estimate was that out of 500–600 first and second tier positions in the administration of Herat in 2004, less than 10% were qualified for the post. This must have compounded the negative effects of patrimonialism on the efficiency of the administration and (even more so) on its accountability and transparency. By July 2003, for example, the Statistics Office had not yet been reactivated and no exact figures were available about how many people were employed by the administration.[2]

The viability of the Emirate rested mainly on a combination of military legitimacy and the ability to provide an administrative framework. Ismail Khan confirmed throughout his period in power his abilities as an energetic

and committed ruler, although he was not as good in choosing his collaborators or in effectively supervising them—their corruption was to tarnish the
image of the first Emirate. His weak military legitimacy instead compromised
his ability to establish solid relations with the military class. Despite his origins as an army captain, he never enjoyed a strong reputation as a charismatic
military leader. There is proof of his personal bravery in the battlefield,[3] but
the majority of the military leaders did not appreciate or understand his
efforts to lead from the back as the general of a complex military organisation. He relied on the charisma of fellow military leaders, first and foremost
Alauddin Khan, for battlefield leadership. Like Ismail, Alauddin was a former
captain and had little experience of how to handle large number of men in
the battlefield. Yet he was far more popular among military leaders and combatants, who liked his more approachable manner. After the creation of the
administrative structure of the Emirate, Ismail mainly busied himself managing that. From 1992 onwards, his battlefield role was usually that of general
commander having the final word on the requests of his subordinates and
often that of commander of the artillery/rocket forces, but he did not lead
troops into battle. Nevertheless, due to his continuous meddling in the planning and conduct of military operations, he remained very exposed to the
consequences of defeat. Consequently, when Herat was lost in 1995, his
authority among his own 'commanders' was in tatters. He was subjected to
heavy and unprecedented criticism. Even those who had not broken with
him during the days of the collapse started adopting a more critical approach
towards him immediately afterwards. A major criticism concerned his failure
to cooperate with the 'officers' dispatched by Massud from Kabul to help
against the Taliban, a fact that in the judgement of many was the main cause
of defeat (see below, 'Centre-periphery and periphery-periphery relations', in
chapter 18). At a meeting held in Iran shortly after the collapse of the Emirate, Alauddin Khan emerged as an alternative political and military leader,
advocating conciliation with Kabul. At least two military leaders went as far
as standing up and fiercely denouncing Ismail, who afterwards disappeared
from public life and remained confined to his house for months, possibly
undergoing a crisis of confidence or meditating on a comeback. With help
from Iran and from Kabul, Alauddin Khan and the remaining military leaders
organised resistance against the Taliban, who were consolidating their position
by bringing in the military leaders who had been marginalised or chased
away by Ismail Khan, especially those belonging to Hizb-i Islami.[4]

The negative implications of Ismail Khan's style of leadership, patrimonial
but centralised rather than 'feudal' like Dostum's, emerged very clearly during
the anti-Taliban insurgency of 1995–2001. When Alauddin and his allies
launched their first attempt to retake Herat in mid-October 1995, attacking
from Islam Qala on the Iranian border, there was no sympathetic military
class left to be mobilised inside Afghanistan. Many had fled in exile, others
were dead, but even those still inside Afghanistan had no appetite for rejoin-
ing Ismail Khan's group. The attack was never more than a raid into enemy

territory; the fighting spread throughout Ghuryan, Guzara and Zendajan districts, but the few hundred fighters who had come from Iran did not have sufficient strength to reach Herat and in the absence of mobilisation inside Afghanistan the offensive rapidly petered out. As an absolute ruler, Ismail Khan was facing absolute defeat. Another attempt was made in April 1996 and faced similar problems. The anti-Taliban forces crossed the Iranian border in the Farah-Nimruz region and penetrated into Herat province. The fighting this time touched Pashtun Zarghoun district east of Herat, but again failed to reach the city or deal any significant blow to the Taliban, who in the end easily defeated it. Throughout the period of Taliban occupation in Herat, the only military leader who managed to keep operating around the city was Qazi Mohammad Askar, who led no more than 200 men in small scale actions against the Taliban. Significantly, he was not one of Ismail Khan's men. In the meanwhile, far from giving ground, after 1995 the Taliban even succeeded in occupying most of Ghor province, with the help of military leaders formerly associated with Hizb-i Islami, an outcome which was ultimately due to Ismail Khan's refusal genuinely to co-opt former enemies in 1992.[5]

Ismail Khan's bitter resentment against any 'interference' might also have spoiled the last serious pre-9/11 attempt to wrest control of Herat away from the Taliban, which occurred in the summer of 1996. This had been planned more ambitiously than the previous ones and involved three concerted attacks, one from a pocket of territory under control of Jami'ati military leaders in Ghor, one from across the Iranian border and one from within the city of Herat itself. The attack had been sponsored by Massud, who provided money and supplies, and had been approved, apparently somewhat grudgingly, by Ismail Khan himself, who was supposed to lead the incursion from Iran. The plan ended in disaster. Alauddin Khan, who was supposed to lead the attack from Ghor, was assassinated in Pashtun Zargoun district as he was preparing the ground for the offensive. Ismail Khan never launched the attack from Iran for reasons that are not fully clear. Some informants allege that he was unhappy with going along with a plan conceived by others and supported by Kabul, others that he assumed the plan would have failed once Alauddin Khan was killed. The planned uprising of Herat was also postponed and then took place in isolation in 2000, under the leadership of the Shiite military leader Mohammad Musa Rezai, ending in a massacre of anti-Taliban militants.[6]

Ismail Khan only fully committed himself again to the struggle once the way was cleared from challenges to his personal leadership, which was the case with the death of Alauddin Khan and the fall of Kabul in the hands of the Taliban. The attractiveness of an alliance with Massud for western Afghanistan's military leaders was now drastically reduced and some of them at least were ready to turn back to Ismail Khan, however reluctantly. Feeling more confident and given his near powerlessness, he showed even a new readiness to adopt a more flexible diplomacy and seek new friends. Although he could still not overcome his suspicion of Massud's motives, the Iranians lobbied

Dostum to let him open an anti-Taliban front in Baghdis. Junbesh had occupied Baghdis at the time of the fall of Herat in 1995, but the Taliban had moved in at the end of 1996 and the frontline was now crossing the districts of Bala Murghab and Ghormach, where Ismail Khan established himself with maybe 1,500 men. However, once again Ismail's long history of bitter relations with the military class returned to haunt him. The military leaders of Faryab were not ready to let the alliance between Junbesh and Ismail Khan blossom. One of the first acts of Abdul Malik, following his coup against Dostum in 1997, was to arrest Ismail Khan and hand him over to the Taliban, who transferred him to prison in Kandahar.[7]

In March 2000 Ismail Khan managed to escape from his Kandahar prison, apparently after bribing the guards. His efforts to prevent the emergence of other leading figures in the region during the 1980s and first half of the 1990s had certainly been detrimental to the cause of the fight against the Taliban, but proved extremely beneficial from a patrimonial standpoint when he made it to Iran to find some restored confidence in his leadership. Three years of almost unchallenged Taliban domination in Herat had strengthened the need for a leader who could gather forces again. Initially, military operations were delayed by the difficult relationship that Ismail still maintained with some old allies, but he found more willing partners among the new generation of military leaders which was emerging from the mountain hideouts. Pockets of guerrilla activity had continued to exist in the mountainous areas of Obeh, Pashtun Zarghoun, Koshk-i Kohne, some parts of Baghdis and Ghor, and Ismail Khan tried to bring such activities under his control. The local military leaders were receiving assistance directly from Massud. In Baghdis, Koshk-i Kohne and Pashtun Zarghoun the Nabizadah brothers, Zahir and Amir Shah, had emerged as the main anti-Taliban military leaders. Their background was in the Emirate of Baghdis, where their father had also been a military leader. Zahir himself had led a battalion of the Hamza in Baghdis, although he had later worked with Junbesh, both joining the short-lived administration of the province in 1995–6 and later cooperating as an insurgent with Junbesh, in particular with Fataullah of Qaysar district (Faryab) and Lal of Jowzjan. A medical school graduate, Zahir had a different background from most of Ismail Khan's men, but he did not refuse to cooperate with him in 2000.[8]

Ismail Khan's autocratic legacy was so strong that not everybody was ready to support his return. In Ghor, the anti-Taliban effort relied on military leaders such as Ahmad Murghabi and Dr Ibrahim, neither of whom had been a warm supporter of Ismail in the past. Ghor was of key importance to the anti-Taliban resistance, as it had become the logistical centre of the resistance of the interior, due to the existence of an air strip in Chaharzada. Ismail Khan travelled to Ghor in 2000 to re-establish his control over the local military leaders, but received a lukewarm welcome from Salam Khan, who had once been one of the military leaders best integrated within the Emirate. Ismail was effectively thrown out of the province after an attempt on his life. Salam

Khan, who accused Ismail Khan of having neglected him and of having with-held supplies in the past, defected to the Taliban shortly thereafter. Zahir Nabizadah, who had accompanied Ismail in the trip, was also forced to leave, a development which prevented the creation of a unified command of all anti-Taliban opposition in the west. Before being thrown out Ismail Khan managed to buy off Murghabi with a delivery of arms and money. Dr Ibra-him, on the other hand, continued to rely on Massud and until well into 2001 even refused to attend Ismail Khan's coordination meetings.[9]

Ismail Khan's limited success in re-establishing himself as undisputed leader was due not only to bad memories he evoked within the ranks of the military class, but also to the absence of a key element in his traditional carrot and stick strategy, namely the stick. Nothing was left of his regular army, the Hamza, after the betrayal in Bala Murghab (1997) (see above). He made an attempt to gather a force under his direct control in Iran, which was ham-pered by Ismail's weak military charisma. In June 2000 UN sources estimated that Ismail Khan had just 600 armed men, although according to Ismail Khan himself these had grown to 3,000 men (effectively led by his son Mirwais) at the beginning of the US-supported 2001 campaign to topple the Taliban regime. The force might have grown further to 4–5,000 men by the time of the final offensive against the Taliban.[10] Cobbled together with financial incentives and led mainly by military leaders of dubious reputation and skills, it played only a modest role in the fighting. The absence of Alauddin Khan and other charismatic military leaders was undoubtedly felt. In the end, the forces with which Ismail Khan entered Herat in October 2001 were Zahir Nabizadah's, not his own.[11] Much of the fighting inside Herat city had been the result of a spontaneous uprising in the bazaar, with the participation of the militias of Hizb-i Wahdat. Ismail Khan's modest role in the conquest of Herat in 2001 would once again affect his relationship with the military class in the following years. On the other hand, his reputation as an organiser and as an administrator, together with a promise to share power, helped Ismail Khan to convince his allies that accepting him as governor of Herat was the best option.[12]

Notes

1. Interviews with former military leaders, government officials, army officers and a relative of Alauddin Khan, Herat and London, Sept. and Oct. 2005.
2. Interviews with former militia leader and Shiite intellectual; J.M. Ledgard, 'Afghan-istan: Future Of Governor Of Herat Hangs In Balance', RFE/RL, 14 July 2003.
3. In an ambush during the 1979–1992 jihad, Ismail Khan was seen by two foreign travellers charging the enemy while his men were fleeing (personal communication with Gilles Dorronsoro, Sept. 2007).
4. Dubuis (1989), p. 147; Zahir Azimi (1377), passim; interviews with former military leaders, government officials, army officers and a relative of Alauddin Khan, Herat and London, Sept. and Oct. 2005.

5. BBC SWB, 19 Oct. 1995; BBC SWB, 14 Oct. 1995; BBC SWB, 21 May 1996; BBC SWB, 16 April 1996; Interviews with former military leaders, government officials, localnotables, army officers and a relative of Alauddin Khan, Herat and London, Sept. and Oct. 2005.
6. Interviews with former military leaders, government officials, local notales, army officers and a relative of Alauddin Khan, Herat and London, Sept. and Oct. 2005.
7. Baigi (2000), pp 265–7; interviews with former military leaders, government officials, local notales, army officers and a relative of Alauddin Khan, Herat and London, Sept. and Oct. 2005.
8. Interviews with former military leaders, government officials, local notales, army officers and a relative of Alauddin Khan, Herat and London, Sept. and Oct. 2005.
9. Ibid.
10. He claimed, quite unrealistically, 12,000 (*The Economist*, 22 Nov. 2001).
11. He entered Herat from the east, not from the direction of the Iran border. See Rory Stewart (2004), p. 140.
12. UNSMA internal document, June 2000; *AFP*, 7 Aug. 2002; Interviews with former military leaders, government officials, local notables, army officers and a relative of Alauddin Khan, Herat and London, Sept. and Oct. 2005.

16

POLITICAL DYNAMICS OF
ISMAIL KHAN'S EMIRATE

Coercive and manipulative coalition-building

Compared to Dostum, Ismail Khan's choice of coalition-building was based more on coercion, in this regard at least resembling Rasul Pahlawan, but he did not shun manipulative tactics either. A very hard worker who took no rest, Ismail Khan demanded much of his subordinates. Through his position of Amir, as well his role as sole supplier of weapons and ammunition and his control of the Hamza, Ismail Khan was also better placed than anybody else to impose his will or manipulate military leaders and turn them against each other. At the beginning of the 1980s there were several relatively large military leaders operating around Herat, some within the framework of the Emirate, some outside it, including several Jami'atis (see Map 15). Whenever military leaders refused to cooperate with him on his own terms and to accept the discipline of the Emirate, Ismail Khan would use a range of ruthless tactics, including divide and rule. This was for example the case of the Popolzai tribal front in Zendajan. Ismail Khan would deliver supplies to some of the front's leaders, but not others, eventually precipitating the front's disintegration. Ismail Khan's near monopoly over external resources was a very effective tool to force the majority of military leaders to obey him, but his tactics were not always successful. While many accepted submission, others responded by intensifying their opposition to Ismail Khan and sometimes even by fighting him. As the relationship deteriorated, Ismail Khan would resort to extreme means to undermine his internal opposition. Of the main military leaders active in Herat under Jami'at-i Islami, only Ghulam Yahya Shawshan survived the jihad, a high casualty rate even compared to other provinces (see Table 5).[1]

Some military leaders whose existence was undoubtedly a liability for the struggle against the government and the Soviet Army were also eliminated. Ghaffar Tufan, for example, had a terrible reputation and had been carrying out executions on a very large scale until his own death. Some of the military leaders who were eliminated had already joined the government militias, so that again this could be seen as a service to the cause of jihad. Among them the most prominent was Sayyed Ahmad.

A few military leaders managed to maintain their autonomy regardless. Apart from the ideologically-driven Niazi and Afzali Islamist fronts, Ghulam Yahya Shawshan was the most important military leader of Jami'at never to join the Emirate. He followed the example of Ismail Khan and created his

Table 5: Deaths of Jami'ati Military Leaders

Name of military leader	Area of activity	Fate
Kamal Gulbagaz	Enjil	ambushed
Ali Khan	Enjil	killed
Saifullah Afzali	Herat province	killed in Iran
Fazel Ahmad Ghorq	Ghuryan	assassinated 1367
Ghulam Farouq	Ghuryan	killed
Awlya	Ghuryan	assassinated
Ghaffar Tufan	Enjil	killed
Latif Karim	Zendajan	killed by a relative in large scale massacre
Sher Ahmad	Zendajan	killed during the Zendajan battle, allegedly shot from behind
Sayyed Ahmad	Guzara	killed while praying at mosque
Haj Faisa	Ghuryan	assassinated

Map 15: Main Military Leaders of Herat Province, circa 1982

own administration, including a judiciary. He would not take orders from Ismail Khan and developed a system of alliances with other commanders and military leaders reluctant to do the same, including the Afzali and Niazi fronts, but also Sayyed Ahmad. Ismail Khan succeeded in cutting him off completely from external supplies but Ghulam Yahya Shawshan reacted by improving his system vis-à-vis the civilian population and relying on community contributions to keep going.[2]

Ghulam Yahya and the Niazi and Afzali fronts were the exceptions. To the average military leader, Ismail Khan's coercive coalition-making presented only two possible courses of action: either accept his impositions or switch sides, joining the government or another party. Some did join other jihadi parties. This was particularly the case of some Pashtun tribal leaders, who were attracted towards the royalist parties, like Mahaz-i Milli or Nejat-i Milli. These parties had little to offer, but since Ismail Khan would not supply these 'undisciplined' tribal strongmen anyway, even their limited resources became more attractive. One of the defectors was Haji Faisa of Ghuryan, who left Jami'at to join Mahaz. He was later assassinated. However, the main competitor of Ismail Khan for the allegiance of military leaders was the government, which invested large resources in the formation of militias. By 1986/87, as the military pressure from the government side was getting stronger, quite a few military leaders were defecting to Kabul (see chapters 3, 14).[3]

Ruthless tactics could only have a significant impact within the central districts of Herat province. By early 1992, at the peak of Ismail Khan's power, his influence was still far from total in every corner of Herat (see Map 16). Even where he had influence, his control was mostly limited except in the districts west of Herat city. After 1986–7, the eastern part of the province was very difficult to reach for Ismail Khan as the government had taken control of the area around Herat, hence military leaders operating there enjoyed de facto autonomy even if formally they were part of the Emirate.

Ismail Khan's approach was similar in the surrounding provinces, although softened with the inclusion of an element of 'feudalism' due to the logistical difficulties of bringing to bear his military superiority. The 'law of decreasing influence' (see chapter 6) inexorably limited his attempts to expand beyond a single province. As long as he did not have control of the main roads and access to large quantities of supplies, extending his influence proved very difficult. In the early 1980s, a separate Emirate had been set up in Baghdis province (which included also the district of Koshk-i Kohne of Herat province), under a local Jami'ati Amir, Sadi Behdudi. This Emirate too had an ulema Council, presided over by Mawlawi Khodabash, but nothing like Ismail Khan's sophisticated administrative system. But the real power in Baghdis rested in the hands of the local Emirate's military responsible, Nik Mohammad. Although the Emirate of Baghdis was just a loose coalition of Jami'ati military leaders, Nik Mohammad's charisma gave him substantial influence. Jami'at had initially been quite thinly spread in the province, but during the 1980s Nik Mohammad attracted many local military leaders from other parties. His popularity prevented Ismail Khan from expanding his influence in Baghdis. Ismail Khan however used his control over supplies to the Baghdis Emirate to impose some form of cooperation throughout the 1980s. Nik resented the fact that Ismail Khan claimed to have the right to control the supplies, which had been dispatched from Pakistan for the mujahidin of Baghdis, but the two men always managed to avoid a direct clash. This might also have been due to the fact that by making a deal with Ismail Khan, Nik himself gained a relatively strict control over Jami'at-i Islami's military leaders in Baghdis and Koshk-i Kohne: he personally received supplies from Ismail Khan and then distributed them.[4]

Only in 1988–89, when Nik Mohammad was killed fighting the government, did Ismail Khan have the opportunity to bring Baghdis under his direct control. Immediately after Nik's death, an attempt was made to choose a successor. The first choice, a Pashtun named Dost Mohammad, lasted just one week, until a rival military leader, Abdul Ahad Khan, attacked and defeated him. Abdul Ahad, in turn, lasted only ten days before another Jami'ati, Khalek, killed him. Immediately Dost Mohammad counter-attacked and proclaimed himself Amir, but the Emirate effectively collapsed in chaos. Ismail Khan at this point succeeded in absorbing Baghdis and Koshk-i Kohne into his own structure, as no one was able any longer to resist his 'army'.[5] Support among the local military class remained precarious: when in 1995 the Taliban were occupying Herat, Junbesh easily marched into Baghdis and found support among the military leaders.

Ismail Khan found it initially easier to expand his influence in Ghor province, a mountainous region where military leaders were mostly confined to their own valleys and no overall dominant figure could emerge. Many military leaders belonged to Jami'at, which facilitated Ismail Khan's task, although there were important areas of Hizb-i Islami influence, especially in Chaghcharan, Taywara and Shahrak districts, while Lal district was completely under the control of Shiite Hazara groups. Harakat-i Enqelab too had some influence. Although Jami'at-i Islami had a provincial political leader in the person of Mawlawi Musa, he had little real power. The very limited resources of this province were one of the sources of frequent infighting among military leaders of Ghor, which again played into Ismail Khan's hands. While these conditions helped him to establish a foothold in the province, in the medium and long term they also prevented Ismail from consolidating his hold, the more so as the government was also actively competing in recruiting military leaders, especially around Chaghcharan. In this case too he tried to use the distribution of supplies as a tool to enforce obedience among the military leaders, but compared to Herat Ghor had access to weapons from alternative sources too. Similarly, the Hamza was not sufficiently strong to take on local military leaders in this mountaineous territory, so remote was it from its bases: Ismail Khan's foray into Tulak district in 1987 did not achieve any appreciable result and he was forced to withdraw. As a result, for all his efforts only a few of the Jami'ati military leaders in Ghor could be described as close to him and more or less collaborating with his Emirate, which in return supplied them. This explains why he reportedly used to describe the Jami'ati military leaders of Ghor as 'selfish and adventurous'. During the time of jihad, in Chaghcharan, Salam Khan was closest to him, while in Shahrak his key ally was Haji Gul and in Taywara Mullah Ahmed Mulgi (see Map 17). Even at the peak of Ismail Khan's influence during the jihad period (1991–1992), his influence over Ghor remained quite patchy, as it did after 2001 (see also Map 16 and Map 17).[6]

Map 16: Areas of Influence of Ismail Khan in the Western Region, Early 1992

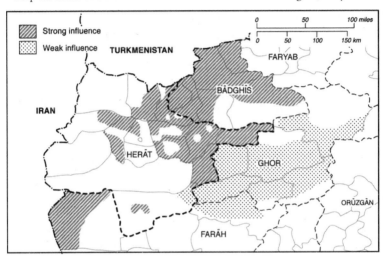

Authoritarianism

As the Emirate emerged from the shadows to become the polity running western Afghanistan in 1992–1995, its greatest weakness was probably its limited inclusiveness. Although all warlords' systems are by definition not very inclusive, they can afford not to take into account at least the interests of the military class only at considerable risk. On the eve of the fall of the Najibullah regime, the majority of the military class in Herat province was most definitely against Ismail Khan. He succeeded in marginalising it by defeating militarily the militias/Hizb-i Islami coalition when they revolted against him a few months after the fall of Najib (see chapter 4) and by gradually sidelining many others, including Jami'atis he did not trust. That would not in itself have been a fatal weakness—in fact it could have turned into a major achievement in terms of primitive accumulation of power—had Ismail Khan established a solid alternative social base and won political legitimacy. He was popular among the man in the street, as a result of the relative law and order ensured by the insurgent Emirate, of the myth of successful military leadership created by the battle of Zendajan and of the enthusiasm that followed the change of regime. He also had a relatively large resource base to tap, as Herat's importance as a conduit for imports into Afghanistan rose after 1992 due to war and the blockade on the Pakistani border. However, this popularity soon wore off and the problem of the Emirate's lack of inclusiveness re-emerged strongly.

During the first Emirate, the limitations implicit in the narrowness of Ismail's social base were compounded by the bad economic situation, exacerbated by the corruption and incompetence of much of the administration. The implementation of rigid religious policies also eroded its initial popularity, especially in Herat city. Although women had more freedom to work and move around than in most of the rest of Afghanistan, one would certainly hesitate to describe the environment of Herat as liberal. For example, men were not allowed to shave. In much of the countryside, Ismail Khan's hold was made precarious by the lack of support among Pashtun tribal leaders and strongmen, who strongly resisted his style of leadership. At times Ismail Khan was able to ally with Pashtun strongmen from Farah and the south, but he never cultivated such alliances sufficiently to turn them into longer-term coalitions. Most of his allies from the Pashtun belt had little love for Ismail Khan himself or tolerance for his authoritarian style; they joined him because they had no alternative, being at odds with the dominant players in their region, that is from 1994 the Taliban. One of them was Mullah Mohammad Shah, a Pashtun military leader from Farah, who led 70th Div. and was affiliated with Harakat-i Enqelab. He had initially aligned with the Taliban, but after they removed him from his position as divisional commander and disarmed his men he defected to Ismail Khan. Nonetheless, he had a major grudge against Ismail Khan too, because he claimed the position of governor of Farah, which the latter was unwilling to concede.[7]

Ismail Khan's strategy was to centralise resources and use at least part of them not to fund patronage politics, but effectively to deliver goods and services to the wider public. On the surface, this might seem a recipe for success. Why then did his authoritarian polity not work? To deliver he would have needed an effective administration, but he failed to develop one. There was a relative abundance of human resources to staff an administrative structure in Herat in 1992, but Ismail Khan failed to mobilise them. Not only the old pro-Soviet leftists, who accounted for a fair share of the local intelligentsia, were left out or forced to flee, but even the Islamists and Ismail's old Maoist friends were poorly treated.[8] This resulted not only in a weak administration and army, but also in an incompetent and unreliable diplomacy. Forming a 'diplomatic corps' would have required a more sympathetic attitude towards both the Herati intelligentsia and the tribal notables than Ismail Khan had. The tribal notables, for example, could have helped him in maintaining good relations with the southern tribes, most of which extended into Herati territory. In the end, he limited his recruitment to a few educated Jami'atis from Herat city. Even they were soon alienated by the rude demeanour of someone whom they considered the son of a villager and who did not pay due respect to people of superior social status (see chapter 18). Once again it is confirmed that the establishment of a successful symbiosis with the city is often a critical determinant of the long term fate of the warlord and his polity.

The same pattern was repeated in 2001–2004. Ismail Khan's base of support within the military class steadily eroded after 2001. Not only the Nabizadahs and various military leaders of Ghor, Nimruz etc., but even some of those who were at the core of the system soon sided with the opposition to Ismail Khan. Sarwar Yakdast, commander of the Herat Airport garrison, joined the opposition to Ismail Khan in 2003 and so did Qazi Mohammad, commander of the border troops in Islam Qala. It appears that the difficulty of mobilizing support for Ismail Khan was widespread, not least because many local military leaders had been alienated by his policy of rotating them between districts, in order to keep them under control and weaken their own power base. In July 2003 the police chief of one of Herat's sub-stations developed a rift with Ismail Khan, who tried to sack him. With Kabul's support, the chief resisted Ismail's pressure and stayed in his job. During the 2004 combined offensive of the anti-Ismail Khan opposition front, Ismail Khan and his men tried to mobilise forces in all the districts, but faced resistance. In Ghuryan, for, example, the local chief of police, a former Jami'ati military leader, refused to fight for Ismail Khan and tried to negotiate between the inhabitants and the authorities, achieving little.[9]

The customs revenue windfall which had benefited Herat after 1992 reached its peak after 2001, so that again Ismail Khan had plenty of resources to build up support among the population on the basis of a 'developmental' model of administration (see chapter 17). Although this time Ismail Khan paid greater attention to reconstruction and development work, once again he failed in the task of involving the intelligentsia of the city in the task. The administration was affected by corruption, but most importantly by lack of accountability and by the low quality of the administrative staff.

Ismail Khan's continuing unwillingness to reach a modus vivendi with the upper and middle social strata of Herat is shown by his refusal to tolerate independent political activities. He maintained a strong control over publishing books and periodicals, which were subject to the authorization of the Herati department of the Ministry of Information and Culture, permission from Kabul not being considered sufficient. The Loya Jirga selections of 2002 showed even more clearly his intolerance of independent views. He used his militias to impose his candidates and tried to prevent the participation of women not affiliated to him. Several candidates were arrested and beaten, others were threatened. Ismail Khan made a particular effort to thwart the ambitions of pro-Zahir Shah candidates,[10] who appeared popular among the Pashtuns and the urban population. Herat city selected mainly independent candidates. The Shiites, better organised, ended up getting six of the twelve seats available, proportionately a higher share than their actual population suggested.[11]

Coalition-building

As pointed out earlier, beyond his core areas Ismail Khan relied on coalition-building rather than on pure coercion, but only half-heartedly. The peak of these efforts was in 1992, as he ascended to power in Herat. In most cases these coalition-building efforts faded quite rapidly. This was for example the case of a remote area like Ghor. In December Ismail Khan organised a shura in Herat to gather the military leaders of the province and request that they granted him full authority as regional leader. This had little lasting effect, to the extent that Ismail Khan was not even able to identify a trusted representative. During the following months he had to rely on a former military leader of Hizb-i Islami with a reputation for infighting and for opportunism, Qayyum Khan, as his main source of support, but he proved totally unreliable and Ismail Khan soon decided that force was the only way to bring order to Ghor (see chapter 18).[12]

After the Taliban took Herat, even that modest level of influence which Ismail Khan had been able to achieve in Ghor waned (see chapters 15, 17 and first paragraph of this chapter). Dr Ibrahim managed to position himself as Massud's proxy in the province and thanks to his direct help emerged as the most prominent opposition military leader, a role which he maintained through to 2001. He managed to get appointed as governor at the end of 2001 in apparent agreement between Kabul and Herat, but soon started displaying signs of restlessness faced with Ismail Khan's intrusions. By the summer of 2003 fighting was already going on in Ghor between Dr Ibrahim and military leaders now supported by Ismail Khan, chiefly Ahmad Murghabi and Maw-

Map 17: Jami'ati Military leaders in Ghor, 1992
(Those allied to Ismail Khan are shown in italics)

Map 18: Areas of influence of Zahir Nabizadah in Baghdis province, 2004

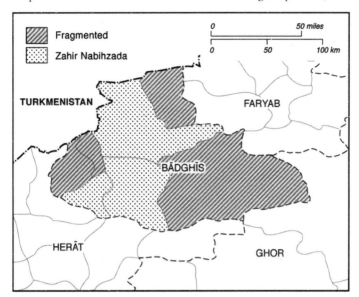

lawi Din Mohammad. Although Murghabi succeeded in forcing Dr Ibrahim to flee from the provincial capital, the latter maintained a relatively strong position in the southern districts and other players also controlled different in parts of Ghor. At this point Ismail Khan's main source of interest in this almost irredeemably turbulent province seem to have been to establish a strategic back yard, presumably based on his experiences of 1995–2001, when he was unable to fight an effective guerrilla war in the open ground surrounding Herat city. One source reported that he asked Murghabi to destroy an NGO-built road from Chaghcharan into the mountains and to buy horses, in order to be ready to use north-eastern Ghor as a remote base for resistance against 'foreign forces'. He also appears to have stockpiled weapons in that area.[13]

If this was his plan, what he lacked were reliable allies. During 2004 the relationship between Ismail and Murghabi too deteriorated, not least because the latter had started receiving support from Shura-i Nezar's Minister of Defence Fahim in Kabul. During the March 2004 clashes in Kabul, some of Murghabi's men were arrested by Ismail Khan's militias, a fact which upset Murghabi and definitely compromised his relationship with Ismail. It might be that the June 2004 fighting, in which Murghabi was in turn chased out of Chagcharan, was instigated by Ismail Khan, as well as by the competition for the control of the main road in Ghor. The most immediate reason appears to be that Rais Abdul Salam, a local military leader formerly affiliated with the Taliban, was not happy with what he had been offered in terms of appointments in exchange for dropping his military ranks and gambled on an attack against the provincial capital. However, Salam was seen by locals as connected to Ismail Khan and was also supported in the attack by Ahmad Sanam, a military leader from Shahrak district close to Ismail Khan. Unable to secure a stable base of support, after 2004 Ismail Khan saw his influence in Ghor decline further. His strategic concerns were not shared by his proxies in Ghor and his ability to buy their support was in steady decline as the control of the narcotics route going through the province became increasingly profitable, removing the incentive to seek support from outside the province (see Map 19).[14]

Elsewhere too Ismail Khan's efforts at 'genuine' coalition-building after 2001 never got very far. In Nimruz he formed an alliance with Abdul Karim Barawi, a former army officer who had led an independent front in the province since the 1980s. Barawi's allegiance was temporary and he soon switched it to Kabul. In Farah, a certain balance of power existed initially between Ismail Khan's and Karzai's supporters, but the former was relying on aspiring tribal strongmen with rather flimsy bases of support and rapidly lost influence. After 2001, Baghdis remained almost entirely beyond Ismail Khan's direct reach. Zahir Nabizadah and his brother Amir Shah maintained control over most of the territory throughout the 2001–5, despite financial difficulties which prevented them from mobilizing large numbers of troops (see Map 18). Amir Shah Nabizadah had to tax the population much more heavily than Ismail's military leaders in order to maintain his forces, but was helped by the popularity of the two brothers with the military class. Initially operating as vassals of Ismail Khan, the brothers soon broke off from the Emirate. It is remarkable that throughout the post-2001 period Ismail Khan's direct influence was limited to a couple of local military leaders, despite his ability to provide support, unmatched in a poor province like Baghdis. Neither of them had more than a few hundred men. Even in remote and mountaineous parts of Herat province Ismail Khan's influence was weak after 2001. In Obeh district, for example, a local military leader called Mustafa, belonging to the new generation which had emerged as the Taliban were collapsing, could easily afford not to align himself with the Amir.[15]

After the emirate

Even after his removal Ismail Khan maintained some influence and leverage, which among other things allowed him to prevent the disarmament of his jihadi brigades in 2004–5, even if they were formally disbanded. He maintained a number of allies among the military class, particularly those whose enemies were also Ismail Khan's enemies. The extent of his overall influence can be gauged by the outcome of the presidential and parliamentary elections of 2004–5. During the presidential elections of 2004, Ismail Khan supported opposition candidate Qanuni, who won 34% of the vote in Herat province, but since he was also supported by groups hostile to Ismail Khan, such as the Afzalis, it can be estimated that support for Ismail Khan was at that time no more than 30%. In the parliamentary elections of 2005, 8 of 17 MPs elected in Herat were linked to Ismail Khan, although they were also supported by other Jami'atis. Overall candidates linked to Ismail received about 20–25% of the vote, but benefited from the extreme fragmentation of other political groupings. Although this was a significant level of support in the context of the extreme political fragmentation of Afghanistan, it was hardly a strong base from which to stage a claim to the leadership of the whole western region. The level of support for Ismail Khan in the other western provinces was appreciably lower. Even if Qanuni did relatively well in most of them, and particularly in Ghor, he was supported by a range of figures hostile to Ismail Khan. In the parliamentary elections, just a single MP directly linked to him was elected in any of these provinces.[16] Ismail Khan has not signalled in any way his desire to create a political party to compete in elections. Moreover, as a popular base from which to start the development of a political organisation able to compete in elections and gain a significant position in national politics, he would only have been able to count on a very modest 1–2%, which does not compare very well with Dostum's electoral weight. It could be argued that Ismail Khan's strongly personalistic attitude and his refusal to produce a political platform beyond his own claim to be the legitimate ruler in Herat greatly limited his electoral appeal and hampered his effort to build a popular base based on the delivery of services (see chapters 14 and 21).

Notes

1. Interviews with Jami'at military leaders of Herat province, Nov. 2004, May 2005 and Oct. 2005.
2. Ibid.
3. Ibid.
4. Interviews with former military leaders from Herat, Ghor and Baghdis.
5. See previous note.
6. Abdul Qadir Alam (nd.); Interview with former government official from Ghor, Herat, Sept. 2005.
7. Interviews with members of the Herati intelligentsia, Nov. 2004, May 2005 and Oct. 2005; Azimi (1377), pp. 48–9
8. Several interviewees allege that Ismail Khan had links to the Maoist movement in the 1970s. Certainly some officers of the group which organised the Herat revolt in March 1979 and which included Ismail were Maoists.
9. UNAMA internal document, July 2003; interview with former military leader from Enjil district, Sept. 2005.
10. Supporters of the former king Zahir Shah wanted the forthcoming Loya Jirga to appoint him head of state, a move fiercely resisted by Islamists.
11. Human Rights Watch (2002), p. 28 and passim; interview with UNAMA political officer, Kabul, May 2003.
12. Abdul Qadir Alam (nd.).
13. Abdul Qadir Alam (nd.); interview with UN official, Herat, 8 May 2004.
14. Interview with UN official, Herat, May 2004; interview with notable from Ghor, knoweledgeable about Farsi, Oct. 2005; interview with former government official from Ghor, Sept. 2005; Human Rights Watch (2002).

15. Parisa Hafezi, 'West Afghan Fighting Threatens Refugees' Return', Reuters, 9 April 2002; 'Afghan refugees return from south Iran', Reuters, 4 May 2002; Guy Dinmore, 'Drought and drugs', *Iran Reporter*, 27 Dec. 2001(http://www.iranreporter.com/story.asp?id=306); Carlotta Gall and Craig S. Smith, 'Rival Flags Stir Afghan Fear', *New York Times*, Feb. 4, 2002; interview with UN officials, Herat, May 2004; Rory Stewart (2004), pp. 107, 136.

16. Amin Tarzi, 'Forces In Herat Province Will Continue 'Resistance' Role In Afghanistan', *RFE/RL NEWSLINE*, Vol. 7, No. 140, Part III, 25 July 2003; personal communication with ANBP official, Kabul, Sept. 2004; Abdul Waheed Wafa, '32 Killed in Factional Fighting in Western Afghanistan', *New York Times*, 23 Oct. 2006; Amin Tarzi, 'Clashes In Western Afghanistan Leave Scores Dead, Including Local Warlord', *RFE/RL Newsline*, 26 Octber 2006; JEMB electoral data (http://www.results.jemb.org/results.asp?ElectionID=1andProvinceID=24andOrder=Voteandoffset=40); personal communication with UN, diplomatic and NGO staff, Dec. 2005–Jano. 2006.

17

THE POLITICAL ECONOMY
OF ISMAIL KHAN'S EMIRATE

During the anti-Soviet jihad (1982–1992), Ismail Khan's financial base was inevitably comparatively modest. According to sources within the Emirate, a quarter of the funds came from the headquarters of Jami'at in Pakistan, another quarter from taxes and the rest from international support organisations, presumably Islamic charities and private donors.[1] On top of this were of course supplies in kind, essentially military ones. Although Herat was certainly not the best supplied of all Afghan regions, there seem to have been sufficient equipment and no need to divert financial resources to that end. If these figures are true, already during the jihad Ismail Khan enjoyed a certain degree of financial autonomy vis-à-vis Peshawar, but was bound to Jami'at-i Islami's leadership by the need to secure military supplies. The Iranians allowed Ismail Khan and his men to move relatively freely across its territory, but never agreed to supply significant quantities of military hardware to any of the Sunni parties during the jihad, probably mainly for considerations of international politics, i.e. the need not to alienate the Soviet Union at a time when Teheran was engaged in a war with Iraq. This attitude deprived Ismail Khan of the possibility of diversifying his sources of supply.

Little is known of Ismail Khan's income in 1992–1995 and the estimates of actual revenue in 2001–2004 also vary widely, but it is no secret that most of his revenue came from customs duties, collected mainly in Islam Qala, but also in Turghundi on the border with Turkmenistan and Kalat-i Nazar in Farah. For the post-2001 period, customs revenue was variously estimated to have ranged between $50–$300 million. The upper end of the range appears quite an exaggeration, since with total imports at just over $2.1 billion and low duties, total revenue might barely have reached that amount nationwide in the early post-Taliban years. An official of the National Bank in Herat estimated the revenue at $600,000 a day for Herat as a whole, but this figure seems incompatible with the results of an enquiry carried out in 2004, which evaluated recorded revenue in Islam Qala at $57 million. The two other customs posts in the region must have been worth much less. An intermediate estimate put the revenue collected at Islam Qala at well over $100 million, based on a traffic of 300–350 imported vehicles a day and on an estimated average duty of $1,000 per vehicle, plus about 100 trucks loaded with goods. This figure might well be close to the truth, if it is true that Ismail Khan once in early 2003 bragged about having a total income of $100 million. It should be remembered that corruption among custom officers would likely have prevented more of this revenue from reaching Herat.[2] One source, based on a discussion with local traders, estimated that 'backhanders' ran to $750 per container, while leakage was estimated by custom officers at around 30% as an average for Afghanistan as a whole. The $100 million figure is also strongly supported by the fact that after control of the customs was at least partially wrested back by the central government, Herat started yielding $100 million a year to the Ministry of Finance in Kabul.[3]

Other sources of revenue were nowhere near as important as customs and were probably pocketed by lower rank officials without ever reaching Ismail Khan. Road taxes likely ranked second to customs in terms of importance, because of the brisk trade with Iran and between Herat and other provinces. In 1992–1995, they were collected without any concern for Kabul, while in 2001–2004 a system was developed whereby police would collect the tax, but largely under-reporting to Kabul, in the end allowing up to 90% of the revenue to be pocketed by local players.[4] A third type of revenue was a monopoly over sales of fuel imported from Iran (where prices were very low). Finally, businesses and farmers were also taxed. Businesses had to pay a corporate tax, while tax on farmers must have been less profitable, especially in the poorest districts.

With such levels of revenue, Ismail Khan likely had no need to extract taxes or bribes from Herat's wealthy. This does not mean that a number of businessmen were not particularly close to him in the construction, fuel and import trades. One example from Herat is that of the Islam Qala-Herat road, where already in 2002 businessmen were complaining about a transport monopoly which was causing the cost of transport to increase greatly.[5] Ismail Khan himself does not appear to have been personally involved in business activities—all the major projects in Herat were awarded to foreign companies, mainly Turkish, which seems to exclude business cronyism being a driving force under him.

While in 1992–5 Ismail Khan's control over local sources of revenue was not challenged, after 2001 he came under pressure from Kabul to hand over customs revenue as early as 2002. He did pass on a small sum, variously reported at $4–5 million, later followed by a second instalment. By early 2003 he had passed on some $8–10 million, or around 10% of his estimated revenue (see above). This far from satisfied the Minister of Finance, Ashraf Ghani, who in May 2003 visited Herat with a group of officials from the Ministry, establishing the amount of recorded revenue in Islam Qala. He managed to return to Kabul with $20 million in cash and the hope that revenue would start flowing regularly from Herat. That did happen, but it took almost a year and the reorganisation of Islam Qala customs. By the summer of 2004, Herat was sending cash to Kabul to the tune of $8 million a month. As a result, Ismail Khan's revenue must have been dramatically reduced. He did not concede graciously, and on one occasion sacked the director of Herat's National Bank for having transferred $3.1 million to Kabul without his authorisation.[6]

It is not certain how much cash Ismail Khan was able to save following the collapse of the Emirate in 1995, or how much he could recover once he took Herat back. Similarly, it is difficult to estimate what percentage of his revenue Ismail Khan may have been spending on managing and improving Herat province; one source in the customs office estimated it at 30%. Certainly the amount spent on Herat was substantial, as shown by the fact that the removal of Ismail Khan and the re-establishment of central control over customs revenue had a major impact in the development of Herat. For example, the new university building started by Ismail Khan and projected to cost $60 million was left half completed after his removal. Another few million dollars a year must have gone into equipping and paying his private ('jihadi') militias, whose full time core was around 3,000 men. If these estimates are correct, he would

Graph 3: Monthly Transfer of Revenue from Herat Province
to the Ministry of Finance in Kabul, US$

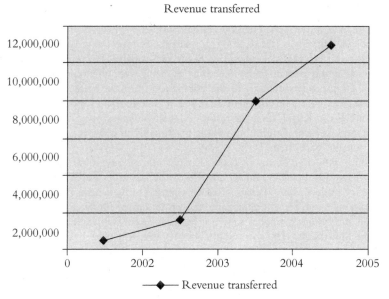

Sources: New York Times 19 Dec. 2002; Washington Post, 19 March 2003; The Times, 25 August 2004; Pajhwok Afghan News 21 March 2005; MSNBC; 20 April 2003; CNN, 12 Sept. 2002; 'In The Balance Measuring Progress In Afghanistan', CSIS, July 2005; Los Angeles Times 28 Dec. 2002.

have pocketed close to $60 million in 2002 and a slightly lower amount in 2003. In 2004, he is likely to have pocketed much less. Part of this revenue was spent on houses, vehicles and other luxury items for himself, his family and the closest circle,[7] but most of it must have been saved. This should not necessarily be taken as a sign of greed: Ismail Khan was likely preparing for a future in which his sources of revenue might dry up, either because of the seizure of the custom posts or because of a change of trade patterns.[8] Saving cash is likely to have been part of larger preparations, including the stockpiling of weapons to arm his full- and part-time militias and ammunition to fight a protracted campaign (see chapter 16).

The role of external 'benefactors' appears to have been less significant in Ismail Khan's case than in Dostum's, except during the jihad, when he was dependent on Rabbani's and others' handouts. There is no indication that in 1992–5 the Iranians provided significant levels of support to Ismail Khan, but that changed after the fall of the Taliban regime. At that point not only Teheran mediated between Ismail and Hizb-i Wahdat, trying to forge some cooperation between the two, but according to sources within Wahdat at some point even decided to suspend aid to the latter and focus it on Ismail. Ismail Khan's fighters remember those as days of plenty, with abundant cash coming from Iran and 'other countries'. A certain number of Ismail's men appear to have even been trained in Iran during the time of the resistance against the Taliban. Apart from the abundant cash, there is also evidence that aid in kind was provided. The Iranians provided for example arms and ammunition for the Baghdis front opened in 1996. The relationship appears to have continued after 2001. Even as late as 2004, Iranian trucks were reported unloading weapons in Ismail Khan's armories. Some pro-Ismail Khan candidates in the provincial and parliamentary elections of 2005 were also reported to have received goods to distribute to the population from the Iranians, although it is not clear who paid for them. If it is true that Tehran's support continued despite Ismail Khan's financial resources, this would suggest that the Iranians were very keen on continuing with it, presumably in order to consolidate his relationship with them.[9]

The political economy of Ismail Khan's influence regionwide was determined not just by his resources, but also by the resources available to the local military leaders. When Ismail Khan proclaimed himself Amir of the western region in 1984/85, encompassing the provinces of Herat, Baghdis, Ghor, Farah and Nimruz, supplies were not the only factor influencing the attitudes of the military class (see chapter 16), but they certainly mattered. His resources were inevitably stretched thin once targeted at the whole region. Unsurprisingly, his claim to be the regional Amir had little impact in Nimruz and Farah, whose supply lines were completely independent of Ismail Khan's. Baghdis was the most dependent, while Ghor had access to other sources of supply, thought modest. With the end of the jihad, external supplies dried up, except for the period of Taliban control, when they were in part re-established from Iran and Kabul or north-eastern Afghanistan. In the absence of external support, in 1992–5 and then again after 2001, internal resources became of paramount importance.

A peculiarity of the region's resources was their extreme concentration along the border with Iran and in Herat itself, that is within easy grab of Ismail Khan. The exception was Nimruz, a long standing smuggling route where local players were hardly interested in Ismail Khan's or anybody else's support. The remaining areas were particularly poor in terms of resources, at least initially. In Baghdis, the Nabizadah brothers, who relied mainly on taxing farmers, always had financially difficulties in maintaining their militias when Ismail Khan was not footing the bill. In Ghor, military leaders tried to control the main provincial road in order first to control the drug route and second to collect road tax. Land tax must have provided little in its extremely impoverished countryside. The rapid shifts in power and control in Ghor after 1992 also suggest that control over the main road was key to the political economy of the province. Sometimes, military leaders would gamble their resources in a bid to seize control of the road, in a 'winner take all' competition which would reward the winner with the ability to buy the support of a majority of other military leaders. As the control of the narcotics route going through the province became increasingly profitable, local military leaders became increasingly independent of external support, including Ismail Khan's (see Map 19). The appearance of the poppy culture in Ghor, albeit on a small scale, might also have contributed to reduce the attractiveness of external 'sponsors', whose ability to manipulate local politics correspondingly declined. Farah followed instead a fate similar to Ghor's, gradually acquiring

Map 19: Areas of influence of main military leaders
and Ismail Khan in Ghor province, 2004

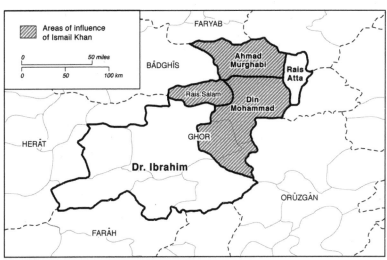

importance as a route for the traffic of narcotics and as a ground for growing the poppies. As in Ghor, Ismail Khan's and other external players' influence within Farah was on the wane by 2004.[10]

Notes

1. Dubuis (1989), p. 159.
2. According to a 'diplomat' cited in Chris Kraul, 'U.S. Afghan Role May Grow', *Los Angeles Times*, 13 May 2003.
3. Andrea Stone, 'Afghan governor de facto ruler in west', *USA Today*, 19 Dec. 2002; 'Afghanistan looks for 30 billion dollars aid and investment', *AFP*, 3 June 2003; Marc Kaufman, 'Karzai's Taxing Probl— Provincial Governor Raises Money Beyond Kabul's Control', *Washington Post*, 19 March 2003; 'The emir of the west', *The Economist*, 19 July 2003; personal communication with customs consultant, Kabul, Feb. 2005; author's interview with a World Bank official in Kabul, Feb. 2005.
4. Interview with former official of the department of transport of Herat, Dec. 2004.
5. Author's interview with former official of the National Bank, Herat, May 2005; AACC, 'Doing business in Afghanistan: Report on Meetings with Afghan Entrepreneurs in Kabul and Kandahar', Afghanistan, Dec. 2002, p. 12, accessed at http://www.cipe.org/regional/nis/aacc.pdf.
6. Waheedullah Massud, 'Warlord Afghan governor slaps and sacks bank director over revenues', AFP, 14 March 2004; Jan Qarabaghi, 'Eyes On Herat', 14 Sept. 2004 (http://www.bassirat.net/news/read_whoswho.php?w=134)
7. 'Les affaires reprennent à Hérat, surtout celles d'Ismail Khan', *Iran reporter*, 23 Nov. 2001; Andrea Stone, 'Afghan governor de facto ruler...', op. cit.; Mark Bendeich, 'Better times, new problems for model Afghan city', *Reuters*, 19 June 2007; Jan Qarabaghi, 'Eyes...', op. cit.
8. The emergence of Islam Qala as by far Afghanistan's main port of entry for goods was a recent development and was largely due to Pakistan's restrictive polices concerning Afghan transit trade.
9. 'Sharing power is hard to do', *The Economist*, 22 Nov. 2001; Rory Stewart (2004), p. 104; Amy Waldman, 'Courted by U.S. and Iran, an Afghan's Influence Rises', *New York Times*, 3 April 2002; Baigi (2000), pp. 266–7; interview with teacher from village in Zendajan, Sept. 2005.
10. Interview with former government official, Herat, Dec. 2004; interviews with former military leaders of Zahir Nabizadah, Herat, Oct. 2005; Rory Stewart (2004), passim; interview with former government official from Ghor, Herat, Sept. 2005; personal communication with UN officials, Herat, May 2004.

18

THE EXTERNAL DYNAMICS
OF ISMAIL KHAN'S EMIRATE

Expansionism and containment

Because Ismail Khan did not rely on direct taxation as much as customs as a source of revenue, territorial expansionism must have been motivated other than by the desire to expand the tax base, with the exception of the capture of the region's few border posts. Having obtained control over Islam Qala and Kalat-i Nazar Khan as the regime collapsed in 1992, he soon moved to seize Turghundi from Hizb-i Islami. By contrast, expanding inland was not rewarding financially, at least not compared to the cost of doing so. Other factors must have driven Ismail Khan towards expanding the area under his control.

Although the boundaries between Junbesh and the Emirate were quite natural ones, with no major road connecting the two areas and with mountains and remote and inhospitable areas dividing them, conflict between Junbesh and Ismail Khan was almost permanent in the area between 1992–5. As already discussed in chapter 10, the conflict with Dostum along the borders of Faryab province was motivated by the involvement of Ismail Khan and Rasul Pahlawan with rival networks of military leaders, as well as by reciprocal mistrust. If Dostum was particularly vulnerable to the desire of his vassals to expand their own areas of influence, due to his reliance on a patronage-driven 'feudal' system, Ismail Khan by contrast seems to have been motivated to a much higher degree than Dostum by personal ambition. His 'ideological' campaign against the remnants of the leftist regime both in the north-west and in the south (see chapter 10) served his purpose ideologically to legitimise his role of regional Amir, as well as to secure for him an advantageous position and moral high ground in any future settlement with Kabul. The 1993 foray against the Khalqis in Lashkargah was a military and political success, because Ismail could enlist the support of local jihadi groups. He succeeded precisely because he did not aim to occupy Helmand, a task well beyond his means. His ambition in organising the expedition was to claim a role of defender of the mujahid in tradition in contrast with the squabbling in Kabul that was leading the country towards civil war. Again in 1995 similar considerations, together with the desire to prevent a Taliban move against Herat or Kabul, prompted him to organise his fateful expedition against the Taliban in Helmand and Kandahar (see chapter 19).

Ismail Khan's ambition is evident in his repeated attempts to develop relations with military leaders both from Jami'at and other parties well beyond western Afghanistan. Even during the jihad he had created Hamza battalions as far as Uruzgan (under Yaqubi) and Kandahar (under Yasir). The rationale for doing so was probably linked to the desire to improve his control over the lines of communication with Pakistan, but also likely to his personal ambition of becoming a national player and to expand beyond the western region. This ambition was probably also playing a role in driving his efforts to attract Jami'ati military leaders from Faryab, an easy task since these military leaders were quite isolated, had very long supply lines to Pakistan and faced the onslaught of Rasul Pahlawan's militias. Receiving help from Baghdis and Ghor was their only chance to resist Rasul and indeed Ismail Khan's help allowed them to keep fighting Rasul longer, although eventually unsuccessfully. Ismail Khan's help for the Jamia'tis of Faryab only exacerbated Rasul's hatred of Jami'at, a party that he had been fighting since the early 1980s, and motivated him to retaliate in kind. When Rasul was approached by the defeated militia leaders of Herat between the end of 1992 and the beginning of 1993, he gave them a warm welcome and started supplying them with weapons and ammunitions, which they used to establish an anti-Ismail Khan front in Bala-i Murghab district of Baghdis province. Moreover, Junbesh became a pole of attraction for all military leaders disgruntled with Ismail Khan's centralisation policies. In Baghdis, such dissatisfaction was quite widespread, as after all Ismail Khan was quite a newcomer to the province and his legitimacy among military leaders was particularly weak. Here, in contrast with what he had done in Herat in 1992, he did not even temporarily appoint the main local military leaders to positions of power, opting instead for some second-tier figures. Moreover, they were left with little autonomy particularly in military and security matters; military operations were led by key figures of the Emirate of Herat, such as Alauddin Khan, Aref Khan and Azizullah Afzali, under whose command the local military leaders had to deploy. Finally, the distance from Herat and bad communications beyond the provincial capital of Qala-i now conspired to make opposition to Ismail Khan a more viable option. Dost Mohammad, the military leader who had tried to claim the role of Amir for the province after the fall of Najib and the death of Nik Mohammad, openly joined Junbesh, but quite a few others also maintained secret relations (see chapter 16). This emerged clearly in 1996 when Junbesh's militias moved in and were welcome by quite a few local military leaders, including Zahir Nabizadah, who were incorporated in the new administration and in the militias.[1]

The pattern was not too different in post-1992 Ghor. Rasul Pahlawan gained some influence through Pir Nezamjah (see chapter 13), but more importantly attracted quite a number of military leaders opposed to Ismail Khan. Yahya and Rais Atta, both from Dawlatyar district,[2] openly joined Junbesh. Others, particularly those who belonged to Hizb-i Islami, maintained contacts with Junbesh through Kamal Mawdudi, the political leader of Hizb-i Islami in the province. It appears that from time to time they even received weapons from Rasul Pahlawan. Clearly the military class of Ghor, like that of Baghdis, preferred Junbesh's loose 'feudalism' to Ismail Khan's centralism. Indeed, after his capture of Herat Ismail Khan did not waste too much time in trying to woo the local military leaders (see chapter 16) and already in 1993 he launched a major operation into Ghor, trying to subdue it with the support of a number of local military leaders, chiefly Rais Abdul Salam from Chaghcharan and Dr Ibrahim from Taywara, who were trying to eliminate their rivals from Hizb-i Islami. The operation succeeded in forcing Hizb-i Islami forces and the former militias to flee, but not to establish a solid hold on the region. The pro-Junbesh military leaders regrouped in Mazar-i Sharif and then with the support of Rasul started staging raids into Ghor, preventing Ismail Khan from fully consolidating his hold on the province. They were to play an important role later, when they contributed decisively in the Taliban's conquest of most of Ghor. Although a pro-Ismail Khan provincial government was established in Chaghcharan, it had virtually no influ-

Map 20: Core Area of Support and Successive Expansion
and Contraction of the Emirate

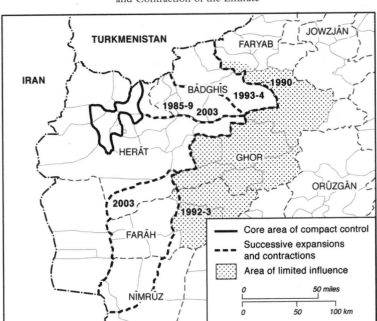

241

ence in the districts, not least because Dr Ibrahim and Rais Abdul Salam both lost interest in cooperating with him.[3]

Ismail Khan's ambitions were not matched by his means, and nor did his preference for a centralist model of governance seem to be working successfully. In the end his attempts to strengthen the control of his borderlands resulted in the weakening of the Emirate, by alienating an ever growing proportion of the military class. Expansion only led to temporary occupation of areas of little economic value, which were then rapidly lost again (see Map 20). This might have been useful in terms of bolstering Ismail Khan's image for wider and higher purposes, but he failed to capitalise on it.

Centre-periphery and Periphery-periphery relations

Ismail Khan was never an Islamist in any real sense. Although the outset of the war appears to have pushed him toward the right end of the political spectrum, he became more of a traditionalist conservative Muslim than anything resembling a revolutionary Islamist. Undoubtedly he always showed little interest in the development of political party structures as a way to mobilise and manage the jihad, which was always one of the key 'selling points' of the Islamists. This does not mean that he maintained hostile relations with the leadership of Jami'at, quite the contrary in fact. He was careful to lobby the upper hierarchy of Jami'at from the outset; and he was one of the first military leaders from the interior, if not the first, to meet Rabbani, the leader of Jami'at. It appears that Ismail travelled to Iran in 1979–80 mainly with the intention of meeting him. The decisive event took place a year later in Pakistan, where Ismail Khan had travelled with a group of other military leaders to meet the leadership of Jami'at and decide who should be in charge of the supplies. Having already secured Rabbani's backing, Ismail Khan was able to arrange for his own selection for the post. His control over supplies from Pakistan might have helped him in getting chosen as Amir of Jami'at in Herat, later that year. In any case, at that point he certainly was the first Amir of Herat to combine both the military-political leadership role and control over supplies. He now had in his hands far more power than previous Amirs had and moved to make as profitable a use of it as possible (see chapter 17). Minor military leaders in Herat province were in no position to compete and establish their own alternative supply routes, even when able to find suppliers in Pakistan. Reportedly, the cost of delivering weapons to Herat was as high as the cost of the weapons themselves, that is if they had been paid for rather than received for free.[4]

Despite having benefited so much from Rabbani's patronage, after 1992 Ismail Khan's challenged his government in several stark ways. In 1992 he reportedly snubbed Rabbani's offer of the post of Defence Minister, clearly an attempt to draw him away from his fiefdom. Symbolic gestures like this abounded after 1992. During the celebrations for the anniversary of Afghanistan's independence, only posters of Ismail Khan were displayed in Herat, and none of Rabbani. He also had the habit of making ministers from Kabul wait for days when visiting him in Herat. An even more clamorous snub to Rabbani was Ismail Khan's endorsement of the hypothesis of Rabbani's replacement as president of the Islamic State with Mr Yusuf. When Ismail Khan organised the Ghazni Shura of multi-party mujahidin representatives to call for an end to internecine fighting, the convocation of a Loya Jirga and the formation of a national army, the main party leaders, including Rabbani, were not among the 4,000 people present. From a more substantial point of view, Ismail Khan's disregard for Kabul's authority was evident in his refusal to hand over custom revenue despite the despatch of a delegation from Kabul to negotiate the issue, as well as in Ismail Khan's refusal to consult Kabul on the appointment of governors in the provinces under his control. He also entertained independent negotiations with neighbouring countries and with the UN. His lack of sympathy for Kabul was unsurprisingly reciprocated. Said Nurullah Emat was Ismail Khan's most bitter adversary in Kabul, but in general he was not very liked very much. Emat, Rabbani and most importantly Massud supported the Afzali group, a fact which must have componded his dislike of the Jami'atis in power in Kabul. Ismail Khan greatly resented the fact that Rabbani, during a visit to Herat, met,with the encouragement of Said Nurullah Emat, some local Jami'ati leaders with whom he was at loggerheads.[5]

Ismail Khan's relations with Massud plunged to new depths, particularly during 1995. As the Taliban were turning their attention to Herat in the spring of 1995, Ismail Khan requested the despatch of reinforcements from Kabul. No more than 1,000 were flown in with light equipment under the command of Gen. Najim, but by the summer a conflict between Ismail Khan and Kabul over who commanded these troops had become manifest. Ismail Khan would not accept an independent command for them, nor would their commanders agree to serve under Ismail Khan's orders. As the situation in the field was parlous (the Taliban had reached Shindand), Massud tried to impose his authority as Defence Minister and interfere with the chain of command in Herat. At the same time a delegation from Kabul was trying to convince some reluctant military leaders to join the frontline. It aroused Ismail Khan's ire by trying to pay them money directly, without routing the funds through him. What Ismail Khan perceived as a combined attempt by Kabul to diminish and maybe even replace him precipitated outrage on his part. The command of the Emirate's army was severely affected, contributing to the collapse of the front.[6]

The vicious circle in the relations between Kabul and Ismail Khan got even worse as the fall of Herat in turn strengthened the ill will between Ismail Khan and Kabul. Shortly after the Taliban took the city, Radio Kabul called Ismail Khan a traitor. Ismail even went public on radio Message of Freedom to attack Massud and accuse him of plotting against Rabbani. Although after 2001 Ismail praised the late Ahmad Shah Massud in public speeches, his hostility to the Shura-i Nezar group remained strong at least as long that represented the core of the Kabul government (2004).[7]

After 2001, Khan's forthright attitude towards Kabul was less than ever matched by his effective strength on the ground, especially in the provinces. When Kabul appointed new governors hostile to Ismail Khan in Baghdis in 2003 and Farah in 2004, he could do little to prevent them from rapidly dismantling his network of influence there. In Farah, Bashir Baghlani successfully prevented Ismail's local proxies from receiving any more funding from him, or forced them out of office. The Ministry of Defence paralleled this effort by replacing most of Ismail's loyalists in the local 71st Div. Ismail Khan's occasional incursions in the neighbouring provinces, while not determined enough effectively to scare his opponents, aroused much hostility, not least in Kabul. He did however organise a far more determined fight to preserve his control over 4th Army Corps in Herat. After he was removed from the position of Corps commander in August 2003, he continued to interfere in its affairs. He first had a provincial Loya Jirga call for his reinstatement and then organized a very unfriendly welcome for the new commander of 4th Corps, Baz Mohammad Ahmadi, who soon took refuge in Kabul and never returned to Herat. In October 2003, Ismail even stormed the barracks of 4th Corps and took away Afs150 million and many cars, which were then transferred to his own private jihadi militia. Finally, in March 2004, following Zahir Nabizadah's flight from Herat after the clash which killed one of Ismail Khan's sons, he appointed Mohammad Omar, one of his men, as new commander of 17th Div., without even consulting the Ministry of Defence, which was inevitably much displeased by the move.[8] Eventually, the disbandment of 4th Corps within the context of the DDR program effectively removed Ismail Khan's influence from MoD units in the west. His uncooperative attitude, won him few friends in Kabul and contributed to his violent removal from power in 2004 (see chapter 20).

One of the most striking features of Ismail Khan's claim to autonomy is his failure to establish anything resembling a reliable diplomatic corps. For example, when he dispatched an envoy (Mir Abdul Khalek) from the sayyid aristocracy of Herat city to Kandahar, seeking negotiations with the Taliban, Khalek ended up striking a deal with the Taliban, who asked him to mobilize anti-Ismail Khan elements within the province. This particular episode had little impact on the patterns of events, both because there was very little chance of Ismail Khan and the Taliban leaders reaching a deal and because Khalek ultimately failed to mobilize people like Ghulam Yahya Shawshan and the Islamists opposed to Ismail Khan,[9] but it reveals how dysfunctional the Emirate's diplomacy was. This reinforces the hypothesis that Ismail Khan might have been thinking of Herat not as de facto state but as a base for entering national politics (see chapter 14).

Notes

1. Mojaddidi (1378), p. 113; interviews with military leaders and officers of Baghdis province, Oct. 2005.
2. An 'unofficial' district which is in the eastern part of Chaghcharano.
3. Alam (nd.).
4. Dubuis (1989), p. 95; interviews with former military leaders from Jami'at and other parties, Herat and Kabul, Nov. 2004, May and Nov. 2005; interview with political activist, Kabul, May 2006.
5. Dorronsoro (2005), p. 253, 251–2; interview with former military leader from Enjil district, Sept. 2005; interview with Qari Masun, former spokesman of IK, Herat Oct. 2005; Zahir Azimi (1377), pp. 111–2, 83.
6. Zahir Azimi (1377), pp. 35, 114; interviews with former military leaders, Herat, Oct. 2005.
7. Baigi (2000), p. 219; *BBC SWB*, 20 Sept. 1995; *Herat TV* in Dari 1730 gmt, 13 July 2003.
8. Personal communication with UN official, Kabul, May 2004; Carlotta Gall and Craig S. Smith, 'Rival Flags Stir Afghan Fear', *New York Times*, 4 Feb. 2002; *RFE/RL Afghanistan Report*, Vol. 2, No. 30, 21 Aug. 2003; *Erada daily* (Kabul), 28 Oct. 2003; *RFE/RL Afghanistan Report*, Vol. 3, No. 13, 01 April 2004.
9. Interview with former government official from Ghor, Herat Sept. 2005.

19

MILITARY DYNAMICS OF THE EMIRATE

The Hamza

The system of military organisation that Ismail Khan tried to implement once he rose to the position of Amir of Herat in the early 1980s was essentially based on his experience as an army officer, even if he had to make adjustments and expand it as time went on. He inherited councils of military leaders, which existed at the provincial and district level, but this type of non-hierarchic organisation was not to his taste and he was quick to leave his mark on the organisation of the Emirate, turning it into something much more structured than before. The figure of the Amir had been established in the early days of the resistance, both at the provincial and district level. They were meant to concentrate political and military powers in the hands of a single man, reproducing at the local level the model adopted for the provincial emirate, but in the absence of supportive institutions their effective powers were limited. Lacking strong personalities, most of these Amirs never emerged as effective leaders and the typical amir worked rather like a *primus inter pares*. Under Ismail Khan, the leadership of the Emirate claimed the right to appoint Amirs in each district, whereas initially they had been elected by the village military leaders. His next step was the creation of something which was meant to resemble a regular army. He argued that fighting around Herat effectively required disciplined military units, which could be manoeuvred on the battlefield and take part in large scale military operations. He even enlisted the support of higher rank former army officers to develop his military system.[1] What was called the Hamza regiment, later to be upgraded to brigade and then to division, was drawn from existing mujahidin units, which kept their military leaders as commanders. The idea was that such units would progressively merge into the larger structure, to form a compact entity. In theory, the Hamza brigade was supposed to count on several regiments (ghunds), which at its peak numbered six, whose bases were distributed as shown in Map 21. The mujahidin serving in the Hamza were paid, although hardly much. Those who were unmarried received just enough to eat, while family heads received much more.[2]

Map 21: Ghunds of the Hamza brigade, circa 1986

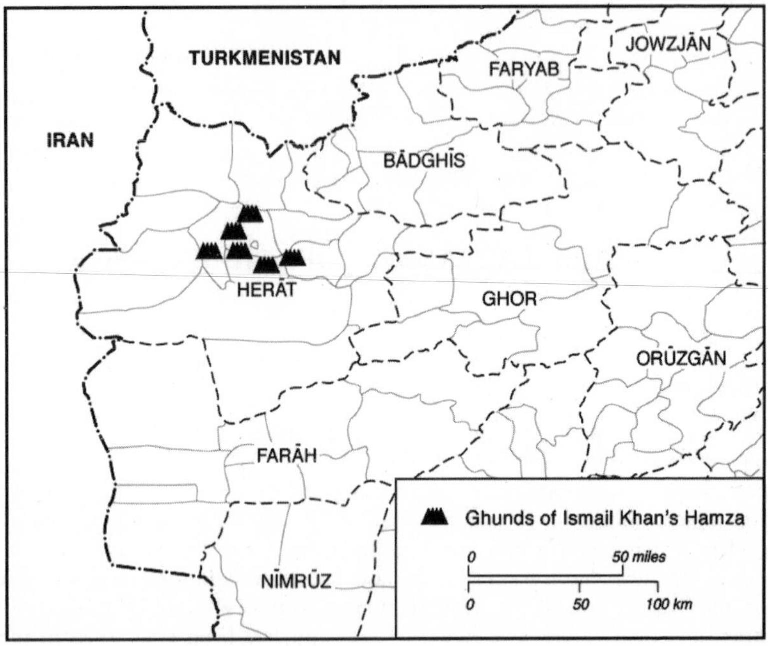

For all his insistence on discipline, what Ismail Khan was effectively demanding from military leaders was loyalty to his person. A greater degree of discipline was achieved with regard to behaviour towards civilians, but the chain of command remained shaky. As a matter of fact, only the first ghund in the Hamza, Qurlus of Enjil, led by Alauddin Khan,[3] really operated as a disciplined unit and fielded several hundred men in a coordinated fashion. The other ghunds existed in theory more than in practice. At best, they would operate at the kundak (battalion) level, that is around 200 men.[4] Often, even that would be impossible. For example, the Ghund of Pashtun Zargoun under Qazi Mohammad gathered mujahidin spread across the whole eastern half of Herat province, especially Pashtun Zarghoun, Obeh and Farsi, making it effectively impossible to carry out large scale operations, not least because the government controlled the only main road. Often, the Hamza's role in fighting in areas remote from Herat, such as Baghdis, Ghor and Farah would be limited to the despatch of Alauddin Khan to lead the fighting as the operational commander and representative of the Emirate. As long as the Soviets were in Herat, for all of Ismail Khan's insistence on the need for a disciplined army able to field thousands of men for large scale battles, armed activities against the Soviet Army were necessarily low scale; few major armed clashes took place which were initiated on the mujahidin side. In fact the only major operations were an offensive in 1986/87 against the outer ring of Herat city's defenses and an attack on Shindand in 1989. The celebrated attack on Shindand airport in 1985 had essentially been a commando raid.[5] The next largest operation, involving a few hundred men, was a large scale ambush in Gulagao (Adraskan district) against a Soviet column, resulting in the death of some Soviet soldiers. Almost all the remaining engagements were fought by small groups of mujahidin, most under a single leader (20–50 men). The situation changed from 1989, when the Soviet Army completed its withdrawal from Afghanistan, but even at that time the ability of the Hamza to take on the Afghan army was at best limited. The largest battle of this period, Zindajan in 1991, was initiated by the government and showed how the Emirate was unable successfully to fight a conventional battle.[6]

In practice, the main impact of the creation of the Hamza brigade was felt in the relations with other insurgent groups and the military leaders. With the even partial creation of the Hamza brigade, Ismail Khan had greatly increased his ability to move armed men away from their villages and manoeuvre them on the battlefield. If throwing in a mobile force of a few hundred extra men did not greatly alter the balance of strength between the Emirate and the Soviets or the Afghan regular army, they would have a much greater impact in the confrontation between Ismail Khan and those military leaders who were reluctant to accept orders from him. One example of Ismail Khan using the new strength provided by the Hamza brigade was in Ghuryan district, where he deployed it to force the reluctant military leader Awlya to obey orders to attack a local rival of the Emirate, Ghulam Farouq. Another example comes from Obeh district, where Hamza units were used against Gulabuddin, a commander of the Afzali front against whom a military leader associated with Ismail Khan, Qazi Obeidullah, had long been fighting.[7]

The Hamza brigade was not just meant for the expansion of Ismail Khan's power, it was also meant as an internal tool of the Emirate for disciplining and policing the mujahidin. The abusive tendencies of many military leaders had created a situation of anarchy and chaos, which in the judgement of Ismail Khan and others would eventually have discredited the cause of jihad and favoured the enemy. The key problem in implementing Ismail Khan's new hierarchical system in the field was that military leaders were reluctant to accept it. Despite his weak military legitimacy (see chapter 15), not only did Ismail Khan pretend to dictate field comanders what to do and that all military operations should be authorised by him, but he also wanted to claim all military actions for himself as leader of the Emirate. He also announced that the military leaders of the Emirate hand over to him all captured supplies and equipment as well as their prisoners. His motivation seems to have been twofold: first to strengthen the image of the Emirate and attract more recruits to it, as well as more funding in terms of voluntary contributions; and second, a patrimonial instict to merge the institution of the Emirate with its leader. In short, he wanted genuinely to turn autonomous military leaders into his 'commanders', i.e. subjects of a hierarchical structure. As a result, Ismail Khan's patrimonialism was perceived as a long-term danger by military leaders, who were often less than keen to become 'commanders' without autonomy. Many however had little choice but to accept the Hamza and Ismail as a leader. In particular the weakest military leaders would not have been able to resist the Hamza, while those operating in remote areas or who were badly networked would have had no chance of attracting alternative funding and supplies (see chapter 16).

The First Emirate 1992–1995

With the fall of the regime of Dr Najibullah, new opportunities were presented to Ismail Khan. He had few military resources immediately available, mainly his exclusive control over the Hamza, of at most 2,000 men, but due to his success in beating the other contenders and chiefly Hizb-i Islami in the race to occupy government positions (see chapter 15), he was able to seize huge depots of weapons and ammunition in Herat; later he also seized similarly large depots in Shindand when the alliance of the militias and Hizb-i Islami was defeated militarily. Thanks to this control over these supplies, for the first time he achieved complete autonomy and was in as dominant a position as ever. The commander of 4th Army Corps, Rahmatullah Raufi, surrendered the forces of the Ministry of Defence to Ismail Khan, which included a few thousands regular army troops available for use even if by now completely demotivated. There was nothing to prevent him from opting to create the same sort of 'feudal' system along the lines which Dostum was following in the north, using his resources to guarantee his position at the centre of it. Characteristically, he moved instead to create a much more centralised system, which was meant eventually to absorb all the various armed groups into a disciplined army. Many military leaders and especially those who had large armed forces at their disposal were however unwilling to give up their power. Among them, those who had something to fear from Ismail Khan were particularly wary of any move on his side towards a monopoly of armed force. The military leaders and commanders of Hizb-i Islami and the majority of the militia leaders of the previous government were convinced that there would have been no future for them had they allowed Ismail to consolidate. During the early months of the post-communist period, some arm-twisting went on between them and Ismail Khan. As their hopes of being given key positions within the army started to fade, these militia leaders and warlords began plotting against the new status quo.[8]

In October 1992, six months after Ismail Khan had seized power, an alliance of Hizb-i Islami and of most of the militias which had fought for Najibullah's regime launched an attempt to drive Ismail Khan from power (see chapter 4). Thanks to the Hamza, to the support of what was left of the regular armed forces and to the unified leadership guaranteed by his absolute predominance, Ismail Khan beat back the challenge after some initial difficulties. Over the next few months, he relentlessly cleaned up the province of his opponents. By the beginning of 1993 his forces had reached the most remote corners of the province, taking areas which had always been outside his influence, such as Turghundi, which he grabbed from Mirhamza, and Shindand, which he took from Farid, the successor of Ghasauddin (see Map 15). He then turned against the remaining potential sources of opposition, attacking Hizb-i Wahdat even if though it had not joined the revolt against him. Dissident elements within Jami'at, such as Gulabuddin, one of the main commanders of the Afzali front who was based in Obeh, were also forced to flee. At this point, no organised opposition was left. Even the Afzali and Niazi fronts had been forced to disband and to renounce the creation of independent political organisations.[9]

Although there were in reality limitations to Ismail Khan's monopoly, at least in the provinces (see chapters 14, 16 and 17), it can be said that as far as Herat province was concerned Ismail Khan had succeeded in ridding himself of rival military leaders and strongmen and effectively enjoyed a monopoly over large scale military force if not over violence altogether. His army was expanded through the introduction of conscription, while weapons were collected from the former militiamen who continued to reside in the countryside, not only in Herat but also to some extent in the neighbouring provinces of Baghdis and Ghor.[10]

If Ismail Khan succeeded in establishing a loyal army and in monopolising large scale violence, he failed to create an effective army. The war being perceived as being over by the population, conscription was unpopular. The 6,000 veteran mujahidin who went on to form the core of the new army of the Emirate were not necessarily happy to be conscripted into the new, more structured, force for an undetermined length of time. Serving away from home seems to have been particularly troubling for many of them. Such discontent resulted in particularly high level of indiscipline, whereas the experienced mujahidin were supposed to be serving as an example to the new conscripts. In fact, the only unit of the army to be purely composed of former mujahidin and meant to become a sort of elite unit, the Jihadi Brigade, was the most indisciplined in the army: its soldiers neglected their duties and often refused to obey orders. The initial conditions of service were fixed at one year with a monthly salary of 15,000*afs*[11] and an allowance of 50 kg. of wheat. In reality, none of the jihadi veteran was ever released from the army until its collapse in 1995. Moreover, the army was not properly funded and many officers were corrupt, a fact that pushed the morale of the rank-and-file even lower.[12] The effectiveness of the Emirate's army was also negatively affected by the fact that even those regular army officers who had been willing to carry on serving were purged from the commanding ranks.[13]

Efforts were made to increase standards in the army, but such efforts fell short of increasing pay or rooting corruption. At the roots of its inefficiency there appears to have been the incorporation of untrained and ill-disciplined military leaders, with little or no bureaucratic supervision. In choosing his

251

'commanders' Ismail Khan had with few exceptions privileged perceived loyalty over ability and military discipline. Bureaucratic supervision was meant to be replaced by raising the ideological (Islamic) consciousness of the rank and file. A list of the achievements of the commander of the army, Alauddin Khan, focused on renovating barracks, the delivery of fresh water and electricity and more remarkably the strengthening of Islamic morals, which was supposed to be achieved with the construction of twenty-two mosques just for 17th Div., the establishment of a Islamic madrasa and of a Quran recital house. Ulema were often invited to deliver speeches about religious rules and regulations in order to strengthen morale and discipline. Clearly Islam was seen as the ideological glue to hold together the army and motivate it and little attention was paid to effective supervision and the fine tuning of command and control mechanisms. This Islamisation of the army proved of modest value as it was implemented from above with little enthusiasm or participation by the foot soldiers. Another flaw of Islamisation as a sources of motivation was that it could only work against an enemy perceived as un-Islamic. Whatever moral edge Islamic indoctrination might have given to the Emirate's army, it was lost when the enemy to be confronted similarly brandished an Islamic banner and perhaps did so in a more convincing manner.[14]

Undoubtedly the Taliban posed a much more serious challenge to the Emirate than Junbesh, if for no other reason than that the south-western approaches to Herat are much more easily negotiable by an invading army and include one of Afghanistan's main highways. Like other major players, Ismail Khan too underestimated the threat posed by the Movement of the Taliban when it emerged in 1994, seeing it as a ragtag force that would be no match for the Emirate's powerful army. This attitude was likely strengthened by the first encounter between the two forces. After failing to take Kabul in early 1995, the Taliban turned towards Herat and in February launched an offensive against the provinces of Farah and Nimruz, which were at that time mostly under the loose influence of Ismail Khan. Having met little resistance, they continued their advance on Shindand, the southern gate to Herat province. Ismail Khan's forces around Shindand easily defeated the unprepared offensive, which ended in disaster. Unhappy about the removal of his influence over Farah and Nimruz and having witnessed the apparent military weakness of the Taliban, Ismail Khan decided that the opportunity presented itself to inflict a decisive blow against the Taliban as well as expand his influence southwards. Immediately following the their defeat he ordered an all out attack against the religious students, with the aim of taking Kandahar and bringing about the disintegration of the Taliban Movement.[15]

The offensive was going to be the first test of the new army of the Emirate as a force capable of large scale operations. Ismail Khan opted to put together an expeditionary force as large as possible, mobilising all the forces at his disposal and disregarding the inevitable consequences in terms of logistical difficulties. The force of 20–25,000 men was drawn from the three provinces under his at least partial control (Herat, Ghor, Baghdis) and from his allies in

Farah, Helmand, Kandahar, Uruzgan and Nimruz and included various types of forces, including army, police, border forces, security troops and airbase protection soldiers (see Table 6). Organising them proved impossible. The motley collection of disparate groups from subordinate military leaders and external allies compounded pre-existing problems linked to the absence of a professional officer corps and effective command and control. The few professional officers were used mainly in reconnaissance, communication and air support tasks, but they were playing an advisory role only. Moreover, as it was the first time the Emirate had attempted to mobilise such a large force, it had no experience of how to manage it. Communication and cõordination were particularly weak; some modern equipment and officers from the old regular army trained to use it were available, but they were not put to good use. Repeatedly over the period of several months the leaders of the Emirate's army lost contact with each other. In fact, often the Emirate's forces had problems in identifying each other, as the external allies from the south wore no uniforms and were completely indistinguishable from the Taliban. Particularly during night fighting this created major problems and favoured enemy infiltration.[16]

The structure of the Emirate was disproportionately based on a very limited number of individuals with any skills to organise and direct. The military structure, for example, was very weakly integrated and rested on the charismatic leadership of a handful of leaders at the top. Even in the best of circumstances this was a primitive system of command and control. When Alauddin Khan, the most popular of the military commanders, was injured during the offensive against Kandahar, the operational effectiveness of the army was affected. Shortly thereafter, when his substitute Nazir Ahmad Khan, the next most popular and effective commander, was killed in action, not only was the morale of the army further damaged, but there was nobody left with the credibility and charisma to lead the expeditionary force as a whole. Moreover the few able and popular military leaders left to lead detachments into battle were not necessarily trusted by Ismail Khan. For example, when Zahir Azimi, who was from the ranks of Harakat-i Islami, played a key role in recovering control of Nimruz and Farah after the first Taliban offensive, Ismail Khan could not bear the fact that he publicly claimed that success for himself and the alliance between the two broke down. Azimi had been a longtime ally of Ismail Khan but was not as willing as Alauddin Khan to allow him to claim all the glory for himself. The rivalry between Ismail Khan and military leaders like Azimi widened as Kabul tried to rely on the latter to expand its influence in Herat and redirect the military effort there. Afzali, Azimi and others travelled to Kabul where Rabbani welcomed them, to Ismail Khan's irritation. Without charismatic leadership, the patchy gathering of armed groups which was the expeditionary force was completely unmanageable on the battlefield. Increasingly aware of the difficulties, during the first half of 1995 Ismail Khan had tried to improve the skills of the army by recalling into service several former officer and specialists of the pro-Soviet army, very few of whom had been left in the armed forces by the end of 1994. However, in true patrimonialist style he was unwilling to accommodate their demand for at least some influence and again tried to limit them to an advisory role. In retaliation, the underground political leadership of the Karmal faction of the HDK advised those serving in the Emirate's forces not to commit themselves seriously to the defence of the Emirate.[17]

The absence of a structured bureaucratic system made manoeuvring on the battlefield very hazardous; often commanding officers had no clue what the rest of the army was doing; in some cases a wing of the army would be advancing, pursuing the enemy, while the rest of the army was withdrawing. Sometimes field officers would lie about the military situation in their sector in order to protect their reputation or to avoid taking risks, as a result endangering the whole army. The same type of problems or worse were of course routinely faced by pre-modern armies, but apart from mismanaging its radio equipment the Emirate made no attempt to establish a system of couriers, nor was the advanced air reconnaissance technology inherited from the state air force integrated with the conduct of operations. Although a headquarters had been established and a high-ranking 'officer' appointed to command it, he had little say in the conduct of operations. Once fighting had started, the field 'commanders' were on their own most of the time. In the event of disorderly withdrawal, a frequent consequence of battlefield difficulties for any ill disciplined army, the troops would often scatter without the headquarters having a clue as to their exact whereabouts; this could have disastrous consequences in case of hot pursuit. On one occasion the leadership of the army tried a relatively sophisticated military tactic, consisting of holding the east wing of the Taliban army while allowing the centre and the western wing to advance, in order to be able to counterattack in the middle and split the Taliban in two. The result was instead a total mess on the battlefield, with the command completely losing control of the Emirate's army. The complex and slow command system, according to which all major decisions had to be taken by 'general commander' Ismail Khan, who was not even based at headquarters, reduced the ability of the Emirate's army to exploit any opportunity arising from the enemy's mistakes and allowed the Taliban to deploy risky tactics, for example showing no regard for securing their flanks. Moreover, Ismail Khan was a strong organiser, but not a decisive military leader. The advantages of the highly centralised command system were therefore rarely exploited and the expeditionary force most of the time was fighting with only the vaguest sense of what their strategic objectives were. While initially it was at least clear that the aim was to take Kandahar and destroy the Taliban, after the initial defeat in Girishk in March there was an absence of clear strategic aims; the leaders of the army never knew whether the aim was to reconquer lost territories, Helmand or even Kandahar, or alternatively to reach an advantageous negotiating position with the Taliban. Typically Ismail Khan would receive suggestions or requests by individual military leaders, consider them and approve or reject, but without providing an overall strategic framework.[18]

Ismail Khan's reliance on fear as a way of instilling discipline was inappropriate for running an army of this size; in practice his ability to enforce discipline was negligible once an operation had started, due to the ensuing chaos. These problems were compounded by the reliance on external allies, who were even less disciplined and were hardly likely to be intimidated by him. His desperate measures to maintain some order among the troops on at least one occasion included firing on his retreating troops, but without result. Indiscipline and abuses against civilians and prisoners were rarely punished because the 'commanders' could appeal to patrons higher up in the hierarchy of the emirate. When the expeditionary force was deployed in Farah for several months during 1995, the badly behaved troops of the external allies from the south did their best to alienate the local population. Many military leaders mobilised for the campaign were actually refusing to join the frontline. A delegation from Kabul, worried about the military situation in the west, even travelled to Herat to try to convince the reluctant military leaders to fight harder and had to pay them extra amounts of cash as an incentive, with dubious results.[19]

Table 6: Military Units Mobilised for the Southern Offensives, Emirate of Herat and Allies

From Herat province
4th Corps units
5th, 17th and 21th divisions
5th, 7th brigades
Police commandment of Herat
State Security of Herat
Heart Airport
Security Unit of Air Defense and those responsible for the airport security.

From Farah province
70th division
Border guard brigade
Jihad brigade
Police
National security

From Nimruz
Border force brigade
Police
National Security
Jihadi Brigade

From Baghdis
Jihadi brigade
Police
National Security

From Ghor
Jihadi Brigade
Police
National Security

From Helmand
90th Div.
Jihadi Brigade
Police
National security

From Kandahar
Halim's militias

Source: Z. Azimi (1377).

Funding such a large force proved difficult and while during the first month of operations the agreed salary of 100,000 Afghanis for mobilised troops was paid on time, during the second month only front line fighters were paid. During the third month even they received only half their salary and by the fourth month no salary was forthcoming at all. Moreover, the Emirate did not have the logistical capability to support such a large number of armed men in a mission a long way away from its base area. Ismail Khan's attitude to logistics, over which he wanted to maintain the tightest control, compounded the problem. He was particularly parsimonious about fuel and would not allow any of it to be distributed without his direct authorisation. As a result the units were operating without the ability to refuel as needed, which in the middle of a battle could lead to disastrous results.[20]

Initially, the Emirate's intelligence of the Taliban was very weak too and no information was available about how many men or weapons the enemy had, although the quality and quantity of the information improved greatly later. Ismail Khan clearly underestimated the mobilisation potential of the Taliban and the hostility that his massive drive southwards would have aroused among the local Pashtun tribes. The advance started in February with the occupation of Dilaram and rapidly reached Girishk, in Helmand province. Here Ismail Khan's forces were met and utterly defeated by a counter-offensive of the Taliban, who in the meanwhile had reorganized, re-equipped and mobilized new forces. An estimated 2,000 men were captured on the first day, the rest were routed and started fleeing back towards Dilaram, where Ismail Khan and his leading commanders tried to reorganise them without success. Although the initial defeat of the Emirate's forces was far from having exhausted its resources, it threw its command system in disarray and both military leaders and troops started losing faith in the leadership. Alauddin Khan, who had been commanding the expeditionary force up to that point, came under very heavy pressure from fellow military leaders until he was injured and had to be evacuated.[21] The withdrawal continued, until a new frontline was organized in Shindand, which held for a few months.

The extent to which the Emirate was dependent on a single man's mood and ruminations showed when, having stopped the advance of the Taliban towards Shindand and Herat for the second time and having even regained control of much of Farah and Nimruz during a counter-offensive, the expeditionary force was left to hang around in the districts of Farah without continuing offensive operations in Helmand, despite appeals to Ismail Khan by his subordinates, by the allies and by Kabul to push the attack further and exploit the disarray of the Taliban. The weakness of the Emirate's military system is evidenced by the fact that during this lull in the fighting no reserve was established, nor was any plan for defence prepared. Orders to improve fortifications particularly around Shindand were not executed by the increasingly demotivated troops, a fact which contributed to the inability to stop the Taliban's advance later. This inactivity badly affected morale too. Without Ismail Khan's or Alauddin Khan's direct orders, not even the most obvious contingencies would be taken care of. When the second attack on Helmand was finally launched in August 1995, it was without appropriate preparations, once again in the expectation of an easy defeat of the Taliban. Ghaffar Akhundzada, the tribal strongman of Helmand, was reassuring his Emirate allies that the local population would support him. The initial advance of the Emirate's army was even on this occasion deceptively easy, but under growing strain the uneasy coalition between Herat and the southern forces started quickly broke down. Shortly after the recapture of Farah's centre, while intervening to prevent the looting Farah's bank, Emirate troops killed two bodyguards of Ustad Abdul Halim Kandahari, a strongman aligned with Sayyaf. Halim never forgave Ismail Khan and the rivalry played a key role in the defeat of Girishk shortly afterwards, when Halim refused to obey Ismail Khan's battle plan and his forces (the 'centre' of the army) failed to advance as planned. As Ismail was busy on the wireless trying to convince Halim to follow the plan, the right and left wings of the army was advancing towards Girishk unaware of the failure of the centre to move. The Taliban were able to listen to the unsecured wireless discussion between Ismail and Halim and to gather all the details of the battle plan. When the Taliban sent a small party to cut off the highway behind the advancing wings, Ismail Khan issued a withdrawal order that caused panic among the troops, which was only exacerbated by the decision to relocate the artillery. Halim and the other military leaders from Kandahar and Helmand at this point fled the scene with their men and mostly crossed the border into Iran, although 300–400 of their militiamen were arrested by the Emirate's forces because of their undisciplined behaviour.[22]

This time the disorganisation of the Emirate's forces was such that an attempt to hold the Taliban in Shindand failed. With the fall of Shindand, a lot of military equipment was lost to the Taliban. The defeat turned in a rout as the troops of the Emirate were fleeing towards Herat. Some attempts to reorganize them still took place just outside Herat, but to no avail. At that point only 300–400 of the once 2000–5,000 strong force were still following their military leaders, who were unable either to communicate among themselves or to establish a defensive line. Utterly demoralised, even these few remaining troops refused to obey orders. Despite his charisma, Alauddin Khan, back from medical treatment in India, in a last attempt to gather a defensive force around him could only field 220 men, mostly friends, relatives and bodyguards, at a time when Ismail Khan himself was fleeing to Iran with a few hundred loyal supporters and the Taliban were completing the occupation of the province. There was not even time to take the money and gold from Herat's bank.[23]

At the root of the collapse of the First Emirate was the fact that Ismail Khan's efforts to centralise power and patronage had alienated many, even among the military leaders who had been fighting with the Emirate throughout the jihad. During the jihad, Ismail Khan's difficult character had been easier to tolerate since they would have little contact with him. After the jihad, however, working day by day with him proved too much for many. He was perceived as selfish and arrogant and many military leaders felt they had not received their fair share of power. While their ambitions might well have been unreasonable, the rude manner in which Ismail Khan treated them for many compounded the situation. The mobilisation of the army from above to fight the Taliban had also left many of them feeling marginalised and without a real role to play. Several military leaders, questioned during the summer of 1995 by an envoy from Kabul, stated frankly that they would not commit themselves to the defence of Herat and the Emirate. The group most likely to be bitterly opposed to the Taliban, the Shiite Hizb-i Wahdat, had also been completely marginalized by Ismail Khan; when its leadership was asked to participate in the defence of the city against the Taliban in the summer of 1995, it demurred. In Farah, even Shiite groups supported the Taliban against Ismail Khan.[24]

The second Emirate 2001–2004

After 2001, Ismail Khan remained committed to the policy of centralisation of power and patronage of his first period in power, as shown by his decision to marginalise the most influential or powerful military leaders, rather than coopting them into his system. This time the surrounding environment was different. While in 1992–1994 he had faced only a weak external challenge from Junbesh, in 2002–2004 Ismail Khan was confronted with a much greater potential for interference from the central government and its international patrons. As a result, he could ill afford to carry out the consolidation of the second emirate as ruthlessly as he had done in 1992–1994, which in turn meant that the military leaders had more leverage to resist him. Zahir Nabi-zadah, who at the time of the fall of the Taliban was the most influential military leader in Baghdis, started breaking away from Ismail Khan in late 2001, when he had a brush with the Amir over his failure to pay the money that he had promised to fund the campaign against the Taliban. Although the matter was apparently settled with Zahir's appointment as commander of 17th Div., he was in reality unhappy with a position that subordinated him to Ismail Khan, who in the meanwhile had appointed himself commander of 4th Army Corps. Later the underlying tension between the two men exploded into conflict. Between the end of 2003 and the beginning of 2004 Nabihzadah openly shifted his allegiance to the central government, joining the newly formed pro-central government *Shura-i Emayat az Markaz* with Azizullah Ludin, Zahir Azimi and Qari Ahmad Ali, to the irritation of Ismail Khan. The exact dynamics of the clashes in Herat of March 2004, which resulted in as many as 150 killed depending on the sources, has not been established beyond doubt. Ismail Khan claimed to have foiled an attempt on his life organized by Nabizadah. In the following botched attempt to arrest the latter, clashes between Zahir's 17 Div. and Ismail's own jihadi units resulted in heavy loss of life, including one of Ismail's sons, Mirwais. The intervention of the central government and the scrutiny of international actors prevented Ismail Khan from pushing the matter to the extreme consequences and Nabihzadah managed to get out of Herat and seek refuge in Baghdis, where he maintained a strong base of support. His ability to support other elements of the anti-Ismail Khan opposition in Herat was from that point onwards severely limited, but he would soon play a role again in the power struggle. Although only a few military leaders remained aligned with the opposition in Herat city and did not have the strength to confront the jihadi units under Ismail Khan's direct orders, at this point the outlying districts and the surrounding provinces were largely controlled by military leaders and strongmen hostile to the Amir (see chapter 16).[25]

The successful joint summer 2004 offensive against Ismail Khan once again evidenced his difficult handling of armies in the battlefield, although the context was completely different from what had happened in 1995. Whereas he had been too daring then, he was too cautious in 2004. Amanullah Khan of Zeerkoh, Zahir Nabihzadah, Dr Ibrahim and others joined hands to challenge Ismail Khan militarily and justify an intervention from the central government. Shindand immediately fell to Amanullah, who then moved on to take Adraskan just south of Herat. Although at the time it was claimed that Herat was very close to falling to Ismail's enemies after the capture of Shindand by Amanullah Khan, Ismail had not committed his Herat-based jihadi troops to the battle yet. Given the past record of his forces and lack of effective military leaders on his side, it should not be assumed that they would have fought the attack off, but by then it was obvious that Dr Ibrahim's and Nabizadah's attacks were little more than faints and the jihadi units could have been committed entirely to defend the city from the southern attack. The outcome of a direct clash would have been uncertain. However, Ismail Khan's slow reaction allowed the situation to be frozen in Amanullah's favour by the intervention of the central government and of the Americans. Amanullah's men even continued to advance in outlying areas for a while, occupying relatively important positions such as Kalat-i-Nazar, a custom post with Iran.[26] The general perception was one of Ismail Khan's utter defeat, for which he paid a heavy political price with his removal from the position of governor shortly thereafter.

Notes

1. Such as Colonel Mohammad Hassan. See Dubuis (1989), p. 149.
2. Dubuis (1989), p. 158.
3. Alauddin Khan was promoted to commander of the Hamza brigade after four years and replaced as *ghund* commander by Abdul Ajan.
4. On this topic see also Roy (1990), pp. 181–182.
5. During the attack, several old Il-28 bombers of the Afghan air force were destroyed and the fact received widespread coverage in the world press.
6. Mojaddidi (1378), p. 113; interview with Zahir Azimi, Kabul, Oct. 2005.
7. Interviews with former military leaders of Ismail Khan, of the militias and of other jihadi groups, as well as government officials and officers of the regular army, Herat, Sept.–Oct. 2005.
8. Nabi Azimi (1998), p. 585; interviews with former militia commanders and military leaders, Herat, Oct. 2005.
9. Interview with former members of the Afzali front, Herat, Oct. 2005.
10. According to one estimate, 60,000 militiamen were disarmed. See Mojaddidi (1378).
11. This salary was at that time considered sufficient to support a family of five for just five days. Zahir Azimi (1377), p. 169.
12. Rashid (2000), p. 39.
13. Zahir Azimi (1377), pp. 168–9, 173–4; interviews with former military leaders and government officials, Herat/Zendajan/Adraskan/Enjil/Guzara, Sept.–Oct. 2005.
14. Mojaddidi (1378), pp. 129–134; interviews with former military leaders and government officials, Herat/Zendajan/Adraskan/Enjil/Guzara, Sept.–Oct. 2005.
15. Zahir Azimi (1377), passim.
16. Ibid.
17. He was interviewed by the BBC. See Zahir Azimi (1377), p. 94; Zahir Azimi (1377), p. 99; Interviews with former army officers and government officials, Herat, Sept.–Oct. 2005.
18. Zahir Azimi (1377), pp. 171–2, 39ff., 83, passim.
19. Ibid., pp. 42, 81, 176, 8, 113–4.
20. Ibid., pp. 82, 92–3.
21. Ibid., pp. 31, 68, 34.
22. Ibid., pp. 94–6, 106–7, 116.
23. Ibid., pp. 117–8, 121–4, 126–8; Interview with Zahir Azimi, Oct. 2005.
24. Zahir Azimi (1377), p. 49.
25. 'Les affaires reprennent à Hérat…', op. cit.; Seymour Hersh, "The Other War," *The New Yorker*, 12 April 2004; interviews with UN officials, Herat, May 2004; interviews with former military leaders of Herat, May and Nov. 2005.
26. Anthony Loyd, 'Afghan warlord closes in on prize city', *The Times*, 25 Aug. 2004.

20

ISMAIL KHAN'S ATTEMPT AT INSTITUTIONALISATION

International recognition

Ismail Khan was not totally oblivious to the need to cultivate international actors. During 1992–5 he received dozens of delegations from foreign countries, including Saudi Arabia, Iran, Pakistan and various European nations. He was initially keen to maintain as much autonomy as possible *vis-à-vis* them, with important consequences for his international legitimisation. Over time he reluctantly accepted that some dependence on the Iranians might be unavoidable, but he kept underestimating the risk of alienating the Americans and the Pakistanis. Amanullah Khan was clearly if discreetly favoured by the Americans in the conflict with Ismail Khan, in part because of his connections in Kabul and because of Ismail Khan's links with Iran, but also because he played his cards better. Twice US troops clashed with Ismail Khan's men in Shindand after 2001 in what might well not have been accidents. On 1 December 2002 a Special Forces patrol was attacked by Ismail's militiamen close to the airport and four militiamen were killed when air support was called in. In June 2003 a second incident took place, as US forces travelling through Zeerkoh and guided by Amanullah's men were attacked by Ismail's militia. Ismail Khan, moreover, never hid his desire to see US troops leave Afghanistan in the not too distant future. Another aspect of his hostility to the international presence in the west was his attempt to limit the operations of international NGOs, whose personnel were sometimes harassed, particularly with regard to the employment of women and dress codes. He also maintained a prohibition on Afghans from inviting foreigners to their homes.[1]

Ismail Khan's foreign relations served to cast him as a rogue rather than institutionalising his role. Given this record, it is unsurprising that with the support of its external allies President Karzai decided to replace Ismail Khan as governor as early as in 2003. At this time there was a first half-hearted attempt to replace him with Dr Azizullah Ludin, a returnee Herati intellectual who had not participated in the conflicts of the 1980s and 1990s. It ended in failure as Ludin was forced to flee Herat after an attempt on his life. Subsequently Karzai repeatedly tried to lure Ismail Khan away from Herat by offering him high ranking positions, including that of head of the National Commission for Disarmament and several ministerial positions, reportedly including that of Minister of the Interior. A major factor in keeping Ismail Khan in power in Herat until September 2004 was American reluctance to risk chaos in the region. The Americans' growing worries about Iran's influence over Ismail Khan and in Afghanistan as a whole might have been a key factor in changing their attitude to him, whose few allies could not do much to help Khan. It came as no surprise therefore that in August 2004 Afghan National Army troops, backed by US air power, intervened to freeze the situation on the ground in terms favourable to Amanullah Khan (see chapter 19). The US embassy gave a green light to replace him as governor that summer, guaranteeing support to Kabul in the event of trouble. The Iranians, who had been consulted beforehand by the UN, thought it better to accept the change in the hope of establishing good relations with his successor and were 'rewarded' with the appointment of the former ambassador of Ismail Khan in Teheran, Khairkhwa.[2] By the time he finally agreed to be 'promoted' to a ministerial post at the end of 2004, Ismail Khan's bargaining power was largely gone and he had to settle for the relatively unimportant position of Minister of Power and Electricity.

Ismail Khan's diplomacy was not always so tactless. After 2001, he avoided repeating the same mistakes of the past in his relationship with Dostum. After his escape from prison in 2000, he publicly announced that Dostum was respected by Afghanistan's Uzbeks and in 2001 agreed to work closely with him. However, it is not clear whether this improvement in his relations with Dostum was a matter of rational diplomacy or was rather dictated by personal considerations.[3]

Institutional self-cooptation

Considering himself to be in no need of any support from a central government that appeared weaker then himself, Ismail Khan consistently showed only a mild interest in being coopted by Kabul. Contrary to Dostum, he did not even try to seek recognition as the head of the western region, which was an official position until 2003, when Karzai and Jalali abolished the job. That position would have provided a reasonable justification for his role as leader of the western provinces, but he preferred to keep calling himself Amir of the West. However, he did occupy the position of commander of 4th Army Corps, which gave him authority over all MoD units in the western region. Together with his cherished position of governor of Herat province, his preference for control over the military suggests that Ismail Khan was after power positions and disregarded mostly symbolic ones such as 'leader of the western zone'. The latter position would have been particularly useful if he had planned to play a role in national politics and in particular in the electoral process or had tried to use regionalism to legitimise his control over the west. But in contrast with the period up to 1995, after 2001 Ismail Khan mostly maintained a low profile in the national political debate. His few interventions were in line with those of other like-minded jihadis, claiming a lasting role for the ex-combatants in the army or at least as an organized group to be active in the reconstruction of the country.[4] His lack of interest in national politics contributed to his main potential ally in Kabul, former President Rabbani of Jami'at-i Islami, deciding that his alliance with Karzai was more important than that with Ismail Khan and endorsing his replacement in 2004.

Although it is unclear whether he envisaged any strategy beyond monopolising as much power as possible in the western region, his attitude concerning institutional self-cooptation and international recognition suggests distrust of the newly re-established Afghan state and of its international alignments, as well as the belief that the new set-up would not last. In 2004, it seemed that Ismail Khan had got it all wrong; by 2007, however, the picture had changed dramatically with the spread of insurgency and insecurity throughout the country and his judgement appeared more likely to have been correct, whether or not for the right reasons.[5]

Institution-building

One of the greatest differences between Ismail Khan and Dostum is certainly the former's distrust of political parties and his refusal to rely on political organisation to consolidate his hold on power and participate in national politics. Ismail's affiliation with Jami'at-i Islami was motivated mainly by the need to access an external source of supply. He never made any use of whatever organization Jami'at had in western Afghanistan and indeed actively antagonised it. Jami'at-i Islami's activists were instead working with the Afzali and Niazi fronts and a few other military leaders opposed to Ismail Khan. On the other hand, he did not really try to organise his own party structures. The closest he came to such an effort was in 2003, when he launched a Shura-ye Eslami-ye Hambastagi-ye Mardom-i Afghanistan (Islamic Council of People's Solidarity of Afghanistan), which was meant as a way to organise support for Ismail Khan. However, it was never registered with the government as a party but only as a social organization, hence it was never meant to take part in elections. In any case, it appears to have been a largely hollow structure and even found it difficult to recruit enough members to staff its councils. One of its most noteworthy activities was the publication of the weekly paper *Payam-i Hambastagi* (Solidarity Message). Ismail also established a Herat Council, to function as an advisory institution to himself. His circle claimed that its members were 'elected', apparently by a number of grand electors selected by Ismail Khan and his associates, so in practice it was representative only of Ismail Khan and his followers. (Ismail's son Mirwais was selected to preside over the Council.)[6]

Needless to say, Ismail Khan had no inclination to tolerate the existence of other organized political groups. Throughout 2001–4, the only one which was allowed to open an office in Herat was Hizb-i Wahdat, by virtue of the uneasy alliance established (probably under Iranian pressure) in 2001. In early 2004, as Wahdat's relationship with Ismail Khan became increasingly difficult, even this office was closed down.[7]

By contrast, Ismail Khan showed a keen interest in the establishment of administrative structures in the area under his control, even during the 1980s.[8] The administration of the Emirate developed over time, but at its peak it included twelve committees (see Table 7). Inevitably, the most important of these was the military one, not because of the (modest) role in planning military operations, but because it was in charge of military supplies. Unsurprisingly, Ismail Khan was at the head of it, although Alauddin Khan was also given the right to distribute supplies after he had become commander of the Hamza.

The head of the provincial administration was Haji Mir Khalek, who was also in charge of propaganda and acted as a sort of 'prime minister'. At the district level the administration existed in a simplified form, with just four committees: finance, culture and propaganda, intelligence and justice. The administration included a rather efficient postal service, even able to deliver letters abroad and used by Ismail Khan to maintain contacts with his subordinates. Every day he would receive many letters from the districts and every military leader used his own personal stamp.[9]

Seizing the state administration

In 1992 Ismail Khan showed little interest in maintaining the military structures of the previous regime, except in a superficial manner (the names of the units were maintained, see chapter 19).[10] The main exception was the security

Table 7: Administrative Committees of the Emirate and their Heads

Committee	Head
Military	Ismail Khan
Political	Khairkhwa, succeeded by Eng. Zia
Cultural/propaganda	Haji Mir
Local administration	Agha Morshed
Vice and virtue	Mawlawi Hafteh Mohammad
Judiciary	Qazi Obeidullah (1 year), succeeded by Qazi Gul Ahmad (killed after 6–7 months), succeeded by Qazi Nazir
Intelligence	Ismail Khan
Education	Nur Ahmad
Investigation	Moallim Abdul Karim
Council of the ulema	Mawlawi Mullah Mohmand
Coomunications	Gul Mohammad
Health	Dr Noor Gul

Source: Interview with Qazi Nazir, village of Guzara district, October 2005.

directorate, which he absorbed into his emirate. By contrast, he showed a much greater interest in seizing and maintaining the existing administrative system. Remarkably, even in the case of the judicial system, despite having created his own during jihad, he decided to adopt the old state's one. As a result, contrary to most of the rest of Afghanistan and similarly to Dostum's, Ismail Khan's judiciary was not exclusively working on the basis of Sharia, but also drew in part from the legislation and the procedures of the previous regimes, as long as these were deemed to be compatible with Islam. What used to be the district amirs became district governors, while former military leaders were appointed as chiefs of police or heads of intelligence. The institutionalisation of Ismail Khan's administration was often only superficial. There was a conflict between formal ranking and an informal hierarchy based on closeness to Ismail Khan. One example is that of a conflict between Nasir Ahmad Alawi, chief of the security directorate, and Faiz Ahmad, head of the criminal department of police. Although according to rank Alawi was superior to Faiz, the latter was personally closer to Ismail Khan and won the day.[1112]

The impact of the decision to maintain the form of the state administration was also drastically reduced by Ismail Khan's tendency to assign positions primarily as a reward for loyal military leaders, who then maintained a military role despite serving in the administration. Heads of departments would participate in military operations with their men when requested to.[13] At the same time, a large-scale purge of former officials of the leftist regime took place. Many were sacked because of suspect disloyalty, others quit because of what they considered unfair treatment. They were replaced by loyal mujahidin, but in part because of an objective shortage of educated and competent people and in part because of Ismail Khan's suspicion of anybody better educated then himself, the standards of the administration fell greatly. Corruption was quite widespread. Ismail Khan himself seems not to have been too happy about the workings of its own administration. In one instance, he was heard asking a group of officials why they could not take a lead from the officials of the previous regime, who were much more honest.[14] At the district level too Ismail Khan appears to have been dissatisfied with the ability of his appointees and kept replacing them frequently. Few of them occupied a position in a district for much longer than a single year. In the case of chiefs of police, he was probably rotating them deliberately, in order to prevent them from consolidating or maintaining a personal power base. The original appointees were locals from the same districts, as Ismail Khan initially had very little control over most of the province, but he soon started to transfer even relatively effective officials away from their home base.[15] Once again his instinct was to centralise power, in stark contrast with Dostum's 'feudalism'.

Notes

1. Zahir Azimi (1377), p. 140; *RFE/RL Afghanistan Report*, Vol. 2, No. 22, 26 June 2003; Pierre Barbancey, 'Ismaël Khan veut un gouvernement 100 % islamique',

L'Humanité, 7 Oct. 2002; Ministerie van Buitenlandse Zaken, Directie Personen-verkeer, Migratie en Vreemdelingenzaken Afdeling Asiel-en Migratiezaken (2002), p. 27; Human Rights Watch (2002b); Julien Bousac, 'Reconstructing States. Afghanistan: emirate of Herat', *Le Monde Diplomatique*, Dec. 2003.

2. Interview with UN official, Kabul, Sept. 2004; Jan Qarabaghi, 'Eyes on Herat', op. cit.; Amy Waldman, 'Courted by U.S. and Iran…', op. cit.; personal communication with UN officials, Kabul, Sept.-Oct. 2004 2004

3. Omar Samad, 'Interview with Ismail Khan', http://membres.lycos.fr/afghanainfo/temoignages.htm; personal communication with UN official, Herat, May 2004; interview with Qari Masun, former spokesman of IK, Herat Oct. 2005, candidate to WJ.

4. *Herat TV* in Dari 1730 gmt, 13 July 2003; *Voice of the Islamic Republic of Iran*, Mash-had, in Dari 0330 gmt 14 Feb. 2004.

5. On the insurgency see Giustozzi (2007d).

6. Personal communication with local notables and booksellers, Herat, Nov. 2005; *Herat TV* in Dari 1600 gmt, 30 Nov. 2003.

7. Interview with UNAMA political officer, Kabul, 7 May 2003.

8. This section is based on interviews with former commadners of Ismail Khan, of the militias and of other jihadi groups, as well as government officials and officers of the regular army, Herat, Sept.-Oct. 2005.

9. Dubuis (1989), p. 158; Kulakov (2003), pp. 141–142; Danziger (1988), p. 149.

10. This practice was widespread in 1992 and again in 2001. The tendency was to see military unit denominations as referring to a set of assets (barracks) or a geo-graphical area of activity rather than as a ensemble of troops able to operate under unified command.

11. Christensen (1995), p. 102.

12. Human Right Watch (2002), p. 38.

13. See for example Zahir Azimi (1377), p. 61.

14. Interviews with former government officials, Kabul, Dec. 2004 and London, March 2005; interview with Herati businessman, London, March 2005.

15. Dorronsoro (2005), p. 127.

21

ISMAIL KHAN'S EFFORT OF LEGITIMISATION

Legitimisation by Cooptation

In his early days in power (1992–3), Ismail Khan looked set to use cooptation extensively as a means to legitimise his rule among the military class. While the civilian administration was staffed by his cronies, clearly he felt the need to make up for his weak military legitimacy. He exploited deftly the uncertainty of those days to secure deals even with the militias most hostile to him, such as the late Sayyid Ahmad's, whose leaders had to accommodate him and accepted a deal. During the days of the confused collapse of Najibullah's regime, there were some scuffles in the race to occupy the centre of local power. In at least two cases there was armed clashes, one resulting in one fatality between the armed men of Ismail Khan and those of Hizb-i Wahdat, who were both claiming control over the headquarters of WAD, and the other, much more important, case in Shindand, where Jami'at and Hizb-i Islami fought bitterly over the airbase. However, on the whole it can be said that Ismail Khan seemed at first to be trying to take all the main players on board. He incorporated the dissident Jami'atis of the Afzali and Niazi front, as well as Ghulam Yahya Shawshan. Azizullah Afzali, at this point the leader of the Afzali front, was appointed chief of police, Sayyid Ahmad Gattali, leader of the Niazi front, became chief of the intelligence, while Ghulam Yahya Shawshan became mayor of Herat city. Among the Shiites, he rewarded those who had been closer to him, such as Zahir Azimi, the main military leader of Harakat-i Islami, who was appointed commander of the border force, but did not forget Hizbollah, which he had had a more troubled relationship with, and appointed their leader Sayed Mahboub Khatib as deputy chief of police. Only Hizb-i Wahdat was excluded from the distribution of the spoils. Even the former officials of HDK/HW were treated with relative magnanimity, despite being relentlessly purged from any position of power. Ismail Khan strongly forbade any execution of former communist officials, although he had many arrested at least temporarily. In at least one case, he had one of his men arrested and hanged over the unauthorised execution of some former HDK members.[1]

In the districts, in most cases he appointed the strongest local military leaders as governors. In Guzara, for example, he appointed Sayyid Ahmad's brother and militia chief Khair Mohammad. In Gulran, he recognised a military leader of Hizb-i Islami, Haji Mohammad Ihlas Noorzai, while he acceded to the control of Hizb-i Islami's Mirhamza over Turghundi, an important border post. However, in a hint of his future plans, he secured complete control over the army by appointing loyalists only. Alauddin Khan was named commander of 17th Div., which had been taken over by the Jami'atis as they entered Kabul, and as his deputy Ghulam Yahya, son of Daoud Ziarjom the deceased militia leader. Soon Kabul endorsed the appointments. Ismail Khan's resort to cooptation, indeed, turned out to be a short-lived trick to stabilise the situation when he felt militarily weak. As soon as he began to feel secure he set out to centralise power in his own hands and in the hands of a small circle around him (see chapters 20 and 16).[2]

The scene was repeated in November 2001, when he was 'acclaimed' as governor. Once again Ismail Khan looked set to coopt other regional players. As the Taliban were fleeing Herat, he had promised one third of the posts to Hizb-i Wahdat, whose militias were only 1,000 strong, but strategically located in the city. He had also promised power and rewards to key military leaders like Zahir Nabizadah and others. Yet despite being advised by close friends to share power and avoid the mistakes of the past,[3] when he distributed the spoils of power among his own men and his allies it became soon evident that some were going to be disappointed. Hizb-i Wahdat, for example, was almost immediately marginalized from power, like all the Shiites in general. Between them, Hizb-i Wahdat, Harakat-i Islami and Hizbollah received only two or three second rank positions in the provincial administration. In general in the civilian administration Ismail Khan practised little cooptation and tried to form a completely loyal and disciplined administration, staffed almost entirely by his closest followers. This had a number of implications in terms of representativeness, not only political but also sectarian and ethnic. Indeed, up to Ismail's removal from power, almost all the administration was Sunni Tajik (see chapter 15).

Once again he initially paid greater attention to the key military leaders. Zahir Nabizadah, for example, was appointed commander of 17th Div. and his brother chief of police of Baghdis. Even some old rivals like Afzali front commanders received some of the spoils: Mahmood Zia was appointed chief of police of Herat, while a member of the Afzali family became head of the Department of Foreign Affairs of the province.[4] Even this time it turned out that Ismail Khan was not trying to set up a system representative of the military class and of the political factions and even less so a 'feudal' system like Dostum's, but was just offering jobs in a highly centralised patrimonial structure and expected obedience. The friendship was short-lived and by 2004 it had all collapsed into enmity (see chapter 16).

Legitimisation by participation or public relations

During the early months of his second period in power (2001–), Ismail Khan appeared to be trying an unprecedented opening to the intelligentsia, among other things encouraging the establishment of a Professional Shura, at the head of which was selected Rafiq Shahrir, a former associate of the Afzali front. The entente did not last long. The relationship with the Professional Shura was the first to crumble. The educated professionals and intellectuals gathered in the Shura expected a role in terms of giving advice and influencing the policies of the governor, but Ismail Khan had not changed his spots. He remained impervious to advice, particularly when it came from the intelligentsia. His old complex of inferiority towards the educated rapidly resurfaced. And he propounded the idea that influence over government should be determined not by technical knowledge, but by piety and merit acquired during the jihad, a clear reflection of his fear of being marginalised by the technocrats and the intelligentsia. When Rafiq Shahrir dared criticise him and run for the Loya Jirga selection of 2002, Ismail Khan had him arrested and thrown in jail. Although Shahrir was soon released, the relationship between the two never recovered and the Professional Shura became a hotbed of opposition to Ismail Khan. The Professional Shura's dream of advising Ismail Khan never materialised, even if after the Loya Jirga of 2002 for a short time he appeared friendlier to its members and even hinted he might be willing to listen to their advice. The relationship between the Shura and Ismail Khan never returned to the lows of spring 2002, as the Shura watered down the content of its criticism towards the administration in public statements. The content of the Shura's paper, *Takhassos*, became reportedly more muted, although it remained to closest thing to a free press in Herat.[5]

A similar story played out with the Women's Council of Herat, except that in its case Ismail Khan initially opposed its creation and then approved it, only to quickly move to establish control over it by appointing its leadership and exercising close supervision over its activities and meetings. He further alienated educated women by banning the celebration of International Women's Day. The disaffection of female activists only grew when Ismail Khan introduced more restrictions affecting women. Some of the initial curbs were eased under international pressure and they were allowed to work for foreign aid groups and enjoy some freedom to speak out publicly about alleged abuses. At the end of 2002, however, he banned wedding parties to prevent males and females from mixing and in January 2003 banned male teachers from teaching girls, including in private schools. Since too few female teachers were available, that meant depriving many girls of education. Nor were women allowed in public accompanied by males who were not their relatives.[6]

Ismail Khan occasionally made some other faint openings to urban opinion and the intelligentsia, but they never went very far. For example, following the publication of a report which accused his administration of being responsible for torture, he established a Human Rights Commission, in January 2003, to investigate the allegations.[7] Needless to say, it never produced a final assessment. Such flimsy efforts are difficult to rank as even a very mild attempt at obtaining legitimisation by participation. It might be more appropriate to describe them as image-driven legitimisation (public relations).

Electoral legitimisation

Ismail Khan never showed much interest in participating in elections and up to the summer of 2007 he does not seem to have ever publicly ventilated the prospect of standing in one. On the other hand, he did not ignore elections altogether. He did his best to get friendly representatives selected in the two Loya Jirgas of 2002 and 2003. In 2002 several candidates not aligned with him were thrown in jail, including a Pashtun mullah from Turghundi and as already mentioned Rafiq Shahir of the Professional Shura. Of those who managed to get elected, six resigned shortly afterwards alleging intimidation. In the presidential election of 2004, he supported opposition candidate Qanuni, despite the latter's background in the Shura-i Nezar group with which he had long entertained difficult relations. Such support was hardly wholehearted and Ismail Khan invested few resources in campaigning for Qanuni. In the parliamentary elections of 2005, Ismail Khan allied with Rabbani and Qanuni in supporting a number of candidates from a Jami'at, background who won almost half of the representatives elected to parliament in Herat province, but did not participate directly in the campaign. The fact that a left-leaning woman, Fawzia Gailani, emerged as the candidate in Herat with most votes must have been a public humiliation to Ismail and his circle. Interestingly, he invested greater resources in the elections for the Provincial Council, where his son was a candidate and won the largest number of votes. By contrast he devoted negligible resources in the campaigns which took place in the other western provinces. In sum, it would seem that Ismail viewed the electoral process as something in which he had to participate but only defensively. He never even went close to conceiving a strategy of legitimisation through electoral participation, as evidenced by the fact that he never developed a platform or a manifest.[8]

Customary legitimisation

For all his neglect of cooptation, participation and elections as sources of legitimisation, one should not assume that Ismail Khan completely disregarded the need to legitimise his rule beyond the mere provision of security. At its core his idea of legitimisation was a very old-fashioned one, resting mainly on the outward respect of Islamic laws and regulations and their imposition on the population. His strategy of customary legitimisation was two-fold: taking the clergy on board and presenting himself as a traditional ruler, but the stress clearly fell on the second aspect.

In the early 1980s, most of the clergy of western Afghanistan was gathered around the Jami'at-i al Ulema, which later merged with Harakat-i Enqelab. The Islamists of Hizb-i Islami and of the Niazi and Afzali fronts had bad relations with the clergy, both because of political and ideological divergences and because of the ulema's hostility to the foreign presence—the Islamists were hosting significant numbers of jihadist volunteers, mostly Arabs. By refusing Saudi aid and the strings attached to it, that is by not accepting foreign jihadist volunteers, Ismail Khan earned some favour with the mullahs and gradually attracted the clergy as Harakat-i Enqelab was losing influence due to its underfunding.[9] Ismail Khan's winning card in terms of relations with the clergy was the creation of a judicial system for the Emirate. A strong current of opinion within the clergy seems to have been arguing at that time that it was necessary to re-establish a judicial system in order to contain abuses against the population, which ranged from excessive taxation[10] to murder and rape. Given the context of the conflict, it is unsurprising that the choice was to use the Sharia as a basis for the judiciary. Many religiously trained judges were available among the ranks of the resistance.

As a result, during the first half of the 1980s a rudimentary judicial system was once again established in areas controlled by the Emirate. The judiciary was supposedly independent of the military-political authorities. Ismail Khan was allowed to attend a trial and express his opinion, but could not reverse the decisions of the judges. A Judicial Committee was created to manage the new institution. Initially it was led by Qazi Obeidullah, who after about one year was replaced by Qazi Gul Ahmad. The latter in turn only lasted a few months, before being killed. Qazi Nazir then replaced him and stayed in the job until the end of Jihad. The demand for judicial services was so strong that even military leaders outside the Emirate had to accept the system run by Ismail Khan, albeit grudgingly. Only in 1986/87, when the government greatly expanded its control over Herat province and cut off the different mujahidin groups from each other, were separate judicial structures created. Especially at the beginning, the quality of the judiciary appears to have left much to be desired, although many would have argued that the system was still better than nothing. The quality of the administration of justice improved slowly over time and played a key role in reducing the number of abuses against the population and of summary executions. It was agreed that prisoners would be executed if it was established that they had killed somebody. The problem was not just that the quality of the judges was on average not very good, but also that the military leaders would not necessarily respect the system. For example, in 1983/84 Qazi Nazir risked an encounter with the military leader Sufi Abdul Ghaffar, who was upset by his accusation of collaborating with the enemy, and was only rescued by Mir Ali Khan Jamju, at that time still one of the key military leaders. In this context, the role of the Hamza brigade as a relatively centralised military force was of major importance in putting pressure on military leaders to comply. Since the Hamza brigade was concentrated around Herat city, at least as far as the really opera-

271

tional ghunds were concerned, the ability of Ismail Khan to enforce his system was limited to this area. The outlying districts were much less affected.[11]

Apart from the judicial system, councils of ulema were also established at
the provincial level and in each district, in order to resolve disputes which the
councils of military leaders were unable to handle. Given the high level of
internecine conflict among military leaders in Herat, it would seem that these
councils were not very effective, although they appear to have done better in
some districts than in others.[12] On the whole, the Islamic judiciary served
Ismail Khan's legitimisation effort well, although even in this case his relations
with the clergy deteriorated after 1992.

Presenting himself as a nineteenth-century Afghan ruler suited Ismail
Khan's political views to perfection, while at the same time also working as a
form of customary legitimisation. He clearly enjoyed holding court at the
governor's palace and receiving all sort of supplicants, from people asking for
his intervention in judicial affairs or in a family dispute, to others just begging
for some practical or financial help. Nonetheless, he improved on the 'tradition' and modernised it, learning from the authoritarian and totalitarian
regimes of the twentieth century. He paid much attention to the choreography of power and his circle arranged for major demonstrations of support on
many occasions, as well as for large crowds to be shepherded to greet him or
to support his claims. His militias would force shopkeepers and shop-owners to
shut down business and attend the gatherings. In at least one case the department of Education of Herat fired a teacher who had refused to let students
attend a rally sponsored by Ismail Khan. His cult of personality was propa-
gated by provincial media, such as state radio and TV and newspapers.[13]

After 2001 the scrutiny of international organisations and foreign embassies
prevented him from fully implementing his model of authoritarianism in
Herat. Without the means of resorting to harsh repression, his attempts to
mobilise Herati society from above were doomed to fail and disaffection
bound to spread. The extent to which Ismail Khan's rural sensibility was out
of tune with urban Heratis is shown by the fate of the newspaper which he
published, *Ittefaq-i Islam*. Very few shops in Herat were selling it, arguing that
nobody wanted to buy a paper which only contained praise for the leader.[14]

Ideological legitimisation and indoctrination

As a conservative Afghan of rural origins, it is perhaps not surprising that
Ismail Khan's view of legitimisation in many regards did not differ very radically from that of the Taliban. Like them, he believed that a state staffed by
well-behaved Muslims would be able to solve every problem. When in 1995
he hesitated before launching a second attack on Helmand (see chapter 19),
he justified his attitude with the belief that the bad Muslims who filled the
ranks of his southern allies (Akhundzada and Halim) would ruin the enterprise. It is worth noting that his reliance on religious legitimisation and the

rigidity with which he interpreted it appears to have increased after the collapse of the Emirate in 1995 and his captivity in Kandahar. He might have thought that his defeat was the outcome of his not having been pious enough. Even in 1992–5 Ismail Khan had stood out in Herat as one of the few supporters, even within the Emirate, of restrictive measures against women, as mentioned above. In July 2002, in order to prevent a society just freed from Taliban domination from becoming 'too libertine', he re-established a moral police, modelled after the Taliban Ministry of Vice and Virtue, which went as far as having the virginity of young females checked in hospital. This force had the power to inflict punishment without going through the courts. Punishments included the shaving of heads, beatings and blackening with coal. A similar moral police had existed during Khan's first emirate (1992–5), but had been milder in its attitudes. At the end of 2002 he banned women from walking in parks after dark and from wearing colourful clothing in public. He also banned the sale of taped and other media containing 'prurient' material, a very wide category in Ismail's definition. Playing music in public was banned and Herat's cinema was not allowed to re-open. In February 2004 he launched a campaign to prevent tailors from taking measures of women's bodies and forbade tailor's shops from having changing rooms for ladies. He also tried to ban women from taking driving lessons.[15]

His idea that modern education was an evil influence and that it had to balanced or replaced by religious education was reflected in his decision in 2004 to launch religious classes for government officials. As their initial launch had failed to attract more then a few participants, he strongly urged officials to attend the courses. And while he did not insist on the exclusive use of Sharia in the courts as the Taliban did, he issued in several instances calls to 'take action' against opponents of Islamic law. Contrary to the Taliban, his fundamentalist attitude should not be taken as implying a clerical leaning. For example in the second half of the 1980s he did not balk at replacing private madrassas run by clerics with his own network of schools, with the purpose of imposing a curriculum more focused on indoctrination.[16] Moreover his autocratic tendencies prevented him from establishing solid, long-term relations with the clergy, despite the latter's importance in his legitimisation effort. Even during the jihad, he never enjoyed much support among the mullahs, who were not terribly attracted by his offer of a marginal role at his service. In 1992–5, all he offered the ulema was partial control over the judiciary and some influence in screening candidates for recruitment in the administration. Khodaidad, head of the ulema council in the 1990s and leading 'alim in Herat, fell out with him in 1995.[17] After 2001, Khodaidad, like many others, was involved in a short-lived attempt to find a modus vivendi with Ismail Khan, but soon broke with him and was forced to flee Herat in March 2004. As a result, the Council of the Ulema stopped supporting Ismail. It is important to stress that this lack of support was not due to the progressiveness of the ulema, whose Council continued to hold conservative views even after breaking with Ismail, for example opposing the screening of

Bollywood movies. The root cause of the split was Ismail's unwillingness to share power.

If his Sunni Islamic conservatism was not enough to win him the support of the clergy, it certainly alienated the large Shiite minority in Herat city. Ismail Khan never entertained good relations with the Shiite minority, which is mostly concentrated there and is very active in trading and professional fields. However, his brand of strictly conservative Sunni Islam succeeded in pushing both the Shiite clergy and the educated middle class into active opposition to his rule. Because this community has long been urbanised, the educated elite had a significant influence within it. Ismail's good relations with Iran allowed him to gain some acquiescence from the Shiite clergy, but did not help with the educated elite, which was mostly strongly hostile to the Iranian clerical regime. When in March 2004 Herat's official media failed to offer any coverage of the anniversary of the killing of Abdul Ali Mazari, a popular leader of Hizb-i Wahdat, Wahdat's clerical leadership was so upset that they moved openly to the opposition camp.[18]

The unpopularity of Ismail Khan's Islamic policies did not stem from a strong liberal leaning among the population of Herat. The political climate of the city remained predominantly conservative even after 2001, and even following Ismail Khan's removal in 2004, if women could now be seen walking around without the veil and people were heard speaking much more freely, demand for more secular oriented policies remained limited.[19] However, much of the population particularly resented Ismail Khan's intrusion in matters which were held to pertain to the exclusive interest of the household.

Delivery-based legitimisation

The most modern aspect of Ismail Khan's legitimisation strategy was his investment of considerable resources in the development of Herat and in the distribution of social benefits. Already during the Jihad, war invalids and families of martyrs received such payments. During the first Emirate, investment on development and service delivery was hampered by high military expenditure, particularly after the emergence of the threat of the Taliban. An educational system was also re-established and by 1993 there were 75,000 students in Herat's schools, of whom half were claimed to be girls, but many children were studying sitting outside and there were no facilities, not even books or stationery. The population seems to have been less than happy about the performance of the administration. Travellers through Herat in 1993–6 reported how the administration was perceived as corrupt and abusive. Heavy taxes were being collected on the roads from lorry drivers, at $300 per truck.[20]

After 2001 Ismail Khan had greater resources at his disposal and invested much larger sums in the reconstruction of the city of Herat. He built several parks, schools and even a library and a university, asphalted all the main roads, restored canals, restored historical sites, repaired water pipes and established public transport. When he was deposed in 2004, he was planning swimming and boating pools, more schools and even the acquisition of sanitation trucks to keep the streets clean. His efforts seem to have been focused on very visible achievements, leaving some essential but not-so-visible requirements not catered for. For example, by the end of 2002 essential facilities were still lacking in Herat's hospital.[21] This seems to confirm that Ismail Khan's interest in Herat city was primarily motivated by the need to have a prestigious capital to show off to the world.

. Ismail Khan's delivery-based legitimisation was probably the most effective of the strategies he adopted, but it did not suffice to consolidate the second emirate for a number of reasons. First, few educated Heratis appear to have been thankful, arguing that Ismail was using public money and only a small portion of that.

Second, even if his resources were considerable by Afghanistan's standards, they would never be enough to buy off everybody. Although Ismail Khan was promising more reconstruction efforts in every village he visited, in the districts his efforts were not evenly distributed, to the extent that one might well speak of patronage politics. The districts which benefited most from Ismail Khan's attention were those immediately to the west of Herat, which had been the theatre of most fighting and where Ismail had most support, but also those close to the Iranian border, presumably for pragmatic considerations— investment in these areas was more easily delivered. Zendajan, Enjil and Ghuryan topped the list of the districts receiving most investment. Telephone, tarmac roads and electricity were in place there by 2005, reaching many villages. Little, however, was done for the districts of eastern Herat. In Obeh, for example, villagers in 2002 still remembered that Ismail Khan's government had not delivered anything to them during his first emirate, except for collecting taxes. In 2002, children were still being taught in the open air and there was no hospital or clinic.[22]

Third, he was unable effectively to supervise the administration, whose corruption and inefficiency ate away much of the legitimisation which could have derived from the delivery of services. Even after 2001 accusations of corruption end embezzlement abounded. Allegations of corruption came from a number of sources, located both in Herat and in Kabul. According to sources within the General Administration of Anti-Bribery and Corruption of the Presidency, corruption reached particularly high levels in the departments of transport and industry and in the municipality. Certainly, many people in Herat seemed to think that the heads of department were enjoying a standard of living absolutely incompatible with their salaries. Quite a few of them were said to have been buying or building several houses and also acquiring several vehicles. Moreover, the administration was perceived as inefficient, especially in the districts, and it was accused of 'doing nothing', a typical view of their administrations among Afghans. The provision of education too remained far from satisfactory, as pupils only received 1–2 hours of teaching each school day.[23]

Fourth, spending proved to be ineffective when focused on infrastructural development and rival local elites were able to maintain access to resources for patronage purposes. A good demonstration of this came from Shindand district, where Ismail Khan started investing heavily in 2004, launching a program which included asphalting the main roads, building forty-eight new minor roads, improving the provision of drinking water, building government offices and installing two electricity generators. It is very significant that just forty-five days after the start of the reconstruction effort in Shindand the power of the emirate was wiped out in Amanullah's offensive, to Ismail's consternation.[24] Most Heratis were in any case unaware of how much worse the administration of other parts of Afghanistan could be and were therefore unable to make comparisons.

Ethnicisation

There are conflicting claims concerning Herat's ethnic breakdown, but it seems likely that Pashtuns represent a majority of the population, probably around 30–40%. Sunni Tajiks are estimated at around 20–25%, Aimaqs at 30%, Shia Tajiks at 10% and Hazaras at 5%.[25] The rest are Turkic speakers and a variety of small groups. The issue is complicated by conflicting views about the identity of the Aimaqs, not just because some consider themselves Tajiks, but also because they are divided into several tribes, which are often considered separate ethnic groups, rather than Aimaqs. Since both have long represented the main base of support for Jami'at-i Islami, adding the two groups together would not be completely arbitrary. While Tajiks dominate the central part of the province, around the city of Herat, Pashtuns are more numerous in the outlying districts. Along the border with Ghor province and in the north reside many Aimaqs (see Map 22).

Whatever the exact figures, this mixed ethnic set-up provided fertile ground for ethnic conflict. It is not clear if or to what extent Ismail Khan had any ideological hostility towards Pashtuns. Since he was born in a Tajik pocket in the middle of Pashtun territory in Shindand, any hostility of this type might reflect his personal experiences.

What is certain is that Ismail Khan's relations with Pashtun tribesmen were most of the time uneasy. He recruited a fair number of Pashtun military leaders into his Emirate during the jihad, but they proved particularly resilient to his attempts to discipline them. By the end of the jihad few were left on Ismail Khan's side; even fewer were still with him by 2002. In areas of mixed ethnic composition, Ismail Khan's militias tended to be recruited largely among Tajiks, but during the period of jihad and the years of the first governorship, clashes between Pashtuns and Tajiks were rare, except in Shindand, where the conflict between Jami'at (Tajiks) and Hizb-i Islami (Pashtuns) had an ethnic connotation from the beginning, even if not all Pashtuns were aligned with Hizb-i Islami. The ethnic character of the confrontation became much more

Map 22: Ethnic Composition of Herat province

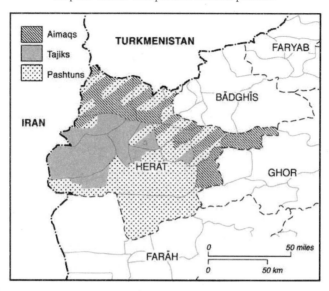

important following the seizure of Herat by the Taliban, when a major source of support for the occupiers were the Pashtun communities, especially at the outset. Although not all the Pashtun communities supported the Taliban, such backing was widespread enough to irritate the Tajik militiamen who were fighting on Ismail Khan's side. As a result, at the time of the fall of the Taliban, Ismail Khan's militias, by then almost entirely Tajik and Aimaq in composition, often indulged in revenge attacks against Pashtun groups in the western part of the province. Such attacks were often indiscriminate and strengthened whatever sentiment against Ismail Khan might have already been there.[26]

During 2002–4, Ismail Khan adopted his classical strategy of coercive coalition-building with Herat's Pashtuns. Certainly, Pashtun militias and tribesmen were targeted in disarmament drives and resilient Pashtun leaders were confronted militarily, as in the case among others of Amanullah Khan of Zeerkoh (Shindand). Although the hostility between Amanullah and Ismail dates back to the early 1990s, in 2001–4 repeated clashes broke out between the two leaders' militiamen. Some more approachable Pashtun leaders would be extended Ismail Khan's patronage, but his own men would sometime sabotage his efforts. In one example from Gulran, Ismail Khan paid travel expenses for some Pashtun nomad elders to reach Kabul and discuss with President Karzai their right to occupy some land, but when they returned the local military leader affiliated with Ismail Khan refused them permission to stay. The land was being assigned to supporters of Ismail Khan and of his proxies. A number of other instances suggest that some at least of the harassment of Pashtuns in

Herat might be due to individual grievances and a desire for revenge on the part of local officials, rather than to Ismail Khan's hatred. Nonetheless, there is no question that Ismail Khan excluded Pashtuns from positions of power and influence in Herat, in the army and police (see chapter 15).[27]

His refusal to coopt Pashtuns into Herat's power structure, together with the harassment by the militias, had a unifying effect on the province's Pashtuns. In July 2002 a group of Pashtun tribal leaders gathered in Herat (probably clandestinely) and prepared a petition to President Karzai, asking for the removal of Ismail Khan and for an enquiry into the abuses of his 'Tajik' militias. Demand for a leader appears to have been high among Pashtun tribal leaders in the region and Amanullah Khan emerged as the only credible choice. Throughout 2002–2004, Amanullah Khan survived all attempts by Ismail Khan to overcome him and even launched occasional counterattacks. His mere ability to survive politically and militarily turned out to be sufficient to attract the support of disgruntled Pashtuns throughout the province and beyond it. Hundreds of Pashtuns from Ghuryan and other districts joined his ranks and at the decisive moment he succeeded in mobilising support through tribal networks from southern strongmen like Gul Agha Shirzai. By the summer of 2004, he was able to field a force of a few thousand motivated fighters, many of whom had suffered at the hands of Ismail Khan's men. Most importantly, Amanullah Khan had succeeded in establishing good connections in Kabul. He claimed to be in constant contact with President Karzai himself, while Ismail Khan alleged that his main source of help was Tribal Affairs Minister Noorzai.[28] Amanullah's role in bringing down Ismail Khan in 2004 was crucial. However, as of mid-2007 there was no sign yet that Ismail Khan's men had reacted by resorting to ethnic strife on a significant scale. This appears to be an indication that his attitude towards Pashtuns was not ideologically motivated, but a reflection of his more general inclination towards personal rule, to the exclusion of all except his closest collaborators.

Notes

1. 'Sharing power is hard to do', op. cit.; interviews with former military leaders and government officials, Herat, Sept.-Oct. 2005.
2. Interviews with former military leaders and government officials, Herat, Sept.-Oct. 2005.
3. 'Sharing power is hard to do', op. cit.
4. Personal communication with administration officials, Herat, May 2005.
5. Ahmed Rashid, 'Civil Society Returns To Herat', *EurasiaNet*, 16 May 2002; Pamela Constable, 'Cracks in a Warlord's Armor. A Local Afghan Ruler Hears Voices of Dissent', *Washington Post*, 9 July 2002; Human Rights Watch (2002b), p. 27.
6. Ibid., section The Women's Shura; John Donnelly, 'Self-styled emir lords it over Herat's poor', *Boston Globe*, 20 May 2002; Andrea Stone, 'Afghan governor de facto ruler in west "Warlords" like him hold fate of central government', *The New York Times*, 19 Dec. 2002; 'New Limits on Female Education in Afghanistan. In Western Province of Herat, School Restrictions; Gender Segregation', *Human Rights Watch*,

NewYork, 16 Jano. 2003; RFE/RL 27 Nov. 2002; 'Mini-skirts, dating in Afghanistan's Herat after warlord leaves', *AFP*, 28 Nov. 2005.

7. 'Afghan warlord Ismail Khan sets up human rights body', *AFP*, 13 Jano. 2003.

8. Rahimullah Samander, 'Loya Jirga Delegates Facing Intimidation', *Afghan Recovery Report*, No. 7, 6 June 2002; Interviews with candidates, Herat, Nov. 2005; interviews with NGO and diplomatic officials, Kabul, Nov. 2005.

9. Interviews with former members of the Afzali front, Herat, Sept.-Oct. 2005.

10. The ulema had authorised the collection of Zakat, that is 10% of harvest, but many military leaders went much beyond that.

11. Dubuis (1989), p. 171; Interview with Qazi Nazar, village in Herat province, Nov. 2005.

12. This section is based on interviews with former military leaders of Ismail Khan, of the militias and of other jihadi groups, as well as government officials and officers of the regular army, Herat, Sept.-Oct. 2005.

13. Pamela Constable, 'Cracks in a Warlord's Armor…', op. cit.; John Donnelly, 'Self-styled emir…', op. cit.; Human Rights Watch (2002a), pp. 15, 35.

14. Ibid., p. 27.

15. Zahir Azimi (1377), p. 96, 162; Fariba Nawa, 'Return of the 'Good Warlord', *The Village Voice*, Nov. 21—27, 2001, http://www.villagevoice.com/news/0147,nawa,30061,1.html; John Donnelly, 'Self-styled emir…', op. cit.; Human Right Watch (2002b); Amy Waldman, 'Courted by U.S. and Iran…', op. cit.; *AFP*, 12 Nov. 2002; Julien Bousac, 'Reconstructing States. Afghanistan: emirate of Herat', *Le Monde Diplomatique*, Dec. 2003; *Hindokosh News Agency*, Kabul, in Dari 0001 GMT, 15 Feb. 2004.

16. Dubuis (1989), pp. 161–2, 165. The curriculum included Persian, arithmetic, drawing, Koran, religious rites and jihad. In areas away from the war, Jami'at claimed that 60% of boys and 5% of girls attended school. While Jami'at claimed to be favourable to girls attending, parents were generally opposed.

17. *Herat TV* in Dari 1600 gmt, 21 Feb. 2004; *RFE/RL*, 27 Nov. 2002; Zahir Azimi (1377), p. 98

18. Interviews with members of Herat's Shiite intelligentsia, Herat, Dec. 2004; 'Ethnic group hits out at Ismail Khan', *AFP*, 21 March 2004. On the hostility towards any idea of Sunni-Shia unity within the Herati administration see also *RFE/RL* 27 Nov. 2002.

19. An example is provided by a public speech of the leader of the Republican Party, Sanjar. He was warmly received by the Herati public at first, but his strong secular tone hit the wrong chord and people were turned against him (interview with UN official, Herat, Dec. 2004).

20. Dubuis (1989), p. 158; Rashid (2000), p. 39; Fariba Nawa, Return of the 'Good Warlord', op. cit.

21. Marc Kaufman, 'Karzai's Taxing Problem…', op. cit.; Barry Bearak, 'Unreconstructed', *New York Times*, 1 June 2003; 'Afghan official lists public works projects completed in Herat', *Etefaq-e Eslam*, 31 May 2003; *RFE/RL*, 27 Nov. 2002.

22. Pamela Constable, 'Cracks in a Warlord's Armor…', op. cit.; interview with political activists, Herat, May 2005; interview with notables from Karokh, Sept. 2005; Borzou Daragahi, 'Afghan governor spurs instability fears', *Washington Times*, 13 April 2002.

23. Julien Bousac, 'Reconstructing States…', op. cit.; interviews with Herati businessmen, May 2005; personal communication with teachers and parents in Herat, Nov. 2004.

24. *Herat TV* at 1730 GMT, 4 Sept. 2004.
25. Based on interviews with local officials and Kulakov (2003), p. 62.
26. Personal communication with relative of Alauddin Khan; For documentation on the attacks see Human Rights Watch (2002a).
27. Beall/Esser (2005), p. 40; Human Rights Watch (2002a), section "Abuses against Pashtuns"; Rahimullah Samander, 'Loya Jirga Delegates Facing Intimidation'. Herat's local power baron is locking up potential opponents in the run-up to the grand assembly', *Afghan Recovery Report*, No. 7, 6 June 2002; interview with UN official, Herat, May 2004; interview with former army officer from Gulran, Sept. 2005; 'Afghans rally in support of Herat governor Ismail Khan', *AFP*, 28 May 2003.
28. *AFP*, 26 July 2002; Amy Waldman, 'Strife Exposes Deep and Wide Ethnic Tensions', *New York Times*, 6 Sept. 2004; Anthony Loyd, 'Afghan warlord closes in on prize city', *The Times*, 25 Aug. 2004.

22

BETWEEN WARLORDISM
AND GUERRILLA WAR

MASSUD AND SHURA-I NEZAR

The origins during jihad

While Ismail Khan and Dostum appear to be clear cut cases of big warlords, Massud's case is more controversial. The military-political organisations operating in the greater north-east[1] differed little from those operating in the north, at least initially. One key difference was geography, given that the north-east is more rugged than the west or the north. Another difference was the lack of a major city to create a 'vortex' and polarise the military class into conflicting coalitions (see Introduction). Also, with the exception of Baghlan province, which was in fact mostly incorporated into Junbesh, no major strategic road crosses this territory. Possibly related to these factors, over time the HDK government in Kabul paid far more attention to the greater north[2] than to the greater north-east, for example investing more resources there in the formation of militias. Apart from Baghlan, large militias also appeared in northern Takhar and some areas of Badakhshan, but compared to the north the overall presence of militias was modest. The lesser strategic importance to Kabul of the provinces of Kunduz, Takhar and Badakhshan and the difficult geography of most of Parwan and Kapisa also explains why no major progovernment warlords emerged in this region. By contrast, the most consistent and successful effort to create a unified command structure among the mujahidin took place in the greater north-east in 1985–1992, exceeding even what Ismail Khan was doing in Herat. This attempt, and the fact that its constituent element (the military class) was the same as in western and northern Afghanistan, makes this region an important test for understanding warlordism in Afghanistan.

An Islamist activist with a gift for military organisation, Ahmad Shah Massud played an essential role in the creation and growth of Shura-i Nezar. In fact, it is certain that without him nothing like Shura-i Nezar would have

281

appeared in the north-east. He resembled a community leader like Naderi in his reliance on a single group (the Panjshiris) as the core of fighting forces and as the leadership of his military-political organisation, although, contrary to Naderi, Massud emerged in such a role only during the war. On the other hand, Massud's importance in the national politics of Afghanistan and his interest in the topic studied in this book derives from his very expansion beyond Panjshir and his transcending of the role of militarised community leader. His transformation into a charismatic military leader well beyond Panjshir cast him in a role that Naderi only remotely approached, even if the latter also managed to some extent to expand his influence beyond the Ismailis of Baghlan. Many factors contributed to Massud's rise: his genuine tactical skills, his capabilities as a speaker and in inter-personal relations, and the failure of the Soviets to subdue him despite the concentration of overwhelming military force.

In 1982 he embarked on a major effort to expand his influence throughout the north-eastern region, which would eventually culminate in the formation of Shura-i Nezar. His rising profile had led to his appointment by the leadership of Jami'at-i Islami as the overall leader of the party in the greater north-east, despite the hostility of more than a few of the Jami'ati political heavyweights based in Peshawar. By 1982 his stock had risen throughout the region, facilitating his task greatly. A key aspect of this growth is that he did not expand his ranks through direct recruitment beyond Panjshir, but by coopting the military class, which continued to operate according to its own criteria. A few exceptions aside, Massud's expansionism was more hegemonic in character than based on coercion. He built military legitimacy, which he earned through his military prowess, into 'military hegemony', which could be described as:

- the acceptance by the military class of his wider leadership role due to the recognition of his superior skills;
- the willingness to imitate his organisational practices and tactics.

Such hegemony was initially (1983) mainly taking the shape of the despatch of instructors to other Jami'atis operating in the surrounding region. Training courses for military leaders from outside the valley were organised in Panjshir.[3] From 1984, Massud also started carrying out military operations beyond the Panjshir valley, a development which, among other effects, had that of allowing a greater number of non-Panjshiris to admire the superiority of his guerrilla force, hence contributing further to strengthen his military hegemony.

In line with Mao's writings, which Massud had carefully studied, he sought to develop his guerrilla forces into an army capable of fighting pitched battles. The conquest of the capital, and hence of state power, was always in Massud's mind, a characteristic which set him apart from Dostum or Ismail Khan. He used his military legitimacy and hegemony to mobilise the troops towards an end of which they were rarely aware, presenting it as the result of the need to attack more rewarding targets such as fortified garrisons. From the very early days, Massud took great care of the organisational aspects of guerrilla war, shaping his Panjshiri fighting force in such a way as to prepare it to become a real army one day. However, his efforts to turn his followers among the military class outside Panjshir into an effective military machine had mixed results. An initial problem derived from using a particular community as the core of his insurgent army, as the sense of superiority of Panjshiri fighters was often resented among combatants from other regions.[4]

Massud's cooptation of a growing number of military leaders outside Panjshir was based not only on his skills as a military leader, but also on his ability to re-distribute resources and build institutions. In this sense, the difference between him and Ismail Khan or Dostum was not very great, although in Massud's case military leadership mattered proportionally more then the redistribution of resources and even more than coercion. By the mid-1980s he had secured control of the distribution of supplies in Parwan and Kapisa, but he never managed to impose on the party leadership in Peshawar the approval for a similar system to cover the greater north-east as a whole. His appointment as regional Amir of Jami'at was meant to be little more then symbolic, and brought with it no substantial powers, concerning supplies or any other matter. As a result, Massud resorted to the creation of an institutional framework under his direction, which would have highlighted his leadership role by reducing personal rivalries and facilitating cooperation. The creation of Shura-i Nezar in 1984 was not sponsored by the leadership of Jami'at. This military-political structure incorporated local military leaders regardless of the party they belonged to and built around them an administrative structure in charge of managing relations with the civilian population. Massud maintained full control of Shura-i Nezar, but by the standards of Afghanistan's civil wars the system was characterised by a relatively high level of institutionalisation.[5]

The Panjshiri core notwithstanding, a largely autonomous military class remained the primary constituency of Shura-i Nezar, a fact which makes it possible to speak of an element of warlordism in the system that Massud progressively built. As a result, beyond Panjshir and few other areas, the structure headed by Massud remained quite loose. The few Islamists in Jami'at were thinly spread across the greater north-east, as most of the old Jawanan-i Muslimun activists belonged to a hostile party (Hizb-i Islami). Abuses, even among those who joined Shura-i Nezar, were frequent. The consequence was that Massud tried to impose stricter discipline on his commanders, preventing the establishment of relationships with the government and abuses towards the population. Although he never tried to enforce the same standards of discipline which he applied to his own mobile forces, his demands were often still seen as excessive. As part of Shura-i Nezar Massud established a military police with his own distinct uniform and a special court, charged with trying undisciplined military leaders. In practice, Massud had only limited success in enforcing the level of discipline that he would have liked. Nor were Shura-i

Nezar's courts and police exempt from criticism. The police was accused of not behaving well itself, while at least until 1989 there were reports of detainees being abused.[6] Massud's demand that all goods and weapons captured from the government convoys ambushed by the mujahidin be turned over to Shura-i Nezar (to him, that is), who would then redistribute them according to need, prevented him from attracting many mujahidin leaders who might have been otherwise interested in linking up with Shura-i Nezar, particularly in the Salang area were booty was abundant.[7]

The consequences of the resilience of the military class vis-à-vis Massud could be long-lasting. The hostility of some military leaders to Massud would lead them to flirt with Dostum after 1992 or join the Taliban after 1996. These military leaders, such as Arif Khan and Naseri of Kunduz, or Agha Shirin Salangi and Karim Qarabaghi of Parwan, would then make up the backbone of Taliban support in the north-eastern region. Even when they did not go as far as joining the enemy or another faction, they would often fail to cooperate with Massud. In 2000, during the war against the Taliban, Jami'at-i Islami's area of control was reduced to Badakhshan, Panjshir and a few districts of Takhar, Baghlan and Parwan, with the Taliban a few kilometres away from Badakhshan. Still, Massud had a hard time trying to mobilise fighters from this province, as local strongmen resisted his call to send more men. Although the potential manpower of Badakhshan represented the greater part of what was available to Massud, in October 2000 only 300 Badakhshanis had been deployed on the frontline, forcing Massud to travel to Faizabad to press for more. Even those who had deployed were described by Massud's commanders at the front as a burden more than an asset due to their poor motivation. The preferred military leaders' answer to the Taliban threat was to apply for visas to Tajikistan, preparing the ground for their flight from Afghanistan. This weak mobilisation might have been due to the reluctance of military leaders, more than of the population itself. In Jurm district, the appointment of a new district commander by the pro-Massud military leader Sardar appears to have been supported by the villagers, despite the latter's greater propensity to send fighters to the battlefront than his predecessor, whom Sardar had forcefully removed. The former district military leader's attempt to reclaim his post was met with hostility by the population. By gradually replacing district commanders and increasing his influence in places such as Jurm and Arghanchkhawah, by the summer of 2001 Massud managed to get a substantial number (2,400) of Badakhshanis deployed on the frontline in Takhar. Badakhshan was not exceptional: during the fighting against the Taliban in Takhar (1998–2001), for example, Massud had to frequently rotate his 'commanders', as he did not trust them to remain loyal. In one occasion, fearing a betrayal, he even summoned to his HQ (in Khwaja Nahauddin) Piram Qul, the military leader of Rustaq and a key player on the Takhar frontline, in order to disarm him. Piram Qul however refused to comply.[8]

There are other similarities between Massud and the warlords. Although Massud started his career as an activist in the ranks of the Afghan Islamist movement, his difficult relations with his political leaders resemble to some extent those of the 'orphan' warlord Dostum or the 'insurgent' warlord Ismail Khan. The Jami'at-i Islami's leader Rabbani had little direct influence over Massud during the jihad. Both in Kabul after 1992 and even more so in Badakhshan after the Taliban captured the capital in 1996, he was increasingly becoming almost a figurehead, wielding little real power compared to Massud. For example, Massud's signature was allegedly required for the release of government money from the state bank. Massud seems to have kept on Rabbani because he was still recognised as President of Afghanistan by a number of countries, he was able to print money (a key source of funding of the war effort after 1992, see chapter 4) and because he guaranteed some international support. He also acted as a conduit for receiving hard currency through Tajikistan.[9] In other words, Rabbani compensated for Massud's relatively weak international connections.

Available evidence also suggests that Massud had in abundance those 'Machiavellian' virtues that are the resort of the state-making warlord. He did not shy away from ruthlessness if necessary. He believed that negotiations and alliances were always merely tactical—he seems to have agreed with Mao that power comes from the barrel of a gun. As he stated in one of his letters, 'experience has shown that alliances among parties of equal strength will not last long. A powerful party should take the initiative to form and lead such an alliance'.[10]

In line with Dostum and Ismail Khan, Massud had his own 'diplomacy'. In fact, sometimes Massud proved to be a cunning diplomat, from the early days when he managed to get invited into Panjshir by the groups which were already active there (which he then proceeded to eliminate), until the days of April 1992 when he managed to seize control of Kabul without fighting. The best known result of his diplomatic activities with Kabul was the 1983 ceasefire, which came at a time when the Panjshiri mujahidin were showing signs of war weariness and general fatigue, allowing him not just to recover and rest the fighters and civilians, but also to intensify his efforts to build a network beyond the valley. Such negotiations continued after the end of the ceasefire in 1984 and culminated in 1988 with the offer by the Soviets of an autonomous Tajik region in north-eastern Afghanistan to be led by Massud and including the provinces of Badakhshan, Takhar, Baghlan and parts of Parwan and Kapisa. Even the appointment of Massud as Defence Minister was on the table. The offer also included participation in the central government, the legalisation of Jami'at Islami, offers of economic aid to the region and, most noteworthily, the creation of 'all Tajik' military units to be incorporated into the armed forces of Afghanistan. This would have been a warlord's dream, but Massud never took the bait. However, the negotiations allowed Massud to open channels of communications with the Russians, which turned out to be useful in 1992 and later. Massud's involvement in the Tajikistan peace process was another smart move, as it opened a Tajikistan conduit to supplies, which would prove crucial to his military effort against the Taliban after the loss of

Kabul. Although the help provided by the government of Tajikistan itself was modest, not going beyond the servicing of Massud's helicopters and some logistical assistance,[11] that government allowed Russian and most importantly Iranian supplies to travel through its territory. Without these supplies Massud would have been defeated long before 2001.[12]

Massud was also very aware of the value of having his own propaganda and public relations operations and was always ready to spend time with journalists, an attitude than in the end cost him his life when two assassins posing as journalists blew him up in 2001. He built a comparatively luxurious guesthouse in Panjshir to host foreign dignitaries and journalists. In some cases he appears to have even paid money in order to get photographed.[13]

In common with the warlords Massud also had an autonomous revenue base. Due to his inability to convince Rabbani of the value of privileging him as a target of his patronage, Massud had a strong incentive to diversify his sources of revenue. Compared to other mujahidin leaders, he was in a favourable position, because of the presence of three lapis lazuli mines and an emerald mine in Panjshir, to which two more lapis lazuli mines in Badakhshan were later added as Massud expanded his influence. Initially Massud also relied on land tax as did many other mujahidin, but subsequently dropped it as the war affected Panjshir's agriculture heavily. However, the tax was later introduced in the territories beyond Panjshir, as they came under Massud's influence. He also taxed traders, again like many other mujahidin. One peculiarity of Massud was the introduction of a tax on Panjshiris working in Kabul, often for the government, in exchange for the safety of their property in the valley (see Table 8). It is hard to estimate Massud's cash revenue, not least because it must have fluctuated widely. Also, the information available might have been contaminated for propaganda purposes, or in order to extract more resources from Rabbani. Bringing together disparate sources, the picture which emerges (see Table 9) is in the range of $2.5–4 million. This figure of course excludes the aid in kind received from Jami'at and other sources, such as weaponry, ammunition and various types of goods and equipment. It also excludes direct foreign aid, which he started receiving towards the end of the 1980s, thanks to the generosity of a number of INGOs and of some Arab supporters of the cause, as well as to the CIA. From 1996 foreign aid appears to have mainly come from Iran; there were two Iranian Revolutionary Guards observers with Shura-i Nezar on the Kabul front in 2001 and they might also have operated as liaison officers to monitor deliveries and distribute cash. A liaison officer from Tajikistan was also based in Panjshir to supervise Russian supplies, but no cash seems to have been provided from this source.[14]

Massud's financial resources were spent to maintain the administration, pay the fighters and feed them, to carry out some reconstruction, but particularly towards the end of the jihad, as resources became more abundant thanks to foreign aid, part of this cash was available to consolidate Shura-i Nezar by offering subsidies to military leaders. Still, as Shura-i Nezar expanded, that money proved far from sufficient. Even as late as 2000–01, when direct foreign aid appears to have peaked, it could not have been enough, otherwise Massud would not have decided that taxation had to be maintained, despite the low returns generated and the friction that it was causing with sections of the population, such as herdsmen from Kunduz in 2001.[15] In fact there are allegations that by the late 1990s Shura-i Nezar had to rely on revenue from the narcotics trade, collected under the supervision of a military leader of Farkhar. One source estimated that narcotics contributed $24 million to Massud's coffers.[16]

Table 8: Taxes Imposed by Massud, 1980–1992

Taxation policy	
Precious stones	5–10%
Land tax	10%
Tax on goods	5–15%
Tax on Panjshiris in Kabul	5%

Sources: Liakhovskii (1995); Clausen (1992); Mansoor (1369), ch. 3; Rubin (1995), p. 236; Gall (1989), p. 95; interview with Hafiz Mansoor, Kabul, May 2006.

Table 9: Massud's Revenue During the Jihad, by source.

Revenue sources	Amount	Period
Sent by Jami'at	30 mill afs	198?-199?
Tax on Panjshiris in Kabul	8 mill afs	beginning of 1983–1992
Locally collected taxes	3–4 mill afs	initially
Taxes on goods	6–7 mill afs	late 1980s–1992
Taxes on precious stones	34–35 mill afs	1979–1992
Looting	up to 35 mill afs	1980–1992
Foreign aid	$ million	1988–1992
Total	100—160 mill afs + direct foreign aid (2.5–4 mill $ + direct foreign aid)	

Sources: As table 8 above.

There were however some key features of Shura-i Nezar that set it apart from the warlord polities of western and northern Afghanistan. As I have already mentioned, Massud enjoyed political legitimacy at least within Panjshir as a community leader. At the top of his organisation, until the end Massud always relied on a small network of educated and trained Panjshiris, or individuals linked to Panjshir, occasionally accommodating a few Badakhshanis among them. In conversations with various state officials from Panjshir during 2004–6, little sense of ideological commitment emerged beyond a vague Islamic conservatism. The point most often raised was about the future and the interests of the people of Panjshir.[17]

Another important feature that separated him from the warlords was Massud's lasting ideological commitment. Massud's career started in the 1970s, when he emerged as one of the leading Islamist activists in the field and was involved in the failed uprising of 1975. There is evidence that he remained an Islamist to the end. For example he long maintained the typical Islamist hostility towards royalist groups and their leadership, despite their common strategic interests, preferring to seek alliances with fellow Islamists such as Rasul Sayyaf and Yunis Khalis. It has also to be taken into account that after 1992 Massud was more exposed to the influence of the conservative core element of Jami'at, as interaction between them intensified once both moved to Kabul. One group of Islamic conservatives, known as the Al Hadith group, was in particular closely associated with him. These had not taken active part in the jihad, being mainly middle class Islamic activists, including some former leftists, such as Dr Abdur Rahman and longer-term Islamists such as Dr Sahar, Dr Mushahid, Dr Mahdi, Ahmad Mossadeq and Sayyed Amanullah Hashimi. Some of them, like Rahman, Mahdi, Hashimi and Mossadeq, became part of the inner circle. Mahdi was then appointed first secretary of the Afghan embassy in Dushanbe, an important position after the arrival to power of the Taliban, because of the supply lines coming through that country. Mossadeq became governor of Takhar province, while Hashemi was appointed chief political officer of the army. This trend towards a stronger Islamic conservatism appears to have negatively influenced his relationship with Dostum and the former officers of Najibullah's army.[18]

It has to be remembered that Massud's own ideological orientation did not extend very deeply into his army. He lacked sufficient numbers of educated and committed cadres and moreover he never invested major resources in carrying out grassroots political work. Massud's chief effort to ensure the ideological awareness and homogeneity of the Panjshiri fighters consisted in the establishment of a network of political commissars. Each unit included one of them accompanying the commander and they were charged with, among other things, lecturing the mujahidin about Islam and politics, but they were never popular. In fact, their presence was deeply resented and they were the object of 'hostility and contempt'. Whatever influence the commissars could muster was the result of the support of the mullahs. Often, the commissars were seen addressing villagers with a mullah beside them.[19] The commissars' system moreover was limited to Panjshir.

Shura-i Nezar after Massud

As long as he was alive, the tension between Massud's role as Islamist activist turned community leader and his role at the helm of a coalition of the north-eastern military class was contained. Inevitably such tension came into the open after his death. Shura-i Nezar was technically dissolved in 1992, but as a network of military leaders associated with Massud it remained in place, within the framework of Rabbani's Islamic State. The first thing to become apparent after Massud's assassination was that he had no real successor. His leading military and political lieutenants (Fahim, Qanuni and Abdullah) represented the group at Bonn, where they succeeded in maintaining their unity and in sidelining both Rabbani and other rivals, on the strength of their militias having already occupied Kabul. In agreement with the Bush Administration, they succeeded in imposing their own candidate to the Presidency, Hamid Karzai, a Popolzai Pashtun whom they perceived as weak and pliable, little more than a figurehead to appease Pashtun opinion.[20] At that time, there was already opposition to the alliance with Karzai among the more ideological elements within their ranks, such as Hafiz Mansoor, who tried to run as a presidential candidate in the Emergency Loya Jirga of June 2002 as an alternative to Karzai, but was forced to give up by the combined opposition of Fahim, Qanuni and Abdullah.[21]

Among his lieutenants who emerged after his death in a prominent position, Yunis Qanuni appears to have been the more genuine product of an Islamist background. Fahim Khan was less interested in ideology. Despite his shortcomings as military commander,[22] during the 1980s he had served Massud well, who had used him not just as head of his intelligence service, but also as an efficient negotiator. He despatched him to resolve delicate situations in places like Kapisa and Andarab. Certainly, he emerged as a pragmatist after 2001, with a penchant for high-profile business dealings and an inclination towards patrimonialism.[23] An apt manipulator inside Shura-i Nazar, Fahim was completely oblivious of the importance of maintaining a good press. By 2003 he was already one of the international press's favourite targets. Qanuni and Abdullah fared much better, although they were rarely able to gain political advantage from good public relations. Their best act was to present themselves as educated, respectable and well dressed men who were qualified for their jobs, in contrast with the mass of warlords and strongmen who were sometimes barely literate.

Fahim was selected as the unofficial leader of the 'shadow' Shura-i Nezar, a move that surprised many given the man's lack of charisma. Initially, Fahim's ability immediately to come up with a pragmatic plan of action in the wake of the shock caused by Massud's death had been the key factor in propelling him to the top. His sound negotiating skills also played in his favour, given the expectation that such a quality could help in keeping Shura-i Nezar and the United Front together. He did indeed manage to reassure the key players in the United Front and to keep it united. However, while his role of military commander of Shura-i Nezar was generally accepted by the other lieutenants of Massud, on political issues his leadership was contested by Qanuni and Abdullah. Fahim was probably accepted precisely because he was perceived as a political lightweight, hence easy to marginalise once the war was over. As he was appointed Minister of Defence, he was in the ideal position to maintain and strengthen relations not only with Massud's former commanders, but also with warlords and strongmen throughout the country, including in the Pashtun belt, where he relied on Islamist and fundamentalist elements to build a network. This, together with the end of the conflict and the weaker ideological commitment of Fahim, resulted in a massive shift towards a patronage-oriented approach. Little was left of Massud's attempt to maintain order and discipline among the military leaders, as well as to establish some meritocratic criteria of selection. The result was seen in a massive increase in abuse and ill-treatment of the civilian population in the north-east and in Kapisa and Parwan.[24] Simultaneously, Fahim's effort to centralise patronage ultimately failed due to the opposition of both international actors and other Afghan players, guaranteeing that he would eventually be unable to consolidate his position. Even during the anti-Taliban campaign of October 2001, Fahim's and his lieutenants' request to act as a channel for all support provided by the Americans to military leaders of the United Front was repeatedly rejected by the US.[25]

Fahim's weak legitimacy was compounded by his controversial appointments, such as Daoud Khan as commander of 6th Army Corps, in charge of the four north-eastern provinces of Kunduz, Takhar, Baghlan and Badakhshan. A young commander who had served under Massud, he suddenly found himself in a position senior to that of many who had fought since the beginning of the jihad. Unsurprisingly, he found it extremely difficult to obtain the support (not to speak of the obedience) of his subordinates. Apart from his home areas and strongholds of Farkhar and Warsaj in southern Takhar, he only effectively commanded the loyalty of the military leaders of Baghlan, who were mostly newcomers themselves, not yet firmly entrenched in their positions and therefore in need of outside support. In Badakhshan, obedience to Daoud was almost non-existent, and the province relapsed into the usual turf wars among local military leaders, this time over the control of the drug routes. In northern Takhar, Uzbek military leaders turned to Dostum for help in their effort to receive a fair share of official appointments, which in their eyes were rewarding only the Tajik old guard of Massud loyalists. In Kunduz, long standing local players such as Mir Alam were particularly jealous of Daoud's appointment, while the Uzbeks and Turkmens of the northern third of the province were busy playing double or treble games between Junbesh, Jami'at and Hizb-i Islami (see Map 23).[26]

As a result, political fragmentation returned to the north-east, preventing the emergence of a figure comparable to Ismail Khan or Dostum. None of the north-eastern provinces had a major leading figure playing a unifying role. At the district level, a multitude of strongmen and military leaders, mostly connected to one or other network, competed over sources of revenue, including official appointments. Missing the catalysing role of a large city (none of the provincial centres of Kunduz, Teluqan, Pul-i Khumri or Faizabad exceed a few tens of thousands of inhabitants), the north-east never saw the emergence of large 'new generation' businesses. As a result the military leaders who populated the region were not as active in the legal economy as their larger counterparts of the north and tended rather to focus on exercising as much control as possible on the drug trade, which was very developed in the region. In the central region, the economic interests of the Panjshiri military

Map 23: Important Military Leaders of the Greater North-east and the Influence of Shura-i Nezar (the grey shade indicates military leaders affiliated to Shura-i Nezar; the lighter shade indicates those responding to Daoud Khan)

class gravitated around Kabul, where some managed to get a firm hold on several key businesses, especially in telecommunications and in the property market.[27]

Smaller military leaders proved to be more interested in occupying positions within the central state than in becoming active in business, possibly because of the lack of financial resources (the drug trade has never been very developed in the central region), and became heavily dependent on their state jobs. Parwan and Kapisa, the two core provinces in Massud's system, remained comparatively more compact politically, but by 2004 signs of tension were emerging there too. Fahim's lack of management of the territory had allowed characters of dubious quality to occupy the ground, often at the expense of other Jami'atis. In Ghorband valley, for example, Satar, who had been one of the few Jami'atis to operate in a corner of the valley solidly under the control of Hizb-i Islami, had eliminated all his rivals by just being the first to return there in 2001. Many Hizbis had cooperated with the Taliban and were therefore marginalised after the change of regime. The signs of fragmentation in Parwan and Kapisa often took the shape of the reappearance of rifts among old and new Jami'atis, that is those who joined in the late 1980s and in the 1990s. The newcomers had not been treated in a satisfactory manner in Jami'at. As the new Jami'atis had mostly been Hizbis before, the attempt of Hizb-i Islami to re-establish itself in 2005–6 might well have appeared as a serious danger to the old Jami'atis. At least two of these former Hizbis, both important military leaders, Agha Shirin Salangi and Karim Qarabaghi, were assassinated in 2004 and 2005 in Kabul, in what could have been a pre-emptive move.[28]

Another sign of fragmentation manifested itself when the Panjshiri core started disagreeing over which option to choose after the fall of Fahim from the post of Defence Minister. Fahim's pre-eminent business interests had earned him little sympathy from the rank-and-file, who even before his removal were beginning to feel threatened by the campaign surrounding demands for reform within the Ministry. Soon a faction emerged among the veteran commanders, advocating a tougher stance against central government and the foreign presence.[29]

Divisions soon became evident even at the top. As early as 2002, after finally openly splitting from Jami'at, Qanuni, Fahim and one of Massud's brothers, Wali, had been involved in the attempt to form a political party on the basis of the old Shura-i Nezar network. Whereas Rabbani was still trying in 2002 to prevent the election of women to the Loya Jirga and to establish limits to the new freedoms, the 'young Turks' of Jami'at criticised the old generations' ineffectiveness and clericalism and tried to promote a more modern image. Faced with a disintegrating base, however, their efforts to establish a functioning political party under the name of Nehzat-i Milli achieved little in organisational terms. As Fahim's weak leadership faded, there was still no consensus over a stronger candidate. From almost the beginning, Wali Massud had on various occasions manifested his hostility to Fahim.[30] In the wake of the Presidential elections of October 2004, his brother Ahmad Zia Massud accepted Karzai's offer of candidacy on his ticket as Vice-president, replacing Fahim and implicitly splitting Shura-i Nezar and Nehzat-i Milli. Qanuni, who like Fahim had been marginalised, but unlike him maintained some support, responded by running for the Presidency. He ended second with 16% of the vote despite Rabbani's support for Karzai. This more than reasonable result catapulted Qanuni to the forefront of Afghan politics, whereas Massud's brothers rapidly lost even the modest level of support that they had. By the parliamentary elections of September 2005, the split between the followers of Qanuni, now the most popular figure within the circle of Shura-i Nezar, and those of Wali and Ahmad Zia Massud, was formalised through the establishment of separate organisations. Qanuni had launched his own party in 2005, Afghanistan-i Newin, to compete with Nehzat-i Milli. In the end Afghanistan-i

Newin overshadowed Nehzat-i Milli by becoming one of the largest groups in parliament, with nineteen members. Nehzat-i Milli managed to elect only four members of parliament, including both of those from Panjshir. The success of Afghanistan-i Newin had been largely due to Qanuni's personal appeal as a widely recognised opposition figure; the party had made little progress in the way of organised party structures. The same is true of Rabbani's Jami'at, which brought seventeen MPs to the parliament. Both fragments of Shura-i Nezar as well as Jami'at remained mainly based on loose networks of military leaders, whose militias played an important role in securing the electoral success, even more so than in Junbesh's case. Neither of them ever managed to produce anything resembling a party program, let alone a clear ideology, while Rabbani only published his own speeches.[31]

The divided and ineffective leadership accelerated the decline of the control exercised by Shura-i Nezar over the militias. Being confident in the leverage deriving from having thousands of militiamen concentrated in and around Kabul, the leadership adopted a defiant posture when confronted with international pressure for reforming the key ministries that they controlled, such as Defence and Interior, and for allowing more space to other ethnic and political groups. They failed to realise, however, that their militias' support could no longer be taken for granted. By 2004, when Fahim was dropped from Karzai's presidential ticket, support for him among the military class had largely eroded. The commanders of the Panjshiri forces thought that Fahim had delivered little or nothing to them and by 2004 most fellow members of Shura-i Nezar regarded him as far too self-interested. Although Fahim had tried to delay the start of the DDR program, in the end he bowed to international pressure and launched it in late 2003. His continuing attempt to slow it down was enough to irritate the international community, but insufficient to reassure the military class, who could still see the loss of their institutional positions coming, even if a few months later than scheduled. When, upset by being dumped by Karzai, Fahim toured the militias headquartered in Kabul and Parwan to enlist their support for a public announcement of their backing for him, he found little support. Only about 15% of the militia leaders declared themselves ready to support him, while the others justified their indifference with Fahim's previous neglect of their interests.[32] As a result, Fahim found himself in a very weak position compared to Karzai, who enjoyed instead the full support of the US Embassy. To all intents and purposes, the episode marked the end of Fahim's political career.

Notes

1. I define this region as the four north-eastern provinces (Kunduz, Takhar, Baghlan and Badakhshan) plus Parwan, Kapisa and northern Kabul.
2. This includes the five northern provinces plus Baghlan and Kunduz.
3. Yusufzai (1985), pp. 111–112.
4. Interview with Hafiz Mansoor, 8 May 2006, Kabul; Mansoor (1369), ch. 6; Walwalji (1378), p. 46.

5. Massud's letter dated 10 Nov. 1982, in Es'haq (1382); Massud's letter dated 5 June 1983, in Es'haq.

6. Interview with Moheiddin Bahdi, former ambassador to Tajikistan, Kabul Feb. 2006; interview with Fahim Doshti, Director of Kabul Weekly, Feb. 2006, Kabul; interview with Akram Kargar,Teluqan, May 2006.

7. See, for the case of Salang, Puig (1994), p. 444.

8. Interview with intellectual and journalist in Kunduz, 20 May 2006; UNSMA internal documents 3 Oct. 2000, 13 June 2001, July 2001, 2 Sept. 2001; interview with UNAMA official, Kunduz, May 2006.

9. Dorronsoro (2005), p. 230; Baigi (2000), p. 75; UNSMA internal document, 11 May 2000.

10. Massud's letter dated 22.04.1365, in Es'haq (1382).

11. Tajikistan's army officers were based in Panjshir as liaison officers (interview with former officer of Tajikistan's army, Kabul, May 2003).

12. Mansoor (1369), ch. 4; Lyakhovskii (1995), p. 511, 518–524.

13. Schroen (2007), p. 11; interview with Hafiz Mansoor, Kabul, May 2006.

14. Gall (1989), p. 67; Rubin (1995), p. 259; Schroen (2007), p. 66, 120; interview with former military officer from Tajikistan, Kabul, May 2005.

15. UNSMA internal document, July 2001.

16. Chouvy (2002), p. 143, who bases his estimates on information provided by Ahmed Rashid. The estimate of $36 million earned from the precious stones trade appears excessive, however.

17. Interviews with officials from Panjshir, Kabul, 2004–2006.

18. Puig (2005), pp. 307–9; Walwalji (1378), p. 59; UNSMA internal document, 2 Sept. 2001; interview with Akram Kargar, Teluqan, May 2006.

19. Puig (2005), pp. 415–6; Puig (1994), p. 440; Ryan (1983), p. 151.

20. See Fazelly (2004).

21. Amanullah Narsat, 'The Mujahedin's Journalist', Afghan Recovery Report No. 139, 6 Oct. 2004.

22. During the war against the Taliban, Fahim performed rather badly on the Farkhar front, repeatedly getting the worst in a number of encounters. His command was then handed over to Daoud Khan. Interview with Fahim Doshti, Feb. 2006, Kabul.

23. UNSMA internal document, 2 Sept. 2001; Massud's letter dated 6 Oct. 1984 to Professor Rabbani; letter dated 20 March 1985 to Professor Rabbani, both in Es'haq (1382); Starr (2003), pp. 45ff.

24. For an example for people's complaints about the behavious of 'gunmen' see BIA News Bulletin, June 15 2004.

25. Schroen (2007), p. 104, 108–9, 98, 275; Interview with Anders Fange, Swedish Committee, Kabul 19 May 2003.

26. Personal communication with UN officials, Kunduz, Oct. 2003–May 2004.

27. On the economic interests of the Fahim clan see Starr (2003), pp. 45–48.

28. Interview with Jan Gul Kargar, Kabul 28 May 2006, MP from Parwan; interview with Fazel Rahman Oriya, NGO Carvan, Kabul 23 Jano. 2006; 'Former Afghan turncoat commander who fought under Taliban gunned down in Kabul', Associated Press, 5 Nov. 2003; 'Ex-Taliban commander gunned down in Afghan capital', Reuters, 21 Aug. 2005.

29. Personal communication with ICG analyst, Kabul, Sept. 2004; personal communication with UN official, Kabul, May 2005.

30. Interview with Asadullah Walwalji, Kabul 13 May 2003; Tanya Goudsouzian, 'Interview with Professor Rabbani', *Gulf News*, 11 Oct. 2002; Abdel Wali, 'Jami'at Faces Break-up', Afghan Recovery Report, No. 18, 9 July 2002; interview with Asadullah Walwalji, Kabul, 13 May 2003.
31. Personal communication with Eckart Schiewek (UNAMA), Kabul, May 2003.
32. Interview with military officer from Tajikistan, May 2003; ISAF source, Kabul, Nov. 2004.

CONCLUSION

A major risk in writing 'national' histories backwards (as it is often done) is that it is easy to underestimate the uncertainty of the early stages of the process of state formation, when a multitude of precarious rulers, made legitimate only by being local community leaders or by their control of military force (warlords), were all trying to outlast their rivals and consolidate or expand their hold. What skills, personal qualities and resources were needed to maximise the chances of such success? Why did some succeed where others failed?

The main argument of this book is that warlordism illustrates well key dilemmas of state-building in Afghanistan and beyond. The warlords of the late twentieth century, like the kings of the eighteenth and nineteenth centuries, all had to prioritise the primitive accumulation of power, to be attained primarily through both the monopolisation of large scale violence and the centralisation of patronage, even if the individual style of each warlord in achieving that could vary hugely as shown by the comparison between Ismail Khan and Dostum. While it is easy to agree that a monopoly on violence and centralised patronage are factors of state strength, the real problem is how to develop them without destroying a polity in the process, as resistance is to be expected. Processes of primitive accumulation of power are particularly difficult, if not impossible, to carry out within institutionalised, bureaucratised, inclusive or representative systems. Patrimonial leadership holds in these contexts a decisive edge. Nonetheless, in a competitive environment patrimonial leaders might be forced to start processes of institutionalisation, bureaucratisation and legitimisation in order to improve the resilience and effectiveness of their own polity. The dilemma faced by these rulers is that the farther they go in implementing these processes, the stronger and the more effective the polity is likely to become, but the weaker their patrimonial hold. The transition from patrimonialism to a more institutionalised, legitimate and bureaucratised (hence more stable) system has always been highly problematic and fraught with difficulties, despite the sweetened up versions often presented by 'national' historians. When both primitive accumulation and institutionalisation/bureaucratisation/legitimisation take place simultaneously, the chances of failure are very high.

The detailed analysis of the Afghan case illustrates how the competitive race created by a stateless environment was characterised by the presence of players endowed with different mixes of skills, capabilities and resources, mostly initially classifiable as patrimonial leaders, but then showing varying degrees of propensity to engage with forms of institutionalisation. If it were possible exactly to measure the degree of patrimonialism and of institutionalisation on which rulers rely, such 'mixes' could be schematically represented by a two-dimensional graph (patrimonial—institutional). My argument is that each ruler would be situated close to the axes: strong patrimonial power is incompatible with strong institutionalisation (see Graph 4). Exceptionally gifted rulers (A in the graph) might be able to combine patrimonialism and institutionalisation in greater measure then most others and therefore would stand out somewhat further, but still be situated not too far from either axis. Rulers close to the 'institutional axis' are developing systems based on the rule of law, while warlords would appear close to the patrimonial axis (B, C), along with other types of patrimonial rulers. Differences nonetheless exist among patrimonial rulers as some are engaging with forms of institutionalisation more than others.

While institutionalised polities are stable, they are weak in terms of decision-making and irresolute; if faced with a crisis situation they are slow and often ineffective in dealing with it. This is why adolescent states, where the primitive accumulation of power has not yet been completed, tend inevitably to be highly patrimonial: ruthlessness and swift decision-making are needed to complete the process; expropriation is the order of the day. On the other hand, institutionalisation, bureaucratisation and legitimisation all contribute to create a much more complex and resilient structure, which allows polities to last for centuries and accumulate a 'capital of civilisation', exemplified by cultural achievements, sophisticated architecture, developed infrastructure, etc. In the absence of such 'civilisation process', polities (including warlords') inevitably tend to remain fragile and fluid, subject to quickly foundering once the charismatic leader at their centre disappears or loses his abilities. Instead of leaving behind benchmarks of civilisation such as roads, temples, mausoleums and palaces, and more importantly institutional development, like the villages from which they arise, these 'empires of mud' can disappear without leaving trace.

Historically a number of partial solutions to the dilemma of combining ruthlessness and fast decision-making with a degree of institutionalisation (hence stability and effectiveness) have emerged; over the twentieth century a popular one has been the development of strongly disciplined political organisations which combine strong/authoritarian leadership with a degree of institutionalisation. 'Leninism' is a typical example of this ideology-based political organisation, although certainly not the only one. While the political organisation can be based on strong institutions, it can in turn be used 'patrimonially' to dominate the polity and steer it in the desired direction. In other terms institutionalisation does not spread to the entire political system and society, allowing for decisive action, but at the same prevents total arbitrariness, regulates succession and offers a degree of predictability. The result of this combination of patrimonialism and institutionalisation is that it escapes to a certain extent the 'zero-sum game' of mixing patrimonialism and institutionalisation in state-building. Hence, it would be situated farther from the axes than other polities (D in Graph 4). Volumes have been filled debating the pros and cos of this approach to state-building and the intrinsic risk of deviation (Stalinism). In the case of Afghanistan, suffice it to say that some key ingredients, necessary to build strong political organisations, were in short supply. As explained in Part I, attempts in this direction were made (HDK, Hizb-i Islami), but faltered because of their limited sustainability. Some elements of residual ideological politics played a role in Junbesh and in Shura-i Nezar, as I have shown in Part II, but they always fell far short of the critical mass required to have a lasting impact.

From the perspective of warlords endowed with different sets of skills and resources, as well as varying personal inclinations in the Afghanistan of the 1990s, much of what happened from 1992 has its own rationale. Civil war is not, after all, a 'stupid thing'.[1] In the very short term, nearly pure patrimonial rule was the safest and easiest option, particularly if strengthened with some political legitimisation. As I have shown throughout part two, partial legitimisation effects can be achieved also in a purely patrimonial context (cooptation, customary legitimisation—on top of course of the provision of security). The positive results of processes of institutionalisation, bureaucratisation or more sophisticated forms of legitimisation are likely to be visible only in the medium and long-term; moreover all these options come at a cost, not only financial but also in terms of the reduction of the arbitrary power of the ruler. They also entail a risk, since the ruler would have to curtail the power of allies and associates, who could react negatively. From this perspective, hesitation and even outright refusal by rulers to move down the road to the 'modern state' is quite understandable. Personality should also be factored in, as

Graph 4: Schematic Positioning of Rulers in Terms of Reliance on Patrimonialism and Institutionalisation

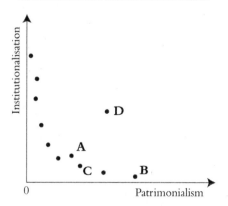

already hinted: certain options might sound more attractive for certain rulers than for others, as discussed in Part II concerning Ismail Khan, for example.

Indeed it is consistent with wider historical knowledge that rulers rarely if ever fully endorse the transformation of their own polities into institutional-ised, bureaucratised and legitimised states. Internal and external pressures are what generally force them to introduce reforms and restructure their polities, while deeper and longer reaching changes are likely to emerge as unplanned side effects. The Afghan warlords of post-1992 were no exception. Internal pressures existed, although as shown in this volume throughout 1992–2007 they never became overbearing. The heaviest pressure exercised on the war-lords came from two external sources: peer competition (i.e. other warlords) and the international environment. Peer competition was important because given the existence of a conflict, warlords were subjected to 'Tillyan' pressure, that is to enhance the military-related performance not only of their armies, but also of their polities as a whole. In this sense it seems to me that the Leander/ Sørensen school of thought,[2] arguing that the competitive pressure cannot have a 'virtous impact' in the context of internal war, is not confirmed by the Afghan case.

The existence of this pressure does not necessarily mean that they all succeeded in achieving such enhancements through reform and restructura-tion, nor even that they all tried; it means however that in the absence of such improvements, the warlord polities were very likely to collapse. Part II shows how the warlords who failed in the 1990s learnt some lessons and tried to improve in the post-2001 period, when they got their second (or third) chance.

International pressure did not prevent Tillyan dynamics from setting off, but impacted on the warlords manly by making it virtually impossible for them to establish fully fledged new states, assuming that they had the capabil-ity to do so anyway. In the post-1945 context, such would-be states would never have received international recognition,[3] an essential component of any definition of the state. Fully aware of this, the warlords were forced to re-di-rect their efforts: self-cooptation into state structures, state seizure (even par-tial) and/or transformation into political leaders within the existing political system. As I have shown, self-cooptation and state seizure were the easiest options, despite some drawbacks, but the transformation into political leaders was also pursued. In both cases a degree of institutional development and some legitimisation efforts were rendered necessary.

Ultimately, these institutionalisation and legitimisation efforts seemed to be failing as of early 2009. There are several reasons why this ended up being the case, including the personal limitations of the warlords themselves. A particu-larly important factor which is worth mentioning is the failure to establish a symbiotic relationship between cities and countryside-based warlords. Proc-esses of this kind have often been key aspects of state-formation. In a sense, the birth of the state has historically often been the result of the union of cities and warlords, even if this union was often a forced marriage. Forced marriages of cities and rural armies occurred several times in Afghanistan's history, and 'rape' of cities too, but were never fertile in terms of giving rise to a solid state. In the case of the warlord polities of the 1990s, one of the causes of their aborted birth seems to be attributable to the constraints created by the new international environment. Although it cannot be said that Afghan cities like Herat or Mazar-i Sharif ever liked the warlords or the military class, they both seemed to be adapting to them in the 1990s. In part through sponsoring the injection of 'new blood' in the urban elites and in part through the cooptation of existing elites, links were created between the warlords and the cities. Mostly 'captive' members of the urban educated class staffed the bureaucracies of the warlords' proto-states, while urban businessmen willingly or not provided trade services. Herat and Mazar-i Sharif became capitals of the two warlord polities and benefited from this in a number of ways, even if opposition to the rule of the warlords never disappeared. 'Married' to cities, warlord polities exhibited an altogether different potential of development and might even have freed those polities from the 'slavery' of the Ibn Khaldun cycle of patrimonial power by making a gradual process of institutionalisation possible. The 'forced marriages' however never had more than three to five years to turn into solid unions and were prevented from consolidating first by the military defeat of the warlords at the hands of the Taliban and second by international intervention. After 2001 old urban elites and professional sectors mostly allied with the central state against the warlords, under the protection of foreign troops. This was seen very clearly in the case of Herat. Without international intervention would the warlord polities have managed to subdue and incorporate the cities in a more organic fashion? The experience of the 1990s, when they failed to do so despite the dearth of international interest in Afghanistan, suggests otherwise, but Ismail Khan's and particularly Dostum's approaches changed after 2001, leaving the possibility open of a different outcome.

The 'victory' of the cities may well have been only a temporary one. The instability of rural Afghanistan continued to represent a threat to the ability of its urban counterpart to shape the developing Afghan state in its own interest. As mentioned in the introduction, previous attempts to alter the balance of the uneasy relationship between the urban and rural worlds in Afghanistan in favour of the former precipitated dramatic backlashes. Repeatedly, sections of urban Afghanistan, encouraged by external support and by the dogmatic absorption of imported ideologies, destabilised the countryside and created the circumstances for their own 'Reconquista' by militarised solidarity groups arising from the villages. At the end of 2007 the question was whether history would once again repeat itself.

The 'divorce' from the cities, the impossibility of giving birth to an internationally recognised polity (a state, that is) and the competition of a re-established central government under international tutelage had all conspired seriously to weaken the warlord polities by the second half of the post-Taliban decade. The prospects of what was left of Dostum's and Ismail Khan's polities were quite grim by 2007; those of Shura-i Nezar only marginally brighter. At the same time, the central government's strategy to weaken the warlords by dissolving their links to the military class had not succeeded in establishing its own firmer hold over the territory. The increasingly floating military class, politically directionless, was becoming a big question mark hanging over the future of Afghanistan. As for the warlords themselves, the gains of peace looked increasingly disappointing. Although Dostum, Ismail Khan and segments of Shura-i Nezar are all known to have flirted with the idea of a return if not to war, at least to the destabilisation of the state (statecide), they had not yet taken any serious action in this direction as of early 2009. The ageing leaders and their increasingly wealthy and comfortably off lieutenants by this time had probably lost the appetite for risk-taking; their brinkmanship tactics appeared unconvincing and increasingly failed to scare anybody in Kabul. Moreover the capital's government and foreign embassies were quite skilled in giving the old warlords and military leaders just enough to keep them away from radical options: a rather unimportant ministerial appointment to Ismail Khan, a ceremonial position to Dostum, an advisory role to Fahim... Compared to the risks entailed by taking on Kabul and the foreign armies garrisoned in Afghanistan, even these modest offerings must have looked attractive to men well beyond their prime, insecure of the loyalty of their followers. Their only chance of re-emerging as key players was linked to the start of a new war cycle and even then with the risk of being overtaken by younger, or more dynamic, actors. Should the foreign presence continue to guarantee peace indefinitely, their disintegration and descent into gunlordism and mafias is bound to continue.

Unexpectedly, such a chance seemed to be emerging as of 2006. By the spring of that year a new war cycle seemed to be taking off. The insurgency was spreading from its heartland in the south and spiralling in violence, while the mood of the population was starting to turn against the government. Several members of the old military class were talking to the Taliban as of 2007, in a clear attempt to hedge their bets. In the event of a foreign withdrawal, it was clear to everybody that Afghan institutional development had clearly progressed too little to avoid a relapse into civil war. At the same time, although as of the end of 2007 there was little sign yet of the emergence of a new generation of warlords to feed into the new war cycle, that clearly remained a possibility. Although Karzai's government was also recruiting militias as its predecessors had done in the 1980s, the scale of the effort was not comparable. As of 2007 the largest militia leaders in southern Afghanistan had never more than 1,000 men each, with just one possible exception. The presence of European forces, who initially at least opposed the reliance on militias, acted as a restraint on their growth even when it failed to eradicate them altogether. By the end of 2007, however, a number of foreign players in Afghanistan, including the UK and the US, seemed to be warming to the idea of arming militias on a large scale, possibly paving the way to the emergence of a new semi-autonomous military class. The disintegration of

Afghanistan's army seemed to be excluded as long as foreign armies were tutoring it, but did not look an unrealistic prospect in the event of a withdrawal of foreign troops. Even if the Taliban leadership of the insurgency (2002–) had obvious difficulties in exercising command and control of its fighters, the rank and file clearly appeared strongly united ideologically,[4] therefore making a drift towards warlordism unlikely, even if not impossible in the event of major disagreements between the political leadership and the field commanders. The main chance of insurgent warlordism resurfacing in Afghanistan was linked to new dissident actors emerging, either rogue elements of the military class, socially marginal strata drawn into the conflict by the prospect of status advancement or local notables arming themselves because of rising insecurity.

Both peace cycles and war cycles resulted from complex social microdynamics linked to local demands for security, predictability and stability. The roots of the civil wars of the 1990s are to be found in the dominant role of the military class after 1992 and in the absence of a central state working both as an effective regulatory and conflict-settling agency. The war cycle was gathering strength in 1992–3 and exploded in the war of all against all from 1994 onwards. (I have illustrated in detail in chapter 9 how a peace cycle emerged during the civil war to threaten the raison d'étre of the warlords.)

The key policy dilemma in post-2001 Afghanistan can be summed up concisely. In the absence of the stabilising effect of a central authority able to claim a monopoly of violence and centralised patronage, as well as of institutionalised authorities, such cycles of war and peace were bound to repeat again. The peace cycle of 1994–2004 was only a window of opportunity, not a permanent post-war condition. However, if institutionalisation, the establishment of a monopoly of violence and the centralisation of patronage can in the long run interrupt such cycles, they are themselves likely starters of conflicts in the short term. The short term / long term dilemma was reflected in the two dominant 'schools of thought' in which the 'international community' divided after 2001, 'rejectionism' and 'collaborationism'. The first school argued that warlords, gunmen and all those involved in the violence of the 1980s and 1990s should be marginalised from politics and power in order to allow a 'clean new start' for the Afghan state. Among those who supported this view were a number of UN officials, especially those with extensive experience of the country, but also human rights activists and some social scientists.[5] The second school argued instead that maintaining stability in Afghanistan was a priority and that could only be achieved with the cooperation of the non-state actors so much despised by the other school. This line of thinking was supported mainly by diplomats (within and without the UN) and international relations experts.[6] As I mention in the introduction, the prospects for an externally managed state-building process in Afghanistan were always remote, a fact which might seem to weigh on the side of the 'collaborationist' school. However, to most of its members 'collaboration' was just a stop-gap measure and not a strategic long-term option; little thinking seems to have gone into how to create the conditions for Afghan allies to work towards medium- and long-term institution-building as opposed to merely occupying the state and starting turf wars over the division of the spoils. On the contrary: feeling protected by international patronage, Afghan factions had no real incentive to sacrifice some of the privileges deriving from direct patrimonial control to the long-term potential gains of institution-building.

The victory in 2001—of the 'collaborationist school' meant that institutionalisation and primitive accumulation of power by the central authority were delayed, avoiding the risk of alienating warlords and other potential losers in such a process. While this minimised the short-term risk of destabilisation, it inevitably increased the long-term risk of the war cycle resurfacing because of the lack of a strong state authority. The threat of a new war cycle, as pointed out above, does not necessarily come from the old warlords and the military class. What matters is that the initial compromise prevented a rapid consolidation of an effective state, leaving the door open to new challenges, and left much of the Afghan countryside in a state of turmoil. This was hardly noticed in Kabul and in the capitals of the world, but was very much felt in many Afghan villages. To be fair, minimising the long-term risk by contrast would have implied emphasising and accelerating the primitive accumulation of power at the centre, reducing as much as possible the window of opportunity for the war cycle to reappear, but risking a short-term conflict with warlords and strongmen. Such risks could have been reduced by offering the warlords and their followers a stake in the development of a working political system in Afghanistan, encouraging for example their transformation into political parties (such as Junbesh for a while tried to do). Instead, the 'international community' busied itself finding as many distractions as possible in 'reconstruction', 'development', 'electoral processes', and so on, which had no chance of ultimately succeeding in the absence of effective state authority. Efforts to build viable political organisations, particularly by warlords but not only, were discouraged.

Any durable post-conflict state (re-)formation will have carefully to craft a combination of institutionalisation and cooptation of local patrimonial or factional leaders. This can only happen in the presence of strong and effective political leadership; only a strong leader can impose the strict delimitation of roles that combining institutionalisation and cooptation requires. The author of this book doubts that strong national leadership will emerge in a context of external intervention in Afghanistan. The other key problem to be resolved is devising incentives for rulers to engage in institution-building. External intervention will likely have the opposite effect, particularly when it is open-ended, with unlimited financial commitment and no conditionalities.

Notes

1. I borrow the expression from Christopher Cramer (2006).
2. Sørensen (2001), Leander (2003).

3. The post-1945 practice has been to recognise only new states which could claim to be emerging from a context of decolonisation; there have been some exceptions (notably Yugoslavia) but Afghanistan's potential claimants to statehood never even remotely had sufficient international support to be granted such an exception.

4. See Giustozzi (2007d) and Giustozzi (2009).

5. Personal communications with UN officials, human right activists and scholars, 2003–2009; see also International Crisis Group (2002a), (2002b), (2003a), (2003b); Human Rights Watch (2002a).

6. Personal communications with diplomats and scholars, 2003–2009; see also Andres et al. (2005); Khalilzad (2005).

BIBLIOGRAPHY

Adams, Richard Newbold (1975), *Energy and Structure: A Theory of Social Power*, Austin: University of Texas Press.

Adkin, Mark and Yussuf, Mohammad (1992), *The Bear Trap*, London: Leo Cooper.

Ahmed Akbar S. (1983), 'Tribes and States in Waziristan', in *The Conflict of Tribe and State in Iran and Afghanistan*, Richard Tapper (ed.), London: Croom Helm.

Alam, Abdul Qadir (n.d.), *Tarikh-i tahwalat-i Ghor az Saur 1357 be iin taraf*, unpublished manuscript.

Adebajo, Adekaye and Keen, David (2000), 'Banquet for Warlords', *The World Today* (July), pp. 8–10.

Allen, C. (1995), 'Understanding African Politics', *Review of African Political Economy*, no. 65.

Amnesty International (2003), 'Police reconstruction essential for the protection of human rights'. London.

Andres, Richard B. et al. (2005), 'Winning with Allies: The Strategic Value of the Afghan Model', *International Security*, Vol. 30, No. 3 (Winter 2005/06), pp. 124–160

Anderson, Jon W. (1978), 'There are no Khans Anymore: Economic Development and Social Change in Tribal Afghanistan', *Middle East Journal*, 2, 1978, pp. 168–70.

Anderson, Mary B. and Duffield, Mark (1998), 'Doing the right thing?', *New Routes*, 3:3.

Arney, George (1989), *Afghanistan*, London: Mandarin Press.

Atseer, Syed 'Allam-ud Din (2005), *Causes of the Fall of the Islamic State of Afghanistan under Ustad Rabbani in Kabul*, Peshawar: Area Study Centre.

Aziz Al-Azmeh (1982), *Ibn-Khaldun: An Essay in Reinterpretation*, London: Frank Cass.

Azevedo, Mario J. (1998), *Roots of Violence: A History of War in Chad*, London: Routledge.

Azimi, Zahir (1377), *taliban: chegune amadan*, Afghan Association Germany.

Azimi, Nabi (1998), *urdu wa syasat dar Afghanistan*, Peshawar: Danesh.

Azoy, Whitney (2002), *Buzkashi: Game and Power in Afghanistan*, Long Grove: Waveland Press Inc., 2nd edn.

Baigi Abd ar Raouf (2000), *Afganistan ba'd az piruzy enqelab-i Islami ta saqute shamal be dost-i Taliban*, Peshavar: Kitaabfuruushi-i Balkh.

Barfield, Thomas (2004), 'Problems in establishing legitimacy in Afghanistan', *Iranian Studies*, vol. 37, no. 2, June, pp. 263–293.

Baali, Fuad (1988), *Society, State and Urbanism: Ibn Khaldun's sociological thought*, State University of New York Press.

Barth, Frederick, (1959), *Political Leadership Among Swat Pathans*, LSE Monograph Series, NY: Humanities Press.

Battera, Federico (2004), 'Le incertezze della deriva warlordista. L'importanza della dimensione locale nei conflitti contemporanei in Africa', paper presented at the Annual Conference of SISP (Società Italiana di Scienza Politica), September. ADD YEAR?

Beall, Jo and Esser, Daniel (2005), *Shaping Urban Futures: Challenges to Governing and Managing Afghan Cities*, AREU Issues Paper, Kabul: Afghanistan Research and Evaluation Unit

Beall, Jo and Fox, Sean (2009), *Cities and Development*. London: Routledge.

Bearden, Milt (2003), *The Main Enemy: The Inside Story of the CIA's Final Showdown with the KGB*, New York: Random House.

Berdal, Mats (2003), 'How "New" are "New Wars"? Global Economic Change and the Study of Civil War', *Global Governance* (October).

Berdal, Mats and Malone, David (eds) (2000), *Greed and Grievance: Economic Agendas in Civil Wars*, Boulder, CO: Westview Press.

Berntsen, Gary and Pezzullo, Ralph (2005), *Jawbreaker*, New York: Three Rivers Press.

Bisher, Jamie (2005), *White terror: Cossack Warlords of the Trans-Siberian Railway*, London: Frank Cass.

Blaum, Paul A. (1994), *The Days of the Warlords, A History of the Byzantine Empire, AD 969–991*, Lanham, MD: University Press of America.

Boot Max (2006), 'Special forces and horses', *Armed Forces Journal*, no. 11.

Buijtenhuijs, Robert (1987), *Le Frolinat et les guerres civiles du Tchad (1977–1984)*, Paris: Karthala.

Centlivres, Pierre and Centlivres-Demont, Micheline (1988), *Et si on parlait de l'Afghanistan?*, Paris: Edns de la Maison des Sciences de l'Homme.

Cerny, Philip G. (1998), 'Neomedievalism, Civil War, and the New Security Dilemma: Globalisation as a Durable Disorder', *Civil Wars* 1:1 (Spring), pp. 36–64.

Chaffetz, David (1981), *A Journey Through Afghanistan: A Memorial*, Chicago, IL: The University of Chicago Press

Chan, Anthony B. (1982), *Arming the Chinese: the Western Armaments Trade in Warlord China, 1920–1928*, Vancouver: University of British Columbia Press.

Ch'en, Jerome (1979), *The Military-Gentry Coalition: China Under the Warlords*, Toronto: University of Toronto-York University Joint Centre on Modern East Asia.

Chouvy, Pierre-Arnaud (2002), *Les Territoires de l'Opium*, Geneve: Olizaine.

Christensen, Aasger (1995), *Aiding Afghanistan. The Background and Prospects for Reconstruction in a Fragmented Society*, Copenhagen: Nordic Institute of Asian Studies.

Claessen, Henri J. M. and Skalniík, Peter (1978), 'Limits, beginning and the end of the early state', in *The Early State*, Henri J. M. Claessen and Peter Skalniík (eds), The Hague: Mouton.

Clapham, Christopher (1998), 'Introduction: analysing African insurgencies', in C. Clapham (ed.), *African Guerrillas*, Oxford: James Currey.

———, (2002), 'I signori della Guerra in Africa', in Maria Cristina Ercolessi (ed.), *I signori della guerra*, Napoli: L'ancora del mediterraneo.

Clausen, Alexander Johannes (1992), *Eine Analyse der politischen Strukturen im Herrschaftsgebiet des Ahmad Shah Massud (Nordostafghanistan)*, Diplomarbeit, University of Salzburg.

Cohen, Youssef et al. (1981), 'The Paradoxical Nature of State-Making: The Violent Creation of Order', *The American Political Science Review*, vol. 75, no. 4 (Dec. 1981), pp. 901–910.

Coll, Steve (2004), *Ghost Wars. The Secret History of the CIA, Afghanistan, and Bin Laden, From the Soviet Invasion to September 10, 2001*, New York: Penguin Press.

Collier, Paul and Hoeffler, Anke (2001), *Greed and Grievance in Civil War?*, Washington, DC: World Bank.

Compagnon, Daniel (1998), 'Somali Armed Movements' in C. Clapham (ed.), *African Guerrillas*, Oxford, James Currey.

Country Information & Policy Unit (2003), Immigration and Nationality Directorate, *Afghanistan Country Report*, London: Home Office, October.

Country Information & Policy Unit (2004), Immigration and Nationality Directorate, *Afghanistan Country Report*, London: Home Office, April.

Coupland, Simon (1998), 'From Poachers to Gamekeepers: Scandinavian Warlords and Carolingian kings', *Early Modern Europe*, vol. 7, no. 1.

Cramer, Chris (2006), *Civil War is Not a Stupid Thing: Making Sense of Violence in Developing Countries*, London: Hurst.

Crumpton, Henry A. (2005), 'Intelligence and war: Afghanistan 2001–2002', in Jennifer Sims et al. (eds), *Transforming US Intelligence*, Washington, Georgetown University Press.

Danziger, Nick (1988), *Danziger's Travels*, London: Paladin.

———, (1992), *Danziger's Adventures*, London: Harper Collins

Daoud, Zemaray (1982), *L'Etat monarchique dans la formation sociale afghane*, Frankfurt am Main: Peter Lang Verlag.

De Waal, Alex (1994), 'Some Comments on Militias in Contemporary Sudan', in M. Daly and A. A. Sikainga (eds) *Civil War in the Sudan*, London: IB Tauris.

DeVries, Kelly (2001), 'Harold Godwinson in Wales: Military Legitimacy in Late Anglo-Saxon England', in Richard p. Abels and Bernard S. Bachrach (eds), *The Normans and Their Adversaries at War: Essays in Memory of C. Warren Holliste*, Woodbridge: Boydell Press, 2001.

Dib, Kamal (2004), *Warlords and Merchants: the Lebanese Business and Political Establishment*, Reading: Ithaca Press, 2004.

Dorenwendt, Thomas (1997), 'Tadschikistan: die Transformationen des Bürgerkrieges', *Orient*, 38:2.

Dorronsoro, Gilles (1993–4), 'Le parti de Dostom: le Junbesh', *Afghanistan Info*, no. 34, Dec.-Jan.

———, (1994), 'La politique de pacification en Afghanistan', in G. Chaliand (ed.), *Stratégies de la guerrilla*, Paris: Payot.

———, (1996), 'Afghanistan: Des réseaux de solidarité aux espaces regionaux', in François Jean and J.C. Rufin (eds.), *Economies des guerres civiles*, Paris: Hachette

———, (2005), *Revolution Unending: Afghanistan 1979 to the Present*, London: Hurst

———, and Lobato, Chantal (1990), 'L'Afghanistan un an après le retrait soviétique', *Est et Ouest*, January.

Duffield, Mark (1997), *Post-Modern Conflict, Aid Policy and Humanitarian Conditionality*, Birmingham: University of Birmingham Press.

Duby, Georges (1980), *The Three Orders: Feudal Society Imagined*, Chicago: University of Chicago Press.

Duverger, Maurice (1976), *Les partis politiques*, Paris: Armand Colin.

Dubuis, Etienne (1989), *Afghanistan terre brûlée*, Lausanne: edns 24 heures.

Edwards, David B. (1998), 'Learning from the Swat Pathans: Political Leadership in Afghanistan, 1978–97', *American Ethnologist*, vol. 25, no. 4.

Eide, Espen Barth (1997), 'Conflict entrepreneurship: On the art of waging civil war', *PRIO Report*, 4 pp. 41–69.

———(1998), *Between Rationalism and Reflectivism—Constructivist Security Theory and the Collapse of Yugoslavia*, Hovedfag-thesis, Institute of Political Science, University of Oslo.

Elias, Norbert (1982), *The Civilising Process, vol. 2: State Formation and Civilisation*, Oxford: Blackwell.

Elmi, Hamid (1997), safarha wa khataraha, Peshawar: Danish KetabKhana, 1997.

Elphinstone, Mountstuart (1815), *An Account of the Kingdom of Kabul*, London: John Murray.

Ellis, Stephen (1999), *The Mask of Anarchy: The Religious Roots of an African Civil War*, London: Hurst.

Es'haq, Mohammad (1382), *Manehay az mas'ud bozorg*, Kabul: Maywand

Ewans-von Krbek, Jeffrey HP (1977), *The social structure and organisation of a Pakhto-speaking community in Afghanistan*, PhD thesis, University of Durham.

FAO/WFP (1997), *Crop and food supply assessment mission to Afghanistan*, 7 August.

Fazelly, Kacem (2004), *L'Afghanistan du provisoire au transitoire*, Paris: l'Asiathéque.

Ferrier, J. p. (1857), *Caravan journeys and wanderings in Persia, Afghanistan, Turkistan, and Beloochistan: with historical notices of the countries lying between Russia and India*, London: John Murray.

Gall, Sandy (1989), *Afghanistan: Travels with the Mujahidin*, London: New English Library.

Gallant, Thomas W. (1999), 'Brigandage, Piracy, Capitalism, and State-Formation' in, Josiah McC. Heyman (ed.) *States and Illegal Practices*, New York: Berg Publishers.

Chabal, Patrick and Daloz, Jean-Pascal (1999), *Africa Works: Disorder as Political Instrument*, London: James Currey.

Gareev, M.A. (1996), *Moya poslednyaya voina*, Moscow: Insan.

Gat, Azar (2006), *War in Human Civilization*, Oxford: Oxford University Press.

Geertz, Clifford (1964), 'Ideology as a cultural system', in David Ernest Apter (ed.), *Ideology and Discontent*, New York: The Free Press, pp. 47–76.

Gélinas, Sylvie (1997), *Afghanistan: du communisme au fondamentalisme*, Paris: L'Harmattan.

Gellner, Ernest (1996), 'War and society', in Ernest Gellner (ed.), *Anthropology and Politics*, Oxford: Blackwell.

Giustozzi, Antonio (2000), *War, Politics and Society in Afghanistan, 1978–1992*, London: Hurst.

————(2003), 'Good state vs. Bad Warlords?', Crisis State Working Paper 51, London: Crisis States Research Centre, LSE.

————(2004), 'The demodernisation of an Army', *Small Wars and Insurgencies*, vol. 15 no. 1 (Spring).

————(2005), 'The ethnicisation of an Afghan faction: Junbesh-i Milli from the origins to the Presidential elections (2004)', Working Paper no. 67, London: Crisis States Research Centre, LSE.

————(2007a), 'Afghanistan: Political Parties or Militia Fronts?', ch. 8 of J. de Zeeuw (ed.), *Transforming Rebel Movements After Civil Wars*, Boulder, CO: Lynne Rienner Publishers.

————(2007b), 'Armed Politics and Political Competition in Afghanistan', working paper, Bergen: Chr Michelsen Institute.

————(2007c), 'Auxiliary force or national army? Afghanistan's 'ANA' and the counter-insurgency effort, 2002–2006', *Small Wars and Insurgencies*, vol. 18, no. 1 (March).

————(2007d), *Koran, Kalashnikov and Laptop: the Rise of the Neo-Taliban Insurgency in Afghanistan*, London and New York: Hurst and Columbia University Press.

————(2007e), 'The missing ingredient: non-ideological insurgency and state collapse in western Afghanistan, 1979–1992', Working Paper Series 2 no. 11, London: Crisis States Research Centre, LSE

————(2007f), 'War and Peace Economies of Afghanistan's Strongmen', *International Peacekeeping*, vol. 14, no. 1, Jan. 2007, pp. 75–89.

————(2008), *Afghanistan: Transition Without End. An Analytical Narrative*, working paper, London: LSE Crisis States Research Centre, 2008.

————(2008b), 'Bureaucratic façade and political realities of disarmament and demobilisation in Afghanistan', *Confict, Security & Development*.

————(2009) 'One or many? The issue of the Taliban's unity and disunity', Brief N. 48, Bradford: Pakistan Security Research Unit (PSRU), April 2009

————(forthcoming 2009a), 'Afghanistan', in Barry Rubin (ed.), *Global Survey of Islamism*, Armonk, NY: ME Sharpe.

————and Ullah, Noor (2006), 'Tribes and warlords in southern Afghanistan', Working Paper 7, Series 2, London, Crisis States Research Centre, LSE.

————and Ullah, Noor (2007), 'The inverted cycle: Kabul and the strongmen's competition for control over Kandahar, 2001–2006', *Central Asian Survey*, n. 2 2007, June

Glatzer, Bernt (1983), 'Political Organisation of Pashtun nomads and the State's in Richard Tapper (ed.), *The Conflict of Tribe and State in Iran and Afghanistan*, London: Croom Helm.

Glatzer, Bernt (2002), 'Centre and Periphery in Afghanistan: New Identities in a Broken State', *Sociologus*, winter.

Goodhand, Jonathan (2004), 'Afghanistan in Central Asia', in M. Pugh *et al.* (eds), *War Economies in a Regional Context. Challenges of Transformation*, Boulder, CO: Lynne Rienner.

Grachev, Oleg (1998), 'Kobal't ukhodit v rassvet', (vecherka/archive/29–04–1998/3/1. DOC.html).

Grevemeyer, *Herrschaft, Raub und Gegenseitigkeit: Die politische Geschichte Badakhshans 1500–1883*, Wiesbaden: Harrassowitz.

Grevemeyer, Jan Heeren (1980), 'Afghanistan: das "Neue Modell einer Revolution" und der dörfliche Widerstand', in Kurt Greussing and Jan-Heeren Grevemeyer (eds), *Revolution in Iran und Afghanistan*, Frankfurt: Syndikat Autoren-und Verlagsgesellschaft.

Griffin, Michael (2000), *Reaping the Whirlwind*, London: Pluto Press.

Grötzbach, Erwin (1986), 'Städte und Basare', in *Afghanistan. Ländermonographie*, Liestal: Bibliotheca Afghanica.

Harlan, J. (1939), *Central Asia: A Personal Narrative of Gen. Josiah Harlan, 1823–1841*, London: Luzac.

Harrison, Selig (1989), 'Fighting to the Last Afghan', in *Peace and Security*, Autumn.

Hawkins, Charles F. (n.d.), 'Toward A Theory Of Military Leadership', The Military Conflict Institute, at http://www.militaryconflict.org/leader.htm.

Hersh, Seymour M. (2004), *Chain of Command*, New York: Harper Collins, 2004.

Hedoyat, Hedayatullah, (n.d.), '*alal saqut-i shamal*, Peshawar.

Hills, Alice (1997), 'Warlords, Militia and Conflict in Contemporary Africa: a Re-examination of Terms', *Small Wars and Insurgencies*, 8:1.

Herbst, Jeffrey (1996–7), 'Responding to State Failure in Africa', *International Security*, vol. 21, no. 3.

Holl, N. H. (2002), *Mission Afghanistan*, Munchen: Herbig.

Hsieh, Winston (1962), 'The Ideas and Ideals of a Warlord: Ch'en Chiung-ming (1878–1933)', *Papers on China*, 16, pp. 198–252.

Human Rights Watch (2001), *Afghanistan: Crisis of Impunity?*, New York, July.

Human Rights Watch (2002a), *All Our Hopes Are Crushed: Violence and Repression in Western Afghanistan*, New York.

EMPIRES OF MUD

————(2002b), *We Want to Live as Humans: Repression of Women and Girls in Western Afghanistan*, New York, December.

————(2002c), *On the Precipice: Insecurity in Northern Afghanistan*, New York.

ibn Khaldūn al-Ha_ramī, Abū Zayd Abdul-Rahman ibn Muḥammad (1377), *The Muqaddimah: An Introduction to History*, translated by Franz Rosenthal, Princeton University Press, 2004.

Ibrahimi, Niamatullah (2006), *The Failure of a Clerical Proto-State: Hazarajat, 1979– 1984*, London: Crisis States Research Centre.

Ibrahimi, Niamatullah (2008 forthcoming), *Divide et impera, State Penetration in Hazarajat (Afghanistan) from the Monarchy to the Taleban*, London: Crisis States Research Centre.

International Crisis Group (2002a), *The Loya Jirga: One Small Step Forward?*, Bruxelles.

International Crisis Group (2002b), *The Afghan Transitional Administration: Prospects and Perils*, Bruxelles

International Crisis Group (2003a), *Peacebuilding in Afghanistan*, Bruxelles

International Crisis Group (2003b), *Afghanistan: the Problem of Pashtun Alienation*, Bruxelles

International Crisis Group (2007), *Reforming Afghanistan's Police*, Bruxelles.

Jackson, Paul (2003), 'Warlords as Alternative Forms of Governance', *Small Wars and Insurgencies*, 14:2 (2003), pp. 133–134.

Johnson, Dominic (1999), 'Warlords außer Kontrolle. Angolas andauernde Tragödie und der Krieg in der Region', *Blätter für deutsche und internationale Politik*, 3 (1999), pp. 336–343.

Jung, Dietrich(2003), 'Confronting a Paradox: The Political Economy of Intra-State Wars', in D. Jung (ed.), *Shadow Globalization, Ethnic Conflicts and New Wars: A Political Economy of Intra-State War*, London: Routledge, 2003.

Kakar, Hassan (1995), *Afghanistan: The Soviet Invasion and the Afghan Response, 1979– 1982*, Berkeley: University of California Press.

Katkov, I.E. (1989), 'Sotsial'nye aspekty plemennoi struktury pushtunov', in *Afganistan: Istoriya, ekonomika, kul'tura (sbornik statei)*, Moscow: Nauka, pp. 54–55.

Keen, David (1998), 'The Economic Functions of Violence in Civil Wars', *Adelphi Paper* 320, Oxford: Oxford University Press.

Khashimbekov, Kh. (1998), *Uzbeki severnogo Afganistana*, Moscow: RAN (Institut Vostokovedeniya), II edn.

Khashimbekov, Kh. (1994), *Uzbeki severnogo Afganistana*, Moscow: RAN (Institut Vostokovedeniya).

Khalilzad Zalmay (1995), 'Afghanistan in 1994: Civil War and Disintegration', *Asian Survey*, vol. 35, no. 2, A Survey of Asia in 1994: Part II (February).

Khalilzad Zalmay (2005), 'How to Nation-Build', *The National Interest*, summer 2005.

Kipp, J.-C. (1989), 'Afghanistan: aprés la guerre', *Politique Internationale*, August.

Kulakov Vyacheslavovich, Oleg (2003), *Geratskii region severo-zapadnogo Afganistana (80–90-ye gody TWENTIETH veka)*, doctoral dissertation, Moscow.

Leander, Anna (2003), 'Wars and the un-making of states: taking Tilly seriously in the contemporary world', in S. Guzzini and D. Jung, *Copenhagen Peace Research: Conceptual Innovations and Contemporary Security Analysis*, London: Routledge.

Lee, Jonathan (1996), *The 'Ancient supremacy': Bukhara, Afghanistan and the Battle for Balkh, 1731–1901*, Leiden: Brill.

Lin, Alfred H.Y. (2002), 'Building and Funding a Warlord Regime. The Experience of Chen Jitang in Guangdong, 1929–1936', *Modern China*, 28:2 (April), pp. 177–212.

312

———(2004), 'Warlord, Social Welfare and Philanthropy. The Case of Guangzhou Under Chen Jitang, 1929–1936', *Modern China*, 30:2, (April), pp. 151–198.

Lintner, Bertil (1994), *Burma in Revolt. Opium and Insurgency Since 1948*, Bangkok: White Lotus.

Lock, Peter (2002), 'From the Economics of War to Economies of Peace. The dynamics of shadow globalisation and the diffusion of armed violence as an obstacle to build peace', text presented at the Hamburg Winterschool on Crisis Prevention and Peace Support, 18 November 2002, (http://www.peter-lock.de/txt/winterschool.html).

Lyakhovskii, Aleksandr (1995), *Tragediya i doblest' Afgana*, Moscow: Iskona.

Machiavelli, Niccoló (1521), *Dell'Arte della Guerra*, Firenze: Giunti.

MacKinlay, John (2000), 'Defining warlords', *International Peacekeeping*, 7:1 (2000).

———(2002), 'Globalisation and Insurgency', *Adelphi Paper*, 352, London: IISS.

Mair, Stefan (2003), 'The New World of Privatised Violence', *Internationale Politik und Gesellschaft*, 2.

Maley, William (2002), *The Afghanistan Wars*, Basingstoke: Palgrave.

Marten, Kimberly (2006–7), 'Warlordism in Comparative Perspective', *International Security*, vol. 31, no. 3 (Winter), pp. 41–73.

Mansoor, Abd al Hafiz (1369), *panjshir dar dawran-i* jihad, Peshawar, s.n.

McChesney, R. D. (1983), 'The Amirs of Muslim Central Asia in the XVIIth Century', *Journal of the Economic and Social History of the Orient*, vol. 26, no. 1. (1983), pp. 33–70.

McCord, Edward (1993), *The Power of the Gun, the Emergence of Modern Chinese Warlordism*, Berkeley, CA: University of California Press.

Menkhaus, Ken (2001), 'Warlordism and the War on Terrorism', *Foreign Policy in Focus* (26 December).

———(2003), 'Warlords and Landlords: Non-State Actors and Humanitarian Norms in Somalia', paper presented at the 'Curbing Human Rights Violations by Armed Groups' Conference, Liu Institute for Global Issues, University of British Columbia, Canada, 14–15 November.

Ministerie van Buitenlandse Zaken (2002), Directie Personenverkeer, Migratie en Vreemdelingenzaken Afdeling Asiel-en Migratiezaken, *Algemeen ambtsbericht Afghanistan*, Den Haag, augustus.

Misdaq, Nabi (2006), *Afghanistan: Political Frailty and External Interference*, London: Routledge

Mojaddidi, Ilhajj Mohammad 'Aisi (1378), *Shahid Dagar Genral alhajj 'Alauddin*, s.n. but printed in Iran.

Noelle, Christine (1997), *State and Tribe in Nineteenth-century Afghanistan: The Reign of Amir Dost Muhammad Khan (1826–63)*, London: Curzon.

Nojumi, Neamatollah (2002), *The Rise of the Taliban in Afghanistan: Mass Mobilization, Civil War, and the Future of the Region*, Basingstoke: Palgrave.

Nourzhanov, Kirill (2005), 'Saviours of the nation or robber barons? Warlord politics in Tajikistan', *Central Asian Survey*, 24:2 (June), pp. 109–130.

Olson, Mancur (1993), 'Dictatorship, Democracy, and Development', *The American Political Science Review*, vol. 87, no. 3. (Sep.), pp. 567–576.

Ottaway, Marina and Lievel, Anatol (2002), *Rebuilding Afghanistan: Fantasy vs, Reality*, Policy Brief 12, Carnegie Endowment for International Peace.

Pereira, N.G.O. (1997), 'Siberian Atamanshchina: Warlordism in the Russian Civil War', in V.N. Brovkin (ed.), *The Bolsheviks in Russian Society*, New Haven: Yale University Press.

Picard, Elizabeth (1996), *Lebanon, a Shattered Country: Myths and Realities of the Wars in Lebanon*, New York: Holmes & Meier.

Puig, Jean-José (1994), 'Le commandant Massud', in G. Chaliand (ed.), *Stratégies de la Guerrilla*, Paris: Payot.

———(2005), *La pêche à la truite en Afghanistan*, Paris: Edns de La Martinière.

Poggi, Gianfranco (1978), *The Development of the Modern State*, Stanford, CA: Stanford University Press.

Poulantzas, Nico (1973), *Political Power and Social Classes*, London: New Left Review.

ProKhanov, Alexander (1988), 'Afghanistan', *International Affairs* (Moscow), August.

Rashid, Ahmed (2000), *Taliban*, London: IB Tauris.

Rais, Rasul Bakhsh (1993), 'Afghanistan and the Regional Powers', *Asian Survey*, vol. 33, no. 9 (September).

Rasuly, Sarajuddin (1997), *Die politischen Eliten Afghanistans*, Frankfurt am Main: Peter Lang.

Rasuly-Paleczek, Gabriele (1998), 'Ethnic identity versus Nationalism: the Uzbeks of north-eastern Afghanistan and the Afghan state', in Touraj Atabaki and John O'Kane (eds), *Post-Soviet Central Asia*, London: IB Tauris.

Reno, William (2002), 'The Politics of Insurgency in Collapsing States', *Development and Change*, 33:5, pp. 837–858.

Riekenberg, Michael (1999), 'Warlords. Eine Probleskizze', *Comparativ*, 5/6.

Roberts, J. A. G. (1989), 'Warlordism in China', *Review of African Political Economy*, 16:45/46 (Summer), pp. 26–34.

Robinson, Cyril D. and Scaglion, Richard (1987), 'The Origin and Evolution of the Police Function in Society: Notes toward a Theory', *Law & Society Review*, vol. 21, no. 1, pp. 109–154,

———(1994), *Police in Contradiction: the Evolution of the Police Function in Society*, Westport, Conn: Greenwood Press.

Roth, Guenther (1968), 'Personal Rulership, Patrimonialism, and Empire-Building in the New States', *World Politics*, vol. 20, no. 2. (Jan.).

Roy, Oliver (1988), 'Nature de la guerre en Afghanistan', *Les Temps Modernes*, June.

———(1989), 'Afghanistan: la guerre comme facteur du passage au politique', *Revue Française des Sciences Politiques*, December.

———(1990), *Islam and Resistance in Afghanistan*, Cambridge: Cambridge University Press.

———(1994), 'The New Political Elite in Afghanistan', in Banuazizi and Wiener (eds), *The Politics of Social Transformation in Afghanistan, Iran and Pakistan*, Syracuse, NY: Syracuse University Press.

———(1995), *From Holy War to Civil War*, Princeton, NJ: Darwin Press.

Rubin, Barnett R. (1995), *The Fragmentation of Afghanistan*, New Haven, Conn: Yale University Press.

———(2000), 'The political economy of war and peace in Afghanistan', *World Development*, vol. 28, no. 10, October, pp. 1789–1803

———(2004), *Road to Ruin: Afghanistan's Booming Opium Industry*, Center for American Progress/Center for International Cooperation, 2004, p. 10, accessed at http://www.globalpolicy.org/security/issues/afghan/2004/1007roadtoruin.pdf

———, and Malikyar, Helena (2003), *The politics of center-periphery relations in Afghanistan*, New York: Center for International Cooperation (New York University), March

Ryan, Nigel (1983), *A Hitch or Two in Afghanistan*, London: Weidenfield and Nicolson.

BIBLIOGRAPHY

624

a

Schroen, Gary C. (2007), *First in: How Seven CIA Officers Opened the War on Terror in Afghanistan*, New York: Ballantine Books.

Salih, M. A. Mohammad and Harir, Sharif (1984), 'Tribal militias. The Genesis of National Disintegration', in Sharif Hariri and Terje Tvedt (eds), *Short-cut to Decay: The Case of Sudan*, Uppsala: Nordiska Institute of African Studies, pp. 186–203.

Schetter, Conrad (2005), 'Warlords and Bürgerkriegökonomie in Afghanistan', in *Unterwegs in die Zukunft*, Claudia Gomm-Ernsting and Annett Günther Berliner (eds), Berlin: Wissenschafts-Verlag

Service, Elman Rogers (1975), *Origins of the State and Civilization: the Process of Cultural Evolution*, New York: W.W. Norton.

Sheridan, James E. (1966), *Chinese Warlord: The Career of Feng Yu-hsiang*, Stanford, CA: Stanford University Press

Simms, Katharine (1987), *From Kings to Warlords. The Changing Political Structure of Gaelic Ireland in the Later Middle Ages*, Woodbridge: Boydell.

Singh, Gandā (1959), *Ahmad Shah Durrani: Father of Modern Afghanistan*, Bombay: Asia Publishing House.

Skalnik, Peter (1978), 'The early state as a process', in Henri J. M. Claessen and Peter Skalniík (eds), *The Early State*, The Hague: Mouton.

Smith, Martin (1991), *Burma, Insurgency and the Politicis of Ethnicity*, London: Zed Press.

Smyth, A. p. (1984), *Warlords and Holy Men: Scotland AD 80–1000*, Edinburgh: Edinburgh University Press.

Sørensen, Georg (2001), 'War and State-Making: Why Doesn't it Work in the Third World?', *Security Dialogue*, vol. 32, no. 3.

Starr, S. Frederick (2003), 'Karzai's Fiscal Foes and How to Beat Them', in M. Sedra (ed.), *Confronting Afghanistan's Security Dilemma*, Bonn: BICC.

Stewart, Rory (2004), *The Places in Between*, London: Picador

Stuvoy, Kirsti (2002), 'War Economy and the Social Order of Insurgencies: An Analysis of the Internal Structure of UNITA's War Economy', *Research Unit of Wars, Armament and Development, Arbeitspapier* 3, Hamburg: Universität Hamburg—IPW.

Swedish Migration Board (Migrationsverket) (2003), Report on Fact-Finding mission to Afghanistan 22–30 November 2002, Stockholm, April.

Spruyt, Hendrik (1994), The Sovereign State and its Competitors: an Analysis of Systems Change, Princeton, NJ: Princeton University Press.

Strayer, Joseph Reese (1970), *On the Medieval Origins of the Modern State*, Princeton, NJ: Princeton University Press.

Szuppe, Maria (1922), *Entre Timourids, Uzbeks and Savafides: questions d'histoire politique et sociale de Hérat dans la prémière moitié du XVIe siécle*, Paris: Association pour l'Avancement des Études Iraniennes.

Tapper, Richard (1983), 'Introduction', in Richard Tapper (ed.), *The Conflict of Tribe and State in Iran and Afghanistan*, London: Croom Helm.

Tarzi, Shah M. (1993), 'Afghanistan in 1992: A Hobbesian State of Nature', *Asian Survey*, Vol. 33, No. 2, A Survey of Asia in 1992: Part II. (February).

TemirKhanov, L. (1984), *Vostochnye pushtuny i novoe vremya*, Moscow

TemirKhanov, L. (1987), *Vostochnye pushtuny: osnovnye problemy novoi istorii*, Moscow: Nauka

Tenet, Charles (2007), *At the Center of the Storm*, London: Harper Collins.

Tilly, Charles (1990), *Coercion, Capital, and European States, AD 990–1990*, Cambridge, MA: Blackwell.

Tumanovich, N. N. (1989), *Gerat v XVI-XVIII vekakh*, Moscow: Nauka.

UNODC (2004), *Afghanistan: Opium Survey 2004*, Wien, November.
UNODC (2007), *World Drug Report 2007*, Wien.
Urban, Mark (1990), *War in Afghanistan*, Basingstoke: Macmillan.
van Creveld, Martin (1991), *The Transformation of War*, New York: Free Press.
Waldron, Arthur (1991), 'The warlord: twentieth-century Chinese understanding of violence, militarism and imperialism', *American Historical Review*, vol. 96 no. 4 (October), pp. 1073–1100.
Walwalji, Asadullah (1378), *Dar ṣafaḥāt-i shimāl-i Afghānistān chih mūguzasht?*, Pishāvar: Kitābfurūshī-i fazl.
Walwalji, Asadullah (n.d.), *Aghaz wa tadawaq-i Ekhtalaafat-i myan-i Genral-i Dustam wa Agaye masood dar sefhaat-i shomal-i afghanesan*, Peshawar.
Walwalji, Asadullah (1380), *ṣafaḥāt-i shimāl-i Afghānistān dar fāṣilah bayn-i ṭarḥ va tahqīq-i barnāmah-i khurūj-i artish-i surkh az ūn kishvar*, Peshawar: Idārah-i Nasharātū-i Gulistān.
Walwalji, Asadullah (2007), *Jaigah-i Junbesh-i Milli Islami Afganistan dar ma'adalat-i siyasi keshvar ba'd az saal 2001*, unpublished manuscript, Kabul.
Wantchekon, Leonard (2004), 'The Paradox of "Warlord" Democracy: A Theoretical Investigation', *American Political Science Review*, 98: 17–33 (www.nyu.edu/gsas/dept/politics/faculty/wantchekon/research/warlord.pdf).
Weber, Max (1994), *Political Writings*, Cambridge: Cambridge University Press.
Whitlock, Monica (2002), *Beyond the Oxus*, London: John Murray.
Whittacker, Dick (1993), 'Landlords and warlords in the later roman empire', in John Rich and Graham Shipley (eds), *War and Society in the Roman World*, London: Routledge.
Wilder, Andrew (2007), *Cops or Robbers?*, Kabul: AREU.
Wily, Liz Alden (2004), *Land Relations In Faryab Province*, Kabul: Afghanistan Research and Evaluation Unit, June.
Volkov, Vadim (2002), *Violent Entrepreneurs: the use of Force in the making of Russian Capitalism*, Ithaca, NY: Cornell University Press.
Woodward, Bob (2002), *Bush at War*, New York: Simon and Schuster.
———(2004), *Plan of Attack*, New York: Simon and Schuster.
Yarn, Douglas H. (1991), *The Dictionary of Conflict Resolution*, San Francisco: Jossey-Bass Publishers
Yunas, S. Fida (nd), *Afghanistan: Political Parties, Groups, Movements and Mujahidin Alliances and Governments (1978–1997)*, Peshawar.
Yusufzai, Rahimullah (1985), 'Resistance in Afghanistan: the Panjshir Model', *Regional Studies*, Summer.

GLOSSARY

Achakzai	Pashtun tribe of southern Afghanistan
Alaqdar	administrative unit (sub-district)
Alizai	Pashtun tribe of southern Afghanistan
Amir	prince, commander
Barakzai	Pashtun tribe of southern Afghanistan
Ghilzai	Afghanistan's largest Pashtun tribal confederacy
Ghund	regiment
Guruh-i Kar	left-wing ethnic nationalist group, which split from HDK in the 1970s.
Hamza	Ismail Khan's 'regular army'
Harakat-Islami	one of the Shiite parties which fought in the war against the Soviet army
Harakat-i Enqelab-i Islami (Islamic Revolutionary Movement)	one of the main opposition parties involved in the jihad, based in Pakistan. Mostly pro-monarchy and conservative
Harakat-i Shamal	Movement of the North, formed by mutinous troops and opposition armed groups in order to overthrow Pres. Najibullah's government in 1992
HDK (Hizb-i Demokratik-i Khalq, People's Democratic Party)	the Marxist party which took power in April 1978 and led the wave of reforms which sparked the resistance and jihad movement in Afghanistan
Hizb-i Islami (Islamic Party)	the largest radical Islamist organisation in Afghanistan.
Hizb-i Wahdat (Unity Party)	the main Shiite/Hazara resistance party from 1988 onwards, active in Heart and elsewhere in Afghanistan.
Ittehad-i Islami	radical Islamist organisation in Afghanistan, formed in the early 1980s and mostly allied with Jami'at-i Islami in 1992–

Ittehadiya Islami-ye Wilayat-i Shamal	a Turkic nationalist party formed in the early 1980s to fight against the Soviet army
Jabh-i Muttahed-i Milli	National United Front
Jabh-i Nejat-i Milli (National Liberation Front)	one of the opposition parties involved in the 1978–1992 jihad, based in Pakistan. Pro-monarchy.
Jami'at-i Islami: (Islamic Society)	one of the main opposition parties involved in the jihad, based in Pakistan. A relatively moderate Islamist party.
Jami'at al ulema (ulema Society)	an insurgent group operating exclusively in western Afghanistan and led by the clergy. In the early 1980s it merged with *Harakat-i Enqelab-i Islami*
Jawanan-i Junbesh	Junbesh Youth
Jawanan-i Muslimun (Muslim Youth)	the first Islamist group to start operating in Afghanistan (1960s)
Jerib	surface unit corresponding to 1953.6 square meters
Jirga	Pashtun tribal assembly.
Junbesh-i Milli-ye Islami	National Islamic Front, a secularist party based in northern Afghanistan
Kalla-pulli	tax to be paid in corvées such as forced recruits
Karmalist	supporter of Babrak Karmal, president of Afghanistan 1979–1986
Khad-i Nezami	military counter-intelligence.
KhAD/WAD (Khedamat-i Etelea'at-i Dawlati/Wazirat-i Amniyat-i Dawlati, State Intelligence Agency/State Security Ministry)	the security services of the HDK-run state.
Khalq	one of the main factions of the HDK and the largest one in southern Afghanistan.
Khan	literally ruler, a grand notable with a large following.
Kuchi	nomad
Kumandan(ha)	commander(s)
Loya Jirga	tribal gathering, assembly.
Mahaz-i Milli (National Front)	one of the main opposition parties involved in the jihad, based in Pakistan. Pro-monarchy.
Madrasa	Islamic school (in Afghanistan only)
Malik	literally ruler, a village notable or man of influence.

Mujahidin	fighters of jihad
Noorzai	Pashtun tribe of southern Afghanistan
Parcham	one of the two main factions of the HDK, strongest in Kabul and the cities
Popolzai	Pashtun tribe of southern Afghanistan
Qazi	Islamic judge
Rutbavi	hierarchical type of Pashtun tribe, with a tendency towards usurpation of the power of the tribesmen by the leader
SAMA (Sazman-i Enqelabi-ye Mardom-i Afghanistan, Revolutionary Organisation of the Afghan People)	an alliance of leftist and nationalist groups which shared their hostility to Soviet influence in Afghanistan.
SAZA (Sazman-i Enqelabi-ye Zahmatkashanha-ye Afghanistan)	left-wing ethnic nationalist party, formed in the 1970s
Sayyid	honorific title given to descendents of Prophet Muhammad
Sharia	Islamic law
Shura (Council)	a type of traditional Afghan council.
Shura-i Emayat az Markaz	(Council for the support of the centre): council established in Heart by the opposition to Ismail Khan
Shura-i Ittefaq	(Unity Council): Shiite jihadi organisation based in Hazarajat
Shura-i Nezar	Supervisory Council, a faction within Jamiat-i Islami, originally created by commander Massud.
Shora-ye-Ahl-i-Hal wa Aqd Shura-ye Eslami-ye Hambastagi-ye Mardom-i Afghanistan (Islamic solidarity council of the Afghan people)	(the council of influential people) social organisation founded by Ismail Khan in Herat
Talib	student of religion
ulema	plural of 'alim
Ushr	religious tax usually consisting of ten percent of agricultural produce payable
Vassal	local leader who maintains a relationship of mutual obligations with a monarch, usually of support in exchange for certain guarantees
Vavassor	local leader who maintains with the vassal the same relationship as the vassal with the monarch
Watan (Hizb-i Watan, Fatherland Party)	new name of HDK from 1991

Wolesi Jirga (People's House)	Afghanistan's lower chamber of Parliament, established in 2005.
Woluswal	administrative unit (district)
Zakat	religious tax on assets and liquidity

INDEX

153, 197, 201, 210, 218, 236,
251, 258, 264, 267–8, 274
Hizb-i Watan see Hizb-i Demokra-
ti-i Khalq
Hobbes, Thomas 2
Human Rights Commission 270

Ibn Khaldun 2, 13, 17, 18, 38, 114
Ibn Khaldunian cycle 18–9, 21, 301
Ibrahim, Dr. 217–8, 228–9, 241–2,
259
Ibrahimi, Haji Latif (Amir Latif)
122, 180
Ideology 13, 23–4
Imam Sahib 122
impact of HRW reports 190
India 155, 257
indoctrination 13
institutional seizure 11
institution-building 10ff
insurgent warlords 16, 18, 32, 43,
208–9, 285, 303
intelligentsia 33, 40, 46, 174, 177,
183, 188, 202, 208, 226, 227,
269
international community 2, 23, 24,
80, 92, 293, 303, 304
international relations 261ff
Iran 44–6, 64, 78–9, 82, 87–8,
114–7, 119, 135–7, 154, 155,
171, 207, 209, 213, 215–8, 222,
233–4, 236–7, 242, 257, 259,
261–2, 264, 274–5, 286
and negotiating role 135–6
ISAF 89, 92, 156
ISI 62
Islam Qala 59, 207, 215, 227,
233–4, 239
Islamists 22, 40, 43, 45, 46, 50,
111, 168, 200, 222, 242, 281,
284, 288–9
Ismail Khan, Mohammad 1, 3, 65,
72, 74–5, 77–9, 87, 90, 95–6,
145–7, 151–2, 154, 163, 191,
207ff

and anti-Taliban insurgency
215ff
and coalition building 221ff
and corruption 275–6
and Council of the Ulema 273
and delivery of services 274ff
and Dostum 262
and elections 270
and ethnicity 276ff
and former officers 253–4, 265
and intelligence 256
and leadership role 213ff
and local administration 214,
264ff, 268
and mass media 272
and military class 250, 268
and political groups 264
and Shiites 258, 274
and supplies 213
and Tajik communities 214
and the central government
209–10, 234–5
and the intelligentsia 208–9, 227,
275
and war with Taliban 252ff
and women 269
authoritarianism 225
centralisation of patronage 226–7
centre periphery relations 242ff,
261–2
choreography of mass support
272
conflict with Amanullah Khan
259ff
emergence 207ff
external support 236
funding 227, 233ff, 256
Herat Council 263
Human Rights Commission, 270
institution building 263ff
international relations 261ff
Judicial Committee 271
judiciary 265, 271–3
legitimisation 267ff
military organisation 247ff

Shahrir, Rafiq 269
Shahzada, Gen. 162
Shamal 180
Shawshan, Ghulam Yahya 221–2, 267
Sher Khan Bander 153, 167
Shiberghan 56–8, 111, 133, 135, 156, 159, 181, 187, 192–4, 198
Shiites 37, 44–5, 209, 214, 216, 224, 227, 258, 267–8, 274
Shindand 54, 70, 72, 207, 209, 243, 249–52, 256–7, 259, 261, 267, 276–7
Shindand attack 249
Shirin Tagab 59, 126, 152, 164, 189, 192, 194
Shirzai, Gul Agha 64, 90, 278
Shora-ye-Ahl-i-Hal wa Aqd 153
Shulgara 104, 150–1, 156
Shura-i Adolat 152
Shura-i Emayat az Markaz 259
Shura-i Ittefaq 37
Shura-i Nezar 3, 32, 74, 79, 87, 89, 95, 118, 156, 162, 172, 174–6, 184, 229, 244, 270, 281ff
and business interests 292
and central government 289ff, 293
and centralization of patronage 290
and military class 283ff, 291ff
and narcotics trade 287
formal disbandment 288
judiciary 284
origins 281
police 284
Shura-ye Eslami-ye Hambastagi-ye Mardom-i Afghanistan 263
Sobhan, Khalif 78
Sources of intra-factional conflict 145ff
Soviet withdrawal 48
Spann, Michael 172
Spin Boldak 62–4
state re-building 2

state security 71
statecide warlords 16, 76, 107, 302
sub-national administration
composition 91
succession 11–2, 19, 119, 163, 298
Sudan 16
Sufi networks 45
Suzma Qala 142
Swats 35

Tajikistan 16, 74, 98, 284–6
Tajiks 36, 37, 146, 165, 200–1, 214, 276
Takhar 45, 82, 87, 94, 106, 145–8, 152, 187, 190, 192, 196, 281, 284–5, 288, 290
Takhassos paper 269
Taleqani, Nurullah 197
Taliban 6, 50, 74, 75, 81–4, 87–90, 92, 98, 108, 112, 113–9, 123–6, 135–7, 140–3, 146, 148, 150, 152, 154–5, 161, 164–9, 172–4, 187, 189, 200–2, 215–8, 224, 226, 228–30, 233, 236, 240–1, 243–4, 252–4, 256–8, 268, 272–4, 277, 284–5, 290, 292, 301–3
High Council 154
Tamerlane 188
Tashkent 133, 136, 138
Tashqurghan (Khulm) 82, 122, 150, 165, 166
taxes 18, 35–6, 48, 65, 74, 75, 79–81, 98, 133, 140, 159, 233, 234, 274–5, 287
Taylor, Charles 7, 20, 24
Taywara 224, 241
Teluqan 37, 290
Termez 136–7
Tilly, Charles 19
Tor Khowtal 63
tribal 'entrepreneurs' 49
tribal leaders 21, 35–6, 49, 64, 66, 124, 223, 226, 278
Tufan, Ghaffar 221